SELECTED
HISTORICAL ESSAYS OF
F. W. MAITLAND

CHOSEN AND INTRODUCED BY

HELEN M. CAM

BEACON PRESS   BOSTON

BEACON SERIES IN CLASSICS OF THE LAW

Charles M. Haar, *General Editor*

William Blackstone: Commentaries on the
Laws of England; Vol. IV, Of Public Wrongs
Selected Historical Essays of F. W. Maitland,
Chosen and introduced by Helen M. Cam

CONTENTS

PREFACE

The Collected Papers of Frederic William Maitland were published by the Cambridge University Press in 1911 in three volumes and are now out of print. More than half of the present selection was not included among them. The date and place of previous publication are noted at the beginning of each essay. Except for Essay VII, Maitland's notes are given in full, with only the slight corrections made necessary by the re-classification of records or the detection of some small error of fact. Notes which have been added by the editor are enclosed in square brackets.   H.M.C.

BIBLIOGRAPHICAL NOTE

Apart from Maitland's own letters, to which full references have been given, the following are the sources I have used:

The Athenaeum (1907), A. J. Butler, p. 4; Anonymous, p. 15.

W. W. Buckland, in *Cambridge Law Journal* (1923), pp. 131–43.

Cambridge University Reporter, p. 790 (5 February 1907); pp. 1301 ff. (22 July 1907), Report of Memorial Meeting.

C. H. S. Fifoot, *Law and History in the Nineteenth Century* (Selden Society Lecture, 1956).

H. A. L. Fisher, *Frederic William Maitland* (Cambridge, 1910).

H. A. Hollond, *Frederic William Maitland* (Selden Society Annual Lecture, 1953).

G. Le Bras, 'Le sens de la vie dans l'histoire du droit—l'œuvre de F. W. Maitland.' *Annales d'histoire économique et sociale* (1930), pp. 279–301.

B. F. Lock (1) Memoir in *Year Books of 3 and 4 Edward II.* Selden Society XXII (edited by Maitland, but published after his death). (2) Life in *Dictionary of National Biography*, 1901–11.

E. Maitland, *F. W. Maitland, a Child's-Eye View* (Selden Society, 1957).

T. F. T. Plucknett, 'Maitland's view of Law and History', *Law Quarterly Review* (1951), pp. 179–94.

F. Pollock (1) in *Law Quarterly Review* (1907), pp. 401–19. (2) In *Proceedings of the British Academy*, vol. II, pp. 455–9.

F. M. Powicke, *Modern Historians and the Study of History* (1955).

Mrs Reynell, 'Frederic William Maitland', *Cambridge Law Journal* (1951), pp. 67–73.

J. H. Round in *Peerage and Pedigree* (1910), vol. I, pp. 145–7.

R. L. Schuyler, 'The historical spirit incarnate; Frederic William Maitland', *American Historical Review* (1952), vol. LVII, pp. 303–22.

T. Seccombe in *The Bookman* (February 1907), pp. 216–21.

J. T. Shotall in *Political Science Quarterly* (1907), pp. 287–90.

Fredegond Shove, *Fredegond and Gerald Shove* (with a preface by Ermengard Maitland, to whom I am indebted for further light on Maitland). Privately printed 1952.

A. L. Smith, *Frederic William Maitland. Two lectures and a bibliography* (Oxford, 1908).

Munro Smith in *Political Science Quarterly* (New York), 1907, pp. 282 ff.

T. F. Tout in *Scottish Historical Review* (1911), pp. 73–5.

P. Vinogradoff in *English Historical Review* (1907), pp. 280–9.

R. J. White, 'F. W. Maitland: 1850–1950', *The Cambridge Journal* (1950), pp. 131–43.

An edition of Maitland's letters is being prepared for the Selden Society, who are also about to reprint his legal essays.

INTRODUCTION

I

This selection is designed to render more accessible those shorter
writings of Maitland's which have the greatest intrinsic value for
students of history and best illustrate his distinctive qualities, thus
serving, it may be, to stimulate a taste for his greater works. It is
lamentable that Maitland should be known to so many mainly by
his lectures on constitutional history. Written in 1888, published
after his death, contrary to his declared judgment, these contain
statements and interpretations quite inconsistent with his mature
opinions and inadequately represent his genius. It is the aim of this
volume to make Maitland better known to a generation that has
entered into his labours without recognising its debt.

When Maitland died, fifty years ago, one friend noted 'the
smallness of the ripple on the general consciousness caused by the
passing of England's greatest historian since Gibbon and
Macaulay'.[1] His indignation was shared on the other side of the
Atlantic; Americans recalled that when Gardiner, Creighton and
Stubbs were still living, Acton had ranked Maitland as the ablest
historian in England.[2] Tributes poured in from the scholars of
France, Italy, Germany, and the United States, and the University
of Oxford sent a special message of condolence on his loss to the
University of Cambridge—a gesture, as far as I know, without
parallel. But *The Times* only accorded him a third of a column.
Spenser has been called the poets' poet; Maitland seems to be the
historians' historian. Today when there is talk of history as
literature it is the rarest thing for Maitland to be named. Yet the
union of grace, wit and humour with the most exacting standards
of scholarship and the most exquisite sense of language is not so
common that we can afford to forget Maitland.

If we attempt to define the peculiar merits of Maitland as a
historian and to estimate his contribution to the interpretation
of English history, we shall find, I think, that there is one and the
same explanation for his special gifts and for his failure to attract

---

[1] T. Seccombe, in *The Bookman* (February 1907), p. 216.
[2] Munro Smith, in *Political Science Quarterly* (1907), p. 282.

the general public. Law was his guiding light; and the legal approach to history is too impersonal for the average reader, who demands incident and characterisation from his historical writers. Maitland came to history by way of law. His sister has traced the stages of the fourteen-year journey; from mathematics (where he did badly), and moral sciences (where he excelled), by conveyancing work in chambers (that admirable introduction to the science of diplomatic),[1] and extension lecturing to workmen and others,[2] to his first brilliant essays in legal journalism and the meeting with Vinogradoff, on a Sunday tramp in January 1884, which 'determined the course of his life'.[3] He was to be not a legal practitioner, but a legal historian; he had 'discovered the work that it was best for him to do'.[4]

Of his great services to the study of law others can speak; we are concerned here with his services to history. He brought law to bear on history. The history of law was not a specialised subsection of the history of England; it was an integral part of it; it was the key to the whole story. Stubbs had traced in masterly fashion the evolution of English self-government from the practices of primitive local communities; Maitland put the common law back in the centre of the picture, and with it the monarchy. It was the king's court that had made the law common to all England: by making himself the protector of the lawful possessor, great or small, the king had bound together the rights of ruler and subject. And the work of Henry II was carried on under his grandson. By dwelling on the great constructive work of the great judges, Bracton's masters, Maitland restored the reign of Henry III to its proper position in English history, taking the eyes of the student off the wearisome involutions of the struggles between king and barons.

Later historians were to pursue in detail the amazing story of the branches thrown out by that central trunk—'the transformations of the Curia Regis'; but even before his great *History of English Law* had appeared Maitland had fitted parliament into the picture. As he had said of the jury, 'it was not popular, but

---

[1] H. A. L. Fisher, *Frederic William Maitland* (Cambridge, 1910) (henceforth cited as Fisher), p. 17.

[2] His lectures on 'The Cause of High and Low Wages' at the Artizans' Institute, Upper St Martin's Lane, when he was twenty-four, seem to have anticipated W.E.A. technique. See H. Solly, *These Eighty Years*, vol. ii, p. 440.

[3] Letter to Vinogradoff, 15 November 1891 (Fisher, p. 51).

[4] Mrs Reynell in *Cambridge Law Journal* (1951), p. 73.

royal'; as his American disciples were to emphasise, it was judicial before it was legislative.

But if Maitland brought law to bear on history, he brought history to bear on law. Again and again he emphasised the danger of imposing legal concepts of a later date on facts of an earlier date—a common fault, before his time, of the majority of legal historians and of many constitutional historians. We must not read either law or history backwards. We must learn to think the thoughts of a past age—'the common thoughts of our forefathers about common things'. 'We must not attribute precise ideas or well defined law to the German conquerors of Britain.' It is as if 'we armed Hengist and Horsa with machine guns or pictured the Venerable Bede correcting proofs'.[1]

The debt of Maitland's two mistresses was mutual. The technique which makes his exposition of general principles so vivid and arresting is that of the lawyer. Every generalisation is seen in terms of the individual, every principle in its application to a particular case. As Vinogradoff said, 'what he wanted most was to trace ideas to their embodiment in facts'.[2] A brilliant example of his method is the imaginary situation arising from a homicide by which Maitland drives home the effects of the impact of feudalism on Anglo-Saxon law and the practical reasons for the substitution of amercement for the old *wite* and *bot* system.

Let us suppose that a man learned in the law is asked to advise upon a case of homicide. Godwin and Roger met and quarrelled, and Godwin slew Roger. What must be paid; by whom; to whom? Our jurist is not very careful about those psychical elements of the case which might interest us, but on the other hand he requires information about a vast number of particulars which would seem to us trivial. He can not begin to cast up his sum until he has before him some such statement as this: Godwin was a free ceorl of the Abbot of Ely: Roger, the son of a Norman father, was born of an English mother and was a vavassor of Count Alan: the deed was done on the Monday after Septuagesima, in the county of Cambridge, on a road which ran between the land which Gerard a Norman knight held of Count Eustace and the land of the Bishop of Lincoln: this road was not one of the king's highways: Godwin was pursued by the neighbours into the county of Huntingdon and arrested on the land of the Abbot of Ramsey: Roger, when the encounter took place, was on his way to the hundred moot: he has left a widow, a paternal uncle and a maternal aunt. As a matter of fact, the result will

[1] *Domesday Book and Beyond*, pp. 356, 520.
[2] *English Historical Review* (1907), p. 282.

probably be that Godwin, unable to satisfy the various claims to which his deed has given rise, will be hanged or mutilated.... The old law consisted very largely of rules about these matters; but it is falling to pieces under the pressure of those new elements which feudalism has brought with it.[1]

This descent to the concrete brings us close to the circumstances and ways of life of the *dramatis personae*, as well as to the rules of law. And the introductions to the Year Books which, he says, 'come to us from life', are also introductions to the mental habits of young lawyers learning the law by listening to older lawyers discussing the cases and of judges illustrating their judgments with anecdotes. As G. M. Trevelyan has said, Maitland uses law as a tool to open the mind of medieval man. He never loses sight of the individuals who created and worked the institutions that he is investigating.

Such a technique could only be used by a master of original material. Maitland's first work had been the editing of legal records,[2] as his last years were to be spent on editing law reports. No one has sung the praises of the Public Record Office more eloquently than Maitland, to whom 'the whereabouts of the first-hand evidence for the law of the Middle Ages' had come as a dazzling discovery seven years after he was called to the bar[3]—it was 'the most glorious store of material for legal history that has ever been collected in one place'.[4]

II

Such an approach to law and history involves intimacy not only with persons[5] but with places. Along with a taste for first-hand evidence Maitland inherited from his grandfather, the ecclesiastical

---

[1] *History of English Law* (2nd edition), vol. i, pp. 106–7.

[2] *Pleas of the Crown for the County of Gloucester, 1221* (1884); *Bracton's Notebook*, containing 2000 cases extracted from the rolls of the King's Court, 1217–40 (1886).

[3] Maitland was working at the Record Office as early as February 1884, well before the May conversation with Vinogradoff described by Fisher, pp. 24 ff. For evidence see Powicke, *Modern Historians and the Study of History* (1955), p. 10; and Plucknett in 'Maitland's view of Law and History', *Law Quarterly Review* (1951), pp. 85–7. For his familiarity with medieval printed court rolls by 1881, see his postcard to Pollock (Fisher, p. 38).

[4] Inaugural lecture, reprinted in *Collected Papers of F. W. Maitland*, vol. i, pp. 495–6.

[5] Maitland's eldest daughter was named after a lady in *Bracton's Notebook*, i, pp. 16, 93–5; iii, no. 1843 (margin). Cf. letter to Vinogradoff, 12 June 1887 (Fisher, p. 40).

historian, an estate in Gloucestershire. The Downing Professor was Lord of the Manor of Brookthorpe.[1] Like Stubbs he comes down to the earth he knows in his picture of his native county in 1221—or rather, as he says, 'a photograph of English life as it was early in the thirteenth century in its most vital parts—the system of local government and police, the organisation of county, hundred and township'. Look again at the two sections of the Ordnance Survey placed between pages 16 and 17 of *Domesday Book and Beyond* to make his point about nucleated villages and hamlets; or at his picture of the open fields of his other home, Cambridge, in the Ford Lectures on *Township and Borough* (No. I, below). Only those who have themselves tried to write the history of the city of Cambridge can justly value the depths of his knowledge of 'the town in which I live'. But both in his study of Cambridge and in that of the manor of Wilburton (No. II) the special local problems are never isolated from the general problems that they may help to elucidate: in the one case the corporation theory, in the other the transformation of villein into copyholder. Maitland's analysis and interpretation of the Wilburton rolls has been the model for and the precursor of many such studies since 1894, but their value is in no sense superseded. Each manor has its own history, and it is as true now as when Maitland wrote that 'the time has not yet come when generalities about *the* English manor and its fortunes will be safe or sound'.

The interest of No. II is mainly economic; that of No. III is mainly legal and administrative. Leet and Tourn are constantly mentioned in manorial and constitutional history, but it is doubtful if they are fully understood. In his introduction to *Select Pleas in Manorial Courts*, the Selden Society volume for 1889, Maitland described their origin and working in fuller detail than he allowed himself in the *History of English Law*. The theory, first stated here, that associated their presenting juries with the Assize of Clarendon (1166) has not been impugned. His description of the double presentment by free and unfree jurors makes clear the functioning of an institution intimately bound up with the king's peace and the king's revenue, and not only the king's. To the sheriff's tourn corresponded the courts leet held by lords of manors to whom the functions and profits of such a court had been delegated by the

---

[1] Strictly speaking, farmer of the manor, which the family held at lease from the see of Gloucester.

king—or who had annexed them without grant. An essential part of the machinery of justice and police in the twelfth century, courts leet and private views of frankpledge had a solid financial value to their holders long after the justices of the peace had made them superfluous for judicial purposes. Maitland's description can stand by itself, without the records which it explains.

III

'Pollock and I have mapped out a big work, too big I fear for the residue of our joint lives.' So Maitland wrote in November 1889,[1] and *The History of English Law before the time of Edward I* was his principal concern for the next five years. He wrote all of it except the chapter on Anglo-Saxon law, about which, he told Vinogradoff in May 1892, he was not too happy. 'My effort now is to shove on with the general sketch of the Norman and Angevin periods so that my collaborator may have little to do before we reach the Year Book period—if we ever reach it.'[2] No student of English history needs an introduction to the First Book; its four last chapters are indispensable reading for anyone who would understand the origins of our constitution. The essays included in this volume are less familiar. No. V, written for the *Encyclopaedia Britannica* in Las Palmas in December 1899—'the work of a bookless imagination, but dates were brought from England'[3]—is a dazzling *œuvre de vulgarisation*. No. VI, published in the second volume of *Social England* in 1894, sketches later medieval developments after Edward I and ends with one of Maitland's happiest paradoxes. It prepares the way for No. VII, the Rede Lecture, given in 1901, in which Maitland drew a picture of English Law against the European background of the sixteenth century; a picture whose colours, critics today agree, are unduly heightened. But in no other essay in this volume do we so unmistakably catch the accents of the speaker who 'heard his words as he wrote them'.[4] Further, it exemplifies its author's dictum 'History involves comparison, and the English lawyer who knows nothing and cares nothing for any system but his own hardly comes in sight of the idea of legal history'.[5] Reading these three essays

[1] Letter to M. M. Bigelow, 24 Nov. 1889, in Boston University Library.
[2] C.U.L. Add. MS. 7005 D, no. 14. The Year Books proper begin after 1272.
[3] Letter to Pollock (Fisher, p. 117).   [4] Miss Ermengard Maitland.
[5] Inaugural Lecture: *Collected Papers*, vol. I, p. 488.

we get a notion of what Pollock meant when he spoke of the transformation that Maitland's genius had accomplished. Twenty-five years ago the early history of the Common Law, he said, had been 'obscure, isolated, a seeming chaos of technical antiquities. Maitland commanded the dry bones to live, and henceforth they are alive.'[1]

IV

If we were to ask what had been Maitland's chief impact on the teaching of history we should, I suppose, put first his presentation of Henry II as founder of the Common Law, and with it of the English monarchy as the effective guardian of justice to all. But today we should unhesitatingly set alongside this his contribution to the history of Parliament in his edition of the Parliament Roll of 1305—The *Memoranda de Parliamento* (No. IV). Yet when the 'trail-blazing' introduction[2] appeared in 1893, it passed largely unregarded. Its wider implications were not perceived. It was a seed cast on barren ground and the germination was slow. Not until McIlwain's *High Court of Parliament* appeared in 1910, three years after Maitland's death, was there any explicit recognition of what it meant for parliamentary studies, which had, in effect, marked time for some twenty years.

The genesis of this volume has not, I think, been traced before now. Early in the New Year of 1889, shortly after his election to the Downing Professorship, Maitland agreed to edit a volume of 'Petitions to Parliament' for the Rolls Series, and the Treasury formally approved the project in May.[3] In August Maitland confided to Vinogradoff, 'I have had a good holiday and am now going to do a little work in the Record Office. I want just to start the edition of the 10,000 odd petitions to King and Council but when it is well started I hope to get out of it.'[4] But on 1 October Maitland reported to Maxwell Lyte that he must suggest a change of plans. It was impossible to produce a scholarly edition of the petitions until they had been dated, and as their original grouping had been disturbed by editors whose identifications must be tested, this would be the work of years. Instead, Maitland proposed to

[1] *Proceedings of the British Academy*, 1905–6, p. 456.

[2] The adjective is Professor Schuyler's. *American Historical Review* (1952), p. 318.

[3] P.R.O. 8/131, pp. 387, 424. I have to thank the Deputy Keeper of the Records for permission to see this correspondence.

[4] C.U.L. Add. MS. 7005 D, no. 10.

edit 'one very early roll of parliament that has not yet been printed' and to 'illustrate the enrolments of the petitions and responses by the petitions themselves and by the writs whereby effect was given to the responses...thus bringing out the connection between the different parts of the government machinery. ...I cannot help thinking that one roll of parliament properly illustrated would be of much greater value than a mere collection of petitions conjecturally dated.'[1] The change of plan was apparently approved before the end of November 1889, but Maitland's other weighty commitments presumably took precedence. In April 1892, however, 'his head was full of it',[2] and by May the printers were receiving the text. Early in 1893 the first part of the introduction was being submitted to Maxwell Lyte[3] and by the end of November the book was out.[4]

In October, while revising the proofs, Maitland had written to Round 'I am trailing my coat through many fairs.'[5] But no one was moved to tread on it. When, in June 1894, Maitland wrote to thank Round for 'an extremely kind review of my parliament roll in the *Athenaeum*' he added 'Your praise is the more welcome because no one else out of Scotland has said one word of the book.'[6] Apart from Round's review, a negligible note in *Notes and Queries* and an admirable notice by Langlois in the *English Historical Review*,[7] it would seem that critics had failed to react to the provocation insinuated by Maitland. Round and Langlois, like Baldwin later, concentrated on the value of the introduction for the history of the Council; Fisher and Tout stressed the value of the text in illustrating the activities of an early parliament. But Stubbs' model parliament in effect held the field until well after Maitland's death. A. L. Smith in his deeply felt eulogium of Maitland, indeed, went so far as to regret that Maitland should

[1] P.R.O. 8/131, pp. 482 ff.

[2] Letter to Round, 10 April 1892, London University Library 653, (henceforth cited as L.U.L. 653).

[3] P.R.O. 8/212. Letters of 7 May 1892, 30 May 1893.

[4] Information from Director of Publications, H.M.S.O.

[5] Letter to Round, 30 October 1893 (L.U.L. 653).

[6] Letter preserved at Girton College, Cambridge. I have been unable to trace any Scottish notice of the *Memoranda*. George Neilson, or possibly Bain, may have written to Maitland.

[7] *The Athenaeum* (March 1894), pp. 273 f.; *Notes and Queries*, 22 September 1894; *E.H.R.* (October 1894), pp. 755–8. Even Langlois, however, failed to appreciate the implications of Maitland's essay for English parliamentary history.

have been put to such hack work. To him it was 'a harnessing of Pegasus to a cart...'. It was 'like finding an electric light left on in a cellar'.[1]

As late as 1911, Tout, criticising Fisher for his failure to appreciate Maitland's permanent contribution to the study of English medieval history, makes no reference to it.[2] In 1920 A. F. Pollard declared that Maitland's essay had been generally ignored by English instructors of youth for nearly a generation.[3] Whatever may have occurred in lecture-rooms—and Lapsley, in 1936, suggests that it was being recommended to students as a 'standard' work before 1910[4]—there seems no evidence in print of the recognition by scholars that it was a turning point in parliamentary studies before McIlwain proclaimed its importance.[5] America and France appear to have been before England. Pasquet in 1914[6] showed a fuller appreciation of Maitland's work than any English writer had so far done. It was not till 1920 that Pollard's lively and readable sketch sent his readers back to the *Memoranda* to discover, as Petit Dutaillis indicated later,[7] that it was as well to take their Maitland first hand. As Baldwin put it, in his review of *The Evolution of Parliament* in 1921, 'The entire history of Parliament must be rewritten;'[8] but it had taken nearly thirty years for that conviction to be generally accepted. The following thirty-five years have seen a laborious and fruitful cultivation of the field that Maitland opened up.[9]

This imperception may in part be attributed to Maitland's modesty[10] and to the seeming tentativeness of his approach.

[1] *F. W. Maitland, Two Lectures* (Oxford, 1908), p. 38.
[2] *Scottish Hist. Rev.* (1911), p. 74. [3] *Evolution of Parliament* (1920), p. vi.
[4] Maitland, *Selected Essays* (Cambridge, 1936), p. 2.
[5] But Baldwin, reviewing *The High Court of Parliament*, observed that the author's views were 'current among various writers of the school of Maitland'. *Amer. Hist. Rev.* (1910–11), p. 598. I have failed to find evidence for this.
[6] *Les origines de la Chambre des Communes* (Paris, 1914, translated by R. G. D. Laffan, 1925).
[7] *Studies Supplementary to Stubbs* (English translation, Manchester, 1930), p. 334.
[8] *Amer. Hist. Rev.* (1921–2), p. 108.
[9] For a brief survey, see Powicke, *The Thirteenth Century* (Oxford, 1953), p. 747; for a more elaborate bibliography, see the *Relazioni* of the Tenth International Congress of Historical Studies (Florence, 1955), vol. I, pp. 36–46.
[10] Even with his reputation established, he could write to Poole, on his election to Ford's Lectureship 'Didst ever feel like a bubble that was going to be pricked?' *Camb. Hist. Jour.* (1952), p. 324. (A letter to Round of the same date—23 February 1897—establishes the reference.)

Twice in his introduction he says that it would not be right for an editor in the Rolls Series to propound theories touching debatable matters.[1] In one footnote only does he define a difference from the accepted views.[2] Moreover, much of what he says is to be found in his magnificent but ambiguous master, Stubbs,[3] who was able to cling to his faith in a 'Model Parliament' whilst supplying a wealth of evidence that proved that concept misleading. Once again, it is the light of the law that Maitland turns on to history, and in that light the parliaments of Edward I's reign look very different from Stubbs' bifocal vision of them.

What was the new light brought to bear on the history of parliament by what McIlwain has called 'the most penetrating of all Maitland's works'? Maitland suggested, only too cautiously, that parliament was in essence royal, not popular; a court of justice before it was a legislature; an expansion of an aristocratic and bureaucratic council before it had any representative character. But if his observation that things were done in full parliament (a characteristically curial phrase) after both representatives and barons not of the council had gone home[4] was outstandingly significant, the statement that a parliament was 'an act rather than a body of persons' was the one most calculated to shake readers out of their established assumptions. Parliament was not an institution, but an event. Things were done *in* parliament, not *by* parliament. 'Parliament' cannot, at this stage, be the subject of a verb, nor the object. 'One cannot address a petition to a colloquy, a debate.'[5]

To whom, then, were the petitions addressed which Maitland had originally been asked to edit?[6] There was in existence in 1305 a body of persons, already an institution, which could be described as taking action; its constitution might be fluctuating, but it could be linked with the king when petitions were addressed to him. 'A session of the king's council is the core and essence of every *parliamentum*.'[7] In its judicial capacity, reinforced by legal experts,

---

[1] Introduction, pp. xxxiv, lxxxiv; for the latter, see below, p. 91.

[2] See below, p. 94, n. 3.   [3] See below, pp. 54, 95.

[4] See below, pp. 53, 55–7, 80, 94.   [5] See below, p. 78.

[6] In writing to Maxwell-Lyte, 6 January 1889, Maitland speaks of petitions *to* parliament; on 7 August 1889, 'having made himself familiar with the already printed petitions', he describes them as petitions *in* parliament; on 1 October 1889 he says 'though these petitions are said to be heard *at* or *in* a parliament they are addressed to the King or the King and council'. P.R.O. 8/131.

[7] See below, p. 94.

it constitutes the king's highest court, in a supremely solemn session, a tribunal superior to the court *coram rege*, 'where judicial doubts are determined, new remedies established for new wrongs, and justice is done to every one according to his deserts'.[1]

Starting from the hearing of petitions, Maitland is mainly concerned with the judicial business of a parliament. But the council has executive and advisory functions, and the wrongs for which remedies are sought may have been committed by the king's own agents.[2] The answer to a petition need not be the outcome of a judgment: the writ that implements it may be purely administrative. 'The whole governmental force of England is brought into a focus' in a parliament.[3]

A caveat ought here to be entered, necessitated by the results of the research which Maitland's essay has stimulated.

The nature of his record, which is far from giving a complete account of the parliament of Easter, 1305,[4] leads him to underestimate the unofficial or political aspects of a parliament. In this he has had distinguished followers; but the evidence not only of the chroniclers but of Edward's own correspondence is clear.[5] The introduction to the Memoranda was a magnificent attack on 'after-mindedness'. We were not to interpret the roll of Edward's reign in the light of those of his grandson's or any later reign.[6] But Edward I 'entered into a traditional inheritance'.[7] Maitland might justifiably have considered the parliaments of Henry III's reign. It had been the magnates who, in 1258, had provided for three parliaments a year, 'to see the state of the realm, and to treat of the common business of the king and the kingdom'. The colloquy or debate might be of a political nature: the judgments, as in Segrave's case,[8] might have political overtones due to the fact that his judges included not only legal experts but the leading men of the land. The 'equitableness' of the tribunal[9] might at times be attributable to political expediency rather than to theories of discretionary power. Perhaps the ultimate supremacy of the king's high court of parliament would owe as much to these factors as to its judicial omnicompetence.

[1] See below, p. 89.   [2] See below, p. 79.
[3] See below, p. 82.   [4] See below, pp. 53, n. 4, 77.
[5] Powicke, *The Thirteenth Century*, p. 343.   [6] See below, p. 91.
[7] Powicke, *The Thirteenth Century*, p. 345. See also J. G. Edwards in the *Bulletin of the Institute of Historical Research* (1954), pp. 35–53.
[8] See below, pp. 85–6.   [9] See below, p. 92.

But in 1893 it was the judicial, the official aspect of parliaments that needed to be emphasised. Stubbs' saving clauses had been generally disregarded, and students of history had to be reminded that in 1305 the 'assembly of estates' had not yet become part of the national council, and that the elected representatives were not necessarily called upon to vote taxes—the function which in the long run was to give the full-grown House of Commons the key to parliamentary sovereignty.

V

Nos. VIII, IX and X deal with ecclesiastical history. In a much quoted phrase, Maitland called himself a dissenter from all the churches. One who knew him intimately describes him as a 'very Protestant agnostic'; but whatever his personal predilections were, his passion for historical truth and legal exactness made him a papalist when determining an issue long obscured by ecclesiastical controversy. In his lectures on constitutional history (1888) he had given a lucid sketch of the relations of church and state in medieval England; in the *History of English Law* (1895) he had traced the frontiers of Common and Canon Law at length. In the summer of 1895, while working on a course of lectures on Canon Law for law students, his study of Lyndwood's *Provinciale*[1] convinced him that Roman or Papal Law had been authoritative in English church courts and that 'any special rules of the Church of England had, in the view of the canonist, hardly a wider scope than the by-laws of London in the eye of the English lawyer'. English Canon Law, in fact, 'was only English because it was universal'.[2] This opinion, expounded fully (1896–7) in the three articles reprinted in the volume *Roman Canon Law in the Church of England* (1898) was 'an assault on the established theory'. Stubbs had said in 1882 that 'in England neither the civil law nor the canon law was ever received as authoritative, except educationally',[3] and had justified this position at length in the historical appendices to the Report of the Royal Commission on Ecclesiastical Courts in 1883. The High Anglican party took this

[1] Written in 1430; the leading English authority on medieval canon law.

[2] Pollock and Maitland, *History of English Law* (2nd edition), vol. I, p. 115.

[3] *Seventeen Lectures on Medieval and Modern History* (1900 edition), p. 354. In 1900 Stubbs, without being fully convinced, deferred to Maitland's superior learning. *Ibid.* p. 335. Maitland is today considered to have proved his case. See Holdsworth, *History of English Law* (1922), vol. I, p. 582.

as proving the legal continuity of the modern Church of England
from that of the Middle Ages. There had been no revolution in the
sixteenth century. As Maitland put it, they held that the Church
of England 'had been Protestant before the Reformation and
Catholic afterwards'. In 1888, Maitland had summed up the
effects of that revolution in the words 'Religion has now become
an affair of statute'.[1] By agreeing to follow up his articles on
Canon Law with a chapter on the Elizabethan Settlement in the
Cambridge Modern History projected by Acton and himself[2] he
was drawn further into the controversy. Acton, he said later, had
induced him to put his hand far into a very nest of hornets.[3] But
he had known from the first that he was 'trailing his coat',[4] and
his correspondence with Round, a Protestant of a very different
kidney, reflects a curious alliance. From 1897 to 1899 Round was
fanning the flames of controversy with articles in the *Nineteenth
Century* and the *Contemporary Review*, on 'The Idolatrous Mass'
and kindred sixteenth-century subjects. Maitland wrote to him in
December 1897 'I do not wonder that your articles should have
won praise in more than one camp. I have lately re-read and
admired. My suspicion is that the Anglican legend of the Reformation has seen its best day, and that its popularizers have done it a
mischief by their recklessness.'[5] One of these popularisers, a
Canon of Ripon with a large reading public, published an article[6]
in which he sought to prove that the Elizabethan Settlement had
been approved by Convocation as well as by Parliament. He had
gone far out of his depth, and his assault on historical fact evoked
a rejoinder written, as Le Bras would say, with 'une verve dis-
crètement impertinente' (No. X). Maitland, who had just offended
Round by his review of the *Commune of London* (No. XI) hoped
that his prickly ally might be mollified by this trouncing of a
common enemy;[7] but apparently in vain. The insensible Mr
MacColl returned to the attack in *The Reformation Settlement
examined in the light of History and Law* in 1900, and the ignorance
of Canon Law revealed in it was well and truly exposed by

[1] *The Constitutional History of England*, p. 512.

[2] 'It will be a very strange book, that *History* of ours,' he wrote to
H. Jackson in 1900 (Fisher, p. 124).　　　[3] Letter to Jackson (Fisher, p. 152).

[4] Letter to Poole, 15 August 1895, *C.H.J.* (1952), p. 322.

[5] Letter at Girton College.

[6] *Fortnightly Review* (October 1899).

[7] Letter to Poole, 26 November 1899 *C.H.J.* (1952), p. 328.

Maitland in a more academic article in the *English Historical Review*.[1]

The chapter on the Anglican Settlement and the Scottish Reformation (No. VIII), Maitland's main concern after the completion of *Domesday Book and Beyond* (January 1897) and *Township and Borough* (February 1898), was being revised in the summer of 1899. 'Just at present', he wrote to Round in July, 'I keep Elizabeth for Sundays.'[2] It was in Acton's hands before Maitland left England for the Canaries in November of that year;[3] it only reached the reading public when volume II of the *Cambridge Modern History* came out in 1903. But its by-products, the first four 'Elizabethan Gleanings' (No. IX) had appeared in the *English Historical Review* in 1900.[4]

Maitland 'liked most centuries better than the sixteenth'.[5] He also doubted his own ability to handle narrative; as to this the reader will judge for himself. Undoubtedly he can create an atmosphere from details skilfully selected. He can drive home a point with an epigram, and hit off a character or a situation in a phrase that provokes delighted laughter in the reader. Competent judges have borne witness to the 'vast erudition' concealed by this lightness of touch. He treads warily, almost daintily, among the complexities of diplomatic and theological rivalries.[6] His interpretation of the steps by which the two great acts of the parliament of 1559 were reached is not accepted by all; but the latest historian to treat of the Elizabethan religious settlement describes it as still 'shrouded in mystery'.[7] Nor does Maitland's detachment from the conflict mean lack of sympathy or doubt of the genuineness of opinions he does not share. He is at home with the personalities of the sixteenth century. Elizabeth, he held, was actuated by religious rather than by political motives in rejecting Rome;[8] and he wrote to Round in February 1898, 'I am among Calvin's letters. I think that he and Elizabeth understood each other.'[9]

---

[1] *E.H.R.* (January 1901). Reprinted, *Collected Papers*, vol. III, pp. 137–56.

[2] 7 July 1899 (L.U.L. 653).

[3] Letter to Jackson (Fisher, p. 125).

[4] The fifth Gleaning was published in July 1903 in the *E.H.R.*

[5] Letter to Round, 29 December 1898 (L.U.L. 653).

[6] As originally drafted, paragraph 1 on p. 203 ended 'So Cox and Knox were satisfied.' *Cambridge Law Journal* (1923), p. 286.

[7] J. E. Neale, *Elizabeth I and her parliaments* (1953), p. 51.

[8] See below, p. 167.   [9] Letter at Girton College.

VI

In the last four articles (Nos. X–XIII) we hear Maitland passing judgment on the work of others. Between 1888 and 1906 he wrote at least thirty-five learned and suggestive reviews of the publications of English and foreign scholars,[1] and his longer writings, both in the text and in the footnotes, constantly, and often warmly, acknowledge his debt to others.[2] From these reviews, and from his correspondence with R. L. Poole, editor of the *English Historical Review*, 1893 to 1906,[3] we can deduce his code for critics. He could master a book with amazing rapidity, and he knew very well what he thought of it, but in pronouncing on its merits his judgments are most delicately balanced between the demands of scholarship and those of the special character and circumstances of the writer. He is reluctant to offer purely destructive criticism. H. B. Simpson on the Constable is 'pretty perverse' but contains 'no corrigible mis-statements'.[4] Apropos of an error that he is intending to correct, he inquires about the writer. 'If he is a young man he might like the opportunity of having a second word about his document, and I should be unwilling to hurt his feelings'; and later, in the same connection, 'I don't like to see that document lying about unqueried, but would not make an unnecessary fuss.'[5] But he took off the gloves when dealing with the egregious errors of the Dean of Lichfield as to the law of marriage in the Middle Ages,[6] and in his exposure of MacColl's discovery of a non-existent convocation (No. X), as we have seen, he could be gaily ruthless, though he admitted to Poole that MacColl was an experienced controversialist and a clever tactician.[7] It is in relation to Round, most learned of scholars and most merciless of critics, that these qualities of Maitland shine out most notably. The two had corresponded since 1888.[8] They had exchanged references on such subjects as early fines, and Maitland had held his hand on

---

[1] See A. L. Smith's bibliography of Maitland in *F. W. Maitland: Two Lectures* (Oxford, 1908).

[2] E.g. Liebermann, Round, Stevenson, Vinogradoff.

[3] Printed in the *C.H.J.* (1952), pp. 318–51.

[4] 7 June 1895 (*C.H.J.*, p. 319).

[5] 29 August 1898, 3 August 1899 (*C.H.J.*, pp. 325–7).

[6] *E.H.R.* (1895), pp. 755–9. Reprinted, *Collected Papers*, vol. III, pp. 21–30.

[7] 30 October 1900 (*C.H.J.*, p. 331).

[8] See correspondence in the London University Library.

Domesday Book until Round's *Feudal England* should appear.[1]
Maitland was a keen admirer of Round's work and that the
admiration was returned appears not only in Round's many
reviews of Maitland's books, but in the eloquent tribute to him
which he published after his death.[2] But Maitland, like many
other scholars, found Round's passion for controversy over the
minutiae of history unedifying and wearisome. 'Is *the* battle over
yet?' he had asked, with some amusement, in June 1894,[3] but
Round's 'terrific conflict' with Freeman and his followers over the
battle of Hastings, opened in 1892, was still raging in 1899 when
amusement had long ceased and the object of dispute had become
'that infernal palisade'.[4]

The controversy between Round and Hubert Hall over the
Red Book of the Exchequer, however, had had uglier aspects and
had caused Maitland acuter discomfort. Hall, the much loved
helper of generations of workers at the Public Record Office, had
been appointed joint editor with Round of the *Red Book* for the
Rolls Series in 1890, but the two differed fundamentally as to the
trustworthiness of Swereford, the thirteenth-century compiler of
the *Red Book*, and after a few months Round resigned. The *Red
Book* was published in April 1897. Round had seen the proofs
beforehand, and his mouth should therefore have been closed on
the subject,[5] but none the less he attacked the editor's errors
savagely in various periodicals and finally in a privately printed
pamphlet. The controversy was opened by Hall's review of *Feudal
England*[6] which had contained observations about the *Red Book*
which 'my friend Mr Hall' was editing, and Maitland, knowing
both men well, foresaw trouble. 'I quite agree', he wrote to
Round privately, 'that the Quarterly Reviewer has a weak spot
in his love for Swereford, but I think this is evident enough and
will do no harm—certainly not to you, nor I think to any one else,
and as there are few people in the world who are of such a right
good sort as he is, I am hoping that you will be content with the

[1] Letter of 18 July 1894, and letter no. 10, which should follow it (L.U.L. 653);
letter to Poole, 15 July 1895 (*C.H.J.*, p. 320); preface to *Domesday Book and
Beyond*, p. v.

[2] *Peerage and Pedigree* (1910), vol. I, pp. 145–7.

[3] Letter at Girton College.

[4] Letter to Poole, 26 November 1899 (*C.H.J.*, p. 328). For a bibliography
of the whole controversy, see *Sussex Archaeological Collections*, vol. xlii.

[5] C. Johnson in *Trans. R. Hist. Soc.* (1946), p. 3.

[6] *Quarterly Review* (July 1896).

status quo. I am thoroughly convinced that you can "afford" to let the matter be. Pray do not think that I am tendering advice—nothing of the kind! I am pleading for a friend.'[1] Maitland's pleadings had no effect and the unedifying conflict continued. Maitland had little doubt that Round was in the right, historically speaking. When he received Round's pamphlet he wrote to him 'I shall learn much, though I expect to feel in my proper person some of the blows that you inflict upon H.H. I fear that what I read will be all too true, and yet of the said H.H. I am fond.'[2] Both parties appealed to the editor of the *English Historical Review* for a judgment, and Poole asked Maitland to act as umpire. Maitland was 'tormented' by the request. He begged Poole to look else-where—'Would not the good Bishop (Stubbs) intervene?'—he had known that 'his very good friend' Hall was incapable of sustaining an argument but had not, when he saw Hall's proofs, suspected the blunders. 'If all that R. says is true, I still think that he is using language that should be reserved for cases of a very different sort.... Poor Hall has a curious fluffy mind, but never scamps work, besides being (but this alas is irrelevant) the most unselfish man I have ever known.'[3] So Poole had to undertake the thankless task himself,[4] and Hall retired wounded from the fray. 'This, alas! is irrelevant.' So Round himself would have said, omitting the 'alas'! When in 1899 the *Athenaeum* sent Maitland Round's *Commune of London* for review,[5] Maitland, we are free to believe, was not sorry to have a chance of saying what he thought of Round's methods.

The review (No. XI), anonymous but unmistakable, has not before been reprinted. It is a learned and appreciative estimate of an important book, but it puts its finger unerringly on Round's weak points—his failure to produce large-scale constructive work,[6] and his bad manners in writing history. Round did history invaluable service by his devotion to exact scholarship, too often

[1] 7 September 1896 (L.U.L. 653).

[2] 31 August 1898 (L.U.L. 653).

[3] 7 September 1898 (*C.H.J.*, 1952, pp. 325 ff.).

[4] *E.H.R.* (1899), p. 148.

[5] The editor was Norman MacColl, Maitland's fellow as one of the 'Sunday Tramps'. The review appeared in the number for 21 October 1899.

[6] The bibliography of Round's writings by W. Page, in *Family Origins and other Studies, by the late J. Horace Round* (1930), pp. xlix–lxxiv, is the best evidence of the truth of this allegation.

displayed in exposing the errors of others.[1] In this he excelled;
but he completely lacked the courtesy and modesty with which
Maitland advanced his corrective views. Now at last Maitland
unsheathes his rapier to counter Round's battle-axe. Too much of
Round's brilliant gifts, he suggests, are devoted to slaughtering
his opponents. 'Gnawing off the nose of a butchered foe' is not
the technique of the good historical critic, 'who executes justice,
in an appendix, as noiselessly and painlessly as may be.' If Round
goes out of his way to sneer at Kate Norgate's 'lady's Latin'
'We do not say that Mr Round's German is gentlemanly' when he
mis-spells the name of a distinguished historian. Did Maitland
really find this part of his task unpleasant? We may doubt it.
But having sheathed his blade, he gives the greater part of his
review to a close and appreciative examination of the valuable
contributions to knowledge in Round's non-controversial sections.[2]
The review appears to have terminated the intimacy of the two.
Round, who was as vain as he was learned, wrote a peevish
rejoinder in the *Athenaeum*,[3] insinuating that the 'erudite critic'
was of those who received only with carping comments the results
of 'the dreary work of exploration'[4] which they were nevertheless
ready to use.

'I am sorry', wrote Maitland to Poole, 'that Round has taken
offence. I tried to do him full justice and thought that by this
time he would have lost the taste for unmitigated praise such as is
rightly bestowed upon promising young persons.'[5] He himself
had warmly welcomed Tait's criticisms of *Domesday Book and
Beyond* in 1897,[6] all the more, because he had, according to Poole,
'suffered from too much adulation'.[7] But Round lacked both the
humour and the generosity of his critic, and six months later
Maitland wrote 'I foresee that I shall have J. H. R. as an assailant
until the end of our joint lives'.[8] Round was to outlive Maitland
by twenty-one years, and was to pay posthumous tribute to the

---

[1] That he sometimes overreached himself as a critic is shown by Powicke,
Modern Historians (1955), p. 57. For an estimate of Round's positive achieve-
ments, see Stenton, *English Feudalism* (1932), pp. 1–6.

[2] Subsequent research has borne out his criticism of Round's view of the bull
Laudabiliter, p. 262 below.   [3] 28 October 1899.

[4] Contrast Maitland's enjoyment in compiling an Anglo-French grammar
for the use of students of the Year Books (Fisher, pp. 166–7).

[5] *C.H.J.*, p. 328. Note 44 on this page misses the allusion.

[6] See his letter to Tait printed by Powicke, *Modern Historians*, pp. 55 ff.

[7] *Ibid.* p. 54.   [8] To Poole, 6 May 1900 (*C.H.J.*, p. 329).

'great genius' of the historian who had 'to prove all things',[1] but he was incapable of valuing justly that combination of absolute intellectual integrity with courtesy, modesty and kindliness in which Maitland the critic has never been excelled.

This modesty is apparent in his obituary notice of Stubbs, worthy of re-reading by a generation that has heard much of that great man's small defects. Maitland writes with the deference, not to say the diffidence, of a pupil. As we have seen, he had upheld a view on the authority of Canon Law diametrically opposed to that of Stubbs. But he 'hated to bark at the heels of a great man whom he admired', and was prepared, in 1898, to destroy all or some of the sheets of his *Canon Law in England* if the reappearance of his articles in book form would make Stubbs 'more unhappy than a sane man is whenever people dissent from him'.[2] As a Cambridge man, and one who had never met Stubbs in person, he only agreed under pressure to write 'four or five pages' for Poole.[3] But what he had to say came to nine pages. Full measure of honour could be given where honour was due without any sacrifice of truth.[4]

On the tribute to the master follows the tribute to the pupil (No. XIII). Schools of graduate study did not exist in England or in Cambridge when Maitland was professor, but there was one Cambridge scholar of his training whose work had to be appraised in the brief notice that Maitland sent to *The Athenaeum* when the news came of her untimely death. In writing of Mary Bateson he, for once, surrendered some of his characteristic reserve. 'I don't feel at all sure that the editor will not suppress what I wrote in a hurry and call it hysterical—and may be he will be right. I was not very cool.'[5]

It was the last thing he wrote; he himself died three weeks later.

[1] *Peerage and Pedigree* (1910), vol. I, p. 145.

[2] Letter to Poole, 12 September 1898 (*C.H.J.*, p. 326).

[3] *C.H.J.*, pp. 331–4.

[4] The same fine discrimination is seen in his private references to Acton, whose obituary notice he wrote for *The Cambridge Review*, 16 October 1902. Reprinted, *Collected Papers*, vol. III, pp. 512–21. Acton had given History an established position at Cambridge (Letters to Poole, *C.H.J.*, pp. 337–9), but he was a man 'who could not bring to birth the multitude of thoughts that were crowding in his mind'. Letter to Jackson (Fisher, p. 135).

[5] To Poole, 5 December 1906 (*C.H.J.*, p. 351).

VII

If, fifty years after his death, we try to recover the aroma of
Maitland—artist and literary craftsman as well as historian—we
may begin by clutching at the personal reminiscences of those
who knew him; who heard him speaking in the Union or in the
Senate House, as in the immortal speech that killed the project
of a Queen's University, for ladies only, in March 1897; of those
who attended his lectures on English law, given 'in a sort of
liturgic rhythm, as though he were some sort of monk reciting the
miracles of his order—but they sent one away feeling that the study
of twelfth-century law was the only thing worth living for'; [1] of
his fellow-walkers in the Alps; of the correspondents with whom
he shared his enjoyment of Spanish grammar and of the many-
coloured landscape of the Canaries; of the friend who found him
reading a musical score with his feet on the fender; of his children
who heard from him the melodies of Mozart and Wagner and saw
with him the drawings of Blake. But in the end we come back to
his writings; it is in his words and works that we can best recognise
Maitland.

The single-minded pursuit of truth of necessity leads to a concern
for words. 'If we speak, we must speak with words. If we think,
we must think with thoughts. Perhaps, as Mr Gilbert suggested,
it is too late to be Early English. Every thought will be too sharp,
every word will imply too many contrasts.' [2] The desire, the determination to describe justly the truth that he had perceived or the
conception he had grasped made Maitland's ear for gradations in
the scale of meaning extraordinarily sensitive, as Mr Schuyler has
said. It made his style at times allusive—only by recalling a series
of analogies can the point be made; at times tentative, as Vinogradoff has described. 'He feels his way, as it were, like a musician
running his fingers over the keys in an improvised prelude towards
leitmotivs and harmonious combinations.' When his children
heard him trying out his lectures orally, what they heard was not
an orator practising his effects before an imaginary audience, but
an explorer eager to communicate his discoveries as he himself
had made them. In an undergraduate speech he had gibed at the

---

[1] J. T. Shotall; another student complained that he could take no notes at
Maitland's lectures because they were so interesting.

[2] *Township and Borough*, p. 22.

'Lords of the realm of tautology'; twenty-seven years later he is 'struggling with the unnecessary adjective; we must have as many substantives and verbs as possible'.[1] It is from this rejection of the superfluous that his lapidary phrases are born. 'The very early concentration of justice in *this conquered country*' gives us the long-distance effects of the Norman Conquest in two words. 'Of the old belief that all the Middle Ages lived at the same time there remains the disposition to think that all "Low Latin" is equally low' kills with one stone two very big birds. 'I doubt if we English-men, who never clean our slates, generally know how clean the French slate was to be' conveys the legal consequences of the French Revolution, but a good deal more. Something has already been said of his use of the concrete, his 'tracing of ideas to their embodiment in facts' (Vinogradoff). In the written word this often flowers into metaphor. Praising a younger historian, he will say 'one of the virtues which is placing Mr Tout in the very front rank of our historians is his determination to leave no stone unturned, no thicket unbeaten. Out of the thicket may fly a bird worth powder and shot. Under the stone may lurk a toad with a jewel in its head.'[2] But the metaphor can also be used with the 'musician's' approach. When describing how Leslie Stephen trained his team of contributors to the *Dictionary of National Biography* (of whom Maitland himself was one),[3] largely by personal example, he will say 'In course of time the stroke was caught. Many could raise the flower. A school has been established.'[4] And, when he reaches the point where words will not serve him, Maitland the poet can still make us share his vision. He is speaking of Leslie Stephen's wife— Virginia Woolf's Mrs Ramsay. 'Her friends Watts and Burne-Jones did their best; Mrs Cameron her best; Leslie himself said a little in the "Forgotten Benefactors"; eyes that saw and ears that heard can never be satisfied.'[5]

We are in the same case with Maitland himself. Let us say with Powicke, 'Maitland is one of the immortals' and leave it at that.

---

[1] Fisher, p. 14; letter to Round, 27 December 1897 (at Girton College).

[2] *E.H.R.* (1906), p. 783: *Collected Papers*, vol. III, p. 488.

[3] Maitland wrote on Le Breton, Fleta, Glanvill and his own father, John Gorham Maitland.

[4] *Life and letters of Leslie Stephen*, p. 372. (A post-Victorian generation may require a note on the reference to Tennyson's 'The Flower'.)

[5] *Ibid.* p. 312.

I

TOWNSHIP AND BOROUGH[1]

On 20 January 1803, Mr Justice Lawrence and a jury of merchants
were sitting at the Gildhall in London to try an issue between the
Mayor, Bailiffs and Burgesses of the Borough of Cambridge and
the Warden, Fellows and Scholars of Merton College in the
University of Oxford.

The value of the matter directly in dispute was not very high;
but the question that was opened was large. A lordship over some
1200 acres, or about two square miles of land, went a-begging.
There were five claimants. There was the municipal corporation
of Cambridge; there was Merton College, Oxford; there were two
Cambridge colleges, Jesus and St John's; there was Sir Charles
Cotton, the squire of a village called Madingley.

This debatable tract of 1200 acres lay, we moderns should say,
immediately outside the town of Cambridge. Our ancestors would
have said that it was a part and a great part, more than a third,
of the town (*villa*) of Cambridge, though it lay outside the defensible
and house-covered area.

What had happened was this: An Act of Parliament had directed
the inclosure of vast 'open and commonable' fields, arable fields,
in which the strips of divers owners lay intermixed. Ring-fenced
plots were to be awarded to these owners in lieu of their scattered
strips. Allotments were also to be made to those who, though
they had owned no strips, had been exercising rights of pasture.
Allotments were also to be made to the owners of the tithe. But
dispersed among the arable strips there were many small pieces of
waste land; there were the balks of green sward, the odds and
ends. Who owned them? Who could claim an allotment in their
stead?

That someone owned them was generally assumed. Suppose

---

[1] [The first of the six Ford lectures delivered at Oxford in the October term
of 1897. Published Cambridge, 1898. For the most recent scholarly accounts
of the boroughs of Oxford and Cambridge, see H. E. Salter, *Medieval Oxford*,
1936; *V.C.H. Cambridge*, vol. IV (in the press).]

that you are inclosing the open field of an ordinary village. Allotments must be made to the owners of the strips, to commoners, to the owners of the tithe; but an allotment should also be made in respect of 'the soil of the waste'. In general you will easily find an owner for it. There will be some obvious manorial lord. But here this ownership goes a-begging. A municipal corporation claims it; three learned corporations claim it; the squire of a neighbouring village claims it. An Act of Parliament directs them to try their claims one against the other. Some one should be lord of this field. *Nulle terre sans seigneur.*

To finish the tale, the municipal corporation was successful. It obtained a verdict, and in consequence it received an allotment of somewhat less than five acres out of the 1200 that were distributed.

At this time on the other side of the town of Cambridge there lay another wide expanse of open arable field. An Act of 1807 provided for its inclosure. Here also the ownership of the waste was in dispute. It was claimed by the municipal corporation; it was also claimed by those who represented the Prior of Barnwell; but the Prior's successors did not go to trial, and out of the 1100 acres that were inclosed nine acres were given to the incorporate Town as an equivalent for its manorial rights.

Thus was decided a question, or one part of a question, that had been simmering for centuries. Briefly we may put it thus: What did King John mean, or rather what did King John really do, when he granted to the burgesses of Cambridge the town of Cambridge with all its appurtenances, to have and to hold it for ever of him and his heirs to them and their heirs at a rent of £40 blanch and £20 by tale? What did he mean, or rather what did he really do, when he commanded that the burgesses and their heirs should have and hold the said town with all its appurtenances well and peaceably, in meadows and pastures, mills, pools and waters with all their liberties and free customs?[1] Were the burgesses collectively or corporatively lords of the town in such sense that they intervened in the feudal scale of land-tenure between the king and any man who held a house within the ditch or an acre-strip without the ditch? Were the burgesses collectively or corporatively the 'tenants in demesne', or, as we should now say,

[1] Cooper, *Annals*, vol. I. p. 33. This charter is closely similar in form to the Oxford charter of 1199: Ogle, *Royal Letters addressed to Oxford*, p. 5.

4

the owners, of whatever land within the ambit of the town was not held in severalty: of the wide pastures, of the balks and odds and ends of sward that lay among the arable strips, of the ditches, of the king's ditch, of the streets and lanes and market places? It was a big question. Happily it was faced in what I may call prehistoric times: I mean in 1803. A jury of merchants at the Gildhall, untroubled by 'the village community' or 'the origin of the borough', made short work of it.

Will you think me ill bred if I talk of the town in which I live? What else have you left me to talk of? What fields has not Oxford made her own?

But Cambridge had fields. I am not telling you that outside what we should call the town of Cambridge, that is, the house-covered space, there were pieces of land which we should call fields and that some of these lay within the boundary of the municipal and parliamentary borough of Cambridge. I am using the words in their medieval sense. Cambridge had fields (*campos*) as the neighbouring villages had fields: vast, hedgeless, fenceless tracts of arable land, in which the strips of divers owners lay interspersed 'hide-meal and acre-meal'. Cambridge had fields which were 'open and commonable': fields such as are depicted on those beautiful maps that Mr Mowat published. Cambridge had fields as Lower Heyford had fields.

David Loggan the engraver drew pictures of Oxford and of Cambridge also. In his general views of Cambridge we see in the background the houses, the colleges and churches, the castle-mound and the remains of the dismantled castle: in the foreground lies the open field, and I do not know that better pictures of an open field were ever drawn.

Celebrated thus by art, our Cambridge field has been celebrated by poetry also, at least if that excellent individualist Thomas Tusser was a poet. In the Cambridge field, if we borrow his eyes, we may see at their worst the evils of the old champion (or, as we say, champain) husbandry: the husbandry, that is, of open and commonable *campi*.

> By Cambridge, a town I do know,
>   Where many good husbands do dwell,
> Where losses by lossels do shew
>   More here than is needfull to tell,
>   . . . .

5

The champion robbeth by night,
  And prowleth and filcheth by day,
Himself and his beast out of sight
  Both spoileth and maketh away
Not only thy grass but thy corn
Both after and ere it be shorn.[1]

Art and poetry left something for modern science. When Mr Seebohm was restoring the open field of the English Village Community, it was I believe a terrier of this Cambridge field that taught him to teach us what butts and gores were like.[2]

Besides fields, Cambridge had meadows or leys which during a part of every year were commonable. Also it had pasture-land which was never inclosed or enjoyed in severalty, 'the green commons of the town'; for the more part they are green and open still. But further, so late as the reign of James I, Cambridge, its fields and its green commons, can upon occasion be treated as an agrarian whole. In 1624 the Vice-Chancellor of the University and the Mayor of the Borough issued an ordinance touching the commons of the town. Every occupier of an ancient tenement having of old time broad gates may turn out two head of cattle. Every occupier of other tenements and cottages may turn out one. Every person having six score acres of land in Cambridge field may turn out six, and so in proportion for any greater or less quantity of land.[3]

Observe what this reverend Vice-Chancellor and this worshipful Mayor are doing. They seem to be legislating for an agrarian commonwealth. They are decreeing that the pasture of the town must still subserve the arable of the town. And what is the unit of arable that gives the normal share of pasture-right? It is six score acres, a long hundred of acres, a hide.

Thus through the crust of academic learning, through the crust of trade and craft, of municipality and urbanity, the rustic basis of Cambridge is displayed. These hereditary enemies, these representatives of Town and Gown, have for once laid their heads together in order that they may stint the common of a community that ploughs.

A curious community it had become. The principal share-

[1] Tusser, 'A Comparison between Champion Country and Severall', stanzas 12–13, in *Five Hundred Points*, ed. Mavor (1812), p. 207.

[2] Seebohm, *English Village Community*, 3rd ed., p. 19.

[3] Cooper, *Annals*, vol. III, p. 164. For the houses 'with broad gates', see also *ibid.*, vol. II, p. 333.

6

holders in the arable were not 'natural persons', but chartered corporations. There are various Cambridge colleges, and this is what brings the Vice-Chancellor into the business. There is Jesus College which represents the Nuns of St Radegund; there is St John's College which represents an ancient Hospital; there is the College of Corpus Christi which ever since its foundation has owned many strips; there is Caius College with a title derived from the Mortimers of Attleburgh. Then there is Merton College, which was endowed by its founder, by Walter of Merton himself, with strips that he had purchased, for reasons that I dare not guess,[1] in the open and commonable fields of Cambridge. The Vice-Chancellor and the Mayor are agreeing in 1624 that he who occupies a hide of such strips may keep six horses or bullocks on the commons of the town. They are also ordaining that every occupier of an ancient tenement in Cambridge 'having of old time broad gates', that is, gates receptive of cattle, may turn out two beasts.

It is a curious case because the strip-owners are for the more part colleges. But does not its curiosity end here? In other words, is it not right and proper that a borough should have fields, arable fields, 'open and commonable fields?' I speak not of the smaller or of the newer boroughs, of the enfranchised manors. I speak of the great, old boroughs, those shire-boroughs, those *civitates*, which already in Domesday Book are sharply separated from the ordinary. villages. I see that when Henry VIII sold the spoils of Godstow and Rewley to Dr George Owen, the conveyance spoke of arable land in Oxfordfield.[2]

Might we not aim yet higher? In the twelfth century when William FitzStephen sings the praises of London, he does not say that somewhere near it lie fertile arable fields; he says that the arable fields of the town of London are fertile.[3]

[1] Rashdall, *Universities*, [1895] vol. II, p. 483 [new ed. (1936), vol. III, p. 194]: 'no doubt in view of the possibility of a migration'.

[2] *Royal Letters*, ed. Ogle, p. 153: 'Ac totum illud messuagium nostrum ac omnes terras arrabiles nostras in Oxfordfylde ac omnia prata pascuas pasturas et pecias terrae in Burge mede et prope Charwell eidem messuagio pertinentia modo vel nuper in tenura Roberti Colyer aut assignatorum suorum scituata iacentia et existencia in parochia S. Egidii iuxta portam borialem ville Oxonie dicto nuper monasterio de Regali loco alias dicto Rewley dudum spectantia et pertinentia.'

[3] *Munimenta Gildhallae*, vol. II, p. 4: 'Agri urbis sationales non sunt ieiunae glareae, sed pingues Asiae campi, qui faciunt laetas segetes, et suorum cultorum repleant horrea Cerealis mergite culmi.'

Historians of our universities will not let us forget that Erasmus accused the Cambridge townsmen of a pre-eminence in boorishness. 'Vulgus Cantabrigiense inhospitales Britannos antecedit, qui cum summa rusticitate summam malitiam coniunxere.'[1] We should distort his words if we took them to mean that there were, in Tusser's phrase, 'many good husbands' in Cambridge, though husband and boor have a common origin. But was the plan, the map, of this ancient borough exceptionally rustic? I shall not admit it until many Inclosure Awards have been studied.

Time was when we in England had a respectably neat system of legal geography, and when we seldom spoke of parishes, except when we were speaking of ecclesiastical affairs. The whole country (this was the theory, if not precisely the fact) was cut up into vills or towns. The law assumed that every acre of land lay in some town, some *villa*. If in a court of law you claimed an acre of land, you were bound to name the *villa* in which it lay. A mistake about this matter would be fatal; your writ would be quashed. Now every borough is a *villa*, a town. Indeed, in course of time we allow the urban places to appropriate to their exclusive use this good old word, and then we awkwardly distinguish the towns from the townships or borrow 'villages' from the French. However, the borough is a *villa*, and if you look at the English boroughs as they stood on the eve of their reformation, as they stood when in 1833 they were visited by the royal commissioners, you will often find that their boundaries have provided wide enough room for fields and meadows and pastures. You will read that 'the local limits of the Borough of Derby contain 1660 statute acres',[2] that the limits of Northampton comprise 1520 acres and include 'a considerable quantity of agricultural land',[3] that 'the Borough of Bedford includes the whole town [that is, the whole house-covered area] which lies nearly in its centre encircled by a broad belt of land; its area being 2164 statute acres',[4] and, to take one last example, that 'the ancient borough' of Nottingham covered no less than 9610 acres and 'included a considerable quantity of forest, meadow and common land without the walls of the town'.[5] On the other hand, the fortified space was never very large. I learn

---

[1] Rashdall, *Universities*, vol. II, p. 553; Mullinger, *Hist. Univ. Camb.*, vol. I, p. 504.

[2] App. to *Munic. Corp. Rep.* (1835), vol. III, p. 1849.

[3] *Ibid.* III, 1965.   [4] *Ibid.* IV, 2103.   [5] *Ibid.* III, 1985.

from Mr Boase that intra-mural Oxford contained little more than 80 acres.[1]

In a legal record of 1426 we may read that there is a highway lying in the town, the *villa*, of Oxford in a certain place called Greenditch within the parish of St Giles outside the North Gate of the town of Oxford, which highway the township (*villata*) of Oxford is bound to repair. Whatever else Oxford may be, it is a *villa*, a town; and, whatever else the community of Oxford may be, it is a *villata*, a township.[2] A township should no more mean a little town than a fellowship should mean a little fellow.

I have been endeavouring to suggest to you that those who would study the early history of our towns (and I now use that word in its modern sense) have fields and pastures on their hands. Perhaps the suggestion is needless. The relationship of the town community, the nascent civic corporation, to the village community, the relationship of the town community to the town lands, the relationship of the oldest *burgenses* to arable strips and green commons, these have been a focus of that vigorous German controversy which we are watching with interest. But it is unnecessary, though it may be profitable, to look abroad. The Bishop of Oxford has taught us that 'the *burh* of the Anglo-Saxon period was simply a more strictly organised form of the township'.[3] If that be so, we must not leave out of view nine-tenths of the borough's territory. After what Mrs Green has written and Mr Stevenson has edited, it is plain that the early history of one ancient shire-borough, I mean Nottingham, cannot be the history of a small house-covered space.[4]

Possibly therefore I may turn your thoughts towards a luminous

[1] Boase, *Oxford*, p. 55: 'The wall enclosed a small rectangular space, measuring about half a mile from east to west, and a little more than a quarter of a mile from north to south.'

[2] *Royal Letters*, ed. Ogle, pp. 339, 340 (A.D. 1426): 'quedam alta via domini Regis iacens in villa Oxonie in quodam loco vocato Grenedyche infra parochiam S. Egidii extra portam borialem ville Oxonie...quam quidem altam viam...villata Oxonie...reparare debet.' For Greenditch, see Wood's *City of Oxford*, ed. Clark, p. 345 [and *Place-Names of Oxfordshire* (1953), p. 21]. In the view of those who endeavoured to make the township of Oxford liable for the repair of this road, the town of Oxford extended far beyond the northern wall.

[3] Stubbs, *Const. Hist.* vol. I, §44.

[4] So of Colchester, Mr Round has written in the *Antiquary*, vol. VI, p. 255: 'Perhaps the most salient feature revealed...is the stamp of a primitive rural community imprinted on a walled and populous town, a former Roman *colonia*.'

point if I try to interest you in the story of this lordship, this ownership, that went a-begging at Cambridge. For a long time past there had been an intermittent dispute. In 1616 the University declared that of the soil of Cambridge 'no certain lord was known'; also that King John's grant of 'the vill of Cambridge' to the burgesses and their heirs was not a grant of 'the soil'.[1] Even in 1826, when the fields had been inclosed, a quarrel among the inhabitants about a toll brought the old documents once more before the courts, and the lawyers were wrangling over the question whether Cambridge was or was not on the ancient demesne of the crown.

All this interests me. Long before I knew of these debates affecting the ground on which I daily walk, certain general considerations had led me to believe, first, that the soil of a truly ancient borough, a shire-borough recognised as such by Domesday Book, would very possibly have no obvious lord, and secondly, that if a king of the twelfth or thirteenth century took upon himself to grant such a borough to its burgesses, he might be sowing the seeds of a pretty law-suit.[2] A certain uncertainty about lordship and ownership, or about somewhat that is neither exactly lordship nor exactly ownership, may, so I think, be a leading thread in the early history of our oldest boroughs. Look at Oxford or look at Cambridge in Domesday Book. Why does the clerk write *Terra Regis* below and not above the account of the borough? Perhaps because there is 'no certain lord', or no certain owner, of the soil.

But I have another and a more general purpose in view when I ask your attention to this disputation. A student of our towns and villages must come to close quarters with some legal ideas, and the task of unravelling their history is not going to be so easy as it looked a while ago. That is a warning which comes to us from many quarters. We may see it in Mr Baden-Powell's book on the Indian Village, and in Dr Gierke's book on the German Community. We may see it everywhere. We shall have to think away distinctions which seem to us as clear as the sunshine; we must think ourselves back into a twilight. This we must do, not in a haphazard fashion, but of set purpose, knowing what we are doing.

Did it not seem to some of us, at all events in the examination room, that the question about the origin of property in land was straightforward? On the one hand, we had something to give

---

[1] Cooper, *Annals*, vol. III, pp. 110–11.
[2] *Hist. Eng. Law* (1st ed.), vol. I, p. 635, [2nd ed., p. 650].

away, 'property' or 'ownership'; on the other, there were various claimants: the tribe, the clan, the village, the family, the individual. We were to give this article, this commodity, to one claimant, and then it was to be passed from hand to hand. The only difficulty lay in the order of succession. Where do you put your family? Before or after the village community?

To be serious, we know now, even if we did not always know, that this is much too simple. Before we have gone far back in our own history, the 'belongs' (if I may so say) of private law begins to blend with the 'belongs' of public law; ownership blends with lordship, rulership, sovereignty in the vague medieval *dominium*, and the vague medieval *communitas* seems to swallow up both the corporation and the group of co-owners. We know or are beginning to know this; but a particular example may bring it sharply before our minds. When King John granted the vill of Cambridge to the burgesses and their heirs, did he mean to confer an ownership of the soil upon a municipal corporation? One point seems certain. Neither John nor his chancellor would have understood the terms of our question. Both the right that is given and the person or persons to whom it is given are hazily and feebly conceived.

You know why I say 'person or persons'. I think that the historian of our towns will have to face that difficulty. Also I fancy that in this country lawyers have done something to deter historians from fairly facing it, by concealing from them its moral and economic interest. The invention of 'fictitious personality', as it is sometimes called, is put before us as a feat of skill, an ingenious artifice of jurisprudence. The inference is readily drawn that it concerns only lawyers. But is that true? Can I in the few minutes that are left to me persuade you that, however meanly you may think of legal technicalities, there is a problem here which deserves patient and sympathetic investigation?

In 1833 Cambridge, like other boroughs, was visited by royal commissioners. Of Cambridge, as of most other boroughs, they reported some evil tidings. In Cambridge, however, they found what was rare, a member of the corporation who courageously defended what they regarded as a bad abuse: namely, the sale of some pieces of the corporation's land to corporators at small prices. 'He thought' we are told 'that the property [of the corporation] belonged *bona fide* to the corporation and that they had a right to do what they pleased with their own.' 'Such', the commissioners

11

exclaim, 'is the theory of a member of the Cambridge common council, which, however frequently it may have been acted upon, has seldom, we conceive, been openly supported by so unflinching an advocate.'[1]

And yet the common-councillor's theory seems verbally plausible. The property of a corporation is unquestionably its property, and are we to be angry whenever a noun in the singular governs a verb in the plural? If so, we had better not read medieval records, for even *universitas* is sometimes treated as a 'noun of multitude'.[2]

I must not carry further the defence of my fellow-townsman. Certainly in this context there is a vast difference between 'its' and 'theirs'. In our eyes this is a difference between decency and scandal. But I think we have reason to believe that it is also a difference between modernity and antiquity, and (if I may so use the words) between urbanity and rusticity. The common-councillor was ignoring a moral and economic achievement accomplished in the medieval boroughs, the differentiation of 'its' from 'ours'.

This was a moral and economic, not primarily a legal achievement. Legally the common-councillor was not so very far wrong. Our law, if I am not mistaken, had never dictated to the boroughs what they should do with their property: it had trusted to their honour. If, observing all constitutional forms, holding duly convened meetings and so forth, the corporators divided among themselves the income or the land of the corporation, they were, I believe, unpunishable and their acts were valid.[3] But, whatever may have been the law, we surely feel that in William IV's reign it was scandalous that the corporators of a great town should think, or act as though they thought, that the property of the corporation, or such remnants of it as had not been squandered, was their property: was their property morally, or as the common-councillor said, *bona fide*.

---

[1] *Munic. Corp. Report*, App. vol. IV, p. 2199; *A Digested Report of the Evidence as to the Corporation of Cambridge*, published by H. Wallis (Cambridge, 1833), p. 63.

[2] Gierke, *Genossenschaftsrecht*, vol. II, p. 49, gives instances, e.g. 'controversia quam universitas villanorum in W. moverunt'.

[3] See Grant, *Corporations* (1850), pp. 129 ff. Mr Grant, writing after the Municipal Reformation, seems to hold that the Court of Chancery would have interfered. But I cannot find among his authorities any that proves this, and, if we consider what the corporations had actually been doing for a long time past, the silence of the law reports will seem eloquent. It will be understood that I am not speaking of cases in which a municipal corporation had been made a trustee for some definite purpose.

From a discourse on personality, the personality of the corporation aggregate, I shrink. Ought we to apply to it such adjectives as 'ideal', 'moral', 'mystical', 'juristic', 'fictitious', 'artificial'? Is it not, on the other hand, as real as the personality of a man? Foreign lawyers, Romanists and Germanists, are disputing strenuously. A great deal of what they are saying is interesting to students of English history, though it is sometimes couched in terms which are more abstract than we like. Just because our own legal history has been continuous, just because there has been no violent breach between 'folk-law and jurist-law',[1] we have never been driven very far into what many of us would contemptuously call legal metaphysics, and I am not going to make the plunge. It is not of the technical shape which lawyers give to the idea, but of the economic and moral substratum that I am speaking. Such a substratum there is: in other words, men will not think of the group or the town as a person until this idea is forced upon them by business and projects and current notions of right and wrong.

Nowadays it is difficult to get the corporation out of our heads. If we look at the doings of our law courts, we may feel inclined to reverse a famous judgment and to say that while the individual is the unit of ancient, the corporation is the unit of modern law. In an university town the difficulty is perhaps at its worst. Oxford and Cambridge are peopled by 'group-persons'. We are not content with what the law does for us. Morally, though not legally, some at least of our multitudinous societies and clubs are persons. The law-student feels a little shock of surprise when he is told that his college is a person and that his college boat club is not—or rather, are not. The club, like the college, seems to have property, to owe and be owed money. The property of the club is not for him exactly and *bona fide* (as the common-councillor said) the property of its members—at least it is not so in all cases.

I say this because we ought to notice that if there is anything that should be called fiction in this matter—and I doubt it—we must not regard that fiction as the work of lawyers. On the contrary, at least in modern England, the lawyer is not the motive force, but the drag on the wheel, and must protest that the layman is (if you please) 'feigning' more rapidly than the law will allow.

---

[1] It was, I believe, Beseler's *Volksrecht und Juristenrecht* (Leipzig, 1843) that opened the controversy about the nature of the German *Genossenschaft*.

It is not the lawyer but the man of business who makes the mercantile firm into a person distinct from the sum of the partners.[1] It is the layman who complains that the club cannot get its clubhouse without 'some lawyer's nonsense about trustees'. Such in these days is our 'propensity to feign' (if I may borrow a famous phrase) that the law can find no place for the new persons, the new *species* and *genera* of persons, whom we are daily calling into existence.

In passing I may observe that in England we have had a second legal expedient for dealing with the affairs of organised groups, an expedient of which our neighbours seem to know little or nothing: I mean the trust. In the fourteenth century, just when we were taking over from the canonists the dogma that the corporation must have its origin in some act of sovereign power, we were hard at work developing the trust, and soon it had become an useful instrument not only in the sphere of private law and family settlements, but also in the sphere of public or semi-public affairs and, if I may so say, of group-organising law.

This by the way, for, leaving the legal machinery out of sight, I would ask your attention for the underlying moral fact. We feel that the disclosures of 1833 were disgraceful. We observe also that few men have had the courage of this common-councillor. Very rarely in the great towns had the property of the corporation been frankly divided among the corporators. Too often it had been sold or let to them at an undervalue. The inadequate price or inadequate rent was a tribute paid to civic virtue. The corporators in the great towns had known and felt that the property of the corporation was not exactly their own *bona fide*.[2]

But it is, so I think, with other feelings that we observe what had happened in some little towns, or rather villages, which long ago received a few chartered privileges from a medieval baron and therefore were allowed a precarious place on the roll of English

---

[1] Lindley, *Partnership*, Bk. I, ch. 7 (6th ed. p. 118): 'Commercial men and accountants are apt to look upon a firm in the light in which lawyers look upon a corporation, i.e. as a body distinct from the members composing it, and having rights and obligations distinct from those of its members....But this is not the legal notion of a firm. The firm is not recognised by lawyers as in any way distinct from the members composing it.'

[2] *Munic. Corp. Rep.* (1835), p. 45: 'Some sense of impropriety, indicated by the secrecy with which such transactions are conducted, has accompanied the execution of long leases for nominal considerations or the alienations in fee of the corporate property to individual corporators.'

boroughs. Economically they were rural villages. In one case we are told that 'most of the senior burgesses were in the rank of labourers'.[1] Well, there used to be a common pasture; it had disappeared; it had been cut up into plots, which had been let on long and highly beneficial leases to burgesses, or rather villagers. Now I should like to put this to you as a question not of law, but of morals: Has any great wrong been done? Do you feel inclined to speak of misappropriation? For my own part I am not prepared to use very hard words, because I do not expect to find in a village community of an old type any clear perception of a difference between 'its' and 'theirs', and, if such a perception I found, I should doubt that it was born in the village.

Perhaps then our best comment on the common-councillor's apology would be *summa rusticitas*.[2]

---

[1] *Munic. Corp. Rep.* (1835), App. vol. I, p. 289 (Laugharne).

[2] I do not mean to imply that the distinction between the property of a corporation and the property of the corporators must always represent a deep moral difference. The modern incorporated trading company aims at making gain which is to be divided between the corporators. They, if unanimous, may put an end to the corporation, and, when its debts have been paid, divide its property; indeed our law enables a majority of a certain strength to extinguish the corporation against the wishes of the few. Here the distinction between 'its' and 'theirs' may be highly technical, and may sometimes be ignored in common discourse. When the idea of a corporation has once been fashioned, it can be employed for the most various purposes; but I do not think that this idea could be fashioned until current morality had perceived that the Town had property which was not co-owned by the existing burgesses. See Gierke, *Genossenschaftsrecht*, vol. II, pp. 573 ff. It will also be understood that I am not an apologist of all that was done in the small boroughs and disclosed by the Reports of 1835 and 1880. Beneficial leases to corporators are not so easily defensible as would have been a frank and final distribution of the common land among the members of the community.

II

THE HISTORY OF A
CAMBRIDGESHIRE MANOR[1]

It is not often that one has the good fortune of being able to study
a series of medieval documents at one's own time and in one's own
house; but this was given to me by the late Mr O. C. Pell, lord of
the manor of Wilburton, in the county of Cambridge. He committed to my care a splendid line of court and account rolls which,
though there were some gaps in it, stretched from Edward I to
Henry VII, and now, the consent of his successor, Mr Albert Pell,
having been very kindly given, I am able to lay before the readers
of this *Review* a fairly continuous history of a particular English
manor during the later Middle Ages; and to me it seems that at the
present time we have some need for histories of particular manors,
for I am convinced that the time has not yet come when generalities
about *the* English manor and its fortunes will be safe or sound.

The manor of Wilburton, on the edge of the fen, formed part
of the ancient estates of the church of Ely. It is fully described in
two 'extents', the one made in 1221, the other in 1277.[2] Of these
its late lord, who was deeply interested in its history, gave an
account in the *Proceedings of the Cambridge Antiquarian Society*.[3]
I shall here speak of them very briefly, for they are but the prelude
to those documents which are the theme of this essay.

The two extents begin by describing the demesne land—that is,
the land which is in the lord's own hand. In the extent of 1277 he
has 216 acres ('by the lesser hundred and the perch of $16\frac{1}{2}$ feet')

---

[1] *English Historical Review* (July 1894): *Collected Papers*, vol. II, pp. 366–406.
[As a guide to recent work in this field, reference may be made to the
bibliographies in the *Cambridge Economic History*, vol. I (1941), and in
E. Miller, *The Abbey and Bishopric of Ely* (1951). See also M. Postan, 'The
Chronology of Labour Services', *Trans. R. Hist. Soc.* (1937); 'The Rise of a
Money Economy', *Econ. Hist. Rev.* (1944); and E. A. Kosminsky, *Studies in
the Agrarian History of England* (1956). For another typical estate study, see
R. A. L. Smith, *Canterbury Cathedral Priory* (1943).]

[2] MS. Cott. Tib. B 2; Claud. C 11.

[3] 'Report and Communications' (1887), p. 162. [These rolls are now
in the Library of the University of Wisconsin.]

of arable land, and besides this he has meadow land and a wide
expanse of fen. In the next place an account is given of the holdings of the 'freeholders' and 'hundredors' (*de hundredariis et
libere tenentibus*). Of these there are nine, one with 16 acres *de wara*,
four with 12 acres *de wara* apiece, two with 6 acres apiece, two
with $2\frac{1}{2}$ acres apiece. This arrangement remained constant during
the half-century which elapsed between the two surveys. These
'freeholders and hundredors' pay small money rents—the holder
of 12 acres pays 2*d.* a year—they owe two days' ploughing in Lent
and two in winter, for which they receive 1*d.* a day; they have to
attend the great boon day in autumn. They owe suit to the court
of Wilburton and must attend the hundred court, which is in the
bishop's hand; hence their designation as *hundredarii*. In the later
extent it is expressly stated that they owe a heriot (best beast,
or 32*d.*), a fine for marrying their daughters (32*d.*), leyrwite and
tallage; the *gersuma*, or fine for marrying a daughter, is mentioned
in the earlier extent.

In the court rolls the existence of freeholders can from time to
time be detected. They owe suit of court; they are often amerced
for not doing it or compound for it with a small sum of money.
There are entries also which show that they still owe ploughing
service and that some of them are very lax in performing it. Again,
descents and alienations are sometimes presented and the heriot
is still due. But on the whole these freeholders seem to have
played only a small part in the manor; the names which occur on
the court rolls are chiefly those of customary tenants.

In the extents the description of the freehold tenements is
followed by the heading 'De Operariis et Plenis Terris'. The full
land (*plena terra*) consists of 12 acres *de wara*. Of this thorny
phrase *de wara* I will here say nothing—its interest lies in a remote
past—save this, that as a matter of fact the full land at Wilburton
really consisted of 24 acres. Of these full lands there are fifteen
and a half. The holder of such a tenement pays 19*d.* a year—12*d.* as
wite penny, 6*d.* as sedge silver, 1*d.* as ward penny. From Michaelmas to Hokeday he does two works a week according to the earlier
survey, three according to the later; from Hokeday to Lammas
three works a week, from Lammas to Michaelmas five works a
week; and besides all this there is a good deal to be done which is
not computed as part of the regular week work. On the whole the
services, which are more elaborately described in the later than in

the earlier of the two surveys, and which perhaps have become heavier during the interval, are of the familiar type.[1]

Then there were ten and a half cottage tenements, which even in Henry VII's days still preserved a relic of the Domesday terminology in the name 'cossetles'. The holder of each such tenement paid 7*d*. a year—4*d*. for wite pound, 2*d*. for sedge silver, 1*d*. for ward penny—and did two works in every week. The holders of the full lands and the cottiers owe suit to the lord's mill, a fine for marrying their daughters, leyrwite and tallage; they cannot sell colt or ox without the lord's leave.

We already see that a basis has been fixed for the commutation of labour into money. Every 'work' in autumn is, we are told, worth one penny, and out of autumn every work is worth a halfpenny; we also see that one half-*cottaria* is held by a tenant who 'at the will of the lord' pays 2*s*. a year in lieu of his labours; but the profit of the manor is reckoned mainly in 'works'. In the way of money rents the lord draws but 31*s*. a year from the manor, besides some small dues; on the other hand 3773½ 'works' are owed to him, by a 'work' being meant the work of one man for one day.

From 1221 down to the very end of the Middle Ages the manor seems to have kept with wonderful conservatism what we may call its external shape—that is to say, at the end of this period the distribution of the customary tenements into 'full lands' and 'cossetles', or cottier tenements, was still preserved, though the 'full land' was often broken into two 'half-lands'.

At the beginning of the fourteenth century we see that some of the 'works' were done in kind, while others were 'sold to the homage'. Thus there is an account for seventeen weeks in the winter of 1303–4 during which the temporalities of the see of Ely were in the king's hand; in this the bailiff and reeve, after charging themselves with the rents of assize (i.e. the fixed money rents),

---

[1] As it seemed that in 1277 the bishop was exacting from the Wilburton tenants a greater amount of 'week work' than he exacted in 1221, I looked through some of the extents of other manors given in the two Cottonian manuscripts, and I found the same phenomenon at Lyndon, Stretham, and Thriplow. Apparently in all these cases the bishop had put on an extra work-day in every week between Michaelmas and Hoketide—and this in the thirteenth century. These Ely extents ought to be printed as soon as possible. [A detailed study of the Ely material has been made by E. Miller, *The Abbey and Bishopric of Ely* (1951).]

proceed to account for 10s. 10d. for 260 'winter works sold to the homage at the rate of a halfpenny per work'. In a later part of the account we see how this number of 'works' is arrived at: the officers account for 1385 works arising from fifteen and a half 'full lands' and ten cottier tenements; they then set against this number the 260 works sold to the homage, 355 works sold to the executors of the late bishop, fifty-seven works excused to the reeve and reaper, thirty-eight works excused to the smith, nineteen works due from a half-*cottaria* which has been let at a fixed rent, fourteen and a half works excused on account of the Christmas holiday, 363½ works the amount of ploughing done, 258 works the amount of harrowing done, twenty works in repairing the ditch round the park at Downham, thus getting out the total of 1385 works.

A little later comes a series of accounts for some consecutive years in Edward II's reign. The basis of these accounts, so far as works come in question, is that 2943 winter and summer works, valued at a halfpenny apiece, are due, and 845 autumn works valued at a penny. These numbers seem subject to some slight fluctuations, due to the occurrence of leap years and other causes. Then the accountants have to show how in one way or another these works have been discharged, and in the first place they must account for 'works sold'. In the year ending at Michaelmas 1322 the accountants charge themselves with the value of 1213 winter and summer works and sixty and a half autumn works which have been 'sold'; in the next year with the value of 1297½ winter and summer works and 170½ autumn works; in the next year with the value of 1496 winter and summer works and 149 autumn works; in the next year with the value of 1225½ winter and summer works and 218½ autumn works; in the next year with the value of 1023 winter and summer works and 247½ autumn works; in the next year with the value of 1381 winter and summer works and sixty-three and a half autumn works. In these and in the later accounts it is not usual to state to whom or in what manner these 'works' were 'sold'; but there can be little doubt that they were sold to those who were bound to do them—that is to say, when the lord did not want the full number of works he took money instead at the rate of a halfpenny for a winter or summer work and of a penny for an autumn work. The phrase 'works sold to the homage', which occurs in the accounts of Edward I's time, may perhaps suggest that the whole body of tenants were jointly liable for the money which thus became due in lieu of works.

It will be seen that the number of 'works sold' does not amount to half the number of works due. How were the rest discharged? In the first place some were released; thus the reeve, the reaper, and the smith stood excused; and then again holidays were allowed on festivals; thus the occurrence of the feasts of St Lawrence and St Bartholomew serves to discharge a certain number of the autumn works. But very many of the works were actually done; thus in one year 203 'diets' of ploughing between Michaelmas and Hokeday discharge 406 works; in the previous year 377 works had been discharged in similar fashion, in the year before that 406, in the year before that 420½. Ploughing, mowing, harrowing, and the like are always wanted; other works are accounted for now in one fashion, now in another. In one year twenty-six works were spent on the vineyard at Ely, in another three works were spent in catching rabbits; but on the whole the *opera* are laid out in much the same manner in each successive year.

I have examined the accounts for the last six years of Edward II's reign; their scheme is as follows: the accountant is the reeve; his year runs from Michaelmas to Michaelmas. He begins by debiting himself with the arrears of previous years. The next item consists of 'Rents of assize'. These are the old money dues payable by freeholders and customary tenants; they amount to no great sum—about £2—but show a slight tendency to increase, owing to the 'arrentation' of some of the minor services; for instance, 19*d*. is accounted for in respect of a release of the duty of collecting sticks in the park at Somersham. Next comes 'Farm of land', a single item of 32*s*. in respect of twenty-four acres of demesne land which have been let at a rent. By far the most important item is 'Sale of crops', a very variable item, fluctuating between £8 and £54. Then follows 'Sale of stock'. Then comes 'Issues of the manor' ('Exitus manerii'). Under this head the reeve accounts for the number of 'works' that have been 'sold', also on occasion for the price of fowls and turf. The 'Perquisites of the court' comprise not only the amercements, but also the fines payable on alienation of the customary tenements and the like. The last item consists of 'Sales accounted for on the back of the roll'; these seem to consist chiefly of sales of malt. The total income varies between very wide limits, rising to £66, falling to less than £20.

On the credit side the first heading is 'Allowances' or 'Acquit-tances'. A sum of 3*d.* has to be allowed because the reeve is excused that sum from his rent. Under 'Custus carucarum' stand the cost of making and repairing ploughs, shoeing horses, and so forth. About 5*s.* per annum is spent in paying 2*d.* per plough per day for every one of the sixteen ploughs of the tenants engaged in the 'boon ploughing' for winter seed and for spring seed. The 'Cost of carts' is sometimes separately accounted for; the cost of 'Repairs of buildings' is by no means heavy. Under 'Minute necessaries' fall the price of various articles purchased, also the wages of the only money-wage-receiving labourers who are em-ployed on the manor—namely, a swineherd at 4*s.* 4*d.* per annum and an occasionally employed shepherd at 5*s.* a year. 'Threshing and winnowing' are paid for as piece work. 'Purchase of corn' and 'Purchase of stock' are headings that need no comment. Under 'Mowing and harvesting' ('Falcatio et autumpnus') we find no heavy charge; all that has to be paid for is the tenant's harvest dinner, and the wages during harvest of the reeve and 'repereve'. Sometimes under the head of 'Forinsec' (or Foreign) 'Expenses' occur a few small sums not expended directly on the manor.

The reeve then accounts for the money that he has paid into the exchequer at Ely, and then the account is balanced and generally leaves him in debt. Apparently the annual profit of the manor varied between very wide limits. The reason of this fluctua-tion is to be found chiefly in the sales of corn. The highest prices of the wheat sold in these six years are as follows:

	s.	*d.*				*s.*	*d.*	
1321–2	12	0	per quarter		1324–5	7	0	per quarter
1322–3	11	0	per quarter		1325–6	5	0	per quarter
1323–4	7	2	per quarter		1326–7	3	4	per quarter

Such figures as these, though they may be familiar enough to economists, are worth notice, for they show us that however stable an institution the manor may have been from century to century, agriculture involved a very high degree of risk.

On the back of the account roll the reeve proceeds to account for the produce of the manor and the 'works' of the tenants. First comes 'Compotus grangie' ('Barn account'). The reeve has received so many quarters of wheat from the barn; so many have gone in seed, so many in provender for the manorial servants, so many remain in the barn. Rye, barley, pease, oats, and malt have to be similarly accounted for; the account is checked by tallies between the reeve, the reaper, and the barn-keeper. There are four ploughmen and one shepherd who are *famuli manerii* and in receipt of corn, each of them getting one quarter per week during some twelve weeks of the year. Next comes 'Compotus Stauri' ('Account of live stock'), under which heading the horses, oxen, and pigs are enumerated. Then under 'Compotus Operum' ('Account of works') the reeve has to show, as explained above, how some 3700 works have been discharged, the autumn works, worth a penny apiece, being distinguished from the winter and summer works, worth a halfpenny. Thus in one of these years he has to account for 814 autumn works; he does so thus:

Excused to reeve, reaper, smith	58	works
Excused in respect of a cottary let at a rent	7½	works
Excused on account of festivals	58	works
Sold	246½	works
Reaping, binding, and stacking 128 acres at two works per acre	256	works
Carrying	96	works
Garnering[1]	22	works
Stacking pease	10	works
Carrying dung	58	works
	812	

Thus out of this batch of works more than half have actually been done.

Now, glancing at the manor as a whole, we see that to a very large extent it is still dependent on the labours of its villeins. The whole amount received by way of rent is but £2. 10*s*., or thereabouts, while the price of works sold brings in some £3 or £4. Almost all the regular agricultural work, with the exception of threshing and winnowing, is done for the lord by his tenants. He is as yet no great 'employer of labour' in the modern sense; wages are a comparatively trifling item in his accounts. He generally employs a hired swineherd and a hired shepherd, and during some part of the year he has ploughmen, who are paid in grain. But the main part of his ploughing, reaping, mowing, harrowing is done by those who are bound to do it by status or tenure.

[1] *In bladis mayand' in grangia.* The word *mayare* is new to me. [See Baxter, *Medieval Latin Word-List, s.v. meia.*]

From the reign of Edward III there are no accounts; but turning to those of Richard II's time we find that the theory of the account, so far as 'works' are concerned, is still the same. It is now reckoned that there are 2970 winter and summer works, worth a halfpenny apiece, and 813 autumn works, worth a penny apiece, to be accounted for. Some of these works are 'sold', some not sold; thus in the year ending Michaelmas 1393 we find 183 works of the one class and ninety-three of the other class accounted for as sold. The number of works sold varies much from year to year. Many hundred works are still done in kind; but the number so done has been diminished, because no less than four full lands and nine cottier tenements 'are in the lord's hand' and have been let out at money rents. This has introduced into the account a new element— namely, 'Rent of bond land' ('Firma terre native' or 'Firma terre nativorum'), which brings in about £9 a year. A large number of *opera* has, therefore, to be subtracted on this score, e.g. 528 winter and summer works in respect of the said four full lands and 836 similar works in respect of the said nine cottier tenancies. Exactly when or how the change occurred the extant accounts do not show. Already in the first year of Richard II there were three full lands and eight and a half cottier tenements let at a rent for short terms of years and doing no work. But by connecting the accounts with the court rolls we are enabled to infer that these lands were vacated by villeins who fled late in the reign of Edward III; thus the first full land on the list is that of John Thorold, who fled in 1376 or thereabouts, and of whose flight the court rolls continue to talk for the next forty years.

Turning, therefore, to the court rolls, we find many entries which seem to show that during the last half of the fourteenth century and the first quarter of the fifteenth the lord had great difficulty in keeping and finding customary tenants on the old terms. Some examples shall be given:

(1364) J. W., who held a full land, has eloigned himself outside the dominion of the lord, and altogether relinquished the said land, which has, therefore, remained in the lord's hand for default of a tenant; N. R. now comes and takes the land.   (1365) N. R., mentioned in the last entry, has now relinquished (*omnino reliquit*) the land; his goods are seized into the lord's hand; they include beasts, swine, household utensils, etc., valued at 33s. 10d., exclusive of the corn.   (1366) H. G., who held a half-land and cottage, has eloigned himself outside the lord's demesne; his goods and crops are seized into the lord's hand.

(1366) R. O., who held a full land, has eloigned himself and abandoned his land, taking with him a plough and a pair of quern stones, against the custom of the manor; let him be attached. (1370) J. C. held a cottage, but has relinquished it because of his poverty (*propter impotenciam*); so it has been seized into the lord's hand and is now let to J. G. for twelve years at a money rent. The tenement abandoned by R. O. is let in the same way. (1370) J. W. takes for twenty years a full land which is in the lord's hand for default of a tenant. In similar circumstances A. L. takes a half-land for twelve years. Several similar entries follow. (1371) S. T. takes for his life a half-land which is in the lord's hand for default of a tenant; he pays no fine, for he takes it unwillingly (*quia invito capit*). Other lands which are in the lord's hands are granted out provisionally until permanent tenants can be found. (1372) One full land, three half-lands, three cottages, and six half-cottages are in the lord's hand for default of tenants, but some of them have been temporarily let; tenants ought to be found for them, and let proclamation be made that any heir or other person who has any right in them do come and claim them. Proclamations to this effect are made at several successive courts. (1380) W. W., who held a messuage and a full virgate of customary land, has left the manor, waived his land, and carried off his chattels to Chesterton [which is ancient demesne]. J. M. removed the chattels for him, knowing him to be the lord's tenant. Let J. M. be distrained to answer for these chattels, and let a writ be sued out against W. W. [for being on the ancient demesne there can be no talk of seizing him]. (1384) W. S. surrenders a cottage and two acres of 'native land', which he held for 5s. a year, for that this was too dear (*eo quod nimis cara*), as the whole homage testifies; it is granted to J. P. and his wife and their sequela at 3s. a year. A case of surrender follows, in which the new tenant is to pay 3s., instead of 5s., paid by his predecessor, the whole homage again testifying that the rent had been too high. (1387) It is ordered in many successive courts that a tenant be found for the lands lately held by J. A., which he has abandoned (*reliquit fugitive*). (1392) It is presented by the reeve that S. T., who holds a messuage and half a 'cossetle', is unable to maintain the said tenement and do the services (*impotens est predictam terram et tenementum manutenere et defendere versus dominum*); therefore the lord's officers must find a new tenant, and in the meantime answer for the issues.

Throughout the court rolls of Henry IV's reign cases continue to occur in which lands have been abandoned or 'waived', and other cases in which rents are reduced. Thus (1401) it is presented that Agnes D., who holds a half-land, is unable to maintain it and do the services due to the lord, and that the jurors have provided R. N. to take the land; he is to pay 12s. rent instead of doing the services which Agnes did, and only pays 2s. by way of fine for admittance, because he is an unwilling tenant. The house is ruinous; the land is out of cultivation; one of his neighbours provides him with the requisite seed. (1409) Mariota, widow of J. N., who held a full virgate for life, has left the lord's domain, gone to Haddenham, taken a husband, and 'waived' the land, so that it has come to the lord's hand. (1410) A cottier tenement formerly held at a rent of 4*s.* is granted out at a rent of 2*s.*

It is not necessary, perhaps not justifiable, to infer from this evidence that the customary tenants of Wilburton were in any absolute sense badly off, that they could not live and thrive upon their tenements. The true explanation may be, not that they were in distress, but that they saw a more attractive prospect elsewhere. An increased demand for hired labour and a consequent rise of wages may have been the forces which drove the peasantry to desert their holdings. Unfortunately there are neither accounts nor court rolls which testify to the immediate effects of the Black Death; but, so far as I can see, the bishop's difficulty in finding tenants who will take the full lands on the old terms begins at a somewhat later time and thenceforth increases.

Nor need we suppose that none of the tenants were contented with their lot. During the same period we find cases in which an heir or surrenderee is willing to promise the old services and to pay a fine on admission. To give a fair idea of the situation I will make notes of the various entries which relate to changes among the tenants of the fifteen and a half full lands between 1364, when the court rolls begin, and the accession of Henry of Lancaster.

(1364) William Starling surrenders half a full land to the use of John Osbern. John Walter, who held a full land, late that of Andrew Cateson, has eloigned himself and relinquished his land; Nicholas of Roydon takes it, to hold at the accustomed services. (1366) Nicholas of Roydon has relinquished a full land; it is seized into the lord's hand. Aubin Willay has eloigned himself and relinquished one half-land; Henry Greneleaf has relinquished another. (1367) Richard Leycester takes the half-land formerly Aubin Willay's, to hold at a rent of 13*s.* until a permanent tenant can be found. (1367) Robert Osbern, who held a half-land, has deserted it. (1368) There are now in the lord's hand for default of tenants a full land late of Nicholas of Roydon, a full land late of John Thorold, a full land late of Robert Osbern, a half-land late of Aubin Willay, a half-land late of Henry Greneleaf, and two cottage tenements. (1369) Robert Tates takes the full land of Nicholas of Roydon for a term of seven years; he is to pay 5*s.* rent and to spend 2*s.* a year on improvements; he pays a fine of 3*d.* (1370) John Frost takes the half-land late of Robert Osbern for a term of twelve years at a rent of 13s. 4d.; he pays a fine of 6d. Aubin Willay takes as tenant for life a half-land, seemingly that which he relinquished in 1366. For half of it he is to pay a rent of 6s.; for the other he is to do the accustomed services. He pays a fine of 6s. John Atwell takes the full land late of John Thorold for twenty years at a rent of 26s. 8d.; fine, 12d. Andrew Lessi takes the half-land late that of Edmund Prat, now in the lord's hand for default of a tenant, to hold for twelve years at a rent of 14s.; fine, 12d. Richard Cokayne takes the half-land late of Henry Greneleaf for twelve years at a rent of 15s.; fine, 12d. John Downham takes a half-land late that of Nicholas of Roydon for twelve years, rendering in the first year 4s. for half of it and the accustomed services for the other half, and afterwards the accustomed services for the whole; fine, 12d.   (1371) Simon Teye takes a half-land, late that of Nicholas of Roydon, for his life at the accustomed services; no fine, for he is unwilling. John Downham, junior, takes a half-land, late that of Nicholas of Roydon, until a tenant shall be found who will do the accustomed services, to hold at a rent of 15s.; fine 6d. There are now in the lord's hand a full land late of John Thorold, a full land late of Robert Osbern, a half-land late of Richard in the Lane, a half-land late of Henry Greneleaf, a half-land late of Nicholas of Roydon, besides seven of the cottage tenements.

[*Hiatus in the rolls*]

(1379) Walter Wiseman marries Alice, widow of Richard Sewyne, tenant of a full land, and is admitted for his wife's life; fine, 2s.   (1381) Walter Wiseman has fled with his chattels to Chesterton; let a writ be sued out against him. The full land known as Thorold's is divided into four portions; one is granted to Richard Tates, another to Nicholas Dony, another to Richard Walter and John Scot, another to John Downham, senior, and John Parsce; in each case the tenure is for ten years at a rent of 6s. 8d.; fine, 6d. John Atwell has been holding the lands, but he could not do the services.   (1382) Alice Cokayne surrenders a half-land, late that of Henry Greneleaf; it is granted to Aubin Willay and John Scot, at a rent of 14s., to hold for their lives or until a tenant be found who will do the ancient services.   (1382) Richard Downham marries Ellen, widow of John Newman, tenant of a full land; he is admitted; fine, 13s. 4d. The full land 'waived' by Walter Wiseman is granted to John Arnold and Margaret, his daughter, for their lives, and the life of the survivor, at a rent of 26s. 8d. and suit of court in lieu of all service.   (1382) John Atwell surrenders a full land to the use of John Warwick, who takes it from the lord for a term of twelve years at the accustomed services; fine, 18d.   (1384) The tenement relinquished by John Arnold is in the lord's hand; the manorial officers answer for the issues.   (1385) Anna Foldyng surrenders a messuage and a full land, for which she has been paying a rent of 29s. 4d., to the use of John Pontefyssche, who is admitted to hold at

26

the same rent; fine, 8s.; John is to erect a chamber which Anna is to hold for her life, and is to demise to her an acre of the said land for life. (1386) Alice Cokayne, who held a full land for life as widow of Richard Cokayne, is dead; her son Andrew is admitted; fine, 6s. 8d. The tenement relinquished by John Arnold is still vacant. Nicholas Dony surrenders a parcel of a full land held by him at a rent of 6s. 8d. to the use of Richard Downham, who is admitted to hold to him and his at the said rent; fine, 12d. Simon Teye, who holds a half-land at the ancient services, is too feeble to do them; John Crombred takes the tenement to hold to him and his at the ancient services; fine, 6s. 8d. (1387) John Arnold's tenement is still vacant. (1389) John Downham, senior, tenant of a full land, is dead; his widow, Anna, is to hold for her life. Richard Downham and Ellen his wife, who in Ellen's right hold a full land, are too feeble to maintain the said land, and they surrender it, Ellen being separately examined; the lord grants it to Jacob Frost, to hold to him and his sequela at the accustomed services; fine, 3s. 4d., and no more, for he is an unwilling tenant; and since Richard and Ellen have let the tenement go out of repair and cultivation, Jacob is to have from them two mares (iumenta), price 15s., and four quarters of drage, price 8s., and they are to hear no more about the waste of which they have been guilty. Aubin Willay, who holds a half-land jointly with John Scot, surrenders his moiety to the use of John Downham, junior, who is admitted to hold at a rent of 7s. until a tenant be found who will do the ancient services; fine, 8d. Richard Downham surrenders his share of Thorold's tenement to the use of William Breche and Catherine his wife, who are admitted to hold to them and their sequela, at the rent of 6s. 8d., at which Richard held; fine, 8d. (1389) John Arnold's tenement is still vacant. (1390) John Atwell surrenders a full land, since he is too feeble to maintain it, to the use of John Warwick, who is admitted to hold to him and his sequela at the accustomed services; fine, 6s. 8d. John Arnold's tenement is still vacant. (1392) John Arnold's tenement is still vacant. (1393) Anna, widow of John Downham, senior, who held a full land for her life, is dead; her son, John Downham, junior, is admitted to hold to him and his sequela at the accustomed services; fine, 6s. 8d. John Arnold's tenement is still vacant. (1396) At the last court it was presented that Aubin Willay, who held a half-land, had gone away and waived it. He is now present, and on being examined states that he refuses and relinquishes the land, and he surrenders it to the use of Richard Scot, to whom it is granted at a rent of 12s., to hold to him and his sequela until some one shall come to take it at the accustomed services; and in case such a one appears, Richard is to have an option of continuing to hold at the said services, and should he reject this option is to receive from the incoming tenant the costs that he has laid out on the tenement; fine, 12d., and no more, because he is to build. John Arnold's tenement is still vacant. (1398) John Crombred, who held a full land, is dead; his widow, Ellen, is admitted to hold for her life; no fine. Richard Dony and Ellen, his wife, late widow of John Crombred, who hold a full land for the life of the said Ellen, surrender their estate, and the lord grants the said land to them and their heirs at the accustomed services; fine 2s. Nicholas Dony, holder of a half-land, is dead; his widow, Agnes, is admitted to hold for her life at the accustomed services; no fine.   (1399) John Starling, holder of a full land, is too feeble to maintain the land, and surrenders it; the lord grants it to John Newman, to hold to him and his sequela at the accustomed services; fine, 6s. 8d. The outgoing tenant 'demises' to the incoming tenant farming utensils and tillages, and pays 60s. to the incoming tenant in respect of waste, which money the incoming tenant is to spend in repairs. John Arnold's tenement is still vacant.

On the whole, after reading these entries our conclusion will probably be that, in the then state of the markets for land, labour, and food, the value of a full land copyhold of the manor of Wilburton, to be held by the ancient services, was extremely small, and was often accounted a negative quantity by the tenant—that is to say, he would rather not have the land than have it. Happy in their posterity were those who endured and got their services commuted into rents.

We may now compare the accounts of Richard II's reign with those of Edward II's. The scheme remains the same, but some new headings have made their appearance. The 'Rents of assize' now bring in £2. 3s. 0¾d.; there is here a trifling increase. The old 'Farm of land', which brought in £1. 12s., is replaced by two headings—'Farm of demesne land' and 'Farm of the natives' land'. Under the former there is an increase during Richard's reign from 6s. 9d. to £1. 1s. 11½d. A good many small pieces, two or three acres apiece, of the old demesne have been granted out by entries on the court roll at money rents of about 1s. per acre. Under the 'Farm of the natives' land' fall the rents paid for those relinquished full lands, half-lands, and cottages which have fallen into the lord's hand and been granted out at money rents; the amount of these rents rises during the reign from £7. 10s. to near £10. 'Sale of corn' brings in some £20, and 'Sale of stock' a very variable amount. The 'Issues of the manor' bring in some £2 and the 'Sale of wool' some £3. The 'Sale of works' is separately accounted for, and at the beginning of the reign still brings in £3 or £4. The 'Perquisites of the court' have fallen rather than risen, and cannot be relied on for more than £2. There are now some sundry receipts which may raise the total by £1 or £2.

The credit side of the account presents some new phenomena.

Under 'Acquittances and decay of rent' we find that the rents with which the reeve now debits himself are by no means pure gain. As tenements fall into the lord's hand and are let out at new rents—rack rents—the old dues have to be forborne; they are not at once struck out of the account, but appear on both sides: it is conceived that the old rents have 'decayed'. Under this heading also various allowances to the tenants are comprised, and a sum is thus shown which rises from 9s. to 15s. Other headings of discharge are 'Purchase of corn and stock' (very variable), 'Cost of ploughs' (£1 to £2), 'Cost of carts', 'Repair of buildings and gates' (usually less than 10s., but rising to £5 when a new pigeon house is built), 'Cost of sheep and fold' (less than £1), 'Necessaries', 'Threshing', 'Servants' wages' (there is a shepherd, sometimes a boy to help him; the whole of this item is 10s. to 15s.), and besides this there is the cost of the 'Boon ploughing' and of the 'Harvesting' (the tenants' dinner).

An attempt has been made to bring out the net result of these accounts in a tabular form, in which are stated (1) the total of the items of charge, less arrears, (2) the total of the items of discharge, less money paid to the lord's use. During the fifteen years of Richard's reign for which accounts exist the excess of income over outgo varies between £23 and £50; its average is about £37.

Year ending Michaelmas

	1378			1379			1381			1382		
Income	47	1	10	45	18	$2\frac{1}{4}$	57	12	$0\frac{3}{4}$	49	19	$10\frac{1}{4}$
Outgo	7	9	$1\frac{3}{4}$	8	18	$11\frac{1}{4}$	16	13	7	12	17	$1\frac{1}{2}$
Balance	39	12	$8\frac{1}{4}$	36	19	3	40	18	$5\frac{3}{4}$	37	2	$8\frac{3}{4}$

	1384			1385			1386			1387		
Income	48	2	$0\frac{1}{2}$	53	6	11	36	19	$3\frac{3}{4}$	46	0	$4\frac{1}{4}$
Outgo	12	8	7	10	10	$2\frac{1}{2}$	13	12	$6\frac{1}{4}$	15	17	$5\frac{1}{4}$
Balance	35	13	$5\frac{1}{2}$	42	16	$8\frac{1}{2}$	23	6	$9\frac{1}{2}$	30	2	11

	1392			1394			1395			1396		
Income	60	17	$9\frac{1}{2}$	40	13	$11\frac{3}{4}$	57	18	6	45	7	$4\frac{1}{4}$
Outgo	11	17	0	7	9	$10\frac{3}{4}$	25	6	$11\frac{1}{4}$	14	9	$9\frac{3}{4}$
Balance	49	0	$9\frac{1}{2}$	33	4	1	32	11	$6\frac{3}{4}$	30	17	$6\frac{1}{2}$

	1397			1398			1399		
Income	48	16	$0\frac{1}{4}$	47	4	$6\frac{1}{2}$	61	8	$1\frac{1}{2}$
Outgo	7	7	9	9	15	11	10	10	$2\frac{3}{4}$
Balance	41	8	$3\frac{1}{4}$	37	8	$7\frac{1}{2}$	50	17	$10\frac{3}{4}$

On the back of the roll, as of old, appear the 'Barn account', 'Stock account', and 'Account of works'. The 'Account of works' for the year ending Michaelmas 1381, the year which saw the peasants' rebellion, is as follows:

Ploughings: [He accounts] for 232½ diets of ploughing, proceeding from 15½ full lands for 30 weeks and two days between Michaelmas and Hokeday, falling this year on the last day of April, from each full land every other week one diet of ploughing reckoned as two works.

Total, 232½ diets.

Of which in acquittance of the reeve and reaper, each of whom holds a half-land in respect of his office, 15 diets; and in default of 4 full lands in the lord's hand and at farm, 60 diets; and in acquittance of 10½ full lands which are in work, in respect of the fortnight at Christmas, 10½ diets; and in ploughing the demesne land for wheat seed, 12 diets; and for spring sowing, 17 diets; and for diets sold, 118 diets.

Balanced.

Somererthe: 15½ diets of ploughing, called Somererthe, proceeding from the said 15½ full lands; to wit, for each full land, 1 acre ploughed and reckoned as 1 work as per the terrier.

Total, 15½ diets.

Of which in acquittance of the reeve and reaper, each of whom holds a half-land in respect of his office, and of the 4 full lands in the lord's hand and at farm, 5 diets of ploughing; and in ploughing the demesne land 10½ diets.

Balanced.

Benerthe: 56 diets of ploughing proceeding from the *custumarii*, as well free as native, according to the teams that they yoke; in the year from each *custumarius* with all the beasts that he yokes, 4 diets, at 1*d.* per diet, as per the terrier.

Total, 56 diets, accounted for by ploughing of the demesne land.

Nederthe: 15½ acres of ploughing and harrowing proceeding from 15½ full lands at two seasons called Nederthe, from each full land at each season ½ acre ploughed and harrowed without food and without being reckoned as a work.

Total, 15½ acres.

Of which in acquittance of the reeve and reaper, each of whom holds a half-land in respect of his office, and of the 4 full lands in the lord's hand and at farm, 5 acres ploughed and harrowed; and in ploughing of the demesne land 10½ acres.

Balanced.

Winter and summer works: [He accounts] for 2936¼ works proceeding from 15½ full lands and 10½ cottaries, from Michaelmas to Lammas (1 Aug.); from each full land 3 works per week and from each cottary 2 works per week; price of each work, a halfpenny.

Total, 2936¼ works; price of a work, one halfpenny.

Whereof in acquittance of the reeve and reaper, each of whom holds a half-land in respect of his office, 130½ works; and in default of the 4 full lands in the lord's hand and at farm, together with the full land of Walter Wiseman, which fell this year into the lord's hand at the end of November, 498½ works; and in default of the 8½ cottaries in the lord's hand and at farm 639½ works, and in acquittance of 10½ full lands which are *in opere* for 147 diets of ploughing, arising from the same as mentioned above, at 2 works per diet, 294 works; and in acquittance of the said 10½ full lands which are *in opere* for 'somererthe' as per the terrier, 10½ works; and in cutting 760 bundles of thatch, called law-thatch, among the full lands that are *in opere*—to wit, each 100 bundles reckoned as 1 work—9 works; in cleansing wheat and rye for seed, 12 works; in harrowing the demesne land for sowing wheat and rye, 46 works; in making a new *murs*[1] for enlarging the lord's sheepfold, 37 works; in covering the same sheepfold, 32 works; in cutting the brush-wood in the grove at Hadenham for inclosing the gardens, rabbit warren, 'et le ponyerd', 36 (?) works; in aiding the carrying of the said brush-wood to the carts which had been brought there, 6 works; in aid in 'shredding' (*shridando*) of the said brushwood at the rabbit warren at Wilburton and drawing it inside, 12 works; in securing the ditch round the said warren, 3 works; in carrying dung outside the manor to the fields within the Christmas fortnight, 40 works; in repairing the wall round the manor, which had fallen down, 61 works; in scouring the ditch round the ponyard, 13 works; in digging the lord's vineyard at Ely, 13 works; in harrowing the lord's land for spring sowing, 102 works; in breaking the ground for the same sowing, 22 works; in carrying pease from the rick in the manor to the barn for threshing, 6 works; in weeding the lord's corn, 60 works; in shearing 173 sheep of the lord, 32 works; in scouring the ditch round the park at Downham, 15 works; in mowing, 7a. 3r. of meadow in Emedwe, 20 works; in cutting, binding, and shocking the forage there, 20 works; in mowing 24½ acres in Landmedwe, 38 works; in making the hay there, in addition to the help given by the servants, 38 works; in carriage of the said forage and hay with two carts for two days, 20 works; in stacking the forage and hay in the manor, 8 works; in collecting dung in the manor in July, 6 works; in winnowing 161 qrs. 2 bus. of divers grain of the issue of the barn, as above, besides the 30 qrs. of barley for malting, 62 works; and in works sold, 484¾ works; and in 23½ works upon the account.

Balanced.

[1] I can only read the word thus.

Autumn works: [He accounts] for 814 works proceeding from the said 15½ full lands and 10½ cottaries from Lammas to Michaelmas, during 8 weeks and 3 days, during which each full land works 5 days per week—to wit, Monday, Tuesday, Wednesday, Thursday, and Friday—and each cottaria works two days per week on days chosen by the bailiff.

Total, 814 works; price of each work, one penny.

Of which in acquittance of the reeve and reaper, each of whom holds a half-land in respect of his office, 41 works; and in default of 4 full lands in the hands of the lord, and at farm, 164 works; and in default of 8½ cottaries in the hands of the lord and at farm, 144½ works; and in acquittance of the 10½ full lands which are *in opere* for two festivals falling on their work days within the said time—to wit, the Assumption of St Mary, on a Thursday, and the Decollation of St John, on a Thursday [21 works]; and in reaping, binding, and shocking 96½ acres of divers grain at two works per acre, 193 works; and in carrying the lord's corn, 28 works, besides the help of the manor carts; and in stacking the lord's corn, as well in the barn as outside, 12 works; and in driving the lord's plough while the servant (*famulus*) of the manor was thatching a rick of pease, 3 works; and in carrying dung out of the manor, 38 works; and in works sold, 169½ works.

Balanced.

We see, then, that at the very end of the fourteenth century many of the old 'works' were exacted. In some years more were 'sold', in some less. In the year ending Michaelmas 1397 only eight out of 2970 winter and summer works were sold: some 800 were actually done; many of the others were discharged by the fact that four of the full lands and no less than ten of the cottage tenements had fallen into the lord's hand and had been let by him either permanently or temporarily at money rents. And on the whole the economy of the manor is far from being an economy of cash payments. The lord is no great payer of wages. For the regular field work he has no need of hired labourers; his only permanent wage-receiving hind is a shepherd, but there are ploughmen who receive allowances of grain.

Passing on now to Henry IV's reign, we find that the old mode of reckoning is still preserved. There are still 2970 winter and summer works due, but five full lands and ten cottier tenements have fallen into the lord's hand and bring in nothing but money; more than £10 has now to be accounted for as 'Rent of bond lands', and a proportionate number of works has to be subtracted. Of the other works some are sold; in one year 204 of the winter and summer works are sold, while 114 have been discharged by harrowing. In 1407, however, the basis of the account was changed; it became a recognised fact that six full lands were no longer *in opere*, and the total number of winter and summer works to be accounted for was reduced to 1188, and that of autumn works to 378.

A great change seems to have taken place soon after this, during a period for which we have no accounts. In the first year of Henry VI (1423) the 'Rent of bond lands' has risen to £22. All the 'works' seem now to be released (*relaxantur custumariis domini*) except the boon ploughing: seventy-six 'diets' of plough-ing due from the customers, whether free or bond. Very shortly after this, in or about 1426, another great change was made. The demesne of the manor, containing 246 acres of arable land and forty-two acres of meadow, was let to farm at a rent of £8, and the demise of the land which had been actually in the lord's hand seems to have carried with it the right to the ploughing service; that service, therefore, no longer concerns the bishop while the lease lasts (*nichil hic quia conceditur firmario terre dominice cum firma sua*). The demesne land is let *cum operibus et consuetudinibus omnium custumariorum operabilium*. This soon leads to a great simplification and abbreviation of the accounts, an abbreviation to be measured in feet. The receipts are now the old assize rents, the rent of the demesne, the rents of the bond lands, the per-quisites of the court; the *opera* are no longer brought into the account, and the purchases and sales of stock and crops disappear, for these of course concern the *firmarius*, not the lord. The *firmarius*, it may be noted, is just one of the men of the vill, one of the copy-holders, as we now may call them; in the first instance he is the same man who is acting as reeve.

Thenceforward the bishop seems to have been able to keep the demesne land in lease, now one and now another of the copyholders taking it for a term of years: thus under Edward IV it was let for sixteen years at a rent of £7. It is always recognised that the subject of this demise comprises 'the customs and works of the customary tenants of the lord'. Meanwhile the 'Rent of bond' or 'natives' land', which has declined from £22 to about £17, remains constant.

Under Henry VII the situation is but little altered; the bond land brings in its £17, the demesne land £8, the demises of the latter are still described as including 'all the works and customs of the customary tenants of the lord'.

The evidence, therefore, seems to point to a great change under

Henry V (1413–22). In the last year of Henry IV the rent of bond lands is entered at £11. 5s. 6d.; it is still reckoned that 1056 half-penny works and 336 penny works are due; many of these are actually done in kind, though some are 'sold'. When the accounts begin again under Henry VI the rent of bond lands is £22. 2s. 10d., almost exactly double the old amount, and all the works that are accounted for are seventy-six diets of ploughing. This change was immediately followed by another—namely, the letting of the demesne—the *scitus manerii*, as it is sometimes called—together with the benefit of whatever *opera* remained uncommuted. Whether the commutation under Henry V was originally regarded as more than a temporary or revocable measure does not appear; practically it seems to have been a final step.

Two cases of commutation which occurred in the reign of Henry IV are noticed on the court rolls. J. N., who holds a full land by services and customs, has requested the lord that he may have his land at farm and not for customs and services, and the lord, seeing his weakness and poverty (*inopiam et debilitatem*), of his special grace has granted that he may hold his land at farm; and upon this comes J. N. and takes the land to hold to him and his by the rod at the will of the lord, according to the custom of the manor, rendering yearly to the lord 20s. rent for all labour services to the said lord belonging, and he gives the lord 2s. The other case is of a similar character: the lord of his special grace grants to J. D. a half-land, to hold to him and his sequela at a rent of 12s. for all services and customs, which land the said J. D. hitherto held by services and customs. It is specially noticed in this case that no fine (*gersuma*) is taken for this new grant.

Then, as already said, we find that in the first year of Henry VI (1422–3) all the customary tenants are paying money rents. It may be interesting to note the fate of the full lands.

The reeve accounts for 26s. 8d. from John Downham and his fellows for the full land late of John Thorold.

For 13s. 4d. from Andrew Somerset for a half-land.

For 13s. 0d. from Thomas Stoney for a half-land, formerly Pratt's.

For 12s. 0d. from Simon Dauntre and William Philip for a half-land, formerly of Henry in the Lane, demised to them for life.

For 13s. 0d. from John Downham, senior, for a half-land, formerly of Henry Greneleaf.

For 26s. 0d. from the full land called Sewyne's, demised to various tenants.

For 12*s*. 0*d*. from Robert Scot for a half-land.

For 12*s*. 0*d*. from Robert Newman for a half-land demised to him and his.

For 12*s*. 0*d*. from Thomas Downham for a half-land demised to him and his sequela.

For 24*s*. 0*d*. from John Newman for a full land.

For 24*s*. 0*d*. from John Downham, senior, for the works of a full land recently released to him.

For 24*s*. 0*d*. from Andrew Cokayne for the works of a full land recently released to him.

For 24*s*. 0*d*. from John Frost for the works of a full land recently released to him.

For 24*s*. 0*d*. from John Downham for the works of a full land recently released to him.

For 24*s*. 0*d*. from Richard Dony for the works of a full land recently released to him.

For 24*s*. 0*d*. from Andrew Frost for the works of a full land recently released to him.

For 24*s*. 0*d*. from Andrew Lessy for the works of a full land recently released to him.

For 24*s*. 0*d*. from Jacob Frost for the works of a full land recently released to him.

For 24*s*. 0*d*. from John Warwick for the works of a full land recently released to him.

Thus the basis of the commutation effected under Henry IV and Henry V seems to have been 24*s*. for the full land—that is to say, a shilling per acre with the messuage thrown in. During the fourteenth century the lord seems to have been able to obtain a higher rent—namely, 26*s*. 8*d*.—for the full land, and 13*s*. 4*d*. for the half-land. But even 24*s*. was too high a rent to be permanently maintained; before the end of Henry VI's reign it had been very generally reduced to 20*s*., and the total 'Rent of natives' land' had fallen from £22 to £17. It might be an anachronism to say that these copyholders of the fifteenth century were paying 'rack rents', but they were paying 'the best rents that could reasonably be gotten'.

When once the commutation has been effected and the demesne demised to a farmer, the manorial accounts cease to have any great legal interest. The lord of the manor has, in effect, become a landlord of the modern type. It can be no part of my undertaking to trace the ups and downs of his income; many of its items were now irrevocably fixed, while the rent that could be obtained for the demesne varied from time to time and lease to lease. On the whole his income seems to have fallen. About the years 1428–32 the excess of income over outgo generally amounts to £30 or little less; thirty years later it has fallen to some £25, and it seems never to recover from this fall. An abstract of the account for the year ending Michaelmas 1507 will show how the matter stood at the beginning of another century.

Debit	£	s.	d.	*Credit*	£	s.	d.
Rents of assize	2	3	2¾	Allowance and decay			
Rents of 'Natives'				of rent		14	0
land'	17	16	1	Repairs of barns	1	0	0
Rents of pieces of				Paid to the lord's			
demesne land	1	6	10	use	28	8	6¾
New rent for small							
parcels of de-					30	2	6¾
mesne		1	8	Balance due		1	11
Farm of the manor	8	0	0				
Issues of the manor							
(only one item, for							
liberty of fold de-							
mised)		1	0				
Perquisites of court		15	8				
Total	£30	4	5¾	Total	£30	4	5¾

The manor was granted by Bishop Martin Heton to Queen Elizabeth in the forty-second year of her reign (1599–1600). This appears from a survey of 8 August 1609, when the manor was in the hand of King James. Its revenue was then estimated as follows:

	£	s.	d.
Rents of assize	2	3	2¾
Rents of assize of 'native tenants'	17	16	1
Farms of demesne lands in the occupation of tenants	1	16	10
New rent		1	8
Issues of the manor		1	0
Farm of the 'scite of the manor' let for a term of years by indenture	8	0	0
Perquisites of the court upon an average	3	9	11¼
Total	£33	8	9

But the surveyor adds, 'Ther is yearly allowed and deducted out of the value aforsayde for a decay of rente within the sayde

mannor the some of xvij.^{s} 9^d ob. but whether it may be repayred
or not I have noe knowledge.'

A good many of the ancient tenements have still to all appearance kept their shape; they are still held as integral wholes, though
several are sometimes in the hand of one man. The full tenement,
or 'virgate', still pays in general a rent of 20s.; it consists of a
house and curtilage, of twenty-four acres of arable scattered about
in the common fields, of a few acres of meadow, and of rights of
common of pasture. What is more, it still owes some labour service,
the remains, so it would seem, of the old 'boon works'. Against
the names of several of the tenants, in addition to the amounts
of their rents, is set '*j. opera seminand' tritici et alt' pro seminand'
ordei*', '*j. opera tritici alt' ordei ut supra*', '*iiij. opera ut supra*',
'4 daye workes *cum carucca firmarii*', '*iiij. opera cum caruca*'.
The benefit of these is enjoyed by the farmer (*firmarius*) of the
demesne, of the *scitus manerii*. But while rents have remained
fixed, the annual values of the copyholds, reckoned in money, have
in all probability increased enormously. Against each tenement
is set not only its rent but what seems to be an estimate of the
amount beyond its rent that it might be expected to bring in if
let at a rack rent. Thus of one small tenement the rent is 12d.,
while after this stands *ann' val' dimittend'* 9s. *ultra r'*—that is, the
annual value of it if demised at a full rent is 9s. beyond the rent
actually paid; in other words, the actual rent is but a tenth of the
possible rack rent. In some cases the virgate which brings in £1
per annum is reckoned as worth £6 or £7 more. Even the demesne
seems to be held by the termor on very beneficial terms (probably
he has paid a substantial fine); as of old he pays but £8, while the
annual value of his tenement seems to be estimated at £66. 13s. 4d.
From a copy of the deed whereby King James sold the manor it
would seem that he got £1261. 18s. 4d. for it, an absurdly large
price if the purchaser was going to get but £33 a year. But whatever the purchaser could get by reletting the demesne or cultivating
it himself, the time was past when he could hope to increase his
receipts from the 'natives' lands', and the evidence goes to show
that the economic catastrophe of the sixteenth century, the influx
of the precious metals, not to mention the debasement of the
coinage, had greatly benefited the representatives of the 'natives'
at the cost of their lord.

At the risk of making this paper intolerably long I must add a few words about the legal status of the villains of Wilburton. There can be no doubt that in the thirteenth century the customary tenants, the holders of the full lands, half-lands, and other tenements, were serfs, *nativi*. This theory was kept up during the whole of the next century, and was brought home to them in practice. Thus in or about the fiftieth year of Edward III a number of *nativi* relinquished their lands and fled; for many years afterwards orders were given at every successive court for their recapture.

(1369) Andrew Thorold, a *nativus* of the lord, dwells at Lindon, Andrew in the Lane at Hidingham, Nicholas Bande at Hempstead, William Coppe at Cottenham; let them be seized and brought to the next court. (1372) Andrew in the Lane, Nicholas Bande, John Thorold and Robert his brother, Andrew Thorold, John and Nicholas, sons of Andrew Frost, *nativi domini*, are missing and ought to be seized. Such entries as these are found on the rolls of the fifteenth century also. (1467) Several *nativi domini* dwell at Crowland, Isleham, and elsewhere, and pay no chevage (head money); let them be attached. (1480) A similar entry. In Henry VII's day care is taken to record the fact that certain persons are serfs, and to state the whereabouts of their progeny. (1491) A. C., a native by blood of the lord, dwells on the lord's demesne, and has three sons and one daughter, whose names and ages are stated; J. B., another native, has two sons and one daughter; R. F., another native, has one daughter; another R. F. has a daughter; Agnes D., a nieve, dwells with W. B.; Joan D., a nieve, dwells at Chatteris; Ellen D., a nieve, dwells at Wilburton; let them be attached by their bodies to do fealty to the lord. Such an entry as this suggests that by this time it has become necessary to enumerate the 'natives'; it is no longer to be assumed that all holders of customary lands are serfs; the difficulty that there had been of finding tenants had probably brought into the manor a number of outsiders who were not the bishop's born bondmen.

The practical incidents of servility are enforced during the fourteenth century. True that when a serf has once run away he is not recaptured; but there is a good deal of talk about recapturing him, though nothing seems to come of it. The 'natives', however, who remain behind cannot marry their daughters, educate their sons, or sell their beasts without the lord's leave.

(1364) It is presented that H. N. sold a foal of his own increase (*de proprio incremento*) without the lord's licence; therefore he is

amerced. (1367–9) Several similar entries. So in 1384 an amercement for selling foals to strangers without leave of the lord or
supervision of the bailiff. (1372) Presentment that Richard
Cokaygne has put his son John, aged eight years, to school without
the lord's leave; he is amerced in 40*d*. At a later court Richard is
licensed to send his son to school on condition that he does not
take any holy orders without the lord's leave, the condition being
enforced by a penalty of 100*s*. (1380) A. L., a *nativus* of the lord,
at the time when he was reeve acquired, without leave of the lord,
a messuage and some freehold land from W. S.; he now makes fine
to the lord with 20*s*., that he may hear no more about this matter
(*ne occasionetur*). (1384) A *nativus* pays 13*s*. 4*d*. for leave to marry
a *nativa*, a widow who holds a full land, and for leave to hold that
land jointly with his wife. (1385) Presentment that A. L. married
his daughter to R. H., a *nativus* of the lord; A. L. pays 3*s*. 4*d*. that
he may hear no more of this (*ne occasionetur de maritacione
predicta*). (1394) J. F., a *nativus domini de corpore*, pays 18*d*. for
leave to marry his daughter, *nativam domini*, to J. C., *nativo
domini*; he pays no more because his daughter has been guilty of
fornication—*comisit leyrwyght*—by reason whereof the lord had 5*s*.
These marks of servility seem to disappear in the fifteenth century.

The terminology employed in the earliest surrenders and
admittances is not stereotyped. The land is sometimes *terra nativa*,
sometimes *terra custumaria*, sometimes simply a 'full land' or
'half-land', as the case may be. The *tenendum* is sometimes *sibi
et suis*, sometimes *sibi et sequele sue*; '*secundum consuetudinem
manerii*' appears at times, and occasionally '*ad voluntatem domini*'.
In Richard II's day, in the case of a grant to a man and his wife,
we already find the full form, *tenendum J. et M. et heredibus et
assignatis eorundem per virgam et ad voluntatem domini secundum
consuetudinem manerii faciendo servicia antiqua pro predicto
integro cotagio*. Thenceforward it is common to mention the rod,
the will of the lord, and the custom of the manor; but the phrases
'*sibi et sequele sue*', '*sibi et suis*' do not at once give way before
'*sibi et heredibus suis*'. In the middle of the fifteenth century it
became common to describe the tenant as holding *per copiam*.

The conclusions to which these rolls would lead us may now be
stated in a summary fashion.

Before 1350 or thereabouts. The lord gets very little by way of money rent. His demesne is cultivated for him by the 'works' of his customary tenants. More works are due than are wanted, and each year he 'sells' a certain number of works at a customary rate—that is to say, he takes from the person liable to work a penny or, as the case may be, a halfpenny in respect of each work that he does not want. The customary tenants are for the more part, if not altogether, unfree men, and are treated as such.

From 1350 to 1410 or thereabouts. There is as yet no permanent commutation of work for rent. The lord, however, finds the greatest difficulty in keeping old and obtaining new tenants; his tenants, more especially the cottagers, run away and relinquish their tenements. The lord still hopes to obtain tenants on the old terms, but in the meanwhile has to make temporary grants or leases at money rents, and from time to time to reduce those rents. From the tenants who still hold on the old terms he still exacts a considerable number of works, while other works he 'sells' to them year by year. Many of the tenants are still unfree, and are treated as such.

After 1410 or thereabouts. It having at last been recognised that many of the tenements are no longer *in opere*, and that there is no prospect of a return to the old state of things, a general commutation of all works (except some ploughing) takes place. Perhaps this is not at once conceived as a final change, but practically it is irrevocable. The rents are the best rents that the lord can get, and in course of time it is necessary to reduce them. The demesne land, together with the benefit of such works as are uncommuted, is now let, for short terms of years, to a farmer. The lord of the manor becomes, in effect, little more than a receiver of rent. Very few practical traces of personal servitude remain, but we read of no formal emancipation of the bondmen, and the lord is careful to preserve a record of their bondage.

In the sixteenth century. Owing to the fall in the value of money, the copyholder gradually acquires a valuable right in his holding. His rent—less than a shilling an acre—becomes light. I will not generalise, but to me it seems that in this instance the copyholder's vendible interest is almost entirely an unearned increment, the product of American mines.

III

LEET AND TOURN[1]

To the student of manorial rolls by far the most interesting
franchise is the 'court leet or view of frank-pledge', because it is
very common, because it has great importance in the history
of society, because its origin is extremely obscure: so obscure
that we may be rash in speaking about it; still a little may be
ventured.

In the sixteenth century the institution can no longer be
described as flourishing; the growth of the commission of the peace
has drawn away its life; still the leet is holden and does business.
It is a royal police court co-ordinate with the sheriff's tourn; the
leet is for 'the franchise' what the tourn is for 'the geldable'; in the
one the lord's steward is judge, in the other the sheriff. In both the
business is transacted by means of presentments and indictments
preferred by a jury. A presentment or indictment of felony the
court cannot try, it must be sent on elsewhere; presentments of
trespasses and nuisances can be disposed of by the court; such
presentments are untraversable if they are made by a jury of
at least twelve and do not touch any question of freehold; the
presented person is amerced there and then. What offences are
presentable in leet and tourn is a question about which there is
learning; to some extent it turns on the words of the apocryphal
statute *De Visu Franciplegii*, the statutory character of which is
asserted and denied; this document contains a list of the *capitula*
or articles which are to be inquired of by the jurors.[2]

[1] [The second section of Maitland's introduction to *Select Pleas in Manorial
Courts*, Selden Society Publications II (1888). Section 1 examines the
seignorial liberties investigated in the Placita de Quo Warranto, for which see
Pollock and Maitland, vol. I, pp. 571–94. For more recent work in this field
see W. A. Morris, *The Frankpledge System* (New York, 1910); H. M. Cam, *The
Hundred and The Hundred Rolls* (1930); *Liberties and Communities* (1944).]

[2] This 'statute' is printed in the Commissioners' edition, I, 246, among
the Statutes of Uncertain Date, along with some other miscellaneous docu-
ments which were at one time regarded as statutes of the last year of Edw. II.
This was due simply to their being found in MSS. inserted between the *Vetera
Statuta* which end with Edw. II and the *Nova Statuta* which begin with
Edw. III, like the Apocrypha between the two Testaments. The statutory

41

THE LEET AND FRANK-PLEDGE

It is still theoretical law that the jury ought to make presentment concerning all who are not in frank-pledge. But beyond this we do not see at first sight that the leet jury or tourn jury has any connection with this obsolete institution. If, however, we look a little below the surface we see that, at least in some parts of the country, the jury is supposed to consist of the chief pledges (*capitales plegii*). A case[1] illustrating this occurred in Coke's day and was 'very obscure and doubtful', for, sighs Coke, 'Tempora mutantur'.

But, as we go backwards from this age, we begin to see an intimate connection between these two institutions, the leet jury and frank-pledge. As regards names we have already remarked this; the term 'leet' disappears and is represented by 'view of frank-pledge'; indeed, to speak with extreme strictness the words 'leet' and 'tourn' were not even in Coke's day the most appropriate terms; the style of the leet was *curia visus franci plegii tenta apud B. coram A.B. senescallo*; that of the tourn was *curia visus franci plegii domini regis apud B. coram vicecomite in turno suo*, 'and not *turnum vicecomitis* for *turnum est nisi perambulatio*'.[2] In the thirteenth century to claim 'view of frank-pledge' is to claim all that was afterwards known as the jurisdiction of a leet.[3] But, to pass from names to facts, we have two descriptions of the sheriff's tourn as it was near the end of the thirteenth century; the one is given us by Fleta, the other by Britton: Bracton unfortunately fails us. Fleta gives the articles of the tourn or view of frank-pledge and then makes clear to us that the persons who have got to make answer to those articles in the first instance are the chief pledges, the *capitales plegii*. But their presentments are not final; they are as it were material for presentments to be made by a jury of twelve free men who can reject these preliminary presentments of the chief pledges or supply omissions in them.[4] Britton's account is substantially similar; the free landowners of the hundred are summoned and the first step is to cause twelve of them to swear

---

character of some of them is often questioned in the Year Books; e.g. the statutory character of the articles in question is denied by Fairfax in Y.B. Mich. 22 Edw. IV. pl. 2, f. 23. See the discussion as to the *Prerogativa Regis* in Y.B. Mich. 15 Edw. IV. pl. 17, f. 11. [See Richardson & Sayles 'The Early Statutes', *Law Quarterly Review* (1934), pp. 563–5.]

[1] *Bullen's Case*, 6 Coke *Reports* 77 b.   [2] Coke, *Fourth Institute*, 260, 265.
[3] *P.Q.W.* 249.   [4] Fleta, f. 113.

that they will make presentment according to the articles. 'Afterwards the rest shall be sworn by dozens [i.e. by frank-pledges, the groups of ten or twelve][1] and by townships, that they will make lawful presentment to the first twelve jurors [i.e. the freeholders] upon the articles.... When the townships [*les villeez*] have given in their verdicts to the first jurors, and they are certified of the truth, let the first jurors go and deliver up their presentment to the sheriff.'[2]

SYSTEM OF DOUBLE PRESENTMENT IN THE TOURN

It will be seen that here we have a system of double presentment. The final presentments are made by twelve freeholders, but the material is provided in the first instance by the tithings, or the chief pledges, or the townships. Elsewhere we have plenty of evidence of the fact that the tourn was attended by the freeholders of the hundred and also by a class of representatives. We are a little perplexed however as to the mode of representation. Sometimes it would seem that the *decennae* were represented by their chief pledges, sometimes that the townships were represented each by its reeve and four men; sometimes again it would seem as if both modes of representation prevailed concurrently. The task of an investigator in this obscure region is much hampered by the fact that in parts of England, the southern counties, the 'tithing' is a geographical district coincident with the township, while in others it is the group of ten or a dozen men; there is the land of the territorial tithing and the land of the personal tithing.[3] But it seems plain that whether the represented unit was tithing or

[1] Britton writes *dozeine*, and the tithing may have been a tenth of the long hundred, and have thus consisted, not of ten, but of twelve men. But there is much evidence against this, e.g. Leg. Edw. Conf. 20, 'ita quod si *unus* ex *decem* forisfecerit, *novem* eum haberent ad rectum'. May not the word which Britton writes *dozeine* be formed from the Latin *decena*, or *decenna*, by the intermediation of such a form as *deciona*? I have seen *decionarius* for a tithingman. In the Year Books both *dizeine* and *dozeine* occur.

[2] Britton, vol. I, pp. 177–82.

[3] See Palgrave, *Commonwealth*, vol. II, p. cxxi; Stubbs, *Const. Hist.* vol. I, §41. In looking through the Hundred Rolls and Placita de Quo Warranto I have been much struck by the truth of the theory, that in the south of England the frank-pledge is territorial, in the midlands personal; and I am also inclined to subscribe the opinion that in the northernmost counties there was no frank-pledge at all; no lord claims to have view of frank-pledge. [This is fully borne out by later research. See Stewart Brown, *The Serjeants of the Peace in Medieval England and Wales* (1936), for the alternative system in the north.]

township or both, the villagers, the peasantry, appeared in the
tourn by their representatives, by the chief pledges or the reeve
and four men.[1] According to strict legal theory perhaps they
could all be compelled to come in person; but our evidence shows
that really they came by their representatives, and so gives us one
more warning as to the extreme caution with which we should read
medieval statements about 'all men', or all men of a great class.
One of the questions to be asked in the tourn was whether all the
chief pledges are come, which seems to imply that each frank-
pledge is sufficiently represented by its head.[2] The duty of appearing seems to have been very generally commuted for a small
money payment, head-money, *capitagium*, *chevagium*, a sum paid
by the frank-pledges *ne vocentur per capita*.[3] In the Hundred Rolls
and Placita de Quo Warranto we constantly read of such representation. There are many entries which show us the freeholders
attending in person and the villagers by their representatives, and
there is one which shows us the system of double presentment
and so bears out the statements of Fleta and Britton:—the
freeholders (*libere tenentes*) of Swavesey and four *homines* and the
reeve go to the tourn and there the free men (*liberi*) shall swear
and the four men and the reeve shall present defaults to the free
men and the free men shall present them to the bailiffs.[4]

[1] On purpose I use vague words such as 'villagers' and 'peasantry'. There
is much to show that at least in the estimation of the greater folk the persons
who were in frank-pledge and who were represented by the reeve and four
men were properly described in the lump as *villani*, and in the Hundred Rolls,
'free man' and 'free holder' are constantly used as synonyms; but had it come
to a *de nativo habendo* many of these *villani* might have proved that personally
they were free.

[2] Statutum de Visu Franciplegii (*Statutes of the Realm*, I, 246); Britton,
vol. I, p. 181; Fleta, f. 112.

[3] 'Capitales plegii et eorum decene nichil dant ad capitagium; ideo vocandi
sunt omnes per capita'; P.R.O., Court Rolls, S.C. 2/179/7. m. 1*d*. [Houghton,
Hunts.]

[4] *R.H.* II, 469. *Ibid.* I, 101 (Dorset), suit to the tourn by twelve liberi of
the hundred and four men and the tithingman of every tithing; *ibid.* I, 141
(Essex), by four villani and the reeve; *ibid.* I, 154 (Essex), by the liberi homines
and four homines and the reeve; *ibid.* I, 100 (Salop), by all the liberi and by
four homines and the reeve. In the southern counties it is often the decenna
that does suit by four men and the tithingman. In *P.Q.W.* 254, we find at
court the reeve, four men and chief pledges. Or again the communitas ville
does suit by its tithingman, *P.Q.W.* 293. The lord is asked whether his chief
pledges *or* four men and the reeve go to the tourn, *P.Q.W.* 10. Presentments
in the tourn are made by the capitales decennarii, *P.Q.W.* 88. See a curious
case of suit by three rudmanni, *P.Q.W.* 780.

THE TOURN CREATED BY THE ASSIZE
OF CLARENDON

Now, with Britton's account before us, are we not compelled to
see the origin of the sheriff's tourn in the Assize of Clarendon?
This may be a new suggestion, but is it not true? Let us observe
the words of the ordinance of 1166:—for the conservation of the
peace and the doing of justice, the king ordains that in every
county and in every hundred inquiry shall be made by twelve of
the most lawful men of the hundred and by four of the most lawful men of every township concerning robbers, murderers and
thieves and the receivers of such, and this inquiry the justices shall
make before themselves and the sheriffs before themselves. The
sheriffs, then, of the thirteenth century are doing just what they
are bidden to do; they are making inquiry in each hundred by
means of the oath of twelve hundredors and by means of the presentments of four men from every township. In accordance with
the charter of 1217 they perambulate the hundreds but twice in
the year, and it is no longer permissible for them to try those who
are presented as felons, for no sheriff may hold pleas of the crown;
but they still receive presentments made in the manner ordained
by Henry II. It may be urged that they do much more than is
prescribed by the Assize; if they receive presentments of robbery,
murder, theft, they also (and this has perhaps become the most
important part of their business) receive presentments about and
finally adjudicate upon many minor offences, nuisances, purpres-
tures, scuffles, and the like. But the same remark will apply to
the justices in eyre; in Henry II's day they are to inquire of robbers,
murderers, and thieves; by the end of Henry III's day the articles
of the eyre have become very numerous and detailed. May we not
infer that the articles of the tourn, like the articles of the eyre, have
received addition from time to time at the hands of the king and his
council, or at the hands of his delegates?

ARTICLES OF THE TOURN

We have in easily accessible places five different sets of articles of
the tourn or of the view of frank-pledge. A set for Wales is
contained in the Statutum Walliae (1284), another set is given
by Fleta[1] (c. 1290), another by Britton[2] (c. 1290), another in

[1] Fleta, f. 112.   [2] Britton, vol. I, p. 177.

Horne's Mirror[1] (temp. Edw. I or Edw. II), and another in the apocryphal undated statute[2] mentioned above. It is a curious fact that though these five documents agree in most points of substance, they are none the less five different documents; they give the articles in very different order, and it is difficult to thread them together by any theory of development.[3] Perhaps the sheriffs were allowed a free hand in settling the articles under the guidance of the general idea that whatever was against the king's peace was presentable at the tourn. Be this as it may, the constitution and procedure of the court that the sheriff holds are the constitution and procedure of the court ordained by the Assize of 1166. And in this context it may be remarked that according to the verdict of a Lancashire jury the sheriff of their county never held a tourn until after Magna Carta was granted[4] and that there was no tourn in Northumberland even in Edward I's day.[5]

THE ASSIZE OF CLARENDON AND THE FRANK-PLEDGE ORGANISATION

Next we may notice how easy it was that the procedure instituted by the Assize should become implicated with the institution of frank-pledge. Already in the Leges Henrici Primi (cap. 8) we find the sheriff holding twice a year a specially full hundred court to see that all are in frank-pledge. We also find (cap. 7) that a lord may send the priest, reeve and four men to represent him in the county court and the hundred court in case neither he nor his steward can be present. In the days of Henry I, therefore (for we may attribute these 'Leges' to his reign), the chief pledges must have attended the hundred court twice a year, and the reeve and four men may often have been there to represent their lord. As yet however there is no talk of any presentment of offences, of any communal accusation. Then upon this state of things is superimposed the procedure of the Assize, which requires the representa-

---

[1] *The Mirror of Justices* [Selden Soc. Publ. VII, 1893], c. 1, §17.

[2] [Above, p. 41, n. 2.]

[3] In the later Middle Ages it was established that the leet could not receive a presentment of homicide; this seems due to an omission of homicide in the apocryphal 'statute', an omission which I strongly suspect to have been accidental, for our four other authorities are clear the other way. In 1367 it was already understood that homicide was not presentable, *Liber Assisarum*, f. 256, pl. 30.

[4] *P.Q.W.* 371.   [5] *R.H.* II, 21.

tion of the townships by their four best men. A certain confusion and interpenetration of the two representative systems would be a very natural result; the *decenna* is represented by its chief pledge, the township by its reeve and four men; but then in a great part of England the *decenna* is the township. So it will not surprise us that while according to Britton the presentments are made in the first instance by the townships (*les villeez*), Fleta says that they are made by the *capitales plegii*; the two accounts may represent local varieties of practice. In Wales there was no frank-pledge and in the Statutum Walliae which established the sheriff's tourn in the principality we find no representation of the peasantry; a jury of twelve freeholders is to be sworn to make presentments and then all the men of the commote are to be sworn to make presentments to these jurors. We may suspect that if in later days we hear nothing of a system of double presentment in the tourn, this is due to the decay of the frank-pledge.

THE PRIVATE LEET AN IMITATION OF THE TOURN

We turn from the sheriff's court to the private courts. Now when we take up a roll of the fourteenth or any later century belonging to a court which has the leet jurisdiction, it is common to find as the first entry under any date, the names of the jurors; commonly there are twelve names, sometimes more, sometimes fewer; on this follow the presentments of these jurors. The same is occasionally the case in rolls of the thirteenth century and often there is nothing on the face of the roll to connect these jurors with the institution of frank-pledge; sometimes however we find that they are the chief pledges; the *juratores* are *capitales plegii jurati*. This is well seen for instance in the Rolls of the City of Norwich which begin in 1288.[1] The city was divided into four leets; for each leet a jury appeared and made presentments, and it is clear that the jurors were the capital pledges of the *decennae*. Then, however, as we pursue our retrogressive course we come across many rolls which show no trace of a formally empanelled jury. Presentments dealing with police affairs, such affairs as belonged to the leets of later times, are made; but they are said to be made by the *capitales*

[1] [See W. Hudson, *The Leet Jurisdiction of the City of Norwich*, Selden Soc. Publ. v, 1891.]

plegii, or by a tithing, or by a tithingman; sometimes each tithing-man comes separately, makes his presentments and offers to prove (*offert probare*) that he has nothing more to present.

THE LEET JURORS AND THE CHIEF PLEDGES

A strong light is thrown upon the situation by an argument repeatedly urged by the king's pleaders when pressing the inquiry *quo warranto*: 'You have no business to be receiving presentments in your court, because you have not got twelve complete tithings; you have not got twelve chief pledges and no one ought to be punished save on the oath of twelve men.' To take one instance: in Bedfordshire the Master of the Templars confesses that in some of the vills in which he holds a view of frank-pledge he has but four *decennarii*, in others five, in others six at most. Gilbert of Thornton, the king's advocate, says that the Master's claim is bad 'since he has not enough chief pledges (*decennarii capitales*) to do judgment on any malefactor; for the custom of England is that everyone shall be judged on the oath of twelve; besides he has to make up his tithings by collecting them out of various vills and he has only two tenants in this vill, three or four in that'.[1] A similar argument is used in Edward III's day. We have this conversation: *Judge*: 'How are presentments made in your leet?' *Counsel*: 'By the reeve and two men of the tithing (*del dosen*).' *Judge*: 'Divers things are presentable in a leet which bind the inheritance, as a purpresture on the highway or the like, to which a man shall have a traverse, and so presentment of these things by the reeve and two men is against law.'[2] The same judge however elsewhere admits that in some districts twelve *dosiners* present the articles of the view, in other districts but two or three according to the usage of the country.[3] Some learning collected round this point which we must not here explore, but even when the presentment was of felony the necessity for a jury of twelve seems to have been regarded as of statutory origin.[4] The Statute of 1285 required that indictments in the tourn or the court of a franchise shall be sworn

---

[1] *P.Q.W.* 5; see also the other cases on pp. 5, 6, 7. A similar doctrine is propounded in Riley's *Munimenta Gildhallae*, I, 116, where Richard Heriet, a judge of John's reign, is made to say that no man may hold a court for a free stranger (outsider) with less than twelve free men.

[2] Keilway, *Reports*, 141.   [3] *Ibid.* 148.

[4] Y.B. Hil. 6 Hen. IV. pl. 4, f.

by twelve at the least.[1] Probably this statute had a great deal to do with fixing for later times the form of 'the leet jury'. In 1367 presentments at the leet are still made by the chief pledges.[2]

CONJECTURAL HISTORY OF LEET JURY

From the point of view that we have now attained some inferences seem possible. Whether the institution of frank-pledge belongs to the days before the Conquest or is the creature of Norman government we need not inquire; that it was in existence before the coronation of Henry II there can be little or no doubt; but nowhere in our earliest accounts of it do we find that the frank-pledges have any duty to make presentments, nor, unless we will put our trust in the well-known and oft-debated passage in the Laws of Ethelred about the twelve eldest thanes,[3] have we any evidence that a procedure by way of presentment, of communal accusation, was known to the English law. Henry II introduced this procedure into the sheriff's court and thereby gave rise to the tourns of later days. The procedure involved a representation of townships which naturally and speedily became implicated with the system of frank-pledge, so that in some districts the *capitales plegii* became the primary presenters. Wholesale the feudal lords grasped at this new procedure; nor can the king or his officers have tried to resist them very seriously. On the whole it was for the good of the peace that there should be as much presenting of offenders as was possible. Every lord of any consideration without troubling himself about charters assumed the right to inquire of all the articles which the sheriff set before the jurors in his tourn; many of them had charters which in a more or less vague fashion exempted their manors from suit to the communal courts and from the incursions of royal officers. Imitate in all respects the procedure of the tourn they could not; their precincts were often too small; they could not impanel twelve freeholders; they had not got so many; seldom could there be any representation of townships; the system of double presentment was too elaborate for their small domains; but the machinery of frank-pledge they could employ, and they did employ, some in this way, some in that; and the sheriff also

---

[1] Stat. West. II, c. 13.
[2] Y.B. Mich. 41 Edw. III. f. 26, Mich. pl. 23.
[3] Ethelred, III, c. 1, §3.

was employing this machinery. The machinery was apt for the purpose; the duty of producing one's neighbour to answer accusations could well be converted into the duty of telling tales against him. Thus the lord made his court a court for the presentment of offences against the peace, in the language of later law 'a court leet'. Some of the smaller and lower lords could not obtain this jurisdiction; their overlords had got it and kept it to themselves; but very generally the lord of a manor possessed himself of a leet and the great Edward could not oust him of it. Statutes and *quo warranto* inquiries introduced a certain uniformity into the procedure; insisted that, at all events for grave cases, there must be a presenting jury of twelve. Thus it is that the leet jury of later days is developed; but even in later days the theory is not always forgotten that the jurors are the chief pledges. The lords turned the new procedure to their own profit; they employed it not merely for the presentment of offences against the general law of the realm but also for the presentment of breaches of manorial custom; when the two courts have fallen asunder there is a presenting jury in the court baron as well as in the court leet.

This theory is put forward tentatively, for it differs in some respects from that sanctioned by the best historians, and it touches an important matter. If what is here said be true, then the last hope of proving that the jury of presentment is an English institution of very high antiquity is gone until someone shall find a stepping stone between the Assize of Clarendon and the Laws of Ethelred.[1]

THE ASSIZE OF BEER

A further insight into the proceedings of the lords may be given us by the fact that they had very generally assumed the right of enforcing the assize of beer. Almost every manorial roll is rich with amercements of those who have brewed against the assize, the offenders being usually women. An assize of bread and beer

---

[1] Dr Stubbs, *Const. Hist.* vol. I, p. 618 [of 1st ed., 662 of 1897 ed.] says, 'The leet juries of the small local courts do not draw their origin from any legal enactment, and bear every mark of the utmost antiquity.' I cannot (reverently be it said) think them very ancient; they seem to me imitations of the jury of the tourn, which seems to me the creature of the Assize of Clarendon. Of course I do not dispute that the half-yearly meetings of the hundred court for the purpose of viewing the frank-pledges were older than this. [See N. D. Hurnard, 'The Jury of Presentment and the Assize of Clarendon', *E.H.R.* 1941, pp. 374–410, for a suggested stepping stone.]

fixing the price of those commodities seems to have been published in 1256 and is commonly printed among the statutes.[1] This, however, was apparently an amended version of an older assize, a copy of which appears in the Malmesbury Register and which we may attribute to John's reign.[2] It said that when wheat sold for 3s. the quarter, barley for 20d. or 2s., and oats for 16d. or 18d., then brewers may well sell two gallons of beer for a penny, in boroughs three gallons, in country and market towns four gallons. The ordinance of 1256 made some change in this tariff. As to bread we need here say nothing; the lords did not as a rule assume that they were to execute the assize of bread, but beer they took under their care. They made profit thereby, for the assize seems to have been broken with as much regularity as the most orthodox of political economists could possibly demand. They often got into a scrape for taking amercements instead of inflicting corporal punishment. The law was that on a fourth conviction the baker should go to the pillory, the brewster to the tumbrel; but this was disregarded. We have seen that in the northern counties the lords claimed the jurisdiction over beer as theirs by common custom.

---

[1] *Statutes of the Realm*, I, 199; *Bracton's Note Book*, vol. I, p. 82.

[2] *Registrum Malmesburiense* (R.S.), I, 134. The date seems fixed by the fact that the ordinance is settled by the bakers of Geoffrey Fitz Peter and Stephen of Turnham.

IV

INTRODUCTION TO
MEMORANDA DE PARLIAMENTO, 1305[1]

THE LENTEN PARLIAMENT OF 1305

On 12 November 1304, King Edward issued from Burstwick writs for a parliament to be holden at Westminster on 16 February 1305.[2] He was on his way back from Scotland. He kept Christmas at Lincoln and was there as late as 12 January. On the 22nd he was at Spalding and thence he issued a second set of writs. Events, he said, had happened which made it impossible for him to be at Westminster on the appointed day, so the parliament was postponed to the 28th of February.[3] Slowly and by a circuitous route he travelled southward, for we hear of him at Walsingham, Swaffham, Thetford, Bury St Edmunds, Exning, Wilbraham, Royston, Braughing, Standon, Wades Hill, Ware, Waltham. On 26 January he addressed a letter under his privy seal to the chancellor, which may perhaps explain the postponement. He expected that in the ensuing parliament the clergy would call him in question and he directed that a search should be made in the chancery for any documents which might bear upon the matters in dispute.[4] By other letters under the privy seal dated on 5 February, of which we must speak at greater length hereafter, he directed the appointment of receivers and auditors of petitions; he desired that the petitions should, so far as was possible, be disposed of before his arrival at Westminster. Meanwhile the

---

[1] *Records of the Parliament holden at Westminster...in the thirty-third year of the reign of King Edward the First*, edited by F. W. Maitland, Rolls Series, 1893. [Reprinted in Maitland, *Selected Essays* (Cambridge, 1936), pp. 1–72. Alternative title, *Memoranda de Parliamento*. References so indicated below are to the Rolls Series volume. Section I of the introduction, dealing with the make-up of the roll, and with the two classes of Ancient Petitions, numbering 16,000 in all, preserved in the Public Record Office, is omitted, as are the Calendar and Lists that make up the last section.]

[2] *Parliamentary Writs*, vol. I, p. 136.   [3] *Parl. Writs*, vol. I, p. 138.

[4] Chancery Warrants, Series I, no. 5263 [*Cal. Chanc. Warrants*, vol. I, p. 246]: 'por ce que nous entendons qe le dit Ercevesqe e autres du clergez nous voudront paraventure aresoner a nostre prochein pallement [*sic*] sur aucunes choses touchantz lour estat.'

sheriffs of Kent, Surrey and Sussex had been bidden to send up great quantities of corn and ale to Westminster for the maintenance of the king's household.[1] On the 27th he entered London and stayed at the Hospital of St Katharine near the Tower. On the 28th the parliament was opened at Westminster.[2]

It was a full parliament in our sense of that term.[3] The three estates of the realm met the king and his council. The great precedent of 1295 had been followed and, if the writs of summons were punctually obeyed, the assembly was a large one. By rights there should have been present some ninety-five prelates, about 145 representatives of the inferior clergy, nine earls (if we include the Prince of Wales and the Earl of Angus), ninety-four barons, seventy-four knights of the shires, and about 200 citizens and burgesses; altogether some 600 men. Besides these we must take account of thirty-three members of the king's council to whom writs were sent, and, as we shall see hereafter, there were yet other men present and performing important duties, men who had a special knowledge of Scotland and Gascony.

This assembly was kept together for just three weeks. On 21 March a proclamation was made telling the archbishops, bishops and other prelates, earls, barons, knights, citizens and burgesses in general that they might go home, but must be ready to appear again if the king summoned them. Those bishops, earls, barons, justices and others who were members of the council were to remain behind and so were all those who had still any business to transact. But the 'parliament' was not at an end. Many of its doings that are recorded on our roll were done after the estates had been sent home.[4] The king remained at Westminster, surrounded by his councillors, and his parliament was still in session as a 'full' and 'general' parliament as late as the 5 and 6 April.[5]

---

[1] *Parl. Writs*, vol. I, p. 407.   [2] *Annales Londonienses*, p. 134.

[3] [The medieval term for describing a parliament containing elected representatives would seem to be *general*. See Powicke, *The Thirteenth Century*, p. 343. The phrase *in full parliament* appears to mean 'in open and formal session'. See below, pp. 58, 80, 94.]

[4] [It must be remembered that the roll does not set out to give a full account of the proceedings. See Richardson and Sayles in *The Bulletin of the Institute of Historical Research* (cited henceforth as *B.I.H.R.*), 1928–9, pp. 132, 149–50, for detailed analysis of the rolls edited by Maitland.]

[5] *Memoranda de Parliamento*, pp. 4, 293, 297. See also *Parl. Writs*, vol. I, p. 158. On 6 April the king releases one of his councillors, Master Robert Pickering, from further attendance.

Easter day fell on the 18th of that month, and its approach seems to have put an end to the prolonged session. Early in May the king began a tour through the home counties. He proposed to hold another 'parliament', which however, so far as we know, was not to be an assembly of the estates, on 15 July, but this he postponed first to 15 August and then to 15 September.[1]

THE KING'S COUNCIL: ITS COMPOSITION

Now if we are to frame any exact conception of the body or various bodies of men by whom the business that is recorded on our roll was transacted, and of the mode in which they dealt with that business, it seems necessary that we should understand the composition of the king's council. Unfortunately, as is well known, the council of Edward I is still for us an ill-defined group of men.[2] Writs of summons and writs for wages will often teach us the names of all the barons who were called to a parliament and enable us to know who it was that represented the pettiest boroughs, and yet we cannot enumerate with any certainty the members of the council. We can indeed make a list of those of its members who, not being prelates or barons, were summoned by name to be present at a given parliament. On the present occasion no less than thirty-three men were thus summoned. The list included Philip Willoughby the chancellor of the exchequer, the justices of the two benches and the barons of the exchequer, several men who were being employed as justices in eyre and thirteen masters of the chancery or clerks of the council. The title 'masters in chancery' is one which may lead us astray by suggesting that those who bear it are, like their successors in later days, principally engaged in performing certain subordinate functions in a great court of law and equity. But this is not so. If, with Dr Stubbs, we say that at this time the chancellor is 'the principal secretary of state for all departments', we may call these masters the 'under-secretaries of state'. Though already a keeper of the privy seal is beginning to intervene between the king and his chancellor, though already the king, at least at times, seems to have one yet more intimate clerk who is known as his secretary, the chancery is still the great secretarial department; it does nearly all the king's writing for him, whether such writing concerns foreign affairs or the govern-

[1] *Parl. Writs*, vol. i, pp. 158–60.   [2] Stubbs, *Const. Hist.* §230.

ment of England.[1] If for a moment we may use such modern terms, we may say that the chancery is Home Office, Foreign Office, Board of Trade, Local Government Board all in one; in short it is a general secretarial bureau, which exercises a certain control even over the only other great official 'department' that there is, namely the exchequer. Thus when the king is surrounded by the masters or principal clerks of the chancery, he has at his side the men who know most about the way in which England is governed and foreign affairs are managed, 'permanent', or fairly permanent, 'under-secretaries of state', and yet men who are on their promotion, for some of them may well look to being chancellors or treasurers before they die. It is among them also that the king finds his diplomatists. The thirty-three names therefore upon our list represent almost all that England has to show in the way of legal learning, official experience and administrative ability.[2]

But then of course it is certain that there are members of the council who are not upon this list. They have been otherwise summoned. In the first place there are the two great ministers. The treasurer, Walter Langton, has been summoned as bishop of Lichfield; he is King Edward's right-hand man. The chancellor, William Hamilton, who, when compared with Langton, seems an insignificant person, can appear as dean of York.[3] But there must be other prelates and there must be lay nobles who are members of the council. On the other hand it is difficult, if not impossible, to believe that every prelate or baron is a member of the council. We see this from that proclamation of 21 March which has already been mentioned. On that day the mass of prelates and nobles is

[1] In 1299 John Banstead is described as 'secretarius regis'; *Foedera*, vol. I, p. 916. In 1306 the same title is given to Philip Martel, doctor of civil law; *Prynne Records*, vol. III, p. 1095. In each case, however, this occurs in a document relating to foreign affairs, and we cannot be sure that in addressing foreign powers the king did not sometimes give to his clerks titles that had no very definite signification in England. As to the title 'clericus Regis', this may be borne at one and the same time by a large number of persons. [According to Tout 'Secretary at that date meant little more than confidant and keepers both of the Great and the Privy seal might be so described'. In 1305 Benstead was Controller of the Wardrobe and keeper of the Privy Seal, and 'in the front rank among Edward's confidential agents'. *Mediaeval Administrative History*, vol. II, pp. 18–19. See also *Essays in History presented to R. L. Poole* (Oxford, 1927), pp. 332–59.]

[2] [On secretaries and king's clerks, see, besides Tout, Powicke, *Henry III and the Lord Edward*, pp. 293–7, 696–7; G. P. Cuttino, *English Diplomatic Administration* (1940); 'King's clerks and the Community of the Realm', *Speculum* (1954), pp. 396–409 and F. Pegues in *E.H.R.* (1956), pp. 529–59.]

[3] The chancellor seems to have had no summons, except as dean of York.

sent home; but the members of the council are to remain behind. Now it would be a hard task were we to seek to recover the names of all those who in any given year were King Edward's sworn councillors. Still certain materials exist, by a circumspect use of which we might arrive at some tentative but serviceable conclusions. We will fix our attention on the months of March and April in the year 1305 and see by whom it is that the king is surrounded. Our parliament roll will give us some help, while some help may be derived from the contemporary charter roll.[1] It is well known that a royal charter—and herein lies the chief formal difference between a charter and a mere patent—purports to have been delivered by the king in the presence of several witnesses whose names are given. We must not for one instant suggest that by merely collecting the names of such witnesses we could frame a list of those men of high station who were sworn members of the council. In the first place a man may be a member of the council and yet for many months together may never be in the king's presence. Sickness, old age, a mission to foreign parts, may keep him away; or again he may be in opposition or disgrace. No law obliges the king to consult all his councillors. For example, during the year in question we hardly ever see the Archbishop of Canterbury in the king's presence. In all likelihood he is still a member of the council; but he is in opposition and disgrace. And then on the other hand we may not infer that a man is a member of the council merely because he witnesses the grant of a charter. Not only may he be a casual visitor to the royal court, but even if his name appears habitually, this may be because he holds some not very important office about the king's person, and we can not be certain that the occupants of all such offices were usually sworn of the council. Still we may reasonably ask what great men were constantly in the king's presence during these two months, and the answer that we get to this question may be of some value.

The parliament, we have said, met on 28 February. Between that date and 21 March, when the assembly of the estates was dissolved, the king's charters were thus witnessed:

5 *March.* Earls of Lincoln, Gloucester, Hereford, and Warwick, Aymer de Valence, Hugh le Despenser, Robert Fitz Roger, Robert de la Warde (steward of the household).

[1] [For an application of this technique to the year 1252–3, see 'History from the Charter Roll', *E.H.R.* (1893), p. 23: *Collected Papers*, vol. ii, pp. 298–312.]

7 *March*. Earls of Lincoln, Gloucester, Hereford, and Warwick, Aymer de Valence, Hugh le Despenser, Robert de la Warde.

8 *March*. Archbishop of Canterbury, Bishop of Lichfield (Treasurer), Bishops of Lincoln, Salisbury, and Carlisle, Earls of Lincoln, Lancaster, Gloucester, Hereford, and Warwick, John of Brittany, Hugh le Despenser, John de Segrave, Roger le Brabazon (C.J.B.R.), Robert de la Warde.

10 *March*. Earls of Lincoln, Gloucester, Hereford, and Warwick, Aymer de Valence, Hugh le Despenser, Robert Fitz Roger, Robert de la Warde.

10 *March*. The same with John of Hastings.

14 *March*. The Treasurer, the Bishop of Durham, the Earls of Lincoln, Lancaster, and Hereford, John of Brittany, Aymer de Valence, Robert Fitz Roger, Robert de la Warde.

20 *March*. The Treasurer, the Bishops of Durham, Carlisle, and Glasgow, the Earls of Lincoln, Gloucester, Hereford, Warwick, and Carrick, John of Brittany, Aymer de Valence, Robert Fitz Roger, Robert de la Warde. [A Scottish charter.]

20 *March*. The Treasurer, the Bishops of Durham and Carlisle, the Earls of Lincoln, Lancaster, Hereford, and Warwick, Aymer de Valence, Hugh le Despenser, Robert Fitz Roger, Robert de la Warde.

On the next day the assembly of the estates was dissolved. We shall see, however, that the king retains all or most of those who have been witnessing his acts.

28 *March*. The Treasurer, the Bishops of Durham, Carlisle, and Glasgow, the Earls of Lincoln, Gloucester, Hereford, Warwick, and Carrick, John of Brittany, Aymer de Valence, Robert de la Warde.

29 *March*. The Treasurer, the Bishops of Durham, Salisbury and Carlisle, Earls of Lincoln, Hereford and Warwick, Henry de Percy, Hugh le Despenser, Robert de Clifford, John de Segrave.

30 *March*. The Treasurer, the Bishops of Durham and Carlisle, the Earls of Lincoln, Hereford, and Warwick, John of Brittany, Aymer de Valence, Hugh le Despenser, John de Segrave, Robert de la Warde.

5 *April*. The Treasurer, the Bishops of Durham and Carlisle, the Earls of Lincoln, Gloucester, and Warwick, Henry de Percy, Robert de Clifford, Robert de la Warde.

5 *April*. The Treasurer, the Bishops of Durham and Carlisle, the Earls of Lincoln, Gloucester, and Hereford, Aymer de Valence, Henry de Percy, John de Hastings, Robert de Clifford, Robert de la Warde.

5 *April*. The Treasurer, the Bishops of Durham and Carlisle, the Earls of Lincoln, Gloucester, Hereford, and Warwick, John of Brittany, Henry de Percy, Hugh le Despenser, Robert de la Warde.

8 *April*. The Treasurer, the Earls of Lincoln and Hereford, John of Brittany, Aymer de Valence, Hugh le Despenser, Robert de la Warde.

10 *April*. The Treasurer, the Bishops of Salisbury and Carlisle, the Earls of Lincoln, Gloucester, and Hereford, Aymer de Valence, Hugh le Despenser and John de Hastings.

15 *April*. The Treasurer, the Bishop of Durham, the Earls of Lincoln and Hereford, John of Brittany, Aymer de Valence, Henry de Percy, Hugh le Despenser, Robert de la Warde.

The Easter holiday now intervenes. In May and June, as in January and February, we may see the king travelling about the country, and when this is the case his charters have fewer witnesses—perhaps the treasurer, perhaps the Bishop of Durham, with an earl or two earls and three or four barons, or some men, it may be officers of his household, who are not of baronial rank. The most regular of all the witnesses to a royal charter is the steward of the household; at this moment he is Robert de la Warde.

We may now turn to the parliament roll and make further pursuit for the names of councillors. Nicholas Segrave has to answer for his offences 'in full parliament, in the presence of the king himself, the Archbishop of Canterbury, and many bishops, earls, barons, and others of the king's council'.[1] Then on Monday, 29 March, certain persons presented themselves 'before the king himself and his council' as willing to go bail for Segrave, and on the following Wednesday their bond was witnessed by the treasurer, the Bishops of Durham and Carlisle, the Earls of Lincoln and Warwick, and the two chief justices.[2] On 13 March Almaric de St Amand is bailed before the treasurer, the chief justice of the king's bench, 'and others of the king's council', by six great men, all of whom may themselves be members of the council, the Earl of Lincoln, John of Brittany, Hugh le Despenser, Hugh de Vere, Thomas of Berkeley, and Adam of Welles.[3] Another case was heard by the treasurer, the chief justice of the king's bench, John of Berwick, 'and others of the king's council'.[4] But by far the longest list of councillors that we get is contained in an elaborate notarial instrument which describes how on 5 April the titular bishop of Byblos appeared 'before the bishops and other prelates, earls, barons, justices, and divers other noble clerks and laymen, councillors of the magnificent prince, the lord Edward, the illustrious king of England', proffered a papal bull, and received a short answer to the effect that this bull was of no avail in England. Then the notary tells us how these things were done in the presence of the treasurer, the Bishops of Durham and Carlisle, the Earls of Lincoln, Hereford, and Warwick, twenty-four persons

---

[1] *Memoranda de Parliamento*, no. 449, pp. 255f.
[2] *Ibid.* no. 449, pp. 258–60.　　[3] *Ibid.* no. 452.　　[4] *Ibid.* no. 420.

who are described as knights, three who are 'discreet men', and three who are clerks. The list is worthy of some further analysis. Of the twenty-four 'knights', ten have received the baronial summons to this parliament (Valence, Percy, Clifford, Vere, Teye, Welles, William de Grandison, Rither, Deyncourt, Burghersh), eight have received the councillor's summons and are justices or barons of the exchequer (Brabazon, de L'Isle, Bereford, Howard, Hengham, Spigurnel, Malorie and Inge). The others are John of Brittany, who apparently was not summoned, but who is the king's nephew and one of his trustiest captains and advisers;[1] John de Botetourte, who is warden of the western parts of the Scottish march;[2] John Wogan, who is justiciar of Ireland; John of Havering, who may be of baronial rank and who at any rate is just being appointed to be seneschal of Gascony;[3] Ralph of Sandwich, who is constable of the Tower; and Nicholas Fermbaud, who is constable of Bristol. The three 'clerks' (Reginald Brandon, Robert Pickering, and William of Kilkenny) have all had the councillor's summons. As to the three 'discreet men', they have none of them been summoned. They are, we may guess, too 'discreet', that is, too intimately connected with the king's person, to need any writ. They are John of Drokenesford, the keeper of the wardrobe, the head, that is, of a department which has a great deal to do with military and other expenditure; John of Banstead, who is or has been the king's secretary, and who before the year is out will be chancellor of the exchequer,[4] and John of Berwick, another clerk, who has long been in the service of the king and queen; possibly he holds the privy seal.[5] Then three notaries of the apostolic see, two of whom, John Bush and John of Caen, are also clerks of the English chancery, perfect the instrument with all due solemnity.

Then we may see a committee of the council appointed. It consists of the treasurer, the Bishop of Durham, the Earl of

[1] His father, John Duke of Brittany, is living, but dies in this year. He is subsequently summoned as Earl of Richmond.

[2] Bain, *Calendar*, vol. II, no. 1659.

[3] *Memoranda de Parliamento*, App. II.

[4] *Foedera*, vol. II, pp. 916, 974.

[5] Already in 1292 he is 'discretus vir', 'clericus Regis'; *Foedera*, vol. II, p. 766. He has lately been negotiating the peace with France. He was dean of Wimborne and a canon of York. He was one of Queen Eleanor's executors; Foss, *Judges*, vol. III, p. 237. [Berwick never kept the privy seal. For further details on the three discreet men, all wardrobe clerks, see Tout, *Administrative History*, vol. II, pp. 42, 83, and the Index in vol. VI.]

Lincoln, Aymer de Valence, John Drokenesford, and John Banstead. They are to discuss the affairs concerning which a certain 'Dominus de Cuk' has come to the king from foreign parts.[1] He, we take it, is Jehan lord of Cuijk in Brabant. He was over here in 1297 as an envoy of the Count of Flanders,[2] and on the present occasion he has apparently come to negotiate about certain debts that are due from the king to the Duke of Brabant.[3]

In the autumn of this year the king held another 'parliament'. So far as we know he did not call in the prelates or barons in mass, nor did he summon any representatives of the shires or the towns. The names of those whom he ordered to appear are for the more part names with which we are by this time growing familiar. The treasurer was summoned and the Bishop of Worcester, the Earls of Lincoln and Hereford, Hugh le Despenser, Henry Percy, John of Hastings, John Botetourte, and William Martin; three justices, two barons of the exchequer; Philip Martel and another master of the chancery;[4] John of Banstead, and John of Sandale, the chamberlain of Scotland; and besides these the Abbots of Westminster and Waverl[e]y and Friar Hugh of Manchester.[5] It was by these twenty men (for John of Hastings was too ill to come), in conjunction with ten representatives of the various estates of Scotland, that the great Ordinance for the affairs of Scotland was drawn up.[6] Almost immediately after this, six out of these twenty men were commissioned as ambassadors to the pope, namely, the treasurer, the Bishop of Worcester, the Earl of Lincoln, Despenser, Banstead and Martel.[7]

Now the constitution of the body which was to treat with the Scottish commissioners may give us a valuable warning; for it is somewhat artificial; the representatives of Scotland are to be

---

[1] *Memoranda de Parliamento*, no. 454.

[2] *Foedera*, vol. I, pp. 853, 856; *Annales de Wigornia*, p. 529.

[3] *Memoranda de Parliamento*, App. III.

[4] [For Philip Martel see Cuttino, *English Diplomatic Administration*, Index. There is no evidence that he was a chancery clerk and no proof that he was a sworn councillor. He was keeper of diplomatic records and attended the king's council in a professional capacity in 1305.]

[5] The 'parliament' was postponed from time to time, and some men who were summoned in the first instance were not (so far as we know) summoned after the postponement, namely, the Bishops of Durham, Salisbury, and Carlisle, the Prince of Wales, the Earls of Lancaster, Gloucester, and Warwick, Aymer of Valence, John of Brittany, Clifford, Burghersh, Thomas of Berkeley, Roger la Warre, and certain justices and clerks; *Parl. Writs*, vol. I, pp. 159–61.

[6] *Parl. Writs*, vol. I, p. 161.   [7] *Foedera*, vol. II, p. 974.

outnumbered by just two to one; there are to be just two English bishops, two English abbots, two English earls. The two abbots are probably not sworn members of the council, but every great interest is to be represented and there are two Scottish abbots to be balanced. We may well believe that according to the notions of this age the king has a clear right to call upon any one of his subjects to give him counsel; and bold would have been the man who either refused to come, or who refused to sit beside any one whom he found at the council board. This makes it exceedingly hard for us to say that one man is while another man is not a permanent councillor.

The difficulty may be illustrated by the case of the most famous of the English nobles. Seven earls were summoned to the parliament, besides the Prince of Wales and Gilbert of Umfraville, who was Earl of Angus in Scotland. Five of these we have seen about the king's court, the Earls of Lincoln, Gloucester, Hereford, Lancaster, and Warwick; and, by the way, it must not escape us that the king is surrounded by his kinsfolk: Thomas of Lancaster and John of Brittany are his nephews, Hereford and Gloucester are his sons-in-law, Aymer de Valence is his cousin. Then the Warenne earldoms of Surrey and Sussex we may perhaps describe as being in suspense. The heir to them, the young John of Warenne, has not been summoned to the parliament; probably he is under age and not yet belted; but we happen to know that he is present, for on 15 March the king 'in his own chamber at Westminster in his Parliament' offers the hand of his granddaughter, Joan of Bar, to the young earl, who gratefully accepts the offer.[1] Edmund, the heir of Arundel, is another infant. The two earls whom we have not mentioned are those of Oxford and Norfolk. We can hardly doubt that the marshal of England is at least a titular councillor; but he is not being consulted; we do not know that he came to this parliament. He has been in disgrace. Three years ago he had to surrender his estate and office to the king, and take them back on terms which will make him the last of his great race.[2] There is no quarrel now. On 14 March the king 'because of his great affection'—so runs the chancery formula—forgives him the debts that he owes.[3]

---

[1] Rot. Cl. 33 Edw. I, m. 18 d.

[2] The surrender was made in April, the regrant in July 1302; *Foedera*, vol. I, pp. 940–1.

[3] Rot. Pat. 33 Edw. I, pt. 1, m. 16: 'ob grandem affectionem'.

He may well be an old, disappointed, broken man; death is at hand and the days of the Bigods are over; but for all this he is probably entitled to call himself one of the king's councillors.

When, however, all due allowance has been made for all our doubts and mistakes, we have to picture to ourselves the council as being in the main a body of officers, of ministers, of men who in one capacity or another are doing the king's work and receiving the king's pay. Even those prelates and barons who remain at Westminster, when their fellows have gone home, are hardly mere prelates and barons. The Bishops of Durham and Carlisle are not just two bishops; the magnificent Anthony Beck, the strenuous John Halton, we might almost call provincial governors, the military governors of districts which are exposed to invasion. Clifford and Despenser are not just two powerful barons; they are the two forest justices, and as such they are at this moment two very important ministers. Valence and Brittany are the king's best generals. The Earl of Lincoln, the faithful Henry Lacy, is as near to being a prime minister as a layman can be. And then the council embraces all the great courts and all the great boards. A full meeting of the council is a full meeting of the king's bench, of the common bench, of the chancery, of the exchequer: it is this and more than this.[1]

So much as to men; one word as to places. The parliament was held at Westminster, and the proclamation that invited petitions was made in 'the great hall'. Nevertheless, it is not in the royal palace that we can lay the one scene of which we have a full account; it was not there that the Bishop of Byblos came before the council. The king, we are told, was dwelling and the council was assembled in the house of the Archbishop of York.[2] Another document tells us that on 22 February a sum of £6. 12s. was paid from the wardrobe to Walter, the chaplain of the palace, in order that the archbishop's house might be prepared for the reception of the king and queen.[3] The temporalities of the archiepiscopal see were in the king's hands; William of Greenfield, the elect archbishop— he had lately resigned the chancellorship—had gone to the pope for

---

[1] I have not come upon any contemporary and official authority which shows that the king has more than one council, or which qualifies the term *consilium* with any such adjectives as *ordinarium*, *privatum*, or the like. [See below, p. 94, n. 3.]   [2] *Memoranda de Parliamento*, no. 464.
[3] Exchequer: Q.R. Various Accounts: Wardrobe and Household. [E 101/366/24.]

confirmation. Already in 1293 the king had held a parliament at the same place,[1] and thus early had York House, standing where the White Hall was to stand in later days, become the scene of royal councils.

THE BUSINESS OF A PARLIAMENT

And now we may ask the question, what does our record tell us of the part played in this parliament by the king's council, and by those who constituted or represented the three estates of the realm? We may bring the business of a medieval parliament under five heads, namely—(1) the discussion of affairs of state, more especially foreign affairs; (2) legislation; (3) taxation or supply; (4) the audience of petitions; (5) judicial business, the determination of causes criminal and civil.

(1) *General discussion*

The king had summoned the estates in order that he might treat 'of certain matters specially touching our realm of England and the establishment of our land of Scotland', and no doubt the state of Scotland was one of the main matters which required his attention and the advice of his councillors. Let us remember that just at this moment Edward was at the full height of his power. All looked well; it seemed as if the evening of his reign was to be peaceful and glorious. He had lately traversed Scotland from end to end hardly finding an enemy, save in the garrison of Stirling Castle, and now even Stirling was his. Wallace, it is true, was in all probability still at large when our parliament was sitting at Westminster; but he was a hunted outlaw and his capture, when it took place soon afterwards, cannot have been an unlooked-for event. As for the young Earl of Carrick, Edward had no reason for suspecting him of a grand ambition; we see him taking part in the parliament as one whom the king trusts. The task in hand was to provide for Scotland a settled form of government, a task that might demand prolonged debates, but not, it would seem, a hopeless task. What Edward did at this parliament was to call upon the Bishop of Glasgow, the Earl of Carrick, and John Mowbray to say how Scotland should be represented at another parliament to be holden later in the year. They reported that two bishops, two abbots, two earls, two barons, and two men elected

[1] *Rolls of Parliament*, vol. i, p. 91.

by the community of Scotland would be representatives enough. As to the place at which the parliament should meet, they left that to the king; as to the time, the Scots could hardly be ready before Midsummer. Thereupon the king fixed London and 15 July as the place and date for the assembly.[1] Afterwards he postponed that date until 15 September, and then at Westminster the ten Scottish representatives and twenty members of the English council drew up the important 'Ordinatio super stabilitate terræ Scotiæ'. However, at the moment what should interest us most is this, that in our lenten parliament the three Scottish spokesmen did not answer the question that had been put to them until after the assembly of the English estates had been dissolved. Those who were not members of the council had been sent home on 21 March; not until the 26th did the Bishop of Glasgow, Robert Bruce, and John Mowbray bring in their report.

Whether Edward had sought advice in this matter from the mass of the clergy, baronage, and commoners, we cannot say; nor do we know that the affairs of Gascony afforded material for a general debate, though there was an enormous mass of Gascon business to be transacted. Edward had lately recovered his French provinces, and was just sending out a new set of representatives. John of Havering, who had been justiciar of Wales, was to be in supreme command as seneschal of the duchy; Richard of Havering, lately the escheator north of Trent, was to be constable of Bordeaux; William Dene, seneschal of the Agenais; Frisot de Montclar, treasurer of Agen. Vast quantities of writs had to be issued for the payment of arrears of many kinds.[2]

To come nearer home, we have seen how the king expected that the clergy would make an attack upon him. He was now quite strong enough to meet, to forestall, such an attack. He had not forgotten the humiliation that he had suffered at the hands of Archbishop Winchelsea. With his very good will, as we may well suppose, a petition was presented by the barons and commons complaining that the monks, more especially the Cistercians, sent large sums of money out of the country to alien mother houses.[3] Of this matter we must speak under another head, but it may have been discussed in many meetings by the assembled laity. The

---

[1] *Memoranda de Parliamento*, nos. 13, 458.
[2] This information is derived from the Gascon Roll. *Memoranda de Parliamento*, App. II.
[3] *Ibid.* no. 486.

treatment of the offending archbishop, who had lately been giving a fresh cause of complaint by 'visiting' the king's free chapel in Hastings Castle,[1] was a subject to be debated rather at the council board than before the estates of the realm.

(2) *Legislation*

In the way of legislation this parliament did little. No statute was passed which at once found a place upon the statute roll; but there are several acts of a more or less legislative character which should be briefly mentioned.

In answer to the petition of the laity touching the revenues of the religious houses the following reply was given: 'The king in his full parliament, by the consent of the prelates, earls, barons, and others of the realm, has ordained and established a certain statute about this matter.'[2] Our roll, as will now be seen for the first time, goes on to add—'in the form that follows'. But nothing follows; a blank space is left; the statute, if drawn up, was kept in abeyance. Two years afterwards it was formally enacted or re-enacted at another parliament and became the well-known Statute of Carlisle, 'De asportatis religiosorum'.[3] The reasons for this delay are not obvious; but we have to remember that at the date of our parliament the papacy was vacant, and that Edward may have had several reasons for keeping in suspense over the future pope a statute which might prevent the flow of money from England to Rome or Avignon.[4]

There has passed into our collections of statutes out of the Vetus Codex an 'Ordinance for Inquests' made at this parliament.[5] It is an answer to a petition presented by Simon Parker, and provides in general terms that an inquest to which the king is

---

[1] *Ibid.* no. 204.   [2] *Ibid.* no. 486.

[3] *Statutes of the Realm*, vol. I, p. 150.

[4] Dr Stubbs, *Const. Hist.* §181, writes thus: 'In the February parliament of 1305 the consent of the barons had been given to a statute forbidding the payment of tallages on monastic property and other imposts by which money was raised to be sent out of the country. Not being fortified by the assent of the clergy or commons this Act was not published until 1307, when in the parliament of Carlisle held in January it was formally passed.' This may be so, and certainly the recitals in the Statute of Carlisle seem to point this way. But our roll very distinctly claims for the statute made in our parliament the consent of the prelates, earls, barons, and others of the realm. Benedict XI died on 7 July 1304; Clement V was not elected until 5 June 1305.

[5] *Statutes of the Realm*, vol. I, p. 143.

party is not to be stayed merely because the king's pleaders assert that some of the jurors are not favourable to the king. This was agreed and ordained 'by the king and his whole council'.[1] Such an ordinance was beneath the dignity of the statute roll, and we should have great difficulty in proving that it had the assent of the estates. But it was a concession by the king, and the king's ordaining power would easily cover the making of such a concession.

An Ordinatio Forestae which is on our roll was placed also upon the close roll; it has been received into our printed statute books.[2] It is the king's answer to certain petitions and does not purport upon its face to bear the authority of the assembled estates or even the authority of the council.[3] The king has been compelled to consent to a perambulation (*puralee*) of his forests, and now some of those who have been 'put out of the forest by the perambulation' want both to be quit of their old burdens and yet to enjoy their accustomed advantages; they do not want to provide 'poture', meat and drink, or money instead of meat and drink, for the foresters as of old, and yet they want to keep their old easements and rights of common within the forest. The king tells them that they must make their choice; they cannot be both inside and outside the forest and the forest law. It was not he who called for the perambulation; the demand for it should not have been made; but he has granted that demand and will keep his word. The justices of the forest are to see that effect is given to this answer. We can hardly treat this as an act of legislation; certainly we cannot treat it as an act in which the estates of the realm took part. But no doubt at their meetings there was much talk about the forests, and discussion of those grievances which in the next year were met by an ordinance of sufficient importance to be placed upon the statute roll.[4]

Lastly, there is, or rather once was, on our roll what was called in the margin thereof 'Ordinatio de trailbastons'.[5] The king has

---

[1] *Memoranda de Parliamento*, no. 10.   [2] *Statutes*, vol. I, p. 144.

[3] *Memoranda de Parliamento*, no. 461.

[4] The Ordinatio Forestae of 1306; *Statutes*, vol. I, p. 145. This is dated on 28 May, that is to say, two days before the day fixed for the parliament. The enacting words are 'concordatum est et statutum', and it calls itself 'istud statutum'.

[5] This seems to be the first appearance in an official document of the curious word 'trailbaston'. There can be little doubt that it signified a 'club-man', a vagabond with a big stick. [For a fourteenth-century miniature showing a trailbaston in action, see H. M. Cam, *The Hundred and the Hundred Rolls* (1930), p. 180.]

appointed justices to inquire of, hear and determine divers felonies and trespasses. Their commissions are upon the patent roll; the earliest is dated on 6 April.[1] The king now gives them certain instructions as to their proceedings. These will be of some importance in later history, for 'a commission of trailbaston' becomes one of the known forms of commission with which justices can be equipped. But this again we can hardly regard as a legislative act. The king has always enjoyed and still enjoys a very large discretionary power of sending justices when and whither he pleases, and of defining the matters about which they are to inquire. Even were we to examine the new commission minutely, we might find in it little that was very new or to us very striking, nevertheless the issue of it was the one thing done in this parliament that all the chroniclers have thought worthy of note; indeed, a certain annalist speaks of this year as the year of trailbaston.[3] This vigorous attempt to free the land of vagabonds takes its place along with the execution of Wallace, the disgrace of the archbishop, and the coronation of a new pope; they are the memorable events of the year, at least so it strikes a contemporary.

(3) *Taxation*

As to taxation, we have every reason to believe that on the present occasion no tax of any kind was imposed, and we have no evidence to show that the king asked for money. He seems to have been very poor. The salaries of his justices and his clerks were in arrear, and they had to be told that they must wait for better times.[4] It is of course possible that some statement of his necessities was laid before the assembled magnates, clergy and commons, but we read nothing of any 'supply' or of any demand.

There are, however, three matters which deserve a brief notice in this context. 'The bishops, abbots, earls, barons, and others of the realm' petitioned that, whereas they had done their military service in Scotland in the campaigns of 1300 and 1303, they might take scutages from their tenants.[5] The request was granted. 'The

---

[1] *Parl. Writs*, vol. I, p. 408.

[2] See Pike, *Introduction to Year Book*, 14–15 Edw. III, pp. xxx–xxxvi.

[3] *Liber de Antiquis Legibus*, App., p. 250: 'L'an de Treyle baton'. See also *Flores Historiarum*, vol. III, p. 122; *Annales de Wigornia*, p. 557; Rishanger, *Chronica*, p. 224; *Annales Londonienses*, p. 134; *Trivet*, p. 404.

[4] *Memoranda de Parliamento*, nos. 80, 175.

[5] *Ibid.* no. 198.

earls, barons, and others who owe the king military service' also complained that though they had done their service, the officers of the exchequer were charging them with scutages for all their fees. The answer was that the king in the presence of the whole council had ordained that relief should be given to them by a writ directed from the chancery to the exchequer, and that the form of the writ was to be settled by the council.[1] Thirdly, 'the archbishops, bishops, prelates, earls, barons, and other good men of the land' asked that, as the king had lately tallaged his demesnes, they also might be allowed to tallage those parts of the ancient demesnes of the crown which were in their hands.[2] To this the response was a simple *Fiat ut petitur*.[3] In all these cases the petitioners seem to have been asking for no more than they were entitled to, though the only procedure by which they could obtain it was a petition.

(4) *Audience of petitions*

But by far the greater part of our parliament roll is occupied by entries which concern the audience of petitions. Before we discuss any of the many questions which such entries suggest we must remember that many of the original petitions exist, and the external form of a petition should be briefly described.

It will in general be a strip of parchment about five inches long, while its breadth will vary from three inches to a bare inch. On the front of this strip and along its length the petitioner's grievance and prayer will be written, usually in French, rarely in Latin, and will be addressed 'to our lord the king' or 'to our lord the king and his council'. On the back of this strip and across its breadth

---

[1] *Memoranda de Parliamento*, no. 203. [For Edward's ultimately unsuccessful attempt to turn the scutage into a general tax, see H. M. Chew in *E.H.R.* (1922), pp. 321 ff.]　　　　　　　　　　　　　　　　　　　　[2] *Ibid.* no. 87.

[3] In 1304 Edward had taken a tallage of a sixth from his demesnes; Stubbs, *Const. Hist.* §181. It would not be true to say that on the present occasion the king allowed the magnates 'to tallage their demesnes'. A landlord may always tallage his villains, and it is by his villains that the greater part of his demesnes are occupied. At all events, though he may thereby be breaking manorial custom, no court of law will prevent him doing this. But when one of the manors which are the ancient demesne of the crown has been granted to a mesne lord, he may only tallage the *homines de antiquo dominico coronae* when their compeers on the manors which have not left the king's hand are being tallaged by the king. And even this, so it would seem, he can only do by the king's permission. See Vinogradoff, *Villainage*, pp. 92–3. [See also R. S. Hoyt, *The Royal Demesne in English Constitutional History* (Ithaca, 1950), pp. 204–6.]

there will almost always be written some words, usually in Latin, rarely at this time in French, which either prescribe the relief which the petitioner is to have or send him away empty. Then below this endorsement there will very often occur the syllable *Irr̃*, while just now and again we find the full *Irrotulatur*.[1] Then, if we are lucky enough to connect this document with an entry on the parliament roll, the relation between the two will be of this kind: By means of the formula, *Ad petitionem A. de B. petentis quod, etc.*, *Ita responsum est quod, etc.*, the roll will first state the substance of the petition, having turned its plaintive French into businesslike Latin and pruned away its immaterial details, and then it will give with absolute accuracy the words of that response which is endorsed on the petition.[2]

And now we may glance at the grave question, How and by whom and when and where was this business, this long and laborious business, transacted? We know that for some time past the multitude of petitions presented at the king's parliaments had been giving trouble and had been met by various expedients. In the eighth year of the reign we hear that 'the folk who come to the king's parliament are often delayed and disturbed to the great grievance of them and of the court by the numerous petitions which are presented to the king, many of which might be " exploited" before the chancellor and the justices'. It is, therefore, provided that these petitions are to be sorted. Those which concern the seal are to come before the chancellor, others are to be sent according to their nature to the exchequer or to the justices, or to the justices of the Jewry. Only those 'which are so great or so much of grace' that they cannot otherwise be dealt with are to come before the king in order that his pleasure may be taken, and they are to be brought before him and his council by the chancellor and the other chief ministers, so that he and his council may have leisure to attend to the great affairs of his realm and of other lands.[3] Then in the twenty-first year it was ordained that all petitions which thenceforth should be proffered at the parliaments should be handed in to receivers appointed by the king in order that they might be examined. Five bundles were to be made, one for the chancery, another for the exchequer, a third for the justices, a

---

[1] On several occasions I have seen *Irrotulatur* at full length, and have never noticed an *Irrotuletur*.   [2] [See below, p. 96, for an example.]
[3] Ryley, *Placita*, p. 442; Stubbs, *Const. Hist.* § 231.

fourth for the king and his council, while the fifth was to contain those which had already been answered.[1]

(a) *Procedure in 1305.* On the present occasion we obtain yet fuller information. Already on 5 February, three weeks before the day fixed for the parliament, Edward, who was then at Swaffham in Cambridgeshire, wrote to his chancellor about this matter.

We bid you [he said] along with the treasurer, to whom we have issued a similar command, proclaim that all those who have petitions to deliver to us and our council at our forthcoming parliament shall deliver them day by day to those who are assigned to receive them between now and the first Sunday of Lent [7 March] at the latest. And do you and the others of our Council in London 'deliver' as many of these petitions as you can before we come, so that no petitions shall come before us in person, save only those which cannot in anywise be 'delivered' without us, and these last you are to have well tried and examined and set in good order. This proclamation should be made in the great hall at Westminster, in the chancery, before the justices of the bench, in the Gildhall, and in Westcheap, and the names of those who are to receive petitions must be declared. You are to let me know without delay in what manner you have fulfilled this command and whom you have appointed to receive the petitions.[2]

From this it would seem that the work of examining and even of answering the petitions—for to 'deliver' a petition is to answer it—was to be taken in hand by those members of the council who were in London some days before the date appointed for the parliament.

Whether this order was obeyed or revoked we cannot say for certain. Our roll opens with just such a proclamation as the king had prescribed, and but for his letter we should naturally have supposed that it was not made until 28 February, the first day of the parliament. Be this as it may, the persons appointed to receive the petitions were Gilbert Roubury,[3] a justice of the king's bench, John Kirkby, the remembrancer of the exchequer, and two clerks of the chancery, who were also notaries of the apostolic see, John Bush and John Arthur of Caen. Their duty was, we take it, to receive and to sort the petitions.

---

[1] Ryley, *Placita*, p. 459; Stubbs, *Const. Hist.* §231.

[2] Chancery Warrants, Series I, no. 5274. [*Cal. Chanc. Warrants*, vol. I, p. 246.]

[3] [Gilbert of Rothbury, justice of king's bench 1295–1316, was the clerk of the parliament 1290–1307. He was also clerk of the king's council 1290–5. See Richardson and Sayles, 'The King's Ministers in Parliament', *E.H.R.* (1931); Sayles, *Select Cases in King's Bench* (Selden Society, 1936), vol. I, p. lxi.]

Then we read that the king has appointed certain men to receive and to answer all those petitions presented by the folk of Gascony that can be answered without the king. These men, we may say, constitute a very strong committee for Gascon affairs. They are the treasurer, the Earl of Lincoln, Aymer de Valence, John of Brittany, John of Havering, Arnaud de Caupenne,[1] the Prior of le Mas, Master Piers Arnaud de Vic, Master Piers Aimery, and John of Sandale. John of Havering is at this parliament appointed seneschal of Gascony; he has some title to be called an English baron, though apparently he has not received the baronial summons on the present occasion. John of Sandale has received no summons; but he is a trusty clerk; he is now chamberlain of Scotland, and will be Bishop of Winchester and Chancellor of England; he has had experience in Gascony.[2] Sir Arnaud de Caupenne, the Prior of le Mas, Piers Arnaud, and Piers Aimery have not received any summons of the ordinary kind and we can in no sense call them Englishmen. Piers Arnaud is provost of Bayonne, he has recently been one of the two royal lieutenants in Gascony and Arnaud de Caupenne has been with him.[3] Piers Aimery has at times been about the king's person[4] and in 1302 he was summoned to a parliament among the king's clerks;[5] but he is or was a canon of the church of St Severin,[6] and is at this moment retiring from the office of constable of Bordeaux. Sir Arnaud de Caupenne is seneschal of the Limousin, Périgord, and Quercy. As to the Prior of le Mas, his name is Bernard Pellet of Pelleti, he is a doctor of both laws, and has lately been engaged for our king's service by the Earl of Lincoln at a yearly salary of £250 tournois. We cannot yet treat the auditors of petitions as a committee of the English house of lords.[7]

---

[1] On p. 3 of the *Memoranda de Parliamento* this name by a deeply regretted error has been given as Campenne. There is more than one Caupenne (Calva Penna) in the south of France.

[2] *Foedera*, vol. II, p. 934.

[3] In 1294 Master Peter Arnaldi 'de Bik' is a king's clerk in Gascony; *Foedera*, vol. II, p. 807. In 1300 and 1301 he was one of the king's 'locum tenentes' in his 'duchy of Aquitaine', *ibid.* pp. 902, 934. On the Gascon Roll for our year (m. 24) he appears as provost of Bayonne on 30 March 1305. I assume that 'de Bik' and 'de Vico' have the same meaning. There are several places called Vic in the south of France.

[4] *Foedera*, vol. II, p. 876.   [5] *Parl. Writs*, vol. I, p. 113.

[6] *Foedera*, vol. II, p. 920.

[7] As to these Gascon auditors, see *Memoranda de Parliamento*, App. II.

To answer those petitions from Ireland and the Channel Islands which can be answered without the king, a less dignified group of men is constituted. It consists of John of Berwick, one of those very 'discreet' clerks who have not received writs of summons, Hervey of Stanton, who has not been summoned, but has been employed as an itinerant justice and will soon be a justice of the common bench, William Mortimer, an itinerant justice who has received the councillor's writ, Roger de Beaufou, who has not been summoned but is going to be employed as a justice of trailbaston, and lastly, William de Dene, who is on the eve of being appointed seneschal of the Agenais; if he was in any sense an Irishman, he was the one Irish member of this Irish committee.[1]

For Scottish petitions a third set of men is appointed. It includes William Inge and Henry of Guildford, English justices, who have been summoned as councillors (Inge is soon to be a justice north of Forth),[2] Richard of Havering who has not been summoned (he is one of the king's clerks, has served him in Scotland,[3] and is now to go out as constable of Bordeaux),[4] and two men neither of whom has been summoned but who probably know more than any other men about the king's proprietary interests in Scotland, namely, James of Dalilegh, escheator south of Forth, and John Weston, the king's receiver; they have lately been taking account of all the king's demesnes as far north as Orkney.[5] We are told that these people are to receive, not that they are to answer, the Scottish petitions, but as it seems plain that in the first instance all petitions are to pass through the hands of Roubury, Caen, Kirkby, and Bush, we may perhaps believe that the committee for Scotland had the same power that was given to the committees for Gascony and for Ireland, that it consisted not merely of receivers and sorters of petitions, but of triers and auditors.

For the English petitions no auditors were, so far as we know, expressly appointed. And here it may be remarked that this roll gives us the first evidence that we have of the appointment of auditors, nor do we get any other evidence for another ten years.[6]

[1] There had been a William de Dene who held land in Ireland; but he was dead; Sweetman, *Calendar*, 1302–7, p. 157.

[2] Bain, *Calendar*, vol. II, p. 457.   [3] *Ibid.* p. 294.

[4] *Memoranda de Parliamento*, App. II.   [5] Bain, *Calendar*, vol. II, p. 438.

[6] At the autumn 'parliament' of this year 1305 Roubury, Kirkby, Caen, and Bush were again appointed to receive the petitions, but of auditors we read nothing; *Parl. Writs*, vol. I, p. 160.

In 1316 there were three parties of auditors; one for England, a second for Gascony and the Isles, a third for Wales, Ireland, and Scotland. On that occasion the English committee consisted of three bishops, two barons, a justice, a baron of the exchequer, and a clerk of the chancery.[1] Perhaps in 1305, without any formal appointment, a small group of councillors was busy over the English petitions, but the constitution of that group may have varied from day to day, as now this man and now that could be spared from other employments. Some of the most important councillors had been told off for the Gascon petitions, the treasurer, the Earl of Lincoln, Aymer de Valence, and John of Brittany. The chancellor may have presided over the English committee and have had with him the Bishops of Durham and Carlisle, the Earls of Hereford, Gloucester and Warwick, some barons, some justices, perhaps the two chief justices, and some clerks. About this matter we cannot be certain; and it is possible that there was more than one committee for England; the endorsements on the various English petitions were not all written by one and the same hand.

Then we can see that some of the petitions were reserved for the king's eye or ear, while others were reserved for plenary meetings of the council. We come across a petition which has an endorsement of the usual character, a response defining the relief that the suppliant is to have, but that response is preceded by the words 'Coram Rege' or 'Coram Consilio', and often we can be sure that those words were not written by the hand that wrote what follows them. Here we seem to have in the first place a statement by the receivers or the auditors that this petition is one which must come before the king himself, or, as the case may be, before a full meeting of the council, followed by the order that was made when the king or when the council had considered the supplication. In one instance the endorsement of a petition which has thus been reserved for the king's audience is followed by an interesting note—'These thirty-two petitions were expedited before the king on the first Sunday of Lent.'[2] It is an interesting note, for it shows us that already on 7 March, just a week after the opening of parliament and on the very day that had been fixed as last for the receipt of petitions, considerable progress had been made in the work of 'delivering' or 'expediting' them;

[1] *Rotuli Parliamentorum*, vol. i, p. 350.
[2] *Memoranda de Parliamento*, no. 77.

already thirty-two of the reserved petitions had come before the king and they, having been duly 'tried' by the auditors, had been answered by him in the course of a single Sunday. Then we find another petition which in effect asks for an original writ of a kind as yet unknown in the chancery.[1] It bears two endorsements made by two different hands. The first says that at the end of the parliament this petition must come before all the justices; the second says that it is agreed by the council that a writ shall be framed to suit the petitioner's case.[2] From this it would seem that towards the end of the parliament, the various committees having done their work, full meetings of the council were held for the discussion of novel and arduous cases. We have seen above how on 5 April the Bishop of Byblos found at least thirty-three men assembled in one place to hear his petition.

(b) *The parliament rolls and the petitions.* However, we must not hope that any study of our roll, however careful, will enable us to set in their true chronological order all the acts done in this parliament. We have but too good reason to believe that a parliament roll is not in the very strictest sense of the term a contemporary record, and that it does not always say first what happened first. In one instance this is clear enough. Our roll begins with the proclamation concerning the delivery of petitions. This is immediately followed by the proclamation of 21 March, which sends all but the king's councillors back to their homes. From this we must not infer that all the subsequent entries on the roll represent events which occurred after that day. On the contrary we have seen that already on 7 March the king had answered a considerable number of petitions. What is more, a glance at the patent or the close roll will show us that long before the 21st the chancery was busily engaged in issuing the writs which carried into execution the responses given to the petitions. Thus, to take one example, we find on the third membrane of our roll an entry telling us how a favourable reply was given to a request by Robert Fitz Walter concerning a chapel in London which had formerly been a synagogue of the Jews; and then on the patent roll we find that Robert had got his writ as early as

---

[1] *Memoranda de Parliamento*, no. 251.

[2] This is just such a case as is contemplated by that famous clause, Stat. West. II, c. 24. The clerks of the chancery will not make a new writ, so the matter is brought before 'the next parliament', and the writ is provided by the 'jurisperiti'.

8 March. We may perhaps suppose that the first membrane with its account of the dissolution of the assembly was prefixed by way of frontispiece to a roll that had been already made up; but we have other reasons for suspecting that the larger part of our parliament roll is in a certain sense a secondhand record. We shall probably come to the conclusion that the entries on the roll stand to the endorsed petitions in the relation of copies to original documents.

Already we have said that on the back of the petition we may generally find the word *Irrotulatur* in some abbreviated form. This, we take it, has been put there by the clerk who wrote the parliament roll. It means, 'I have enrolled this petition and answer'. He did not sit writing his roll in the room in which the petitions were being heard. They were brought to him as they were 'expedited', perhaps at the close of each day's session, and his *Irrotulatur* serves as a 'tick' to show which of them he has already entered on his roll. Then he sends the originals to the chancery. In the margin of the roll, whenever that margin is still undecayed, we may read opposite almost every entry that concerns a petition, *Lib' in Canc'*, which we may expand into *Liberatur in Cancellariam*. The clerk having done with the petitions sends them off to the chancery, and we may say puts a 'tick' on his roll to show that this has been done. Then in the chancery the original endorsed petition will be the warrant for further proceedings. The chancellor will seal some patent writ or some close writ, or, it may be, some charter and vouch his warrant for so doing by the words *per petitionem de consilio*, or *per petitionem retornatam de consilio*. He finds his authority not in the entry on the parliament roll, which perhaps is not in his custody, but in the original endorsed petition. The endorsement itself is the order that has been made, the entry on the roll is a copy of that order. We are putting no slight upon the parliament roll by saying this and must hasten to add that the roll now before us shows every sign of having been drawn up while the work of hearing petitions was still in progress. To take one example, on the sixth membrane of the roll we read how an addition was made to the response given to a petition of the prior of Bridlington. That petition has been reported on the third membrane, and looking back to the report of it we find that the additional words stated on the sixth membrane have also been introduced by way of postscript into the entry on the third membrane.[1] The third

[1] *Memoranda de Parliamento*, nos. 49, 170.

membrane of our roll, therefore, had been written before the addition was made to the response that had been given to the prior. Still it seems that the endorsement itself and not the entry on the roll should be considered as the first hand and the authoritative document.

This may serve to explain a remarkable fact in the history of the parliament rolls. To all seeming the practice of enrolling such petitions as those which are entered on the roll that is now before us was abandoned early in the course of the fourteenth century. Such rolls as we have of Edward II's day are very like this roll, that is to say, they are largely occupied by the petitions of private persons who are seeking redress or favours at the hands of the king or at the hands of the king and his council. On later rolls we may find petitions enough; we shall find many petitions presented by one or more of the estates, and also a few petitions which the estates have in effect made their own; but we shall not find, at least not in any number, petitions addressed by private persons to the king or the king and council. We have every reason to believe that such petitions were still presented, for large quantities of them still exist, and some of them have been printed, also that they were presented in parliament, for we find auditors still appointed to hear them; but they are not entered on the parliament roll. If the printed book be a safe guide, there is no parliament roll even of Edward III's day that in this most important respect resembles our roll.[1] The explanation of this we take to be that the enrolment of the petition and its response is all along somewhat of a luxury, for it is not the entry on the roll but the writing on the back of the original petition that serves as a warrant for all subsequent proceedings.[2]

---

[1] If the printed *Rotuli Parliamentorum* give a different impression, this is because their editors have hardly distinguished with sufficient emphasis the matter that they took, at first or second hand, from parliament rolls, from the matter which they took, at first or second hand, from the original petitions. I do not think that they used, at first or second hand, as many as 1600 petitions, while the two classes of 'Ancient Petitions' and 'Ancient Petitions —Exchequer' contain together about 16,000 documents.

[2] See Hale, *Jurisdiction of the House of Lords*, p. 64: 'Some [petitions] were delivered over by the receivers of petitions either to the *consilium regis* or the *auditores petitionum* and by them indorsed. And these petitions are not entered on the parliament roll, but were entered [that is, were preserved] *in bundellis petitionum parliamenti* with their answers.' This seems to describe correctly the practice which obtained from Edward III's day onwards; but in earlier days the petitions disposed of by the auditors or by the council were not only endorsed but also enrolled; at least so it seems to me.

We may venture on one other speculation. May it not be that the many sad gaps which occur in the series of parliament rolls are due partly to the fact that at many parliaments, even of the later years of Edward I, no roll was made, and that if a roll was made, it was not treated as being of very high value?[1] The suggestion has been offered that many early rolls were deliberately destroyed by kings who wished to be quit of uncomfortable precedents. But this hardly accords with the nature of those rolls which have come down to us. By far the greater part of them is filled by what we may call private petitions, and no great store may have been set by them because what they recorded was sufficiently recorded elsewhere. If any dispute arose about a petition, the original could be found upon the chancery file, and possibly the reason why our oldest parliament rolls come from the exchequer and not from the chancery is that they were intended to serve as a check on a chancellor who had got the original documents and was bound to execute the orders endorsed upon them. Then a statute would go on to the statute roll, an ordinance would go on to the patent or the close roll, while as to the *placita*, those heard by the king in parliament were sometimes put upon the 'coram rege' roll, the roll of the king's bench.[2] May it not be then that the first parliament roll was a somewhat superfluous document? At any rate it is a most remarkable fact that we have at this day got most of the membranes that were used by the maker of the Vetus Codex and very few membranes that he did not use. Miserably defective though our series may seem, it may be nearly as perfect as it was in the middle of the fourteenth century; it may perhaps be nearly as perfect as it ever was.

(c) *Petitions are to king and council.* The petitions of which our roll speaks are neither petitions by parliament nor yet are they petitions addressed to parliament. We see at once that they are very different from those petitions of the commons (*petitions de la commune, petitions des communes*) which will occupy the greater part of almost any

---

[1] [For a close examination of the early records of the parliaments see Richardson and Sayles in *B.I.H.R.* vols. v and vi (1927–9), and their introduction to *Rotuli Parliamentorum Anglie hactenus inediti* (Camden Series, 1935).]

[2] Hale, *Jurisdiction*, p. 53: 'And it is observable that most of the great cases, which are recorded *inter placita parliamenti E. i.*, which were in their nature cognizable by the king's bench, are likewise entered *inter placita coram rege*, as if transacted and judged in that court.'

parliament roll of Edward III's day. But again they are not addressed to 'parliament', or to 'the lords of parliament', or to either house of parliament. They are addressed either 'to the king' or 'to the king and his council'. In a certain sense they are parliamentary petitions, they are presented in or at a parliament. But at present 'parliament' or 'a parliament' is not conceived as a body that can be petitioned. A parliament is rather an act than a body of persons. One cannot present a petition to a colloquy, to a debate. It is but slowly that this word is appropriated to colloquies of a particular kind,[1] namely, those which the king has with the estates of his realm, and still more slowly that it is transferred from the colloquy to the body of men whom the king has summoned. As yet any meeting of the king's council that has been solemnly summoned for general business seems to be a parliament.[2] These petitions are not addressed to parliament, nor are they addressed to the assembled estates, nor are they addressed to the earls, barons, and prelates. They are addressed either simply to the king or to the king and his council. The formal title for them which is in use in the chancery is 'petitiones de consilio', 'council petitions'.

When we examine the character of these petitions we soon see that for the more part they were not fit subjects for discussion in a large assembly. They do not ask for anything that could be called legislation; the responses that are given to them are in no sort 'private acts of parliament'. Generally the boon that is asked for

---

[1] [The thesis of Richardson and Sayles that *parliamentum* had acquired a technical meaning before the accession of Edward I has been forcibly contested by Powicke, *Henry III and the Lord Edward*, p. 341, and by Plucknett, who considers the term still equivocal in 1336. See *The English Government at Work, 1327–1336* (Cambridge, Mass., 1940), vol. I, pp. 82–90.]

[2] Stubbs, *Const. Hist.* § 230: 'The name of parliament, the king's parliament, belonged to the sessions of each of the three bodies thus distinguished, the terminal session of the select council, the session of the great council, the session of the commune consilium of the three estates.' Langlois, *Revue Historique*, vol. XLII, p. 90: 'Parlement, ce mot vague, synonyme barbare, à l'origine, d'assemblée et de *colloquium*, s'est précisé vers la même époque en Angleterre et en France.' The personification of 'parliament', which enables us to say that laws are made by, and not merely in, parliament, is a slow and subtle process. The same process is now at work upon other words; we begin to personify the Church Congress and so forth; even our 'meetings' pass resolutions. As to the word 'council', it is important to remember that in the Middle Ages no distinction was or could be drawn between 'council' and 'counsel'; both were *consilium*. [On the word 'parliament', see Langlois, reviewing the *Memoranda* in *E.H.R.* (1894), pp. 755 ff., and H. G. Richardson on 'The Origins of Parliament', *Trans. R. Hist. Soc.* (1928).]

is one which the king without transcending his legal powers might either grant or deny. Sometimes we may say that, if the facts are truly stated by the petitioner, the king is more or less strictly bound by the rules of common honesty to give him some relief: The king owes him wages, or his lands have been wrongfully seized by the king's officers. At other times what is asked for is pure grace and favour: The petitioner owes the king money and asks that he may be allowed to pay it by instalments, or that in consideration of his poverty part of his debt may be forgiven, or perhaps the University of Cambridge asks that the king will found a college.[1] As yet no hard line is drawn between the true petition of right which shall be answered by a *Fiat justitia* and all other petitions. 'Right' and 'grace' shade off into each other by insensible degrees, and there is a wide field for governmental discretion. Probably there would be an outcry if the religious houses could not pretty easily obtain licences for the acquisition of a reasonable quantity of land; if the nobleman who is going abroad were not suffered to appoint a general attorney; if the burghers of this or that town could not without much difficulty get leave to tax themselves and their neighbours by way of murage, pontage, or pavage; still, in any particular case the request may be refused and no reason given for the refusal.

(*d*) *The responses to the petitions.* Further, we see that the response to the petition seldom gave to the suppliant all that he wanted. He had only, we may say, 'made a *prima facie* case' for relief, and he obtained only a preliminary order. He did not get what he wanted, he was merely put in the way of getting it. Hale has stated this matter very well:

But although the council received the petitions from the hands of the receivers, yet they rarely (if at all) exercised any decision or decisive jurisdiction upon them, but only a kind of deliberative power, or rather direction, transmitting them to the proper courts, places, or persons where they were proper to be decided.... Hence it is, that most of the answers that the council gave were in the nature of remissions of the petitions to those persons or courts that had properly the cognizance of the causes.[2]

That is so; but it does not imply that, had there been no petitions, those persons or courts would have been competent to entertain

---

[1] [The enrolment, answer, petition and endorsement are given below (p. 96).]
[2] *Jurisdiction*, pp. 67–8.

those causes or to have given relief to the aggrieved. These petitions and responses are not nugatory. Nothing in the age that we are studying is more remarkable than the narrowly limited powers of the courts of law, of the exchequer, of the chancery, more especially in all such matters as concern the king. The courts of law can in general only entertain such causes as are laid before them by a writ issued from the chancery. For ordinary cases the chancery has a store of 'writs of course', and no doubt they are issued as a mere matter of routine upon receipt of the proper fees; but if anything that is in the least unusual is required, the chancellor will do nothing without a warrant from the king or council, and this warrant will be carefully noted at the foot of the writ. Some day, when the excellent work of calendaring the patent and close rolls has been completed, we shall know how much and how little a chancellor dared to do without an express warrant; apparently he dared do but little. This roll of ours contains a memorandum telling how on 6 April 'in full parliament' (it was a full parliament though the assembly of the estates had been dissolved a fortnight ago) the king prohibited his chancellor, William Hamilton, from issuing letters of protection for men who were in Ireland.[1] At present the warrant upon which the chancellor proceeds may well be oral instructions given to him immediately by the king, or brought to him by a member of the council, by John of Banstead, Henry Percy, the Bishop of Durham, Aymer de Valence, the Earl of Lincoln, or it may be a writ under the privy seal, or again it may be an endorsed petition.[2] Hence the need for so many petitions. As to the exchequer, the man who wants any relief there which is not to be had as a mere matter of routine must petition the king, and if his petition receives a favourable reply, even this will not send him directly to the exchequer; on the

---

[1] *Memoranda de Parliamento*, no. 459.

[2] I understand the note *per ipsum Regem* to mean at this time, 'My warrant is the king's word of mouth heard by me'; *per ipsum Regem nunciante J. de Benstede*, 'I act upon an oral message brought to me from the king by John of Banstead'; *per breve de privato sigillo*, 'For this I have a writ under the privy seal'; *per consilium*, 'I heard the council authorise me to do this'; *per petitionem de consilio* or *per petitionem retornatam de consilio*, 'I rely upon the endorsement of a petition presented to the council'. The 'sign manual' does not belong to this age. [For the beginning of the sign manual, under Edward III, see Tout, *Administrative History*, vol. v, p. 61; for various forms of chancery warrant, see Maxwell-Lyte, *Historical Notes on the use of the Great Seal of England* (1926), pp. 141 ff., 179 ff.]

contrary it will send him first to the chancery for a writ directed to the treasurer and barons.[1] The king has a very tight and immediate control not only over all purely governmental affairs, but also over all 'administrative justice'. This control is exercised for him in his 'parliaments' by his council or by committees of his council, the greater cases and those which have most of 'grace' in them being reserved for his own hearing. The exchequer, the financial department, is controlled by the chancery, the secretarial department, and the chancery is controlled by king and council. Often enough the man who wishes for relief in the exchequer must go first to the council for an endorsement and then to the chancery for a writ. There is already a great deal of what an impatient reader may call circumlocution and red tape. The petition will perhaps in the first instance be endorsed with a *Coram Rege*; it will then be taken before the king and another endorsement will be made upon it; a note of it will then be made upon the parliament roll; then it will be delivered into the chancery; from the chancery a writ will be sent to the exchequer but not until it has been copied on the close roll; when it gets to the exchequer, copies of it will be made by the remembrancers upon their memoranda rolls; and after all this the treasurer and barons will only begin to consider whether justice requires that the suppliant should have any relief. All this formalism is worthy of study; it is the necessary ground work for ministerial responsibility and government by discussion.

The petitioner, we have said, had only 'to make a *prima facie* case'. Occasionally we find him sending in some evidence along with his petition, for example, a copy of a charter, or of an inquisition. This, however, is rare, and a petition hardly ever ends with a formal offer of proof such as that which every plaintiff makes in the courts of law. Still it seems plain that those who heard the petitions must have had before them more than the suppliant's bare and unsworn word about the facts of his case. True that they were seldom going to give him any final relief; usually they would do no more than set some inquiry going in the courts of law, the chancery or the exchequer. But then the institution of such inquiries cannot possibly have been a mere matter of course; had it been such, a clerk of the chancery might have been set to endorse the petitions with cut and dried formulas.

---

[1] See the learned and triumphant argument of Lord Somers in The Bankers' Case, *State Trials*, vol. xiv, p. 1.

The truth probably is that as regards the king's interests—and it is just because the king has some interest in the matter that most of these petitions are presented—the council is exceedingly well informed; potentially it is almost omniscient. In these parliaments the whole governmental force of England is brought into a focus. Not only are all the great officers there, but most of their principal subordinates are there or within call. A petitioner can hardly make a statement about the king's finances, the king's estates, or even the course of justice, that cannot at once be checked, if not by one of the auditors, then by some judge, clerk, remembrancer or escheator who is close at hand, or by a few recent rolls which are within easy reach. This, we take it, is what is meant by that 'trying' of petitions of which we hear. The petitions reserved for the king himself are not to be placed before him until they have been sufficiently 'tried', that is to say, he expects that when a petition is brought before him there will be some minister at hand to say whether there is any truth in the petitioner's allegations. We know that the work of hearing petitions was long and laborious; it had threatened to deprive the king and his chief advisers of any leisure for the great affairs of state; and we may well believe that the four hundred and fifty endorsements recorded by our roll represent the work of many hours.

When a petition was to be heard, did the petitioner appear either in person or by attorney prepared to supplement or support by oral argument the written statement of his grievance? Probably this was unusual, but still we seem to have evidence that the petitioner's presence might be required and that his petition might be 'dismissed for want of prosecution'. An entry on our roll tells us how one William of Whitewell presented a petition complaining of the misconduct of John Bacon, a clerk of the court, who was seemingly lying in gaol for his offences, and by way of response we have this: 'William of Whitewell being solemnly called has not prosecuted this petition, therefore let the said John go quit thereof for the present.'[1] Then the next entry is concerned with another charge against this same John Bacon. Ralph of Cokethorpe accuses him of making fraudulent erasures on the plea rolls and asks for relief. 'Roger de Fresnes', we are told, 'has presented this petition before the council on Ralph's behalf, but on being asked whether he is Ralph's attorney, he says that he is not;

[1] *Memoranda de Parliamento*, no. 266.

therefore he is told to cause the said Ralph to appear and prosecute the petition should Ralph wish to do so.' 'Afterwards', says our record, 'it was testified by [the chief and another justice of the king's bench] that Ralph came before them and confessed that it was not by his authority that Roger prosecuted the said petition, nor had he any complaint to make. Therefore let the said John go quit thereof for the present.'[1] These two cases stand a little outside the general run of petitions, in that a very definite complaint is brought against a royal officer, but still it is evident that at least in some instances a petitioner was expected to be at Westminster by himself or his attorney, and that his petition might be rejected if he was not there to explain and support it.

(e) *Petitions by communities.* Sometimes the petition comes from an individual, sometimes from a community. Of petitions presented by communities we have a considerable number. To say nothing of the religious houses and the two universities, we have petitions by the communities of boroughs and by the communities of counties. And here we may perhaps see one of the duties of the knight who appears on behalf of a shire and of the representative burgess: he brings in and, it may be, urges by oral argument the petitions of that community which has sent him to the parliament. Then, again, we seem to have petitions which must have been drawn up during the parliament. Some instances we have already mentioned. 'The bishops, abbots, earls, barons, and others of the realm' ask the king's aid in collecting their scutages. 'The archbishops, bishops, prelates, earls, barons, and other good men of the land' ask that they may tallage such of the ancient demesnes of the crown as are in their hands. Such petitions seem to imply meetings at Westminster of those who were interested in them: they may imply regular sessions of the lords and the commons. By some resolution or another someone must have been authorised to write down these demands on strips of parchment. But so far as we can see these petitions are treated like the other petitions; on the parliament roll they are indiscriminately mixed up with the other petitions. We pass from a petition of the rector of Winchelsea, asking that the king will not take quite all the tithes of his church, to a petition presented by the magnates, and thence to a petition by the Abbot of Osney concerning certain financial operations in which he has taken part on the king's behalf. Then again wedged

[1] *Memoranda de Parliamento*, no. 267.

between a petition of Roland of Okestead and a petition of the citizens of Lincoln we find two petitions which seem to come from the assembled commons and to be the outcome of their deliberations. 'The poor men of England' complain that juries are corrupted by the rich, and that ecclesiastical judges meddle with temporal suits.[1] In each case the king civilly refuses to do anything. If juries are corrupt, those who are injured can have a writ of attaint; a writ of prohibition will confine the courts christian within their proper bounds. By no sharp line can the petitions of the assembled lords and commoners be marked off from the general mass of those petitions which are to be 'expedited' in the parliament by the king and his council. At a somewhat later date the line will be drawn; the petitions of the assembled commons, the petitions of 'the community of the land', will be enrolled along with the king's answers to them; petitions addressed to either of the two houses will be enrolled, if they have received the assent of both houses and of the king; but the ordinary petitions presented to the king and council by those who have grievances will not be enrolled, though as of old many of them will be answered in parliament by committees of auditors.

(*f*) *Action of the commoners.* As to what was done by the assembled commoners during the three weeks that they spent at Westminster, we shall hardly get beyond guess-work. All that we learn from our roll is, first, that they joined in a petition with the magnates about the exportation of the wealth of the monasteries, to which petition the king gave his assent, though he did not at once convert it into a statute; and secondly, that they presented two petitions of their own, which were refused. The king, so far as we know, did not ask them for money, nor did he desire their consent to any new law. The doctrine that in these days the representatives of the shires and towns were called to parliament not in order that they might act in concert on behalf of the commons of England, but in order that each might represent before the king in council the grievances and the interests of the particular community, county or borough, that sent him thither,[2] may easily be pressed too far, but we shall

---

[1] *Memoranda de Parliamento*, no. 472. The 'pauperes homines terrae Angliæ' seem to be the assembled commons. The original French petition may have run somewhat as follows: 'A nostre seigneur le Rei prient les povres gentz de sa terre.'

[2] [For a sound criticism of this doctrine see G. L. Haskins, 'Petitions of representatives in the parliaments of Edward I', *E.H.R.* (1938).]

probably think that there is no little truth in it, if we ask what the knights and burgesses were doing while the king and his councillors were slowly disposing of this great mass of petitions, many of which were presented by shires and boroughs. Official testimony the council can easily obtain; but it wants unofficial testimony also; it desires to know what men are saying in remote parts of England about the doings of sheriffs, escheators, and their like, and the possibilities of future taxation have to be considered. Then, again, there are many appointments to be made; for example, it is the fashion at this time to entrust a share in the work of delivering the county gaol to some knight of the county, very often to one of the knights who is representing or has represented that county at a parliament. Without denying that the germ of a 'house' of commons already exists, without denying that its members hold meetings, discuss their common affairs and common grievances, without denying that Edward has encouraged them to do this—at the present moment he has a quarrel with the clergy, at least with the archbishop, and no doubt is glad when the assembled commons protest that there are abuses in the church—without denying all this, we may still believe that the council often gives audience, advice, instructions to particular knights and burgesses. After all we have to fall back upon the words of the writ of summons: the commoners have been told to come in order that they may do what shall be ordained.

(5) *Judicial business*

We pass to judicial business, noticing that the line between this and the hearing of petitions is not very sharp.

(*a*) *The Placita.* The *Placita* which came before this parliament were few but miscellaneous.

In the first place we have the very famous case of Nicholas Segrave.[1] Segrave and Cromwell had been serving with the king in his Scottish campaign; Segrave had brought an accusation against Cromwell and a judicial combat had been waged between them in the king's court.[2] Then, however, Segrave, perhaps because he knew that the king would stop the duel, challenged his adversary

---

[1] *Memoranda de Parliamento*, no. 449.

[2] ['Waged' is used here in the technical sense of giving an undertaking to prove your charge by your body or otherwise as the court may determine, at an appointed time.]

to fight him in the court of the king of France; he withdrew himself from the English host and was endeavouring to make his way to France when he was captured. He confessed this grave offence—it was nothing less than treason. Edward then asked his council what was the punishment meet for such a crime. Their answer was—Death. The king, however, of his special grace was content that Segrave should find seven manucaptors who would undertake that he would render himself to prison if ever the king should call upon him to do so.[1]

As regards the tribunal before which Segrave stood we can say this much: The sheriff of Northampton was told to bring him before the king in the forthcoming parliament at Westminster, so soon as the king should arrive there: He made his appearance 'in full parliament in the presence of the king, the archbishop of Canterbury, and divers earls, barons and others of the king's council': When sentence was to be pronounced the king asked the advice of 'the earls, barons' (not, it will be observed, the prelates, for there was like to be a judgment of blood), 'and others of his council': it is said by a chronicler that they discussed the matter for three days:[2] Segrave's manucaptors appeared 'before the king and his council' on 29 March and executed their bond on the 31st in the presence of the treasurer, three other bishops, the two chief justices, and others. The assembly of the estates had been dissolved on the 21st. It is very possible, however, that the trial took place while all the magnates were still at Westminster; Segrave was a baron and had been summoned as such to the parliament.[3]

The citizens of Salisbury had refused to submit to a tallage set upon them by the bishop under the authority of a charter granted to one of his predecessors by Henry III. On 5 March a writ went to the sheriff of Wiltshire bidding him summon the mayor, citizens, and the whole community of the city to be 'before us and our council' at Westminster on Mid Lent Sunday (28 March). On that day four men appeared bearing full powers from the civic com-

---

[1] [See Pollock and Maitland, vol. II, p. 508; and, for the setting and sequel of the case, Powicke, *The Thirteenth Century*, pp. 331–2.]

[2] *Flores Historiarum*, vol. III, p. 122.

[3] Nicholas Kingston, accused of complicity in Segrave's crime, waged his law (*Memoranda de Parliamento*, no. 450). It is said that he made his law on Friday, 2 March. The 2 April was a Friday; the 2 March was a Tuesday and the third day of the parliament. As Segrave had been convicted before Kingston was accused, it seems probable that 2 April is the true date.

munity; two of them were, if we may already use such a phrase, the sitting members for Salisbury, a third had represented the town at a former parliament.[1] They and the bishop plead, and then the matter having been discussed 'before the king and his council', a judgment is pronounced. 'The king wills and commands' that the citizens do pay the tallage on this occasion, while as to the future they must choose between submitting to tallage and abandoning their franchises. They take the latter course, and on 6 April 'before the whole council' the mayor surrendered the mayoralty into the king's hand. It is clear that in this case the trial did not take place until the assembly of the estates had been dissolved.[2]

Next we read how on 13 March certain great folk, all of whom may themselves have been members of the council, undertook in the presence of the treasurer, the chief justice of the king's bench, 'and others of the king's council', to produce Almaric of St Amand and William of Montacute before the king whenever they should be called upon to do so; and then how on the 19th Almaric undertook to produce John of St Amand.[3] Almaric was the governor of Oxford castle, and in and about Oxford castle there had been a serious riot, in which some clerks of the university had taken their full and accustomed share. The subsequent proceedings assumed the form of an information—and, be it noted, an information of felony—lodged by the king's serjeant in the court of king's bench, and one offender of humble rank went to the gallows. As we read the record which tells this picturesque tale, we shall notice that between the king's council and the king's bench there was still in Edward I's day a very close connection.

A citizen of Bayonne, a hostage in the king's hand, had been committed to the care of the citizens of Winchester, but had escaped. For his escape the citizens were to answer by their mayor, bailiffs and six other representatives 'before us and our council in our forthcoming parliament at Westminster' on the last day of February. At that day nine of the Winchester folk appeared 'before the king and his council in the said parliament'. Further proceedings took place on 4 March, and on a yet later day the citizens made fine with the king 'before the king himself and his council'.[4]

(b) *The council and the courts.* Such records as these—and many

---

[1] *Parl. Writs*, vol. i, p. lxxxi.
[2] *Memoranda de Parliamento*, no. 451.
[3] *Ibid.* nos. 452–3.
[4] *Memoranda de Parliamento*, no. 456.

others of a like kind might be cited from other rolls—bring us within sight of an often debated and still debatable question. What in Edward I's day was the jurisdictional competence of the king's council, and in particular what was the relation in matters of judicature between the council and the nascent house of lords?[1]

Perhaps some new light might fall upon this old question were we to view it from what might be called the archivist's standpoint, were we to say for the moment that every one of the high courts in England must have a separate set of rolls. If we take up this not indefensible position, and leave out of sight the chancery and the exchequer and also the courts of the itinerant justices, we shall then hold that Henry III during the last half of his reign has two, and only two, high courts of law. The one of these is 'the bench'; it has a separate set of records, 'the *de banco* rolls'. The other is professedly held before the king himself; it follows him in his movements; it has a separate set of records, 'the *coram rege* rolls'. For ordinary purposes this latter court consists of a few professional justices; later in the reign a chief justice is definitely appointed to hold the pleas *coram rege*; but at any moment this court can be afforced by the presence of the king, of his councillors, of numerous barons and prelates. Now and again its roll will bear as a title 'Pleas before the King and his Council'.[2] It is superior to 'the bench', for it can correct the errors of 'the bench'.[3] Then early in Edward I's reign a further differentiation takes place. The court held *coram rege* when it assumes its everyday shape—that of a tribunal consisting of a few professional justices—becomes 'the king's bench'; what has formerly been 'the bench', though it always preserves this title, becomes, in common parlance, 'the common bench'; at a later day it will be the court of common pleas. But there is a greater change than this. A new set, unfortunately a meagre, disjointed set, of plea rolls (which, however, are not pure plea rolls, for they deal also with petitions and other

---

[1] [See *Select Cases before the King's Council*, 1243–1482, ed. J. F. Baldwin and I. S. Leadam, Selden Society, 1918; G. O. Sayles, Introduction to *Select Pleas in King's Bench* (Selden Society, 1936), vol. I.]   [2] Hale, *Jurisdiction*, p. 51.

[3] I may perhaps be allowed to refer to what I have elsewhere written about this matter; Bracton's *Note Book*, vol. I, p. 56; *Select Pleas of the Crown*, Selden Society, p. xii. Two points seem to be too easily forgotten. (1) *The Bench* is the formal title, not of the King's Bench, but of the Court of Common Pleas. (2) The two benches were not in all respects courts of co-ordinate jurisdiction; error lay from the Common Pleas to the King's Bench. See Blackstone's *Commentaries*, vol. III, pp. 410–11; Hale, *Jurisdiction*, p. 126.

matters) begins to appear. A court which is to stand above the king's bench is being evolved out of the old court held *coram rege*; its rolls are the 'parliament rolls'. But the process is slow. For a while this highest tribunal is hardly distinct from the king's bench. Every plea in the king's bench is in theory a plea *coram ipso domino rege*, and the rolls of the king's bench never cease to be the *coram rege* rolls. The superior tribunal is rather, if we may so speak, an afforced, an intensified form of the inferior tribunal than a separate court; a plea that is put upon the parliament roll may be put upon the king's bench roll also; the justices of the king's bench are members of the council, and a case heard at a full meeting, a parliament, of the council, is heard by, among others, the justices of the king's bench. A plea may be adjourned from a parliament to the king's bench or from the king's bench to a parliament without breach of continuity.

A new tribunal is evolved, or rather, two tribunals become three. We can see this development taking place in the pages of Bracton and Fleta. Bracton knows but two of those courts of which we are speaking: there are justices resident at the bench; there are yet more exalted justices attending the king's person.[1] Fleta knows three: there are justices resident at the bench; there are other justices who fill the king's own place, but above even them there is another tribunal, 'for the king has his court in his council in his parliaments, in the presence of prelates, earls, barons, nobles, and other learned men, where judicial doubts are determined, and new remedies are established for new wrongs, and justice is done to every one according to his deserts'.[2] Bracton has to account for two sets of rolls; Fleta for three. Whether we ought to say that the highest of the three tribunals is the new one, whether we ought to describe the process as the deposit of a middle tribunal between the lowest and the highest, whether both of these phrases are not too definite and too modern to describe the real facts—these are grave problems which must be left to others. Our imaginary archivist would perhaps say that he could not decide them until

---

[1] Bracton, f. 108.

[2] Fleta, lib. II, c. 2: 'Habet enim Rex curiam suam in consilio suo in parliamentis suis, præsentibus prælatis, comitibus, baronibus, proceribus, et aliis viris peritis, ubi terminatæ sunt dubitationes judiciorum et novis injuriis emersis nova constituuntur remedia, et unicuique justitia, prout meruit, retribuetur ibidem.' In many handwritings *viris peritis* and *iurisperitis* would be indistinguishable.

he had made up his mind on the humbler question whether many parliament rolls have been lost. Our present point must be that before the end of Edward's reign there are three courts each with its roll.

(c) *The highest tribunal.* What is the nature of the highest of these three? Is it council, is it house of lords? Fleta will warn us that we are asking an almost unanswerable question. 'Habet enim Rex curiam suam in consilio suo in parliamentis suis, præsentibus prælatis, comitibus, baronibus, proceribus et aliis viris peritis', that is all that we can safely say. The highest tribunal of the realm is the king in council; it is the king in his council in his parliaments, in the presence of prelates, barons, and other learned men. To deny that it is the king in council is impossible; to deny that it is the king in parliament, or rather that its sessions are parliaments, is impossible.

Events which were still in the future when the great Edward died, decided that the highest ordinary tribunal of the realm should be 'the king in parliament', and that this term should mean the house of lords; they decided that this tribunal should become for the more part but a court of error, and during the rest of the Middle Ages and far into modern times should have exceedingly little to do;[1] they decided also that the king in council should dispense an extraordinary justice and this on a very large scale. If asked to mark the difference between ordinary and extra-ordinary justice, we can hardly do better at the present moment than place ourselves once more in the archivist's room, and say that the court of ordinary jurisdiction keeps a proper Latin plea roll and that the council keeps none. This is no insignificant detail. When the time has come for abolishing that court of star chamber which is one of the forms that the council has assumed, this will be charged against it as one of its many irregularities—it has no proper Latin plea roll.[2] In the eyes of the lawyers of the seven-teenth century this want of a roll goes far to prove that the council board is an upstart tribunal. What has been its strength in time gone by when, having no stiff Latin record to draw up, it could modify its procedure to suit every new want, has become its weakness in the age of Coke and Prynne, an age which demands a parchment title for every unpopular institution.

---

[1] Hale, *Jurisdiction*, chap. xxx; see also Hargrave's Introduction, p. vi.

[2] Stat. 16 Car. I, c. 10: 'And by another statute...it is...enacted...that all pleas...shall be entered and enrolled in Latin.'

Long ago the parliament roll has passed from the custody of the council. Long ago it has become the record of those meetings of the estates of the realm which have acquired an exclusive right to the name of parliaments, and more particularly it has become the record of the house of lords. Long ago the rule has been that those members of the council who are not peers of the realm, but yet are summoned to parliament, are to sit in the house of lords as 'mere assistants', are not to vote, are not to speak unless their opinions are demanded. This being so, we are apt to approach the parliament rolls of Edward I's reign with a certain prejudice in our minds. They ought, so we think, to be the records of the estates of the realm; in so far as they are judicial records, they ought to be the records of the house of lords. It is hard to think away out of our heads a history which has long lain in a remote past but which once lay in the future; it is hard to be ever remembering that such ancient terms as *house of lords* and *peers of the realm* were once new terms; it is hard to look at the thirteenth century save by looking at it through the distorting medium of the fourteenth. And so we are apt to approach our earliest parliament rolls with a belief that they ought to be rolls of the house of lords and not rolls of the king's council, that the supreme tribunal of England ought to be the house of lords and not the king's council, that whatever upon our record makes against this belief should be explained away as irregular or anomalous.

Even if he had settled opinions about debatable questions of constitutional history, it would be wrong for the editor of such a book as this is to thrust them forward. The most that he can legitimately do is to provide materials for the formation of opinions. In so doing, however, it may perhaps be lawful and desirable that he should remind his readers of some facts that are like to be forgotten. And in the present case he may be allowed to say once more that we have very few parliament rolls of Edward I's reign, to remark that his son's reign was filled with momentous events, and to plead that those events may not be suffered to cast their shadow over the past. We must judge the rolls of Edward I's reign on their own merits, without reference to the parliament rolls of his grandson's, or of any later, reign. As regards the matter that is now before us, the jurisdictional competence of the parliaments, there seem to be some special reasons why this warning should not be neglected.

We are dealing with something that is new. However ancient may be the roots whence the jurisdiction of 'the king in his council in his parliaments' draws its nourishment, it is a new thing that men should see three different tribunals rising one above the other; it is a new thing that they should see a yet higher court above that court which is held in theory *coram ipso domino rege*. The competence of this highest court is as yet indefinite. Fleta uses vague words about it. He has a fairly clear view of the competence of the king's bench; it hears criminal causes; it corrects the errors and false judgments of all justices, except when such matters are brought before the king himself and his council or before auditors specially assigned for the purpose. But of the justice that is done by the king 'in his council in his parliaments' we must speak loosely: Judicial doubts are there decided, new remedies are provided for new wrongs, and justice is done to every one according to his merits. We can see, however, that this tribunal is not solely a court of error; it has a far wider power than the house of lords will have in later days. This doctrine is fully borne out by the parliament rolls. The causes which come before the parliaments do not usually come there by writ of error. The jurisdiction that is exercised is more commonly than not a jurisdiction of first instance. If we ask why a case comes before a parliament rather than before the king's bench or the common bench, often we can give no certain answer. We may say perhaps—to take examples from our own roll—that Nicholas Segrave is tried in a parliament because he is a baron charged with treason; but why should the citizens of Winchester be haled before a parliament for suffering a prisoner to escape, and why should not the Bishop of Salisbury urge his claim to tallage the men of Salisbury before one of the two benches, or even before the exchequer? Seemingly all that we dare say is that the causes heard in parliament are important causes, important because they concern the king, or because they concern very great men, or because they involve grave questions of public law, or because they are unprecedented. We must not miss the 'equitableness' of this tribunal. When Fleta says that it provides new remedies for new wrongs, and that justice is done to every man according to his deserts, he means that this supreme court can look at 'the merits of the case' with some disregard for technicalities. We are dealing with a court that has large, indefinite powers.

And then we are dealing with Edward I, the wise and vigorous king. Under his hand institutions which to our eyes seem to have in them many flaws, flaws which may easily become yawning clefts, are doing their appointed work without much friction. We can hardly look back to his time through the fourteenth century without imagining that there must be some jealous dislike of the council, an aristocratic jealousy on the part of the nobles, a professional jealousy on the part of the judges and common lawyers. But do we really see this? If not, then our problem as to the constitution of the supreme tribunal becomes simpler. It may be further simplified if we try to make it a concrete problem. Indubitably this supreme tribunal is the council. The question whether it is also the house of lords may be divided into two. First, we ought to ask whether every prelate and baron had a right to sit in the council though he had not been invited to do so. Secondly, we ought to ask whether those members of the council who were neither prelates nor barons were fully competent members of the tribunal.

To neither of these questions must we here give a dogmatic answer, but in connection with the first it may be right that we should ask a yet further question, namely, whether we are not introducing an inappropriate idea and burdening ourselves with an unnecessary anachronism when we talk of any man having a right to sit in this or any other court of law? We must put duty in the first line, right in the second. We have learnt to do this when discussing the constitution of those county courts which send knights to the house of commons; must we not also do it when we are discussing the constitution of the house of lords and of the council? In 1305 the baron, who had come from Yorkshire or Devonshire, had been compelled to spend three weeks in London at his own cost, for he was paid no wages. Did he very much want to spend another three weeks there hearing dreary petitions concerning the woes of Scots and Gascons? At a later time a desire for political power and for social pre-eminence will make the English baron eager to insist on his right to a writ of summons, eager to take a part, however subordinate, in all that is done by the house of lords. But in Edward I's day the baronage is hardly as yet a well-defined body, and it may be that there are many men who, unable to foresee that their 'blood' is being 'ennobled' for ever and ever, are not pleased when they receive a writ which tells them that, leaving their homes and affairs, they must journey and labour in the king's service, and all this at their own cost. Thus for many years one great constitutional question can remain in suspense. It is not raised, no one wishes to raise it. So long as the king does not impose taxes or issue statutes without the consent of the baronage, the baron hopes that the king will mind his own business (and it is his business to govern the realm) and allow other folk to mind theirs.[1]

Of the second of our two questions but one word can here be said. If we fix our gaze on the council which remains in constant session and 'in full parliament' at Westminster for several weeks after the generality of prelates and barons have departed, we shall have some difficulty in believing that those councillors who are neither prelates nor barons are taking but a subordinate part in the work that is done; for example, that when the council is sitting as a judicial tribunal, the opinions of the two chief justices, Brabazon and Hengham, are of less importance than the opinions of two barons who are no lawyers. Once more let us remember that until very lately the jurisdiction of the king's council has been regarded as being substantially the same thing as the jurisdiction of that court over which Brabazon presides.[2]

CONCLUSION

Perhaps more than enough has already been said about these controverted matters; but it seemed necessary to remind readers, who are conversant with the 'parliaments' of later days, that about the parliaments of Edward I's time there is still much to be discovered, and that should they come to the opinion that a session of the king's council is the core and essence of every *parliamentum*, that the documents usually called 'parliamentary petitions' are petitions to the king and his council, that the auditors of petitions are committees of the council, that the rolls of parliament are the records of the business done by the council—sometimes with, but much more often without, the concurrence of the estates of the realm—that the highest tribunal in England is not a general assembly of barons and prelates, but the king's council, they will not be departing very far from the path marked out by books that are already classical.[3]

[1] [For evidence, however, as to the active co-operation of the baronage in Edwardian parliaments, see Powicke, *The Thirteenth Century*, pp. 343–8.]

[2] Hale, *Jurisdiction*, pp. 59, 156, holds that the judges were in Edward I's day the most important members of the tribunal which heard pleas in parliament.

[3] The one point about which I venture to differ from what seems to be the general opinion of modern historians (and I am uncertain as to whether this

Those who have done most for the constitutional history of the middle ages would probably be the first to admit that much more remains to be done. And much more can and will be done in due course. Only a very small portion of the records that bear on the history of the council of the thirteenth and fourteenth centuries has yet been published.[1] It is true that the parliament rolls are in print, but we have no such rolls for Henry III's reign, very few from the days of the first two Edwards, and even when we have a parliament roll it does not tell us by any means all that we ought to know if we are to know the council. On the other hand there is an inexhaustible supply of rolls of other kinds. The contents of this book, for example, represent but a little part of the writing that was done at Westminster in consequence of one particular session of the council, that which was held in the spring of the year 1305. It would have been easy to have filled another volume with documents occasioned by that session, writs of all sorts and kinds issued *per consilium* or *per petitionem de consilio*, including the very numerous letters that were sent to Gascony, inquisitions of all sorts and kinds that were made under the authority of those writs, proceedings before the king's bench and proceedings in the exchequer which took place because the council had ordered them. I am persuaded that if the charter, patent and close rolls, the privy

difference is real) is that I cannot find in the official language of Edward I's time any warrant for holding that the king has more than one *concilium*, or rather *consilium*; any warrant, that is, for holding that this term is applied to two or three different bodies of persons, which are conceived as permanently existing bodies, or any warrant for holding that the term should be qualified by some adjective, such as *commune*, or *magnum*, or *ordinarium*. We might like to ask the question whether every prelate and every baron is a member of *the* magnum consilium, whether every representative of a shire or a borough is a member of *the* commune consilium regni. The Latin language knows no article definite or indefinite; the language of the time knows no difference between counsel and council. One thing is clear: an order sending to their homes the prelates, earls, barons, knights, burgesses, and other commoners, 'sauve les Evesques, Contes et Barouns, Justices et autres, qui sount du Counseil nostre seigneur le Roy' is an intelligible order. [Maitland's statement here differs hardly at all from that of Stubbs in §§230–1 of the *Constitutional History*. On the question of council or councils, his view is now generally accepted.]

[1] [Since Maitland wrote, the series of calendars of the medieval close, patent and charter rolls have been completed. The curia regis rolls down to 1220 have been printed in full, and a selection of pleas from the *coram rege* rolls is being published by the Selden Society. No comprehensive collection of early council proceedings has been published, nor any memoranda roll of the exchequer later than 1200.]

seals, the memoranda of the exchequer, and the *coram rege* rolls were used skilfully and in combination, our historians would be able to give us an account of many a session or parliament of the council of which we have not yet heard, to tell us who were present and what business was transacted. The task that has to be performed is indeed a gigantic task, that of calendaring mile after mile of closely written parchment, and fitting thousands of undated documents into their proper places; but it can be accomplished by prolonged, sustained, and well-directed efforts, and it ought to be accomplished. He would be a bold man who said that there is any question about the government of England by Edward I which cannot be answered.

APPENDIX[1]

Ad petitionem Universitatis de Cantebrigia petentis auxilium domini Regis quod ipse velit esse fundator unius domus quam eadem Universitas ordinavit pro pauperibus scolaribus in eadem Universitate commorantibus sustentandis et quod domus illa dotari possit de terris et redditibus usque ad summam xl. lib. vel plus vel minus pro voluntate Regis:—

Ita responsum est: Rex vult certiorari per vicecomitem si sit ad commodum vel ad dampnum Regis.

Ancient Petitions, 13758.

A nostre seignur le Roy qe Deu gard moustrent le Chaunceler, Mestres, e Clers de sa Universite de Cauntebrige par la ou il ount...e purveu pur lestat de Seynt Eglise e profit de la terre al eyde de Deu, une collegion de povres escolers a estre trovez sustenance en la dite Universite, parmy vostre eyde chere Syre si vous plest, e autries almoignes des clers e des lays qe lur voylent pur Deu eyder et [avaun]cer, vous prions pur lamour de Dieu, e les almes vostre piere, miere, cumpaigne e vos auncestres voyllet de cele mesun estre fundur e qe ele seit en vostre proteccion e qe ele puisse estre dowe par purchas en almoignee de ceaux qe les voillent avauncer des terres ou des rentes a la value de quaraunte livrees, ou plus, ou meyns, a vostre vollente, nient countre-esteaunt vostre estatuz des teres e tenemens alyenez en morte mein, dount les escolers la demoraunz puissent estre sustenuz, issint qe ceaux escolers soient esluz, receus, demoraunz e governez par le Chaunceler e la fraunchise de la dite Universite, cum autres escolers iloqes estudiaunz.

(*Endorsement.*) Rex vult certiorari per vicecomitem si sit ad commodum vel ad dampnum Regis.

Domino Cancellario.[2]

----

[1] *Memoranda de Parliamento,* no. 50.
[2] At the foot of the back of the petition, by way of address.

HISTORY OF ENGLISH LAW[1]

In English jurisprudence 'legal memory' is said to extend as far as, but no further than the coronation of Richard I (3 September 1189). This is a technical doctrine concerning prescriptive rights, but is capable of expressing an important truth. For the last seven centuries, little more or less, the English law, which is now over-shadowing a large share of the earth, has had not only an extremely continuous, but a matchlessly well-attested history, and, moreover, has been the subject matter of rational exposition. Already in 1194 the daily doings of a tribunal which was controlling and moulding the whole system were being punctually recorded in letters yet legible, and from that time onwards it is rather the enormous bulk than any dearth of available materials that prevents us from tracing the transformation of every old doctrine and the emergence and expansion of every new idea. If we are content to look no further than the text-books—the books written by lawyers for lawyers—we may read our way backwards to Blackstone (d. 1780), Hale (d. 1676), Coke (d. 1634), Fitzherbert (d. 1538), Littleton (d. 1481), Bracton (d. 1268), Glanvill (d. 1190), until we are in the reign of Henry of Anjou, and yet shall perceive that we are always reading of one and the same body of law, though the little body has become great, and the ideas that were few and indefinite have become many and explicit.

Beyond these seven lucid centuries lies a darker period. Nearly six centuries will still divide us from the dooms of Æthelberht (c. 600), and nearly seven from the Lex Salica (c. 500). We may regard the Norman conquest of England as marking the confluence of two streams of law. The one we may call French or Frankish. If we follow it upwards we pass through the capitularies of Carlo-vingian emperors and Merovingian kings until we see Chlodwig and his triumphant Franks invading Gaul, submitting their Sicambrian necks to the yoke of the imperial religion, and putting their traditional usages into written Latin. The other rivulet we

[1] [*Encyclopaedia Britannica*, 10th ed., supplement (1902), vol. xxviii, pp. 246–53; 11th ed. vol. ix, pp. 600–7.]

may call Anglo-Saxon. Pursuing it through the code of Canute (d. 1035) and the ordinances of Alfred (*c.* 900) and his successors, we see Ine publishing laws in the newly converted Wessex (*c.* 690), and, almost a century earlier, Æthelberht doing the same in the newly converted Kent (*c.* 600). This he did, says Beda, in accordance with Roman precedents. Perhaps from the Roman missionaries he had heard tidings of what the Roman emperor had lately been doing far off in New Rome. We may at any rate notice with interest that in order of time Justinian's law-books fall between the *Lex Salica* and the earliest Kentish dooms; also that the great pope who sent Augustine to England is one of the very few men who between Justinian's day and the eleventh century lived in the Occident and yet can be proved to have known the Digest. In the Occident the time for the Germanic 'folk-laws' (*Leges Barbarorum*) had come, and a Canon law, ambitious of independence, was being constructed, when in the Orient the lord of church and state was 'enucleating' all that was to live of the classical jurisprudence of pagan Rome. It was but a brief interval between Gothic and Lombardic domination that enabled him to give law to Italy: Gaul and Britain were beyond his reach.

The Anglo-Saxon laws that have come down to us (and we have no reason to fear the loss of much beyond some dooms of the Mercian Offa) are best studied as members of a large Teutonic family. Those that proceed from the Kent and Wessex of the seventh century are closely related to the continental folk-laws. Their next of kin seem to be the *Lex Saxonum* and the laws of the Lombards. Then, though the eighth and ninth centuries are unproductive, we have from Alfred (*c.* 900) and his successors a series of edicts which strongly resemble the Frankish capitularies —so strongly that we should see a clear case of imitation, were it not that in Frankland the age of legislation had come to its disastrous end long before Alfred was king. This, it may be noted, gives to English legal history a singular continuity from Alfred's day to our own. The king of the English was expected to publish laws at a time when hardly any one else was attempting any such feat, and the English dooms of Canute the Dane are probably the most comprehensive statutes that were issued in the Europe of the eleventh century. No genuine laws of the sainted Edward have descended to us, and during his reign England seems but too likely to follow the bad example of Frankland, and become a loose congeries of lordships. From this fate it was saved by the Norman duke, who, like Canute before him, subdued a land in which kings were still expected to publish laws.

In the study of early Germanic law—a study which now for some considerable time has been scientifically prosecuted in Germany—the Anglo-Saxon dooms have received their due share of attention. A high degree of racial purity may be claimed on their behalf. Celtic elements have been sought for in them, but have never been detected. At certain points, notably in the regulation of the blood-feud and the construction of a tariff of atonements, the law of one rude folk will always be somewhat like the law of another; but the existing remains of old Welsh and old Irish law stand far remoter from the dooms of Æthelberht and Ine than stand the edicts of Rothari and Liutprand, kings of the Lombards. Indeed, it is very dubious whether distinctively Celtic customs play any considerable part in the evolution of that system of rules of Anglian, Scandinavian and Frankish origin which becomes the law of Scotland. Within England itself, though for a while there was fighting enough between the various Germanic folks, the tribal differences were not so deep as to prevent the formation of a common language and a common law. Even the strong Scandinavian strain seems to have rapidly blended with the Anglian. It amplified the language and the law, but did not permanently divide the country. If, for example, we can today distinguish between *law* and *right*, we are debtors to the Danes; but very soon *law* is not distinctive of eastern or *right* of western England. In the first half of the twelfth century a would-be expounder of the law of England had still to say that the country was divided between the Wessex law, the Mercian law, and the Danes' law, but he had also to point out that the law of the king's own court stood apart from and above all partial systems. The local customs were those of shires and hundreds, and shaded off into each other. We may speak of more Danish and less Danish counties; it was a matter of degree; for rivers were narrow and hills were low. England was meant by nature to be the land of one law.

Then as to Roman law. In England and elsewhere Germanic law developed in an atmosphere that was charged with traditions of the old world, and many of these traditions had become implicit in the Christian religion. It might be argued that all that we call progress is due to the influence exercised by Roman civilisation;

that, were it not for this, Germanic law would never have been set in writing; and that theoretically unchangeable custom would never have been supplemented or superseded by express legislation. All this and much more of the same sort might be said; but the survival in Britain, or the reintroduction into England, of anything that we should dare to call Roman jurisprudence would be a different matter. Eyes, carefully trained, have minutely scrutinised the Anglo-Saxon legal texts without finding the least trace of a Roman rule outside the ecclesiastical sphere. Even within that sphere modern research is showing that the church-property-law of the Middle Ages, the law of the ecclesiastical 'benefice', is permeated by Germanic ideas. This is true of Gaul and Italy, and yet truer of an England in which Christianity was for a while extinguished. Moreover, the laws that were written in England were, from the first, written in the English tongue; and this gives them a unique value in the eyes of students of Germanic folk-law, for even the very ancient and barbarous *Lex Salica* is a Latin document, though many old Frankish words are enshrined in it. Also we notice—and this is of grave importance—that in England there are no vestiges of any 'Romani' who are being suffered to live under their own law by their Teutonic rulers. On the Continent we may see Gundobad, the Burgundian, publishing one law-book for the Burgundians and another for the Romani who own his sway. A book of laws, excerpted chiefly from the Theodosian code, was issued by Alaric the Visigoth for his Roman subjects before the days of Justinian, and this book (the so-called *Breviarium Alarici* or *Lex Romana Visigothorum*) became for a long while the chief representative of Roman law in Gaul. The Frankish king in his expansive realm ruled over many men whose law was to be found not in the *Lex Salica* or *Lex Ribuaria*, but in what was called the *Lex Romana*. 'A system of personal law' prevailed: the *homo Romanus* handed on his Roman law to his children, while Frankish or Lombardic, Swabian or Saxon law would run in the blood of the *homo barbarus*. Of all this we hear nothing in England. Then on the mainland of Europe Roman and barbarian law could not remain in juxtaposition without affecting each other. On the one hand we see distinctively Roman rules making their way into the law of the victorious tribes, and on the other hand we see a decay and debasement of jurisprudence which ends in the formation of what modern historians have called a

Roman 'vulgar-law' (*Vulgärrecht*). For a short age which centres round the year 800 it seemed possible that Frankish kings, who were becoming Roman emperors, would be able to rule by their capitularies nearly the whole of the Christian Occident. The dream vanished before fratricidal wars, heathen invaders, centrifugal feudalism, and a centripetal church which found its law in the newly concocted forgeries of the Pseudo-Isidore (*c.* 850). The 'personal laws' began to transmute themselves into local customs, and the Roman vulgar-law began to look like the local custom of those districts where the Romani were the preponderating element in the population. Meanwhile, the Norse pirates subdued a large tract of what was to be northern France—a land where Romani were few. Their restless and boundless vigour these Normans retained; but they showed a wonderful power of appropriating whatever of alien civilisation came in their way. In their language, religion and law, they had become French many years before they subdued England. It is a plausible opinion that among them there lived some sound traditions of the Frankish monarchy's best days, and that Norman dukes, rather than German emperors or kings of the French, are the truest spiritual heirs of Charles the Great.

THE NORMAN AGE

In our own day German historians are wont to speak of English law as a 'daughter' of French or Frankish law. This tendency derived its main impulse from H. Brunner's proof that the germ of trial by jury, which cannot be found in the Anglo-Saxon laws, can be found in the prerogative procedure of the Frankish kings. We must here remember that during a long age English lawyers wrote in French and even thought in French, and that to this day most of the technical terms of the law, more especially of the private law, are of French origin. Also it must be allowed that when English law has taken shape in the thirteenth century it is very like one of the *coutumes* of northern France. Even when linguistic difficulties have been surmounted, the Saxon Mirror of Eike von Repgow will seem far less familiar to an Englishman than the so-called Establishments of St Louis. This was the outcome of a slow process which fills more than a century (1066–1189), and was in a great measure due to the reforming energy of Henry II, the French prince who, in addition to England, ruled a good half of France. William the Conqueror seems to have intended to govern Englishmen by English law. After the tyranny of Rufus, Henry I promised a restoration of King Edward's law: that is, the law of the Confessor's time (*Lagam Eadwardi regis vobis reddo*). Various attempts were then made, mostly, so it would seem, by men of French birth, to state in a modern and practicable form the *laga Eadwardi* which was thus restored. The result of their labours is an intricate group of legal tracts which has been explored of late years by Dr Liebermann. The best of these has long been known as the *Leges Henrici Primi*, and aspires to be a comprehensive law-book. Its author, though he had some foreign sources at his command, such as the *Lex Ribuaria* and an epitome of the Breviary of Alaric, took the main part of his matter from the code of Canute and the older English dooms. Neither the Conqueror nor either of his sons had issued many ordinances: the invading Normans had little, if any, written law to bring with them, and had invaded a country where kings had been lawgivers. Moreover, there was much in the English system that the Conqueror was keenly interested in retaining—especially an elaborate method of taxing the land and its holders. The great product of Norman government, the grandest feat of government that the world had seen for a long time past, the compilation of *Domesday Book*, was a conservative effort, an attempt to fix upon every landholder, French or English, the amount of geld that was due from his predecessor in title. Himself the rebellious vassal of the French king, the duke of the Normans, who had become king of the English, knew much of disruptive feudalism, and had no mind to see England that other France which it had threatened to become in the days of his pious but incompetent cousin. The sheriffs, though called *vice-comites*, were to be the king's officers; the shire-moots might be called county courts, but were not to be the courts of counts. Much that was sound and royal in English public law was to be preserved if William could preserve it.

ROYAL JUSTICE

The gulf that divides the so-called *Leges Henrici* (*c.* 1115) from the text-book ascribed to Ranulf Glanvill (*c.* 1188) seems at first sight very wide. The one represents a not easily imaginable chaos and clash of old rules and new; it represents also a stage in the development of feudalism which in other countries is represented chiefly by a significant silence. The other is an orderly, rational book, which through all the subsequent centuries will be readily understood by English lawyers. Making no attempt to tell us what goes on in the local courts, its author, who may be Henry II's chief justiciar, Ranulf Glanvill, or may be Glanvill's nephew, Hubert Walter, fixes our attention on a novel element which is beginning to subdue all else to its powerful operation. He speaks to us of the justice that is done by the king's own court. Henry II had opened the doors of his French-speaking court to the mass of his subjects. Judges chosen for their ability were to sit there, term after term; judges were to travel in circuits through the land, and in many cases the procedure by way of 'an inquest of the country', which the Norman kings had used for the ascertainment of their fiscal rights, was to be at the disposal of ordinary litigants. All this had been done in a piecemeal, experimental fashion by ordinances that were known as 'assizes'. There had not been, and was not to be, any enunciation of a general principle inviting all who were wronged to bring in their own words their complaints to the king's audience. The general prevalence of feudal justice, and of the world-old methods of supernatural probation (ordeals, battle, oaths sworn with oath-helpers), was to be theoretically respected; but in exceptional cases, which would soon begin to devour the rule, a royal remedy was to be open to anyone who could frame his case within the compass of some carefully worded and prescript formula. With allusion to a remote stage in the history of Roman law, a stage of which Henry's advisers can have known little or nothing, we may say that a 'formulary system' is established which will preside over English law until modern times. Certain actions, each with a name of its own, are open to litigants. Each has its own formula set forth in its original (or, as we might say, originating) writ; each has its own procedure and its appropriate mode of trial. The litigant chooses his writ, his action, and must stand or fall by his choice. Thus a book about royal justice tends to become, and Glanvill's book already is, a commentary on original writs.

The precipitation of English law in so coherent a form as that which it has assumed in Glanvill's book is not to be explained without reference to the revival of Roman jurisprudence in Italy. Out of a school of Lombard lawyers at Pavia had come Lanfranc the Conqueror's adviser,[1] and the Lombardists had already been studying Justinian's Institutes. Then at length the Digest came by its rights. About the year 1100 Irnerius was teaching at Bologna, and from all parts of the West men were eagerly flocking to hear the new gospel of civilisation. About the year 1149 Vacarius was teaching Roman law in England. The rest of a long life he spent here, and faculties of Roman and Canon law took shape in the nascent University of Oxford. Whatever might be the fate of Roman law in England, there could be no doubt that the Canon law, which was crystallising in the *Decretum Gratiani* (*c.* 1139) and in the decretals of Alexander III, would be the law of the English ecclesiastical tribunals. The great quarrel between Henry II and Thomas of Canterbury brought this system into collision with the temporal law of England, and the king's ministers must have seen that they had much to learn from the methodic enemy. Some of them were able men who became the justices of Henry's court, and bishops to boot. The luminous *Dialogue of the Exchequer* (*c.* 1179), which expounds the English fiscal system, came from the treasurer, Richard Fitz Nigel, who became Bishop of London; and the treatise on the laws of England came perhaps from Glanvill, perhaps from Hubert Walter, who was to be both primate and chief justiciar. There was healthy emulation of the work that was being done by Italian jurists, but no meek acceptance of foreign results.

BRACTON

A great constructive era had opened, and its outcome was a large and noble book. The author was Henry of Bratton (his name has been corrupted into Bracton), who died in 1268 after having been for many years one of Henry III's justices. The model for its form was the treatise of Azo of Bologna ('master of all the masters of the laws', an Englishman called him), and thence were taken many of the generalities of jurisprudence: maxims that might be regarded as of universal and natural validity. But the true core of the work was the practice of an English court which had yearly been extending its operations in many directions. For half a century past diligent record had been kept on parchment of all that this court had done, and from its rolls Bracton cited numerous decisions.

[1] [This identification is disputed. For bibliography, see R. W. Southern in *Studies in Medieval History presented to F. M. Powicke* (Oxford, 1948), pp. 28–30.]

He cited them as precedents, paying special heed to the judgments of two judges who were already dead, Martin Pateshull and William Raleigh. For this purpose he compiled a large Note Book, which was discovered by Professor Vinogradoff in the British Museum in 1884. Thus at a very early time English 'common law' shows a tendency to become what it afterwards definitely became, namely, 'case law'. The term 'common law' was being taken over from the canonists by English lawyers, who used it to distinguish the general law of the land from local customs, royal prerogatives, and in short from all that was exceptional or special. Since statutes and ordinances were still rarities, all expressly enacted laws were also excluded from the English lawyers' notion of 'the common law'. The Great Charter (1215) had taken the form of a grant of 'liberties and privileges', comparable to the grants that the king made to individual men and favoured towns. None the less, it was in that age no small body of enacted law, and, owing to its importance and solemnity, it was in after ages regarded as the first article of a statute book. There it was followed by the 'provisions' issued at Merton in 1236, and by those issued at Marlborough after the end of the Barons' War. But during Henry III's long reign the swift development of English law was due chiefly to new 'original writs' and new 'forms of action' devised by the chancery and sanctioned by the court. Bracton knew many writs that were unknown to Glanvill, and men were already perceiving that limits must be set to the inventive power of the chancery unless the king was to be an uncontrollable law-maker. Thus the common law was losing the power of rapid growth when Bracton summed the attained results in a book, the success of which is attested by a crowd of manuscript copies. Bracton had introduced just enough of Roman law and Bolognese method to save the law of England from the fate that awaited German law in Germany. His book was printed in 1569, and Coke owed much to Bracton.

The comparison that is suggested when Edward I is called the English Justinian cannot be pressed very far. Nevertheless, as is well known, it is in his reign (1272–1307) that English institutions finally take the forms that they are to keep through coming centuries. We already see the parliament of the three estates, the convocations of the clergy, the king's council, the chancery or secretarial department, the exchequer or financial department, the king's bench, the common bench, the commissioners of assize and gaol delivery, the small group of professionally learned judges, and a small group of professionally learned lawyers, whose skill is at the service of those who will employ them. Moreover, the statutes that were passed in the first eighteen years of the reign, though their bulk seems slight to us nowadays, bore so fundamental a character that in subsequent ages they appeared as the substructure of huge masses of superincumbent law. Coke commented upon them sentence by sentence, and even now the merest smatterer in English law must profess some knowledge of *Quia emptores* and *De donis conditionalibus.* If some American states have, while others have not, accepted these statutes, that is a difference which is not unimportant to citizens of the United States in the twentieth century. Then from the early years of Edward's reign come the first 'law reports' that have descended to us: the oldest of them have not yet been printed; the oldest that has been printed belongs to 1292. These are the precursors of the long series of Year Books (Edw. II–Hen. VIII) which runs through the residue of the Middle Ages. Lawyers, we perceive, are already making and preserving notes of the discussions that take place in court: French notes that will be more useful to them than the formal Latin records inscribed upon the plea rolls. From these reports we learn that there are already, as we should say, a few 'leading counsel', some of whom will be retained in almost every important cause. Papal decretals had been endeavouring to withdraw the clergy from secular employment. The clerical element had been strong among the judges of Henry III's reign: Bracton was an archdeacon, Pateshull a dean, Raleigh died a bishop. Their places begin to be filled by men who are not in orders, but who have pleaded the king's causes for him—his serjeants or servants at law—and beside them there are young men who are 'apprentices at law', and are learning to plead. Also we begin to see men who, as 'attorneys at law', are making it their business to appear on behalf of litigants. The history of the legal profession and its monopoly of legal aid is intricate, and at some points still obscure; but the influence of the canonical system is evident: the English attorney corresponds to the canonical proctor, and the English barrister to the canonical advocate. The main outlines were being drawn in Edward I's day; the legal profession became organic, and professional opinion became one of the main forces that moulded the law.

The study of English law fell apart from all other studies, and the impulse that had flowed from Italian jurisprudence was ebbing. We have two comprehensive text-books from Edward's reign: the one known to us as *Fleta*, the other as *Britton*; both of them, however, quarry their materials from Bracton's treatise. Also we have two little books on procedure which are attributed to Chief-Justice Hengham, and a few other small tracts of an intensely practical kind. Under the cover of fables about King Alfred, the author of the *Mirror of Justices* made a bitter attack upon King Edward's judges, some of whom had fallen into deep disgrace. English legal history has hardly yet been purged of the leaven of falsehood that was introduced by this fantastic and unscrupulous pamphleteer. His enigmatical book ends that literate age which begins with Glanvill's treatise and the treasurer's dialogue. Between Edward I's day and Edward IV's hardly anything that deserves the name of book was written by an English lawyer.

FOURTEENTH AND FIFTEENTH CENTURIES

During that time the body of statute law was growing, but not very rapidly. Acts of parliament intervened at a sufficient number of important points to generate and maintain a persuasion that no limit, or no ascertainable limit, can be set to the legislative power of king and parliament. Very few are the signs that the judges ever permitted the validity of a statute to be drawn into debate. Thus the way was being prepared for the definite assertion of parliamentary 'omnicompetence' which we obtain from the Elizabethan statesman Sir Thomas Smith, and for those theories of sovereignty which we couple with the names of Hobbes and Austin. Nevertheless, English law was being developed rather by debates in court than by open legislation. The most distinctively English of English institutions in the later middle ages are the Year Books and the Inns of Court. Year by year, term by term, lawyers were reporting cases in order that they and their fellows might know how cases had been decided. The allegation of specific precedents was indeed much rarer than it afterwards became, and no calculus of authority so definite as that which now obtains had been established in Coke's day, far less in Littleton's. Still it was by a perusal of reported cases that a man would learn the law of England. A skeleton for the law was provided, not by the Roman rubrics (such as public and private, real and personal, possessory and proprietary, contract and delict), but by the cycle of original writs that were inscribed in the chancery's *Registrum Brevium*. A new form of action could not be introduced without the authority of parliament, and the growth of the law took the shape of an explication of the true intent of ancient formulas. Times of inventive liberality alternated with times of cautious and captious conservatism. Coke could look back to Edward III's day as to a golden age of good pleading. The otherwise miserable time which saw the Wars of the Roses produced some famous lawyers, and some bold doctrines which broke new ground. It produced also Sir Thomas Littleton's (d. 1481) treatise on Tenures, which (though it be not, as Coke thought it, the most perfect work that ever was written in any human science) is an excellent statement of law in exquisitely simple language.

LEGAL EDUCATION

Meanwhile English law was being scholastically taught. This, if we look at the fate of native and national law in Germany, or France, or Scotland, appears as a fact of primary importance. From beginnings, so small and formless that they still elude research, the Inns of Court had grown. The lawyers, like other men, had grouped themselves in gilds, or gild-like 'fellowships'. The fellowship acquired property; it was not technically incorporate, but made use of the thoroughly English machinery of a trust. Behind a hedge of trustees it lived an autonomous life, unhampered by charters or statutes. There was a hall in which its members dined in common; there was the nucleus of a library; there were also dormitories or chambers in which during term-time lawyers lived celibately, leaving their wives in the country. Something of the college thus enters the constitution of these fellowships; and then something academical. The craft gild regulated apprenticeship; it would protect the public against incompetent artificers, and its own members against unfair competition. So the fellowship of lawyers. In course of time a lengthy and laborious course of education of the medieval sort had been devised. He who had pursued it to its end received a call to the bar of his inn. This call was in effect a degree. Like the doctor or master of a university, the full-blown barrister was competent to teach others, and was expected to read lectures to students. But further, in a manner that is still very dark, these societies had succeeded in making their degrees the only steps that led to practice in the king's courts. At the end of the Middle Ages (*c.* 1470) Sir John Fortescue rehearsed the praises of the laws of England in a book which is one of the earliest efforts of comparative politics. Contrasting England with France, he rightly connects limited monarchy, public and oral debate in the law courts, trial by jury, and the teaching of national law in schools that are thronged by wealthy and well-born youths. But nearly a century earlier, the assertion that English law affords as subtle and civilising a discipline as any that is to be had from Roman law was made by a man no less famous than John Wycliff. The heresiarch naturally loathed the Canon law; but he also spoke with reprobation of the 'paynims' law', the 'heathen men's law', the study of which in the two universities was being fostered by some of the bishops. That study, after inspiring Bracton, had come to little in England, though the canonist was compelled to learn something of Justinian, and there was a small demand for learned civilians in the court of admiralty, and in what we might call the king's diplomatic service. No medieval Englishman did anything considerable for Roman law. Even the canonists were content to read the books of French and Italian masters, though John Acton (*c.* 1340) and William Lyndwood (1430) wrote meritorious glosses. The Angevin kings, by appropriating to the temporal forum the whole province of ecclesiastical patronage, had robbed the decretists of an inexhaustible source of learning and of lucre. The work that was done by the legal faculties at Oxford and Cambridge is slight when compared with the inestimable services rendered to the cause of national continuity by the schools of English law which grew within the Inns of Court.

CHANCERY

A danger threatened: the danger that a prematurely osseous system of common law would be overwhelmed by summary justice and royal equity. Even when courts for all ordinary causes had been established, a reserve of residuary justice remained with the king. Whatever lawyers and even parliaments might say, it was seen to be desirable that the king in council should with little regard for form punish offenders who could break through the meshes of a tardy procedure, and should redress wrongs which

corrupt and timid juries would leave unrighted. Papal edicts
against heretics had made familiar to all men the notion that a
judge should at times proceed *summarie et de plano et sine strepitu
et figura justitiae*. And so extraordinary justice of a penal kind
was done by the king's council upon misdemeanants, and extra-
ordinary justice of a civil kind was ministered by the king's
chancellor (who was the specially learned member of the council)
to those who, 'for the love of God and in the way of charity',
craved his powerful assistance. It is now well established that the
chancellors started upon this course, not with any desire to intro-
duce rules of 'equity' which should supplement, or perhaps
supplant, the rules of law, but for the purpose of driving the law
through those accidental impediments which sometimes unfortunately beset its due course. The wrongs that the chancellor
redressed were often wrongs of the simplest and most brutal kind:
assaults, batteries and forcible dispossessions. However, he was
warned off this field of activity by parliament; the danger to law,
to lawyers, to trial by jury, was evident. But just when this was
happening, a new field was being opened for him by the growing
practice of conveying land to trustees. The English trust of land
had ancient Germanic roots, and of late we have been learning how
in far-off centuries our Lombard cousins were in effect giving
themselves a power of testation by putting their lands in trust.
In England, when the forms of action were crystallising, this
practice had not been common enough to obtain the protection
of a writ; but many causes conspired to make it common in the
fourteenth century; and so, with the general approval of lawyers
and laity, the chancellors began to enforce by summary process
against the trustee the duty that lay upon his conscience. In the
next century it was clear that England had come by a new civil
tribunal. Negatively, its competence was defined by the rule that
when the common law offered a remedy, the chancellor was not to
intervene. Positively, his power was conceived as that of doing
what 'good conscience' required, more especially in cases of
'fraud, accident or breach of confidence'. His procedure was the
summary, the heresy-suppressing (not the ordinary and solemn)
procedure of an ecclesiastical court; but there are few signs that
he borrowed any substantive rules from legist or decretist, and
many proofs that within the new field of trust he pursued the ideas
of the common law. It was long, however, before lawyers made

a habit of reporting his decisions. He was not supposed to be tightly bound by precedent. Adaptability was of the essence of the justice that he did.

THE TUDOR AGE

A time of strain and trial came with the Tudor kings. It was questionable whether the strong 'governance' for which the weary nation yearned could work within the limits of a parliamentary system, or would be compatible with the preservation of the common law. We see new courts appropriating large fields of justice and proceeding *summarie et de plano*; the star chamber, the chancery, the courts of requests, of wards, of augmentations, the councils of the North and Wales; a little later we see the high commission. We see also that judicial torture which Fortescue had called the road to hell. The stream of law reports became intermittent under Henry VIII; few judges of his or his son's reign left names that are to be remembered. In an age of humanism, alphabetically arranged 'abridgments' of medieval cases were the best work of English lawyers: one comes to us from Anthony Fitzherbert (d. 1538), and another from Robert Broke (d. 1558). This was the time when Roman law swept like a flood over Germany. The modern historian of Germany will speak of 'the Reception' (that is, the reception of Roman law), as no less important than the Renaissance and Reformation with which it is intimately connected. Very probably he will bestow hard words on a movement which disintegrated the nation and consolidated the tyranny of the princelings. Now a project that Roman law should be 'received' in England occurred to Reginald Pole (d. 1558), a humanist, and at one time a reformer, who with good fortune might have been either king of England or pope of Rome. English law, said the future cardinal and archbishop, was barbarous; Roman law was the very voice of nature pleading for 'civility' and good princely governance. Pole's words were brought to the ears of his majestic cousin, and, had the course of events been somewhat other than it was, King Henry might well have decreed a reception.[1] The role of English Justinian would have perfectly suited him, and there are distinct traces of the civilian's Byzantinism in the doings of the Church of England's supreme head. The academic study of the Canon law was prohibited; regius professorships of the civil

[1] [See below, pp. 137 ff., 149.]

111

law were founded; civilians were to sit as judges in the ecclesiastical courts. A little later, the Protector Somerset was deeply interested in the establishment of a great school for civilians at Cambridge. Scottish law was the own sister of English law, and yet in Scotland we may see a reception of Roman jurisprudence which might have been more whole-hearted than it was, but for the drift of two British and Protestant kingdoms towards union. As it fell out, however, Henry could get what he wanted in church and state without any decisive supersession of English by foreign law. The omnicompetence of an act of parliament stands out the more clearly if it settles the succession to the throne, annuls royal marriages, forgives royal debts, defines religious creeds, attaints guilty or innocent nobles, or prospectively lends the force of statute to the king's proclamations. The courts of common law were suffered to work in obscurity, for jurors feared fines, and matter of state was reserved for council or star chamber. The Inns of Court were spared; their moots and readings did no perceptible harm, if little perceptible good.

COKE

Yet it is no reception of alien jurisprudence that must be chronicled, but a marvellous resuscitation of English medieval law. We may see it already in the Commentaries of Edward Plowden (d. 1585) who reported cases at length and lovingly. Bracton's great book was put in print, and was a key to much that had been forgotten or misunderstood. Under Parker's patronage, even the Anglo-Saxon dooms were brought to light; they seemed to tell of a Church of England that had not yet been enslaved by Rome. The new national pride that animated Elizabethan England issued in boasts touching the antiquity, humanity, enlightenment of English law. Resuming the strain of Fortescue, Sir Thomas Smith, himself a civilian, wrote concerning the Commonwealth of England a book that claimed the attention of foreigners for her law and her polity. There was dignified rebuke for the French jurist who had dared to speak lightly of Littleton. And then the common law took flesh in the person of Edward Coke (1552–1634). With an enthusiastic love of English tradition, for the sake of which many offences may be forgiven him, he ranged over nearly the whole field of law, commenting, reporting, arguing, deciding,—disorderly, pedantic, masterful, an incarnate national dogmatism tenacious of continuous life. Imbued with this new spirit, the lawyers fought the battle of the constitution against James and Charles, and historical research appeared as the guardian of national liberties. That the Stuarts united against themselves three such men as Edward Coke, John Selden and William Prynne, is the measure of their folly and their failure. Words that, rightly or wrongly, were ascribed to Bracton rang in Charles's ears when he was sent to the scaffold. For the modern student of medieval law many of the reported cases of the Stuart time are storehouses of valuable material, since the lawyers of the seventeenth century were mighty hunters after records. Prynne (d. 1669), the fanatical Puritan, published ancient documents with fervid zeal, and made possible a history of parliament. Selden (d. 1654) was in all Europe among the very first to write legal history as it should be written. His book about tithes is to this day a model and a masterpiece. When this accomplished scholar had declared that he had laboured to make himself worthy to be called a common lawyer, it could no longer be said that the common lawyers were *indoctissimum genus doctissimorum hominum.* Even pliant judges, whose tenure of office depended on the king's will, were compelled to cite and discuss old precedents before they could give judgment for their master; and even at their worst moments they would not openly break with medieval tradition, or declare in favour of that 'modern police-state' which has too often become the ideal of foreign publicists trained in Byzantine law.

HALE

The current of legal doctrine was by this time so strong and voluminous that such events as the Civil War, the Restoration and the Revolution hardly deflected the course of the stream. In retrospect, Charles II reigns so soon as life has left his father's body, and James II ends a lawless career by a considerate and convenient abdication. The statute book of the restored king was enriched by leaves excerpted from the acts of a lord protector; and Matthew Hale (d. 1676), who was, perhaps, the last of the great record-searching judges, sketched a map of English law which Blackstone was to colour. Then a time of self-complacency came for the law, which knew itself to be the perfection of wisdom, and any proposal for drastic legislation would have worn the garb discredited by the tyranny of the Puritan Caesar. The need for the yearly renewal of the Mutiny Act secured an annual session of parliament. The mass of the statute law made in the eighteenth century is enormous; but, even when we have excluded from view such acts as are technically called 'private', the residuary matter bears a wonderfully empirical, partial and minutely particularising character. In this 'age of reason', as we are wont to think it, the British parliament seems rarely to rise to the dignity of a general proposition, and in our own day the legal practitioner is likely to know less about the statutes of the eighteenth century than he knows about the statutes of Edward I, Henry VIII and Elizabeth. Parliament, it should be remembered, was endeavouring directly to govern the nation. There was little that resembled the permanent civil service of today. The choice lay between direct parliamentary government and royal 'prerogative'; and lengthy statutes did much of that work of detail which would now be done by virtue of the powers that are delegated to ministers and governmental boards. Moreover, extreme and verbose particularity was required in statutes, for judges were loth to admit that the common law was capable of amendment. A vague doctrine, inherited from Coke, taught that statutes might be so unreasonable as to be null, and any political theory that seemed to derive from Hobbes would have been regarded with not unjust suspicion. But the doctrine in question never took tangible shape, and enough could be done to protect the common law by a niggardly exposition of every legislating word. It is to be remembered that some main features of English public law were attracting the admiration of enlightened Europe. When Voltaire and Montesquieu applauded, the English lawyer had cause for complacency.

The common law was by no means stagnant. Many rules which come to the front in the eighteenth century are hardly to be traced farther. Especially is this the case in the province of mercantile law, where the Earl of Mansfield's (d. 1793) long presidency over the king's bench marked an epoch. It is too often forgotten that, until Elizabeth's reign, England was a thoroughly rustic kingdom, and that trade with England was mainly in the hands of foreigners. Also in medieval fairs, the assembled merchants declared their own 'law merchant', which was considered to have a supernational validity. In the reports of the common law courts it is late in the day before we read of some mercantile usages which can be traced far back in the statutes of Italian cities. Even on the basis of the excessively elaborated land law—a basis which Coke's Commentary on Littleton seemed to have settled for ever—a lofty and ingenious superstructure could be reared. One after another delicate devices were invented for the accommodation of new wants within the law; but only by the assurance that the old law could not be frankly abolished can we be induced to admire the subtlety that was thus displayed. As to procedure, it had become a maze of evasive fictions, to which only a few learned men held the historical clue. By fiction the courts had stolen business from each other, and by fiction a few comparatively speedy forms of action were set to tasks for which they were not originally framed. Two fictitious persons, John Doe and Richard Roe, reigned supreme. On the other hand, that healthy and vigorous institution, the Commission of the Peace, with a long history behind it, was giving an important share in the administration of justice to numerous country gentlemen who were thus compelled to learn some law. A like beneficial work was being done among jurors, who, having ceased to be regarded as witnesses, had become 'judges of fact'. No one doubted that trial by jury was the 'palladium' of English liberties, and popularity awaited those who would exalt the office of the jurors and narrowly limit the powers of the judge.

EQUITY

But during this age the chief addition to English jurisprudence was made by the crystallisation of the chancellor's equity. In the seventeenth century the Chancery had a narrow escape of sharing the fate that befell its twin sister the Star Chamber. Its younger sister, the Court of Requests, perished under the persistent attacks of the common lawyers. Having outlived troubles, the Chancery took to orderly habits, and administered under the name of 'equity' a growing group of rules, which in fact were supplemental law. Stages in this process are marked by the chancellorships of Nottingham (1673–82) and Hardwicke (1737–56). Slowly a continuous series of Equity Reports began to flow, and still more slowly an 'equity bar' began to form itself. The principal outlines of equity were drawn by men who were steeped in the common law. By way of ornament a Roman maxim might be borrowed from a French or Dutch expositor, or a phrase which smacked of that 'nature-rightly' school which was dominating continental Europe; but the influence exercised by Roman law upon English equity has been the subject of gross exaggeration. Parliament and the old courts being what they were, perhaps it was only in a new court that the requisite new law could be evolved. The result was not altogether satisfactory. Freed from contact with the plain man in the jury-box, the Chancellors were tempted to forget how plain and rough good law should be, and to screw up the legal standard of reasonable conduct to a height hardly attainable except by those whose purses could command the constant advice of a family solicitor. A court which started with the idea of doing summary justice for the poor became a court which did a highly refined, but tardy justice, suitable only to the rich.

BLACKSTONE

About the middle of the century William Blackstone, then a disappointed barrister, began to give lectures on English law at Oxford (1758), and soon afterwards he began to publish (1765) his *Commentaries*. Accurate enough in its history and doctrine to be an invaluable guide to professional students and a useful aid to practitioners, his book set before the unprofessional public an artistic picture of the laws of England such as had never been drawn of any similar system. No nation but the English had so eminently readable a law-book, and it must be doubtful whether any other lawyer ever did more important work than was done by the first professor of English law. Over and over again the *Commentaries* were edited, sometimes by distinguished men, and it is hardly too much to say that for nearly a century the English lawyer's main ideas of the organisation and articulation of the body of English law were controlled by Blackstone. This was far from all. The Tory lawyer little thought that he was giving law to colonies that were on the eve of a great and successful rebellion. Yet so it was. Out in America, where books were few and lawyers had a mighty task to perform, Blackstone's facile presentment of the law of the mother country was of inestimable value. It has been said that among American lawyers the *Commentaries* 'stood for the law of England', and this at a time when the American daughter of English law was rapidly growing in stature, and was preparing herself for her destined march from the Atlantic to the

Pacific Ocean. Excising only what seemed to savour of oligarchy, those who had defied King George retained with marvellous tenacity the law of their forefathers. Profound discussions of English medieval law have been heard in American courts; admirable researches into the recesses of the Year Books have been made in American law schools; the names of the great American judges are familiar in an England which knows little indeed of foreign jurists; and the debt due for the loan of Blackstone's *Commentaries* is being fast repaid. Lectures on the common law delivered by Mr Justice Holmes of the Supreme Court of the United States may even have begun to turn the scale against the old country. No chapter in Blackstone's book nowadays seems more antiquated than that which describes the modest territorial limits of that English law which was soon to spread throughout Australia and New Zealand and to follow the dominant race in India.

BENTHAM

Long wars, vast economic changes and the conservatism generated by the French Revolution piled up a monstrous arrear of work for the English legislature. Meanwhile, Jeremy Bentham (d. 1832) had laboured for the overthrow of much that Blackstone had lauded. Bentham's largest projects of destruction and reconstruction took but little effect. Profoundly convinced of the fungibility and pliability of mankind, he was but too ready to draw a code for England or Spain or Russia at the shortest notice; and, scornful as he was of the past and its historic deposit, a code drawn by Bentham would have been a sorry failure. On the other hand, as a critic and derider of the system which Blackstone had complacently expounded he did excellent service. Reform, and radical reform, was indeed sadly needed throughout a system which was encumbered by noxious rubbish, the useless leavings of the Middle Ages: trial by battle and compurgation, deodands and benefit of clergy, John Doe and Richard Roe. It is perhaps the main fault of 'judge-made law' (to use Bentham's phrase) that its destructive work can never be cleanly done. Of all vitality, and therefore of all patent harmfulness, the old rule can be deprived, but the moribund husk must remain in the system doing latent mischief. English law was full of decaying husks when Bentham attacked it, and his persistent demand for reasons could not be answered. At length a general interest in 'law reform' was excited; Romilly and Brougham were inspired by Bentham, and the great changes in constitutional law which cluster round the Reform Act of 1832 were accompanied by many measures which purged the private, procedural and criminal law of much, though hardly enough, of the medieval dross. Some credit for rousing an interest in law, in definitions of legal terms, and in schemes of codification, is due to John Austin (d. 1859) who was regarded as the jurist of the reforming and utilitarian group. But, though he was at times an acute dissector of confused thought, he was too ignorant of the English, the Roman and every other system of law to make any considerable addition to the sum of knowledge; and when Savigny, the herald of evolution, was already in the field, the day for a 'Nature-Right'—and Austin's projected 'general jurisprudence' would have been a Nature-Right—was past beyond recall. The obsolescence of the map of law which Blackstone had inherited from Hale, and in which many outlines were drawn by medieval formulas, left intelligent English lawyers without a guide, and they were willing to listen for a while to what in their insularity they thought to be the voice of cosmopolitan science. Little came of it all. The revived study of Germanic law in Germany, which was just beginning in Austin's day, seems to be showing that the scheme of Roman jurisprudence is not the scheme into which English law will run without distortion.

RECENT CHANGES

In the latter half of the nineteenth century some great and wise changes were made by the legislature. Notably in 1875 the old courts were merged in a new Supreme Court of Judicature, and a concurrent administration of law and equity was introduced. Successful endeavours have been made also to reduce the bulk of old statute law, and to improve the form of acts of parliament; but the emergence of new forces whose nature may be suggested by some such names as 'socialism' and 'imperialism' has distracted the attention of the British parliament from the commonplace law of the land, and the development of obstructive tactics has caused the issue of too many statutes whose brevity was purchased by disgraceful obscurity. By way of 'partial codification' some branches of the common law (bills of exchange, sale of goods, partnership) have been skilfully stated in statutes; but a draft criminal code, upon which much expert labour was expended, lies pigeon-holed and almost forgotten. British India has been the scene of some large legislative exploits, and in America a few big experiments have been made in the way of code-making, but have given little satisfaction to the bulk of those who are competent to appreciate their results. In England there are large portions of the law which, in their present condition, no one would think of codifying: notably the law of real property, in which may still be found numerous hurtful relics of bygone centuries. So omnipresent are statutes throughout the whole field of jurisprudence that the opportunity of doing any great feat in the development of law can come but seldom to a modern court. More and more, therefore, the fate of English law depends on the will of parliament, or rather of the ministry. The quality of legal text-books has steadily improved; some of them are models of clear statement and good arrangement; but no one has with any success aspired to be the Blackstone of a new age.

LAW REPORTING

The Council of Law Reporting was formed in the year 1863. The council now consists of three *ex-officio* members—the attorney-general, the solicitor-general and the president of the Incorporated Law Society, and ten members appointed by the three Inns of Court, the Incorporated Law Society and the council itself on the nomination of the general council of the bar. The practitioner and the student now get for a subscription of four guineas a year the reports in all the superior courts and the House of Lords and the judicial committee of the privy council, issued in monthly parts, a king's printer's copy of the statutes, and weekly notes, containing short notes of current decisions and announcements of all new rules made under the Judicature Acts and other acts of parliament, and other legal information. In addition the subscriber receives the chronological index of the statutes published from time to time by the Stationery Office, and last, but not least, the Digests of decided cases published by the council from time to time. In 1892 a Digest was published containing the cases and statutes for twenty-five years, from 1865 to 1890, and this was supplemented by one for the succeeding ten years, from 1891 to 1900. The digesting is now carried on continuously by means of 'Current Indexes', which are published monthly and annually, and consolidated into a digest at stated intervals (say) of five years. The Indian appeals series, which is not required by the general practitioner, is supplied separately at one guinea a year.

LEGAL EDUCATION

In the sixteenth and seventeenth centuries the corporate life of the Inns of Court in London became less and less active. The general decay of the organisation of crafts and gilds showed itself among lawyers as among other craftsmen. Successful barristers, sharing in the general prosperity of the country, became less and less able and willing to devote their time to the welfare of their profession as a whole. The Inns of Chancery, though some of their buildings still remain—picturesque survivals in their 'suburbs'—ceased to be used as places for the education of students. The benchers of the Inns of Court, until the revival towards the middle of the nineteenth century, had wholly ceased to concern themselves with the systematic teaching of law. The modern system of legal education may be said to date from the establishment, in 1852, of the council of legal education, a body of twenty judges and barristers appointed by the four Inns of Court to control the legal education of students preparing to be called to the bar. The most important feature is the examination which a student must pass before he can be called. The examination (which by degrees has been made 'stiffer') serves the double purpose of fixing the compulsory standard which all must reach, and of guiding the reading of students who may desire, sooner or later, to carry their studies beyond this standard. The subjects in which the examination is held are divided into Roman law; Constitutional law and legal history; Evidence, Procedure and Criminal law; Real and Personal Property; Equity; and Common law. The council of legal education also appoint a body of readers and assistant readers, practising barristers, who deliver lectures and hold classes.

Meanwhile the custom remains by which a student reads for a year or more as a pupil in the chambers of some practising barrister. In the eighteenth century it first became usual for students to read with a solicitor or attorney, and after a short time the modern practice grew up of reading in the chambers of a conveyancer, equity draftsman or special pleader, or, in more recent times, in the chambers of a junior barrister. Before the modern examination system, a student required to have a certificate from the barrister in whose chambers he had been a pupil before he could be 'called', but the only relic of the old system now is the necessity of 'eating dinners', six (three for university men) in each of the four terms for three years, at one of the Inns of Court.

The education of solicitors suffered from the absence of any professional organisation until the Incorporated Law Society was established in 1825 and the following years. So far as any professional education is provided for solicitors or required from them, this is due to the efforts of the Law Society. As early as 1729 it was required by statute that any person applying for admission as attorney or solicitor should submit to examination by one of the judges, who was to test his fitness and capacity in consideration of a fee of one shilling. At the same time regular preliminary service under articles was required, that is to say, under a contract by which the clerk was bound to serve for five years. The examination soon became, perhaps always was, an empty form. The Law Society, however, soon showed zeal for the education of future solicitors. In 1833 lectures were instituted. In 1836 the first regular examinations were established, and in 1860 the present system of examinations—preliminary, intermediate and final—came into effect. Of these only the last two are devoted to law, and both are of a strictly professional character. The final examination is a fairly severe test of practical acquaintance with all branches of modern English law. The Law Society makes some provision for the teaching of students, but this teaching is designed solely to assist in preparation for the examinations.

VI

ENGLISH LAW, 1307–1600[1]

The desire for continuous legislation is modern. We have come to think that, year by year, parliament must meet and pour out statutes; that every statesman must have in his mind some programme of new laws; that if his programme once become exhausted he will cease to be a statesman. It was otherwise in the middle ages. As a matter of fact a parliament might always find that some new statute was necessary. The need for legislation, however, was occasioned (so men thought) not by any fated progress of the human race, but by the perversity of mankind. Ideally there exists a perfect body of law, immutable, eternal, the work of God, not of man. Just a few more improvements in our legal procedure will have made it for ever harmonious with this ideal; and, indeed, if men would but obey the law of the land as it stands, there would be little for a legislator to do.

During the fourteenth century a good deal is written upon the statute roll, and a good deal can still be said in very few words. 'Also it is agreed that a parliament shall be holden once a year or more often if need be.' This is a characteristic specimen of the brief sentences in which great principles are formulated and which by their ambiguity will provide the lawyers and politicians of later ages with plenty of matter for debate. Many of these short clauses are directed against what are regarded as abuses, as evasions of the law, and the king's officers are looked upon as the principal offenders. They must be repeated with but little variation from time to time, for it is difficult to bind the king by law. Happily the kings were needy; in return for 'supply' they sold the words on the statute roll, and those words, of some importance when first conceded, became of far greater importance in after times. When we read them nowadays they turn our thoughts to James and Charles, rather than to Edward and Richard. The New Monarchy was not new. This, from its own point of view, was its great misfortune. It had inherited ancient parchment rolls which had uncomfortable words upon them.

---

[1] [From *Social England* (1894), vol. ii, pp. 476–89: *Collected Papers*, vol. ii, pp. 477–96.]

But parliament by its statutes was beginning to interfere with many affairs, small as well as great. Indeed, what we may consider small affairs seem to have troubled and interested it more even than those large constitutional questions which it was always hoping to settle but never settling. If we see a long statute, one guarded with careful provisos, one that tells us of debate and compromise, this will probably be a statute which deals with one particular trade; for instance, a statute concerning the sale of herring at Yarmouth fair. The thorniest of themes for discussion is the treatment of foreign merchants. Naturally enough our lords, knights, and burgesses cannot easily agree about it. One opinion prevails in the seaports, another in the upland towns, and the tortuous course of legislation, swaying now towards free trade and now towards protection, is the resultant of many forces. The 'omnicompetence', as Bentham called it, of statute law was recognised by all, the impotence of statute law was seen by none. It can determine the rate of wages, the price of goods, the value of money; it can decide that no man shall dress himself above his station.

On the other hand, the great outlines of criminal law and private law seem to have been regarded as fixed for all time. In the twentieth century students of law will still for practical purposes be compelled to know a good deal about some of the statutes of Edward I. They will seldom have occasion to know anything of any laws that were enacted during the fourteenth or the first three-quarters of the fifteenth century. Parliament seems to have abandoned the idea of controlling the development of the common law. Occasionally and spasmodically it would interfere, devise some new remedy, fill a gap in the register of writs, or circumvent the circumventors of a statute. But in general it left the ordinary law of the land to the judges and the lawyers. In its eyes the common law was complete, or very nearly complete.

And then as we read the statute roll of the fifteenth century we seem for a while to be watching the decline and fall of a mighty institution. Parliament seems to have nothing better to do than to regulate the manufacture of cloth. Now and then it strives to cope with the growing evils of the time, the renascent feudalism, the private wars of great and small; but without looking outside our roll we can see that these efforts are half-hearted and in-effectual. We are expected to show a profound interest in 'the making of worsteds', while we gather from a few casual hints that the Wars of the Roses are flagrant. If for a moment the parliament of Edward IV can raise its soul above defective barrels of fish and fraudulent gutter tiles, this will be in order to prohibit 'cloish, kayles, half-bowl, hand-in-hand and hand-out, quekeboard', and such other games as interfere with the practice of archery.

In the end it was better that parliament should for a while register the acts of a despot than that it should sink into the contempt that seemed to be prepared for it. The part which the assembled Estates of the Realm have to play in the great acts of Henry VIII may in truth be a subservient and ignoble part; but the acts are great and they are all done 'by the authority of parliament'. By the authority of parliament the Bishop of Rome could be deprived of all jurisdiction, the monasteries could be dissolved, the king could be made (so far as the law of God would permit) supreme head of the English Church, the succession to the Crown could be settled first in this way, then in that, the force of statute might be given to the king's proclamations. There was nothing that could not be done by the authority of parliament. And apart from the constitutional and ecclesiastical changes which everyone has heard about, very many things of importance were done by statute. We owe to Henry VIII—much rather to him than to his parliament—not a few innovations in the law of property and the law of crime, and the parliaments of Elizabeth performed some considerable legal exploits. The statutes of the Tudor period are lengthy documents. In many a grandiose preamble we seem to hear the voice of Henry himself; but their length is not solely due to the pomp of imperial phrases. They condescend to details; they teem with exceptions and saving clauses. One cannot establish a new ecclesiastical polity by half-a-dozen lines. We see that the judges are by this time expected to attend very closely to the words that parliament utters, to weigh and obey every letter of the written law.

Just now and then in the last of the Middle Ages and thence onwards into the eighteenth century, we hear the judges claiming some vague right of disregarding statutes which are directly at variance with the common law, or the law of God, or the royal prerogative. Had much come of this claim, our constitution must have taken a very different shape from that which we see at the present day. Little came of it. In the troublous days of Richard II a chief justice got himself hanged as a traitor for advising the king that a statute curtailing the royal power was void. For the rest, the theory is but a speculative dogma. We can (its upholders seem to say) conceive that a statute might be so irrational, so wicked, that we would not enforce it; but, as a matter of fact, we have never known such a statute made. From the Norman Conquest onwards, England seems marked out as the country in which men, so soon as they begin to philosophise, will endeavour to prove that all law is the command of a 'sovereign one', or a 'sovereign many'. They may be somewhat shocked when in the seventeenth century Hobbes states this theory in trenchant terms and combines it with many unpopular doctrines. But the way for Hobbes had been prepared of old. In the days of Edward I the text-writer whom we call Britton had put the common law into the king's mouth: all legal rules might be stated as royal commands.

Still, even in the age of the Tudors, only a small part of the law was in the statute-book. Detached pieces of superstructure were there; for the foundation men had to look elsewhere. After the brilliant thirteenth century a long, dull period had set in. The custody of the common law was now committed to a small group of judges and lawyers. They knew their own business very thoroughly, and they knew nothing else. Law was now divorced from literature; no one attempted to write a book about it. The decisions of the courts at Westminster were diligently reported and diligently studied, but no one thought of comparing English law with anything else. Roman law was by this time an unintelligible, outlandish thing, perhaps a good enough law for half-starved Frenchmen. Legal education was no longer academic—the universities had nothing to do with it, they could only make canonists and civilians —it was scholastic. By stages that are exceedingly obscure, the inns of court and inns of chancery were growing. They were associations of lawyers which had about them a good deal of the club, something of the college, something of the trade-union. They acquired the 'inns' or 'hospices'—that is, the town houses— which had belonged to great noblemen: for example, the Earl of Lincoln's inn. The house and church of the Knights of the Temple came to their hands. The smaller societies, 'inns of chancery', became dependent on the larger societies, 'inns of court'. The serjeants and apprentices who composed them enjoyed an exclusive right of pleading in court; some things might be done by an apprentice or barrister, others required a serjeant; in the Court of Common Pleas only a serjeant could be heard. It would take time to investigate the origin of that power of granting degrees which these societies wielded. To all seeming the historian must regard it as emanating from the king, though in this case, as in many other cases, the control of a royal prerogative slowly passed out of the king's hand. But here our point must be, that the inns developed a laborious system of legal education. Many years a student had to spend in hearing and giving lectures and in pleading fictitious causes before he could be admitted to practice.

It is no wonder that under the fostering care of these societies English jurisprudence became an occult science and its professors 'the most unlearned kind of most learned men'. They were rigorous logicians, afraid of no conclusion that was implicit in their premises. The sky might fall, the Wars of the Roses might rage, but they would pursue the even course of their argumentation. They were not altogether unmindful of the social changes that were going on around them. In the fifteenth century there were great judges who performed what may seem to us some daring feats in the accommodation of old law to new times. Out of unpromising elements they developed a comprehensive law of contract; they loosened the bonds of those family settlements by which land had been tied up; they converted the precarious villein tenure of the middle ages into the secure copyhold tenure of modern times. But all this had to be done evasively and by means of circumventive fictions. Novel principles could not be admitted until they were disguised in some antique garb.

A new and a more literary period seems to be beginning in the latter half of the fifteenth century, when Sir John Fortescue, the Lancastrian Chief Justice, writing for the world at large, contrasts the constitutional kingship of England with the absolute monarchy of France, and Sir Thomas Littleton, a Justice in the Court of Common Pleas, writing for students of English law, publishes his lucid and classical book on the tenure of land. But the hopes of a renascence are hardly fulfilled. In the sixteenth century many famous lawyers added to their fame by publishing reports of decided cases and by making 'abridgments' of the old reports, and a few little treatises were compiled; but in general the lawyer seems to think that he has done all for jurisprudence that can be done when he has collected his materials under a number of rubrics alphabetically arranged. The alphabet is the one clue to the maze. Even in the days of Elizabeth and James I Sir Edward Coke, the incarnate common law, shovels out his enormous learning in vast disorderly heaps. Carlyle's felicity has for ever stamped upon Coke the adjective 'tough'—'tough old Coke upon Littleton, one of the toughest men ever made'. We may well transfer the word from the man to the law that was personified in him. The English common law was tough, one of the toughest things ever made. And well for England was it in the days of Tudors and Stuarts that this was so. A simpler, a more rational, a more elegant system would have been an apt instrument of despotic rule. At times the judges were subservient enough: the king could dismiss them from their offices at a moment's notice; but the clumsy, cumbrous system, though it might bend, would never break. It was ever awkwardly rebounding and confounding the statecraft which had tried to control it. The strongest king, the ablest minister, the rudest Lord Protector could make little of this 'ungodly jumble'.

To this we must add that professional jealousies had been aroused by the evolution of new courts, which did not proceed according to the course of the common law. Once more we must carry our thoughts back to the days of Edward I. The three courts—King's Bench, Common Bench, and Exchequer—had been established. There were two groups of 'justices', and one group of 'barons' engaged in administering the law. But behind these courts there was a tribunal of a less determinate nature. Looking at it in the last years of the thirteenth century we may doubt as to what it is going to be. Will it be a house of magnates, an assembly of the Lords Spiritual and Temporal, or will it be a council composed of the king's ministers and judges and those others whom he pleases for one reason or another to call to the council board? As a matter of fact, in Edward I's day, this highest tribunal seems to be rather the council than the assembly of prelates and barons. This council is a large body; it comprises the great officers of state—chancellor, treasurer, and so forth; it comprises the judges of the three courts; it comprises also the masters or chief clerks of the chancery, whom we may liken to the 'permanent under-secretaries' of our own time; it comprises also those prelates and barons whom the king thinks fit to have about him. But the definition of this body seems somewhat vague. The sessions or 'parliaments' in which it does justice often coincide in time with those assemblies of the Estates of the Realm by which, in later days, the term 'parliaments' is specifically appropriated, and at any moment it may take the form of a meeting to which not only the ordinary councillors, but all the prelates and barons, have been summoned. In the light which later days throw back upon the thirteenth century we seem to see in the justiciary 'parliaments' of Edward I two principles, one of which we may call aristocratic, while the other is official; and we think that, sooner or later, there must be a conflict between them—that one must grow at the expense of the other. And then again we cannot see very plainly how the power of this tribunal will be defined, for it is doing work of a miscellaneous kind. Not only is it a court of last resort in which the errors of all lower courts can be corrected, but as a court of first instance it can entertain whatever causes, civil or criminal, the king may evoke before it. Then lastly, acting in a manner which to us seems half judicial and half administrative, it hears the numerous petitions of those who will urge any claim against the king, or complain of any wrong which cannot be redressed in the formal course of ordinary justice.

In the course of the fourteenth century some of these questions were settled. It became clear that the Lords' House of Parliament, the assembly of prelates and barons, was to be the tribunal which could correct the mistakes in law committed by the lower courts. The right of a peer of the realm to be tried for capital crimes by a court composed of his peers was established. Precedents were set for those processes which we know as impeachments, in which the House of Lords hears accusations brought by the House of Commons. In all these matters, therefore, a tribunal technically styled 'the King in Parliament', but which was in reality the House of Lords, appeared as the highest tribunal of the realm. But, beside it, we see another tribunal with indefinitely wide claims to jurisdiction—we see 'the King in Council'. And the two are not so distinct as an historian, for his own sake and his readers', might wish them to be. On the one hand, those of the king's council who are not peers of the realm, in particular the judges and the Masters of the Chancery, are summoned to the Lords' House of Parliament, and only by slow degrees is it made plain to them that, when they are in that house, they are mere 'assistants' of the peers, and are only to speak when they are spoken to. On the other hand, there is a widespread, if not very practical, belief that all the peers are by rights the king's councillors, and that any one of them may sit at the council board if he pleases. Questions enough are left open for subsequent centuries.

Meanwhile the council, its actual constitution varying much from reign to reign, does a great deal of justice, for the more part criminal justice, and this it does in a summary, administrative way. Plainly there is great need for such justice, for though the representative commoners and the lawyers dislike it, they always stop short of demanding its utter abolition. The commoners protest against this or that abuse. Sometimes they seem to be upon the point of denouncing the whole institution as illegal; but then there comes some rebellion or some scandalous acquittal of a notorious criminal by bribed or partial jurors, which convinces them that, after all, there is a place for a masterful court which does not stand upon ceremony, which can strike rapidly and have no need to strike twice. They cannot be brought to admit openly that one main cause of the evils that they deplore is the capricious clumsiness of that trial by jury which has already become the theme of many a national boast. They will not legislate about the matter, rather they will look the other way while the council is punishing rich and powerful offenders, against whom no verdict could have been obtained. A hard line is drawn between the felonies, for which death is the punishment, and the minor offences. No one is to suffer loss of life or limb unless twelve of his neighbours have sworn to his guilt after a solemn trial; but the council must be suffered to deal out fines and imprisonments against rioters, conspirators, bribers, perjured jurors; otherwise there will be anarchy. The council evolves a procedure for such cases, or rather it uses the procedure of the canon law. It sends for the accused; it compels him to answer upon oath written interrogatories. Affidavits, as we should call them, are sworn upon both sides. With written depositions before them, the Lords of the council, without any jury, acquit or convict. The extraction of confessions by torture is no unheard-of thing.

It was in a room known as the Star Chamber that the council sat when there was justice to be done, and there, as 'the Court of Star Chamber', it earned its infamy. That infamy it fairly earned under the first two Stuart kings, and no one will dispute that the Long Parliament did well in abolishing it. It had become a political court and a cruel court, a court in which divines sought to impose their dogmas and their ritual upon a recalcitrant nation by heavy sentences; in which a king, endeavouring to rule without a parliament, tried to give the force of statutes to his proclamations, to exact compulsory loans, to gather taxes that the Commons had denied him; a whipping, nose-slitting, ear-cropping court; a court with a grim, unseemly humour of its own, which would condemn to an exclusive diet of pork the miserable Puritan who took too seriously the Mosaic prohibition of swine's flesh. And then, happily, there were doubts about its legality. The theory got about that it derived all its lawful powers from a statute passed in 1487, at the beginning of Henry VII's reign, while manifestly it was exceeding those powers in all directions. We cannot now accept that theory, unless we are prepared to say that for a century and a half all the great judges, including Coke himself, had taken an active part in what they knew to be the unlawful doings of the council—the two Chief Justices had habitually sat in the Star Chamber. Still we may be glad that this theory was accepted. The court was abolished in the name of the common law.

It had not added much to our national jurisprudence. It had held itself aloof from jurisprudence; it had been a law unto itself, with hands free to invent new remedies for every new disease of the body politic. It had little regard for precedents, and, therefore, men were not at pains to collect its decisions. It had, however, a settled course of procedure which, in its last days, was described by William Hudson in a very readable book. Its procedure, the main feature of which was the examination of the accused, perished with it. After the Civil War and the Restoration no attempt was made to revive it, but that it had been doing useful things then became evident. The old criminal law had been exceedingly defective, especially in relation to those offences which did not attain the rank of felonies. The King's Bench had, for the future, to do what the Star Chamber had done, but to do it in a more regular fashion, and not without the interposition of a jury.

Far other were the fortunes of the Star Chamber's twin sister, the Court of Chancery. Twin sisters they were; indeed, in the fourteenth century it is hard to tell one from the other, and even in the Stuart time we sometimes find the Star Chamber doing things which we should have expected to be done by the Chancery. But, to go back to the fourteenth century, the chancellor was the king's first minister, the head of the one great secretarial depart-

ment that there was, the president of the council, and the most
learned member of the council. Usually he was a bishop; often
he had earned his see by diligent labours as a clerk in the chancery.
It was natural that the lords of the council should put off upon
him, or that he should take to himself, a great deal of the judicial
work that in one way or another the council had to do. Criminal
cases might come before the whole body, or some committee of it.
Throughout the Middle Ages criminal cases were treated as simple
affairs; for example, justices of the peace who were not trained
lawyers could be trusted to do a great deal of penal justice, and
inflict the punishment of death. But cases involving civil rights,
involving the complex land law, might come before the council.
Generally, in such cases, there was some violence or some fraud to
be complained of, some violence or fraud for which, so the com-
plainant alleged, he could get no redress elsewhere. Such cases
came specially under the eye of the chancellor. He was a learned
man with learned subordinates, the masters of the chancery. Very
gradually it became the practice for complainants who were seeking
the reparation of wrongs rather than the punishment of offences,
to address their petitions, not to the king and council, but to the
chancellor. Slowly men began to think of the chancellor, or the
chancery of which he was president, as having a jurisdiction
distinct from, though it might overlap, that of the council.

What was to be the sphere of this jurisdiction? For a long time
this question remained doubtful. The wrongs of which men usually
complained to the chancellor were wrongs well enough known to
the common law—deeds of violence, assaults, land-grabbing, and
so forth. As an excuse for going to him, they urged that they were
poor while their adversaries were mighty, too mighty for the
common law, with its long delays and its purchasable jurors. Odd
though this may seem to us, that court which was to become a
byword for costly delay started business as an expeditious and a
poor man's court. It met with much opposition: the House of
Commons did not like it, and the common lawyers did not like it;
but still there was a certain half-heartedness in the opposition.
No one was prepared to say that there was no place for such a
tribunal; no one was prepared to define by legislation what its
place should be.

From the field of the common law the chancellor was slowly
compelled to retreat. It could not be suffered that, merely because

there was helplessness on the one side and corruptive wealth on
the other, he should be suffered to deal with cases which belonged
to the old courts. It seems possible that this nascent civil jurisdiction of the chancellor would have come to naught but for a
curious episode in the history of our land law. In the second half
of the fourteenth century many causes were conspiring to induce
the landholders of England to convey their lands to friends, who,
while becoming the legal owners of those lands, would, nevertheless,
be bound by an honourable understanding as to the uses to which
their ownership should be put. There were feudal burdens that
could thus be evaded, ancient restrictions which could thus be
loosened. The chancellor began to hold himself out as willing to
enforce these honourable understandings, these 'uses, trusts or
confidences' as they were called, to send to prison the trustee who
would not keep faith. It is an exceedingly curious episode. The
whole nation seems to enter into one large conspiracy to evade its
own laws, to evade laws which it has not the courage to reform.
The chancellor, the judges, and the parliament seem all to be in the
conspiracy. And yet there is really no conspiracy: men are but
living from hand to mouth, arguing from one case to the next case,
and they do not see what is going to happen. Too late the king,
the one person who had steadily been losing by the process, saw
what had happened. Henry VIII put into the mouth of a reluctant
parliament a statute which did its best—a clumsy best it was—to
undo the work. But past history was too strong even for that
high and mighty prince. The statute was a miserable failure. A
little trickery with words would circumvent it. The chancellor,
with the active connivance of the judges, was enabled to do what
he had been doing in the past, to enforce the obligations known as
trusts. This elaborate story we can only mention by the way; the
main thing that we have to notice is that, long before the Tudor
days—indeed, before the fourteenth century was out—the
chancellor had acquired for himself a province of jurisdiction
which was, in the opinion of all men, including the common lawyers,
legitimately his own. From time to time he would extend its
boundaries, and from time to time there would be a brisk quarrel
between the Chancery and the law courts over the annexation of
some field fertile of fees. In particular, when the chancellor forbade
a man to sue in a court of law, or to take advantage of a judgment
that he had obtained in a court of law, the judges resented this,

and a bitter dispute about this matter between Coke and Ellesmere gave King James I a wished-for opportunity of posing as the supreme lord of all the justice that was done in his name and awarding a decisive victory to his chancellor. But such disputes were rare. The chancellors had found useful work to do, and they had been suffered to do it without much opposition. In the name of equity and good conscience they had, as it were, been adding an appendix to the common law. Every jot and tittle of the law was to be fulfilled, and yet, when a man had done this, more might be required of him in the name of equity and good conscience.

Where were the rules of equity and good conscience to be found? Some have supposed that the clerical chancellors of the last Middle Ages found them in the Roman or the Canon law, and certain it is that they borrowed the main principles of their procedure from the canonists. Indeed, until some reforms that are still very recent, the procedure of the Court of Chancery was the procedure of an ecclesiastical court. In flagrant contrast to the common law, it forced the defendant to answer on oath the charges that were brought against him; it made no use of the jury; the evidence consisted of written affidavits. On the other hand, it is by no means certain that more than this was borrowed. So far as we can now see, the chancellors seem to get most of their dominant ideas from the common law. They imitate the common law whenever they can, and depart from it reluctantly at the call of natural justice and common honesty. Common honesty requires that a man shall observe the trust that has been committed to him. If the common law will not enforce this obligation it is failing to do its duty. The chancellor intervenes, but in enforcing trusts he seizes hold of and adopts every analogy that the common law presents. For a long time English equity seems to live from hand to mouth. Sufficient for the day are the cases in that day's cause-list. Even in the seventeenth century men said that the real measure of equity was the length of the chancellor's foot. Under the Tudors the volume of litigation that flowed into the chancery was already enormous; the chancellor was often sadly in arrear of his work, and yet very rarely were his decisions reported, though the decisions of the judges had been reported ever since the days of Edward I. This shows us that he did not conceive himself to be straitly bound by precedents: he could still listen to the voice of conscience. The rapid increase in the number of causes that he had to decide began to make his conscience a technical conscience. More and more of his time was spent upon the judgment-seat. Slowly he ceased to be, save in ceremonial rank, the king's first minister. Wolsey was the last chancellor who ruled England. Secretaries of State were now intervening between the king and his Great Seal. Its holder was destined to become year by year more of a judge, less of a statesman. Still we must look forward to the Restoration for the age in which the rules of equity begin to take a very definite shape, comparable in rigour to the rules of the common law.

Somehow or another, England, after a fashion all her own, had stumbled into a scheme for the reconciliation of permanence with progress. The old medieval criminal law could be preserved because a Court of Star Chamber would supply its deficiencies; the old private law could be preserved because the Court of Chancery was composing an appendix to it; trial by jury could be preserved, developed, transfigured because other modes of trial were limiting it to an appropriate sphere. And so our old law maintained its continuity. As we have said above, it passed scatheless through the critical sixteenth century, and was ready to stand up against tyranny in the seventeenth. The Star Chamber and the Chancery were dangerous to our political liberties. Bacon could tell King James that the Chancery was the court of his absolute power. But if we look abroad we shall find good reason for thinking that but for these institutions our old-fashioned national law, unable out of its own resources to meet the requirements of a new age, would have utterly broken down, and the 'ungodly jumble' would have made way for Roman jurisprudence and for despotism. Were we to say that equity saved the common law, and that the Court of Star Chamber saved the constitution, even in this paradox there would be some truth.

VII

ENGLISH LAW
AND THE RENAISSANCE[1]

Were we to recall to life the good Sir Robert Rede who endowed lecturers in this university, we might reasonably hope that he would approve and admire the fruit that in these last years has been borne by his liberality. And then, as in private duty or private interest bound, I would have him speak thus:

Yes, it is marvellous and more than marvellous this triumph of the sciences that my modest rent-charge stimulates you annually to record; nor do I wonder less at what my lecturers have said of humane letters and the fine arts, of the history of all times and of my time, of Erasmus whom I remember, and that age of the Renaissance (as you call it) in which (so you say) I lived. But there is one matter, one science (for such we accounted it) of which they seem to have said little or nothing; and it happens to be a matter, a science, in which I used to take some interest and which I endeavoured to teach. You have not, I hope, forgotten that I was not only an English judge, but, what is more, a reader in English law.[2]

Six years ago a great master of history, whose untimely death we are deploring, worked the establishment of the Rede lectures into the picture that he drew for us of The Early Renaissance in England.[3] He brought Rede's name into contact with the names of Fisher and More. That, no doubt, is the right environment, and this pious founder's care for the humanities, for logic and for philosophy natural and moral was a memorable sign of the times. Nevertheless the fact remains that, had it not been for his last will and testament, we should hardly have known Sir Robert except as an English lawyer who throve so well in his profession that he became Chief Justice of the Common Bench. And the rest of the acts of Robert Rede—we might say—and the arguments that he urged and the judgments that he pronounced, are they not written in

---

[1] [The Rede Lecture for 1901, delivered in the Senate House, Cambridge (Cambridge, 1901). Reprinted in *Anglo-American Legal Essays* (Cambridge, 1907), vol. I, pp. 168–203. For notes 2–29 see pp. 149–51.]

queer old French in the Year Books of Henry VII and Henry VIII? Those ancient law reports are not a place in which we look for humanism or the spirit of the Renaissance: rather we look there for an amazingly continuous persistence and development of medieval doctrine.

Perhaps we should hardly believe if we were told for the first time that in the reign of James I a man who was the contemporary of Shakespeare and Bacon, a very able man too and a learned, who left his mark deep in English history, said, not by way of paradox but in sober earnest, said repeatedly and advisedly, that a certain thoroughly medieval book written in decadent colonial French was 'the most perfect and absolute work that ever was written in any human science'. Yet this was what Sir Edward Coke said of a small treatise written by Sir Thomas Littleton, who, though he did not die until 1481, was assuredly no child of the Renaissance.

I know that the names of Coke and Littleton when in conjunction are fearsome names or tiresome, and in common honesty I am bound to say that if you stay here you will be wearied. Still I feel that what is at fault is not my theme. A lecturer worthy of that theme would—I am sure of it—be able to convince you that there is some human interest, and especially an interest for English-speaking mankind, in a question which Coke's words suggest: How was it and why was it that in an age when old creeds of many kinds were crumbling and all knowledge was being transfigured, in an age which had revolted against its predecessor and was fully conscious of the revolt, one body of doctrine and a body that concerns us all remained so intact that Coke could promulgate this prodigious sentence and challenge the whole world to contradict it? I have not the power to tell and you today have not the time to hear that story as it should be told. A brief outline of what might be said is all that will be possible and more than will be tolerable.

Robert Rede died in January 1519. Let us remember for a moment where we stand at that date. The Emperor Maximilian also was dying. Henry VIII was reigning in England, Francis I in France, Charles I in Spain, Leo X at Rome. But come we to jurisprudence. Is it beneath the historic muse to notice that young Mr More, the judge's son, had lately lectured at Lincoln's Inn? Perhaps so. At all events for a while we will speak of more resonant exploits. We could hardly (so I learn at second-hand) fix a better date than that of Rede's death for the second new birth of Roman law. More's friend Erasmus had turned his back on England and was by this time in correspondence with two accomplished jurists, the Italian Andrea Alciato and the German Ulrich Zäsi. They and the French scholar Guillaume Budé were publishing books which mark the beginning of a new era. Humanism was renovating Roman law. The medieval commentators, the Balduses and Bartoluses, the people whom Hutten and Rabelais could deride, were in like case with Peter Lombard, Duns Scotus and other men of the night. Back to the texts! was the cry, and let the light of literature and history play upon them. The great Frenchmen who were to do the main part of the work and to make the school of Bourges illustrious were still young or unborn; Cujas was born in 1522; but already the advanced guard was on the march and the flourish of trumpets might be heard.[4] And then in 1520—well, we know what happened in 1520 at Wittenberg, but perhaps we do not often remember that when the German friar ceremoniously and contumeliously committed to the flames some venerated law-books—this, if an event in the history of religion, was also an event in the history of jurisprudence. A current of new life was thrilling through one Corpus Juris; the other had been sore stricken, and, if it escaped from violent death, might perish yet more miserably of a disease that becomes dangerous at the moment when it is discovered.

A few years afterwards an enlightened young humanist, of high rank and marked ability, a man who might live to be pope of Rome or might live to be king of England, was saying much evil of the sort of law that Rede had administered and taught; was saying that a wise prince would banish this barbaric stuff and receive in its stead the civil law of the Romans. Such, so we learn from one of his friends, was the talk of Reginald Pole, and a little knowledge of what was happening in foreign countries is enough to teach us that such talk deserves attention.[5]

This was the time when Roman law was driving German law out of Germany or forcing it to conceal itself in humble forms and obscure corners. If this was the age of the Renaissance and the age of the Reformation, it was also the age of the 'Reception'.[6] I need not say that this Reception—the reception of Roman law—plays a large part in modern versions of German history, and by no means only in such as are written by lawyers. I need not say that it has been judged from many different points of view, that it has been connected by some with political, by others with religious and by yet others with economic changes. Nor need I say that of late years few writers have had a hearty good word for the Reception. We have all of us been nationalists of late. Cosmopolitanism can afford to await its turn.

Then we observe that not long after Pole had been advocating a Reception, his cousin King Henry, whose word was law supreme in church and state, prohibited the academic study of one great and ancient body of law—the canon law—and encouraged the study of another—the civil law—by the foundation of professorships at Oxford and Cambridge.[7] We observe also that his choice of a man to fill the chair at Cambridge fell on one who was eminently qualified to represent in his own person that triad of the three R's —Renaissance, Reformation and Reception. We know Professor Thomas Smith as a humanist, an elegant scholar with advanced opinions about the pronunciation of Greek. We know the Reverend Thomas Smith as a decided, if cautious, Protestant whose doings are of some interest to those who study the changeful history of ecclesiastical affairs. Then we know Dr Thomas Smith as a doctor in law of the university of Padua, for with praiseworthy zeal when he was appointed professor at Cambridge he journeyed to the fountain-head for his Roman law and his legal degree. Also he visited those French universities whence a new jurisprudence was beginning to spread. He returned to speak to us in two inaugural lectures of this new jurisprudence: to speak with enthusiasm of Alciatus and Zasius: to speak hopefully of the future that lay before this conquering science—the future that lay before it in an England fortunately ruled by a pious, wise, learned and munificent Prince. Then in Edward VI's day Thomas Smith as a Master of Requests was doing justice in a court whose procedure was described as being 'altogether according to the process of summary causes in the civil law' and at that moment this Court of Requests and other courts with a like procedure seemed to have time, reason and popularity upon their side.[8] Altogether, the Reverend Professor Dr Sir Thomas Smith, Kt., M.P., Dean of Carlisle, Provost of Eton, Ambassador to the Court of France and Secretary of State to Queen Elizabeth was a man of mark in an age of great events. Had some of those events been other than they were, we might now be saying of him that he played a prominent part in Renaissance, Reformation and Reception, and a part characteristic of that liberal and rational university of which he was professor, public orator and vice-chancellor.[9]

Some German historians, as you are aware, have tried to find or to fashion links that will in some direct and obvious manner connect the Reformation and the Reception. In one popular version of the tale Protestantism finds a congenial ally in the individualism and capitalism of the pagan Digest. In truth I take it that the story is complex. Many currents and cross-currents were flowing in that turbid age. It so happens that in this country we can connect with the heresiarchal name of Wyclif a proposal for the introduction of English law, as a substitute for Roman law, into the schools of Oxford and Cambridge.[10] On the other hand, the desire for a practical Reception of the civil law is ascribed to the future cardinal, who in his last days reconciled England for a moment, not with the Rome of the Digest, but with the Rome of the Decretals. And by the way we may notice that when the cardinal was here upon his reconciliatory errand he had for a while as his legal adviser one of the most learned lawyers of that age, the Spaniard Antonio Agustin. But we in England take little notice of this famous man, who, so foreigners assure us nowadays, began the historical study of the canon law and knew more about the false Isidore than it was comfortable for him to know. Our Dr Smith was Protestant enough; but his Oxford colleague Dr John Story showed zeal in the cremation of Protestants, helped Alva (so it is said) to establish the Inquisition in the Netherlands, was hanged as a traitor at Tyburn in 1571 and beatified as a martyr at Rome in 1886. Blessed John Story was zealous; but his permanent contribution to the jurisprudence of his native land was (so far as I am aware) an early precedent for the imprisonment of a disorderly member by the House of Commons, and a man may be disorderly without being a jurist. Ulrich Zäsi went part of the way with Luther; but then stayed behind with Erasmus. He had once compared the work that he was doing for the Corpus Juris with the work that Luther was doing for the Bible. The great Frenchmen answered the religious question in different ways.[11] One said 'That has nothing to do with the praetor's edict.' His rivals charged him with a triple apostasy. Three or four of them were stout Huguenots, and we must not forget that Calvin and Beza had both been at Bourges and had both studied the civil law. Melanchthon also was a warm admirer of Roman jurisprudence. It is reported that Elizabeth invited Francis Hotman to Oxford.[12] He was Protestant enough, and fierce enough to exchange letters with a tiger. He is best known to English law-students as the man who spoke light words of Littleton and thus attracted Coke's thunderbolt; but if he thought badly of Littleton, he thought badly of Tribonian also, and would have been the last man to preach a Reception. Professor Alberigo Gentili of Oxford, he too was Protestant enough and could rail at the canonists by the hour; but then he as an Italian had a bitter feud with the French humanisers, and stood up for the medieval gloss.

Plainly the story is not simple and we must hurry past it. Still the perplexity of detail should not obscure the broad truth that there was pleasant reading in the Byzantine Code for a king who wished to be monarch in church as well as state: pleasanter reading than could be found in our ancient English law-books. Surely Erastianism is a bad name for the theory that King Henry approved: Marsilianism seems better,[13] but Byzantinism seems best. A time had come when, medieval spectacles being discarded, men could see with the naked eye what stood in the Code and Novels of Constantinople. In 1558 on the eve of an explosive Reformation 'the Protestants of Scotland', craving 'remedy against the tyranny of the estate ecclesiastical', demanded that the controversy should be judged by the New Testament, the ancient fathers 'and the godly approved laws of Justinian the emperor'.[14] University-bred jurists, even such as came from an oldish school, were very serviceable to King Henry in the days of the great divorce case and the subsequent quarrel with the papacy. Tunstall, Gardiner, Bonner, Sampson and Clerk, to say nothing of the Leghs and Laytons, were doctors of law and took their fees in bishoprics and deaneries.[15] Certainly they were more conspicuous and probably they were much abler men than those who were sitting in the courts of the common law. With the one exception of Anthony Fitz Herbert, the judges of Henry's reign are not prominent in our legal history, and we have little reason for attributing deep knowledge of any sort of law to such chancellors as Audley, Wriothesley and Rich. I doubt our common lawyers easily accommodated themselves to ecclesiastical changes. Some years after Elizabeth's accession the number of barristers who were known to the government as 'papists' was surprisingly large and it included the great Plowden.[16] But we must go back to our main theme.

A Reception there was not to be, nor dare I say that a Reception was what our Regius Professor or his royal patron desired. As to Smith himself, it is fairly evident that some time afterwards, when he had resigned his chair and was Elizabeth's ambassador at the French court, he was well content to contrast the public law of England with that of 'France, Italy, Spain, Germany and all other countries which' to use his words 'do follow the civil law of the Romans compiled by Justinian into his Pandects and Code'. The little treatise on the Commonwealth of England which he wrote at Toulouse in 1565[17]—a remarkable feat for he had no English books at hand—became a classic in the next century, and certainly did not underrate those traditional, medieval, Germanic and parliamentary elements which were still to be found in English life and law under the fifth and last of the Tudors. Nevertheless I think that a well-equipped lecturer might persuade a leisurely audience to perceive that in the second quarter of the sixteenth century the continuity of English legal history was seriously threatened.*

Unquestionably our medieval law was open to humanistic attacks. It was couched partly in bad Latin, partly in worse French. For the business Latin of the Middle Age there is much to be said. It is a pleasant picture, that which we have of Thomas More puzzling the omniscient foreigner by the question 'An averia carucae capta in withernamio sunt irreplegibilia'.[18] He asked a practical question in the only Latin in which that question could have been asked without distortion. Smith's acute glance saw that *withernamium* must have something to do with the German *wiedernehmen*; for among his other pursuits our professor had interested himself in the study of English words. But this business Latin was a pure and elegant language when compared with what served our lawyers as French. Pole and Smith might well call it barbarous; that it was fast becoming English was its one redeeming feature. You are likely to know what I must not call the classical passage: it comes from the seventeenth century. In all the *Epistolae Obscurorum Virorum* there is nothing better than the report which tells how one of Sir Robert Rede's successors was

---

* [The following estimate of the threat to the English common law in the sixteenth century is today regarded as exaggerated. See Holdsworth, *History of English Law*, vol. IV, pp. 253–62, and note 23, below, p. 151.]

assaulted by a prisoner 'que puis son condemnation ject un brick-bat a le dit justice que narrowly mist'.[19] It is as instructive as it is surprising that this jargon should have been written in a country where Frenchmen had long been regarded as hereditary foes. This prepares us for the remark that taught law is tough law. But when 'Dunce' had been set in Bocardo (and it was a doctor of civil law who set him there), why should the old law-books be spared? They also were barbarous; they also were sufficiently papistical.

Turning to a more serious aspect of affairs, it would not I think be difficult to show that the pathway for a Reception was prepared. Not difficult but perhaps wearisome. At this point it is impossible for us to forget that the year 1485, if important to students of English history for other reasons, is lamentably important for this reason, that there Dr Stubbs laid down his pen. In his power of marshalling legal details so as to bring to view some living principle or some phase of national development he has had no rival and no second among Englishmen.* Howbeit, we may think of the subjected church and the humbled baronage, of the parliament which exists to register the royal edicts, of the English *Lex Regia* which gives the force of statute to the king's proclamations, of the undeniable faults of the common law, of its dilatory methods, of bribed and perjured juries, of the new courts which grow out of the King's Council[20] and adopt a summary procedure devised by legists and decretists. Might not the Council and the Star Chamber and the Court of Requests—courts not tied and bound by ancient formalism—do the romanising work that was done in Germany by the Imperial Chamber Court, the *Reichskammergericht*? This was the time when King Henry's nephew James V was establishing a new court in Scotland, a College of Justice, and Scotland was to be the scene of a Reception.

It seems fairly certain that, besides all that he effected, Henry had at times large projects in his mind:[21] a project for a great college of law (possibly a College of Justice in the Scotch sense), a project for the reformation of the Inns of Court, which happily were not rich enough to deserve dissolution, also perhaps a project for a civil code as well as the better known project for a code ecclesiastical. In Edward VI's day our Regius and German Professor of Divinity,

---

* [Maitland to Poole, 9 June 1901: 'I spoke warmly of W.S. in the Rede Lecture and was rewarded by what French reporters call a movement of adhesion. I heard a purr from the Master of Trinity' (H. M. Butler).]

Dr Martin Butzer, had heard, so it seems, that such a scheme had been taken in hand, and he moved in circles that were well informed. He urged the young Josiah to go forward in the good work; he denounced the barbarism of English law and (to use Bentham's word) its incognoscibility. The new ecclesiastical code, as is generally known, was never enacted; but we know equally well that the draft is in print.[22] Its admired Latinity is ascribed to Professor Smith's immediate successor, Dr Walter Haddon. I take it that nowadays few English clergymen wish that they were living—or should I not say dying?—under Dr Haddon's pretty phrases. Codification was in the air. Both in France and in Germany the cry for a new Justinian was being raised, and perhaps we may say that only because a new Justinian was not forthcoming men endeavoured to make the best that they could of the old. How bad that best would be Francis Hotman foretold.

And then we see that in 1535, the year in which More was done to death, the Year Books come to an end: in other words, the great stream of law reports that has been flowing for near two centuries and a half, ever since the days of Edward I, becomes discontinuous and then runs dry. The exact significance of this ominous event has never yet been duly explored; but ominous it surely is. Some words that once fell from Edmund Burke occur to us: 'To put an end to reports is to put an end to the law of England.' Then in 1547 just after King Henry's death a wail went up from 'divers students of the common laws'. The common laws, they said, were being set aside in favour of 'the law civil' insomuch that the old courts had hardly any business. Ten years later, at the end of Mary's reign, we read that the judges had nothing to do but 'to look about them', and that for the few practitioners in Westminster Hall there was 'elbow room enough'. In criminal causes that were of any political importance an examination by two or three doctors of the civil law threatened to become a normal part of our procedure. In short, I am persuaded that in the middle years of the sixteenth century and of the Tudor age the life of our ancient law was by no means lusty.[23]

And now we may ask what opposing force, what conservative principle was there in England? National character, the genius of a people, is a wonder-working spirit which stands at the beck and call of every historian. But before we invoke it on the present occasion we might prudently ask our books whether in the sixteenth century the bulk of our German cousins inherited an innate bias towards what they would have called a Welsh jurisprudence. There seems to be plentiful evidence that the learned *doctores iuris* who counselled the German princes and obtained seats in the courts were cordially detested by the multitude. In modern times they often have to bear much blame for that terrible revolt which we know as the Peasants' War.[24] No doubt there were many differences between England and Germany, between England and France, between England and Scotland. Let us notice one difference which, if I am not mistaken, marked off England from the rest of the world. Medieval England had schools of national law.

The importance of certain law schools will be readily conceded, even to one who is in some sort officially bound to believe that law schools may be important. A history of civilisation would be miserably imperfect if it took no account of the first new birth of Roman law in the Bologna of Irnerius. Indeed there are who think that no later movement—not the Renaissance, not the Reformation—draws a stronger line across the annals of mankind than that which is drawn about the year 1100 when a human science won a place beside theology. I suppose that the importance of the school of Bourges would also be conceded. It may be worth our while to remark that the school of Bologna had a precursor in the school of Pavia, and that the law which was the main subject of study in the Pavia of the eleventh century was not Roman law but Lombard law: a body of barbaric statutes that stood on one level with the Anglo-Saxon laws of the same age. This I say, not in order that I may remind you what sort of law it was that Archbishop Lanfranc studied when as a young man he was a shining light in the school of Pavia,[25] but because this body of Lombard law, having once become the subject of systematic study, showed a remarkable vitality in its struggle with Roman jurisprudence. Those Italian doctors of the middle age who claimed for their science the fealty of all mankind might have been forced to admit that all was not well at home. They might call this Lombard law *ius asininum* and the law of brute beasts, but it lingered on, and indeed I read that it was not utterly driven from the kingdom of Naples until Joseph Bonaparte published the French code. Law schools make tough law.

Very rarely do we see elsewhere the academic teaching of any law that is not Roman: imperially or papally Roman. As a matter of course the universities had the two legal faculties, unless, as at Paris, the Pope excluded the legists from an ecclesiastical preserve. The voice of John Wyclif pleading that English law was the law that should be taught in English universities was a voice that for centuries cried in the wilderness. It was 1679 before French law obtained admission into the French universities. It was 1709 before George Beyer, a pandectist at Wittenberg, set a precedent for lectures on German law in a German university. It was 1758 before Blackstone began his ever famous course at Oxford. The chair that I cannot fill was not established until the transatlantic Cambridge was setting an example to her elderly mother. But then, throughout the later middle age English law had been academically taught.

No English institutions are more distinctively English than the Inns of Court; of none is the origin more obscure.[26] We are only now coming into possession of the documents whence their history must be gathered, and apparently we shall never know much of their first days. Unchartered, unprivileged, unendowed, without remembered founders, these groups of lawyers formed themselves and in course of time evolved a scheme of legal education: an academic scheme of the medieval sort, oral and disputatious. For good and ill that was a big achievement: a big achievement in the history of some undiscovered continents. We may well doubt whether aught else could have saved English law in the age of the Renaissance. What is distinctive of medieval England is not parliament, for we may everywhere see assemblies of Estates, nor trial by jury, for this was but slowly suppressed in France. But the Inns of Court and the Year Books that were read therein, we shall hardly find their like elsewhere. At all events let us notice that where Littleton and Fortescue lectured, there Robert Rede lectures, Thomas More lectures, Edward Coke lectures, Francis Bacon lectures, and highly technical were the lectures that Francis Bacon gave. Now it would, so I think, be difficult to conceive any scheme better suited to harden and toughen a traditional body of law than one which, while books were still uncommon, compelled every lawyer to take part in legal education and every distinguished lawyer to read public lectures. That was what I meant when I made bold to say that Robert Rede was not only an English judge but 'what is more' a reader in English law.

Deus bone! exclaimed Professor Smith in his inaugural lecture, and what excited the learned doctor to this outcry was the skill in disputation shown by the students of English law in their schools at London. He was endeavouring to persuade his hearers that in many ways the study of law would improve their minds. If, he urged, these young men, cut off as they are from all the humanities, can reason thus over their 'barbaric and semi-gallic laws', what might not you, you cultivated scholars do if you studied the Digest and Alciatus and Zasius? And then the professor expressed a hope that he might be able to spend his vacation in the Inns of Court. His heart was in the right place: in a school of living law. Even for the purposes of purely scientific observation the live dog may be better than the dead lion.

When the middle of the century is past the signs that English law has a new lease of life become many. The medieval books poured from the press, new books were written, the decisions of the courts were more diligently reported, the lawyers were boasting of the independence and extreme antiquity of their system.[27] We were having a little Renaissance of our own: or a Gothic revival if you please. The Court of Requests in which Professor Smith and Professor Haddon had done justice was being tried for its life. Its official defender was, we observe, Italian by blood and Parisian by degree: Dr Adelmare, known to Englishmen as Sir Julius Caesar.[28] That wonderful Edward Coke was loose. The medieval tradition was more than safe in his hands. You may think it pleasant to turn from this masterful, masterless man to his great rival. It is not very safe to say what Thomas More did not know, less safe to say what was unknown to Francis Bacon, but I cannot discover that either of these scholars, these philosophers, these statesmen, these law reformers, these schemers of ideal republics, these chancellors of the realm, these law lecturers, had more than a bowing acquaintance with Roman law.

If Reginald Pole's dream had come true, if there had been a Reception—well, I have not the power to guess and you have not the time to hear what would have happened; but I think that we should have had to rewrite a great deal of history. For example, in the seventeenth century there might have been a struggle between king and parliament, but it would hardly have been that struggle for the medieval, the Lancastrian, constitution in which Coke and Selden and Prynne and other ardent searchers of mouldering records won their right to be known to schoolboys. In 1610 when the conflict was growing warm a book was burnt by the common hangman: it was written by an able man in whom Cambridge should take some pride, Dr Cowell, our Regius Professor, and seemed to confirm the suspicion that Roman law and absolute monarchy went hand in hand.[29]

The profit and loss account would be a long affair. I must make no attempt to state it. If there was the danger of barbarism and stupidity on the one side, there was the danger of pedantry on the other: the pedantry that endeavours to appropriate the law of another race and galvanises a dead Corpus Juris into a semblance of life. Since 1 January 1900 the attempt to administer law out of Justinian's books has been abandoned in Germany. The so-called 'Roman-Dutch' law of certain outlying parts of the British Empire now stands alone, and few, I imagine, would foretell for it a brilliant future, unless it passes into the hand of the codifier and frankly ceases to be nominally Roman. Let us observe, however, that much had been at stake in the little England of the sixteenth century.

In 1606 Coke was settling the first charter of Virginia. In 1619 elected 'burgesses' from the various 'hundreds' of Virginia were assembling, and the first-born child of the mother of parliaments saw the light. Maryland was granted to Lord Baltimore with view of frank-pledge and all that to view of frank-pledge doth belong, to have and to hold in free and common socage as of the castle of Windsor in the county of Berks, yielding yearly therefor two Indian arrows of those parts on the Tuesday in Easter week. The port and island of Bombay in one hemisphere, and in another Prince Rupert's Land stretching no one knew how far into the frozen north were detached members of the manor of East Greenwich in the county of Kent. Nearly 2500 copies of Blackstone's *Commentaries* were absorbed by the colonies on the Atlantic seaboard before they declared their independence. James Kent, aged fifteen, found a copy, and (to use his own words) was inspired with awe; John Marshall found a copy in his father's library; and the common law went straight to the Pacific.

A hundred legislatures—little more or less—are now building on that foundation: on the rock that was not submerged. We will not say this boastfully. Far from it. Standing at the beginning of a century and in the first year of Edward VII, thinking of the wide lands which call him king, thinking of our complex and loosely-knit British Commonwealth, we cannot look into the future without serious misgivings. If unity of law—such unity as there has been—disappears, much else that we treasure will disappear also, and (to speak frankly) unity of law is precarious. The power of the parliament of the United Kingdom to legislate for the colonies is fast receding into the ghostly company of legal fictions. Men of our race have been litigious; the great Ihering admired our litigiousness; it is one of our more amiable traits; but it seems to me idle to believe that distant parts of the earth will supply a tribunal at Westminster with enough work to secure uniformity. The so-called common law of one colony will swerve from that of another, and both from that of England. Some colonies will have codes. If English lawyers do not read Australian reports (and they cannot read everything), Australian lawyers will not much longer read English reports.

Still the case is not yet desperate. Heroic things can be done by a nation which means to do them: as witness the mighty effort of science and forbearance which in our own time has unified the law of Germany, and, having handed over the Corpus Juris to the historians, has in some sort undone the work of the Reception. Some venerable bodies may understand the needs of the time, or, if I may borrow a famous phrase, 'the vocation of our age for jurisprudence and legislation'. Our parliament may endeavour to put out work which will be a model for the British world. It can still set an example where it can no longer dictate, and at least it might clear away the rubbish that collects round every body of law. To make law that is worthy of acceptance by free communities that are not bound to accept it, this would be no mean ambition. *Nihil aptius, nihil efficacius ad plures provincias sub uno imperio retinendas et fovendas.* But it is hardly to parliament that our hopes must turn in the first instance. Certain ancient and honourable societies, proud of a past that is unique in the history of the world, may become fully conscious of the heavy weight of responsibility that was assumed when English law schools saved, but isolated, English law in the days of the Reception. In that case, the glory of Bourges, the glory of Bologna, the glory of Harvard may yet be theirs.*

* ['At this point, when he seemed about to address an exhortation of a like sort to the Universities, Maitland interrupted himself in a tone of apologetic surprise, "But, Mr Vice-Chancellor, I perceive there are strangers present." Not too many speakers could carry off such a piece of by-play—and in the Senate House. It was entirely successful and more significant than any formal peroration.' Pollock, *Quarterly Review* (April 1906), p. 417.]

NOTES

[Maitland's notes, twice the length of the text, cite authorities for its statements and allusions, or elaborate suggestions made in it. In view of their bulk and of their partial supersession by the later work that they have evoked, it seemed better to omit or abridge the greater part, adding references to bring them up to date. The original notes may be found in full in the editions of 1901 and 1907 (see p. 135 above).]

² Rede was a Reader at Lincoln's Inn in 1481 and 1486. [See S. E. Thorne, *Readings and Moots at the Inns of Court* (Selden Society, 1952), vol. I, p. x.]

³ Creighton, *The Early Renaissance in England* (Cambridge, 1895).

⁴ For these Renaissance jurists, see Dareste, *Essai sur François Hotman*, pp. 17–31; [Olivier-Martin, *Histoire du droit français*, pp. 430–8; Holdsworth, *History of English Law*, vol. IV, pp. 225–8].

⁵ Thomas Starkey was employed in the endeavour to win Reginald Pole to King Henry's side in the matter of the divorce from Catherine and the consequent breach with Rome. The negotiation failed, but Starkey took the opportunity of laying before Henry a dialogue which he (Starkey) had composed. The interlocutors in this dialogue were Pole and the well-known scholar Thomas Lupset, and Pole was represented as expounding his opinions touching political and ecclesiastical affairs. How far at all points Starkey fairly represented Pole's views may be doubted. Still we have respectable evidence that Pole had talked in the strain of the following passage, and at any rate Starkey thought that in King Henry's eyes he was befriending Pole by making him speak thus.

'Thys ys no dowte but that our law and ordur thereof ys over-confuse. Hyt ys infynyte, and without ordur or end. Ther ys no stabyl grounde therin, nor sure stay; but euery one that can coloure reson makyth a stope to the best law that ys before tyme deuysyd. The suttylty of one sergeant schal enerte [enerve?] and destroy al the jugementys of many wyse men before tyme receyuyd. There is no stabyl ground in our commyn law to leyne vnto. The jugementys of yerys [i.e. the Year Books] be infynyte and ful of much controuersy; and, besyde that, of smal authoryte. The jugys are not bounden, as I vnderstond, to folow them as a rule, but aftur theyr owne lyberty they haue authoryte to iuge, accordying as they are instructyd by the sergeantys, and as the cyrcumstance of the cause doth them moue. And thys makyth jugementys and processe of our law to be wythout end and infynyte; thys causyth sutys to be long in decysyon. Therefor, to remedy thys mater groundly, hyt were necessary, in our law, to vse the same remedy that Justynyan dyd in the law of the Romaynys, to bryng thys infynyte processe to certayn endys, to cut away thys long lawys, and, by the wysdome of some polytyke and wyse men, institute a few and bettur lawys and ordynancys. The statutys of kyngys, also, be ouer-many, euen as the constytutyonys of the emperorys were. Wherefor I wold wysch that al these lawys schold be brought into some smal nombur, and to be wryten also in our mother tong, or els put into the Latyn, to cause them that studye the cyuyle law of our reame fyrst to begyn of the Latyn tong, wherin they myght also afturward lerne many thyngys to helpe thys professyon. Thys ys one thyng necessary to the educatyon of the nobylyte, the wych only I wold schold be admyttyd to the study of thys law. Then they myght study also the lawys of the Romaynys, where they schold see al causys and controuersys decyded by rulys more conuenyent to the ordur of nature then they be in thys barbarouse tong and Old French, wych now seruyth to no purpos els. Thys, Mastur Lvpset, ys a grete blote in our pollycy, to see al our law and commyn dyscyplyne wryten in thys barbarouse langage, wych, aftur when the youth hath lernyd, seruyth them to no purpos at al; and, besyde that, to say the truth, many of the lawys themselfys be also barbarouse and tyrannycal, as you haue before hard. [Here follows an attack on primogeniture and entail.] The wych al by thys one remedy schold be amendyd and correct, yf we myght induce the hedys of our cuntrey to admyt the same: that ys, to receyue the cyuyle law of the Romaynys, the wych ys now the commyn law almost of al Chrystyan natyonys. The wych thyng vndowtydly schold be occasyon of infynyte gudness in the ordur of our reame, the wych I could schow you many-festely, but the thyng hyt selfe ys so open and playn, that hyt nedyth no decla-ratyon at al; for who ys so blynd that seth not the grete schame to our natyon, the grete infamy and rote that remeynyth in vs, to be gouernyd by the lawys gyuen to vs of such a barbarouse natyon as the Normannys be? Who ys so fer from rayson that consyderyth not the tyranycal and barbarouse instytutionys, infynyte ways left here among vs, whych al schold be wypt away by the receyuyng of thys wych we cal the veray cyuyle law; wych ys vndowtydly the most auncyent and nobyl monument of the Romaynys prudence and pollycy, the wych be so wryte wyth such grauyte, that yf Nature schold herselfe pre-scrybe partycular meanys wherby mankynd schold obserue hyr lawys, I thynke sche wold admyt the same: specyally, yf they were, by a lytyl more wysedome, brought to a lytyl bettur ordur and frame, wych myght be sone downe and put in effect. And so ther aftur that, yf the nobylyte were brought vp in thys lawys vndoubtydly our cuntrey wold schortly be restoryd to as gud cyuylyte as there ys in any other natyon; ye, and peradventure much bettur also. For though thes lawys wych I haue so praysyd be commyn among them, yet, bycause the nobylyte ther commynly dothe not exercyse them in the studys thereof, they be al applyd to lucur and gayne, bycause the popular men wych are borne in pouerty only doth exercyse them for the most parte, wych ys a grete ruyne of al gud ordur and cyuylyte. Wherefor, Master Lvpset, yf we myght bryng thys ij. thyngys to effecte—that ys to say, to haue the cyuyle law of the Romaynys to be the commyn law here of Englond with vs; and, secon-dary, that the nobylyte in theyr youth schold study commynly therein— I thynk we schold not nede to seke partycular remedys for such mysordurys as we haue notyd before; for surely thys same publyke dyscyplyne schold redresse them lyghtly; ye, and many other mow, the wych we spake not yet of at al.'

Lupset thereupon objects that, seeing we have so many years been governed by our own law, it will be hard to bring this reform to pass. Pole replies that the goodness of a prince would bring it to pass quickly: 'the wych I pray God we may onys see'.

(*Starkey's England*, Early English Text Society, 1878, pp. 192 ff.)

[6] [On the Reception see Holdsworth, *op. cit.* vol. IV, pp. 240–52.]

[7] In 1535 and 1540. See C. H. Cooper, *Annals of Cambridge*, vol. I, pp. 375, 397; Ellis, *Original Letters*, Ser. II, vol. II, p. 60.

[8] See Leadam's introduction to *Select Cases in the Court of Requests* (Selden Society, 1898), p. *cxxiii.*

[9] [On Smith's career, see Maitland's Preface to Smith's *Commonwealth of England*, ed. Alston (Cambridge, 1906).] For a summary of his inaugural orations, see Mullinger, *History of the University of Cambridge*, vol. II, pp. 129–32.

[10] Wyclif, *Select English Works*, ed. Arnold, vol. III, p. 326: 'It semeth that curatis schulden rathere lerne and teche the kyngis statutis, and namely the Grete Chartre, than the emperours lawe or myche part of the popis.' [See also 'Wyclif on English and Roman law', *Collected Papers*, vol. III, pp. 50–3.]

[11] On the French lawyers and the Reformation see Dareste, *op. cit.*; Haag, *La France protestante*, ed. 2, vol. IV, col. 957–70; vol. V, cols. 508, 783–9; Brissaud, *Histoire du droit français*, pp. 349–57.

[12] Dareste, *op. cit.*, p. 5. The 'tiger' was the Cardinal of Lorraine.

[13] The translation of Marsiglio's *Defensor Pacis*, published July 1535, was backed by Cromwell. *Letters and Papers of Henry VIII*, vols. VII, pp. 6, 178; IX, p. 171. [See F. Baumer, *Early Tudor Theory of Kingship* (New Haven, 1940), p. 44.]

[14] *Calendar of State Papers, Foreign series* 1558–9, p. 8.

[15] See lives of Cuthbert Tunstall, Stephen Gardiner, Edmund Bonner, Thomas Thirlby, Richard Sampson, John Clerk (†1541), Richard Layton, Thomas Legh, James Denton, in *Dict. Nat. Biog.*

[16] See lives of Edmund Plowden, William Rastell and Anthony Browne (d. 1567) in *Dict. Nat. Biog.*; *Calendar of Inner Temple Records*, vol. I, p. 470.

[17] [See *note* 9.]

[18] Blackstone, *Commentaries*, vol. III, p. 149; J. H(oddesdon), *Tho. Mori Vita*, London, 1652, p. 26.

[19] Dyer's *Reports* (1688), p. 188*b*.

[20] [See Holdsworth, vol. I, pp. 409–26, 492–508; vol. IV, pp. 272–83.]

[21] [For these projects, see Holdsworth, vol. IV, pp. 269, *n.* 1, 572–86; Plucknett in *Trans. R. Hist. Soc.* (1936), pp. 121–44.]

[22] Printed 1571; see Cardwell, *The Reformation of the Ecclesiastical Laws.*

[23] For the students' petition see *Acts of the Privy Council*, 1547–1550, pp. 48–50. [On all the evidence cited by Maitland in this paragraph see Holdsworth, vol. IV, pp. 253–9.]

[24] [On Roman Law and the Peasants' War see *Cambridge Medieval History*, vol. VII, p. 737.]

[25] See above, p. 104, *n.* 1.

[26] [On the Inns of Court, see Holdsworth, vol. II, pp. 493–512 and S. E. Thorne, Introduction to vol. II, *Readings and Moots at the Inns of Court* (Selden Society, now in the press).]

[27] [See J. H. Beale, *Bibliography of early English Law-books* (Cambridge, Mass., 1926).]

[28] See Caesar, Sir Julius, in *Dict. Nat. Biog.*; and Leadam, *op. cit.*

[29] See S. R. Gardiner, *History of England, 1603–1642*, vol. II, pp. 66–8.

VIII

THE ANGLICAN SETTLEMENT
AND THE SCOTTISH REFORMATION[1]

When at the beginning of 1560 there was a new pope, pledged to convoke the Council for a third time and to stem and repel the tide of heresy, the latest disaster that met his eye was no mere relapse of England followed by a lapse of Scotland; for what was shaping itself in the northern seas already looked ominously like a Protestant Great Britain. Two small Catholic Powers traditionally at war with each other, the one a satellite of the Habsburg luminary, the other a satellite of France, seemed to be fusing themselves in one Power that might be very great: great perhaps for good, but more probably for evil. 'Earnest embracing of religion', wrote a Scottish to an English statesman, 'will join us straitly together.' The religion that William Maitland meant when he sent these words to Sir William Cecil was not the religion of Pius IV and the General Council.

Suddenly all farsighted eyes had turned to a backward country. Eyes at Rome and eyes at Geneva were fixed on Scotland, and, the further they could peer into the future, the more eager must have been their gaze. And still we look intently at that wonderful scene, the Scotland of Mary Stewart and John Knox: not merely because it is such glorious tragedy, but also because it is such modern history. The fate of the Protestant Reformation was being decided, and the creed of unborn millions in undiscovered lands was being determined. This we see—all too plainly perhaps—if we read the books that year by year men still are writing of Queen Mary and her surroundings. The patient analysis of those love letters in the

<hr />

[1] [*Cambridge Modern History* (1903), vol. II, ch. XVI. For recent work on the Scottish reformation, see Gordon Donaldson, 'The Scottish Episcopate at the Reformation', *E.H.R.* (1945); 'The attitude of Whitgift and Bancroft to the Scottish Church', *Trans. R. Hist. Soc.* (1942); 'The Polity of the Scottish Church, 1560–1600', *The Record of the Scottish Church History Soc.* (1953), vol. XI, part III. The most recent discussion of the Anglican Settlement is by J. E. Neale: 'The Elizabethan Acts of Supremacy and Uniformity', *E.H.R.* (1950); *Elizabeth I and her Parliaments 1559–1581* (1953). His interpretation of Elizabeth's policy differs from that of Maitland.]

casket may yet be perturbed by thoughts about religion. Nor is the religious the only interest. A new nation, a British nation, was in the making.

We offer no excuse for having as yet said little of Scotland. Called upon to play for some years a foremost part in the great drama, her entry upon the stage of modern history is late and sudden. In such phrases there must indeed be some untruth, for history is not drama. The annals of Scotland may be so written that the story will be continuous enough. We may see the explosion of 1559 as the effect of causes that had long been at work. We might chronicle the remote beginnings of heresy and the first glimmers of the New Learning. All those signs of the times that we have seen elsewhere in capital letters we might see here in minuscule. Also, it would not escape us that, though in the days of Luther and Calvin resistance to the English and their obstinately impolitic claim of suzerainty still seemed the vital thread of Scottish national existence, inherited enmity was being enfeebled, partly by the multiplying perfidies of venal nobles and the increasing wealth of their paymasters, and partly also by the accumulating proofs that in the new age a Scotland which lived only to help France and hamper England would herself be a poor little Power among the nations: doomed, not only to occasional Floddens and Pinkies, but to continuous misery, anarchy, and obscurity.

All this deserves, and finds, full treatment at the hands of the historians of Scotland. They will also sufficiently warn us that the events of 1560 leave a great deal unchanged. Faith may be changed; works are much what they were, especially the works of the magnates. The blood-feud is no less a blood-feud because one family calls itself Catholic and another calls itself Protestant. The 'band' is no less a 'band' because it is styled a 'Covenant' and makes free with holy names. A king shall be kidnapped, and a king shall be murdered, as of old: it is the custom of the country. What is new is that farsighted men all Europe over, not only at London and at Paris, but at Rome and at Geneva, should take interest in these barbarous deeds, this customary turmoil.

Continuity there had been and to spare. In that mournful procession of the five Jameses there is no break (1406–1542). The last of them is engaged in the old task, and failing as his forbears failed. It is picturesque; sometimes it is heroic; often it is pathetic;

but it is never modern. Modern history sees it as a funeral procession
burying a dead time, and we are silent while it passes. In a few
sentences we make our way towards the momentous years.

Scotland had been slow to emerge from the Middle Age. A
country which of all others demanded strong and steady government had been plagued by a series of infant kings and contested
regencies. In the sixteenth century its barons still belonged to
the twelfth, despite a thin veneer of French manners. Its institutions were rudimentary; its parliaments were feudal assemblies.
Since the close of the War of Independence there had been hardly
anything that could properly be called constitutional growth.
Sometimes there was a little imitation of England and sometimes
a little imitation of France, the king appearing as a more or less
radical reformer. But the king died young, leaving an infant son,
and his feudatories had no desire for reformation. The Scottish
monarchy, if monarchy it may be called, was indeed strictly
limited; but the limits were set much rather by the power of
certain noble families and their numerous retainers than by an
assembly of Estates expressing the constant will of an organised
community. The prelates, lords, and represented boroughs formed
but one chamber. Attempts to induce the lesser tenants-in-chief
to choose representatives who would resemble the English knights
of the shire had been abortive, and a bad habit prevailed of
delegating the work of a parliament to a committee known as
'the Lords of the Articles'. Normally the assembly of Estates was
but the registrar of foregone conclusions. In troublous times
(and the times were often troublous) the faction that was in power
would hold a parliament, and the other faction would prudently
abstain from attendance. When in 1560 an unusually full, free and
important parliament was held for the reformation of religion, an
elementary question concerning the right of the minor barons to
sit and vote was still debatable, and for many years afterwards
those who desire to see the true contribution of Scotland to the
history of representative institutions will look, not to the blighted
and stunted conclave of the three Estates with its titular bishops
and abbots commendatory, but to the fresh and vigorous Assembly
of the Presbyterian Church.

Steady taxation and all that it implies had been out of the
question. The Scots were ready to fight for their king, unless they

happened to be fighting against him; but they would not provide him with a revenue adequate for the maintenance of public order. He was expected 'to live of his own' in medieval fashion, and his own was not enough to raise him high above his barons. Moreover, Douglases and Hamiltons and others, hereditary sheriffs and possessors of 'regalities', were slow to forget that these crowned stewards of Scotland were no better than themselves. What had 'come with a lass' might 'go with a lass', and was in no wise mysterious. We shall see Queen Mary, widow of a king of France, giving her hand first to a Lennox-Stewart whose mother is a Douglas and then to a Hepburn, while the heir presumptive to the throne is the head of the Hamiltons. We shall see Queen Elizabeth having trouble with northern earls, with Percies and Nevilles, who set up an altar which she had cast down, and belike would have cast down an altar which she had set up; but their power to disturb England was as nothing to the power of disturbing Scotland which was exercised by those near neighbours and like-minded fellows of theirs who joined the bellicose Congregation of Jesus Christ. And even in the briefest sketch we must not omit to notice that, as beyond England lay Scotland, so beyond the historic Scotland lay the unhistoric land of 'the savages'. The very means that had been taken by Scottish kings to make Scotsmen of these 'red-shanks' and to bring these savages within the pale of history had raised up new feudatories of almost royal rank and of more than baronial turbulence. Thenceforward, the king would have to reckon, not only with an Albany, an Angus, and an Arran, but also with an Argyll and with a Huntly. When we see these things we think of the dark age: of Charles the Simple and Rolf the Pirate.

Neither valorous feats of arms which overtaxed a people's strength nor a superabundance of earls and barons should conceal from us the nakedness of the land. It is more than probable that in the middle of the sixteenth century the whole of the Scottish nation, including untamable Highlanders, was not too large to be commodiously housed in the Glasgow of today. Life was short, and death was violent. It is true that many hopeful signs of increasing prosperity and enlightenment are visible in the days of James IV (1488–1513). But those days ended at Flodden. The flowers of the forest were once more mown down. The hand went back upon the dial towards poverty and barbarity. An aptitude for letters we may see. Of a brief springtime of song Scotland may fairly boast, for as yet no icy wind was blowing from Geneva. Universities we may see: more universities indeed than the country could well support. By a memorable, if futile, act of parliament James IV attempted to drive the sons of the gentry into the grammar-schools. But an all-pervading lack of wealth and of the habits that make for wealth was an impediment to every good endeavour. The printing press had been in no hurry to reach England (1477); but thirty years more elapsed before it entered Scotland. An aptitude for jurisprudence we might infer from subsequent history; but it is matter of inference. Of lawyers who were not ecclesiastics, of temporal lawyers comparable to the professionally learned justices and serjeants of England, we can hardly read a word. When at length James V founded the College of Justice (1532), half the seats in it, and indeed one more, were allotted to the clergy, and in later days foreign science was imported from the continental universities to supply the deficiencies of an undeveloped system. Scotland had been no place for lawyers, and the temporal law that might be had there, though it came of an excellent stock, had for the more part been of the bookless kind. And as with jurisprudence, so with statesmanship. The Scottish statesman who was not a bishop was a man of a new kind when Lethington began his correspondence with Cecil; for, even if we employ a medieval standard, we can hardly attribute statecraft or policy to the Albanys and Anguses and Arrans.

In this poor and sparsely peopled country the Church was wealthy; the clergy were numerous, laic, and lazy. The names of 'dumb dogs' and 'idle bellies' which the new preachers fixed upon them had not been unearned. Nowhere else was there a seed-plot better prepared for revolutionary ideas of a religious sort. Nowhere else would an intelligible Bible be a newer book, or a sermon kindle stranger fires. Nowhere else would the pious champions of the Catholic faith be compelled to say so much that was evil of those who should have been their pastors. Abuses which had been superficial and sporadic in England were widely spread and deeply rooted in the northern kingdom. In particular, the com-mendation of ecclesiastical benefices to laymen, to babies, had become a matter of course. The Lord James Stewart, the king's base-born son, who at the critical moment is Prior of St Andrews and sits in parliament as a member of the spiritual Estate, is a typical figure. The corslet had 'clattered' beneath the archbishop's cassock, and when bishops and abbots lie among the dead on Flodden field they have done no less but no more than their duty. We say that the Scottish Church was rich, and so it nominally was, for the kirk-lands were broad; but when the Protestant ministers, much to their own disappointment, had to be content with a very small fraction of the old ecclesiastical revenues, they had probably secured a larger share than had for a long time past been devoted to any purpose more spiritual than the sustentation of royal, episcopal, and baronial families. We exclaim against the greedy nobles whose lust for the kirk-lands is one of the operative forces in the history of the Scottish Reformation. They might have said that they were only rearranging on a reasonable and modern basis what had long been for practical purposes the property of their class. Their doings send back our thoughts to far-off Carolingian days, when the 'benefice' became the hereditary fief. To the king it was, no doubt, convenient that the power of those nobles who would leave heirs should be balanced by the power of other nobles, called prelates, whose children would not be legitimate. But such a system could not be stable, and might at any time provoke an overwhelming outcry for its destruction, if ever one bold man raised his voice against it. Men who are not themselves very moral can feel genuine indignation when they detect immorality among those who, though no worse than themselves, pretend to superior holiness. Prelates, and even primates of Scotland, who were bastards and the begetters of bastards, were the principal fore-runners and coadjutors of John Knox; and unfortunately they were debarred by professional rules from pleading that they, or the best among them, were in truth the respectable husbands of virtuous wives.

Lollardy too there had been, and in some corners of the land it had never been thoroughly extirpated. Also there had been a little burning, but far from enough to accustom the Scots to the sight of a heretic tortured by the flames. Then the German leaven began to work, and from 1528 onwards a few Lutherans were burnt. The protomartyr was Patrick Hamilton, the young and well born abbot of Ferne. Like many another Scottish youth he had been at the University of Paris. Afterwards he had made a pilgrimage, if not to Wittenberg, at all events to Marburg. It is characteristic of time and place that historians have to consider whether a feud between Douglases and Hamiltons counts for nothing in his martyrdom. 'The reek of Patrick Hamilton', we are told, infected many; and we can well believe it. The College of St Leonard was tainted with humanism and new theology. Young men fled from Scotland and made fame elsewhere. Such were Alexander Aless, who as Alesius became the friend of Melanchthon, and John Macalpine, who as Machabaeus professed divinity at Copenhagen. Such also was George Buchanan, the humanist and the Calvinist, the tutor and the calumniator of Queen Mary. And we see the Wedderburns who are teaching Scotsmen to sing ballads of a novel kind, 'good and godly ballads', but such as priests are loth to hear. And we see Sir David Lindsay, the herald, the poet, the king's friend, scourging the lives and sometimes the beliefs of the clergy with verses which rich and poor will know by heart. In short, there was combustible material lying about in large quantities, and sparks were flying.

But the day of revolt was long delayed. What held in check the rebellious and even the Reforming forces, was the best of Scottish traditions, the undying distrust of an England which claimed an overlordship; and in the days of Henry VIII no wholesomer tradition could there be. His father had schemed for amity by way of matrimonial alliance, and Margaret Tudor had become the wife and mother of Scottish kings. It was plain that in the age of great monarchies England would be feeble so long as she had a hostile Scotland behind her. But the Tudor would not see that he could not annex Scotland, or that a merely annexed Scotland would still be the old enemy. Just as in the days of the Great Schism England had acknowledged one, and Scotland the other, of the rival popes, so in the new days of a greater schism James V became the better Catholic because his bullying uncle had broken with Rome. As was natural for a king of Scots, he leant upon the support of the clergy, and thereby he offended his barons. They failed him in his hour of need. After the shameful rout at Solway Moss, he turned his face to the wall and died, a worn-out desperate man at the age of thirty years (14 December 1542).

His wife, Mary of Lorraine, the sister of those Guises who were to be all-powerful in France, had just borne him a daughter: she was the ill-fated Mary Stewart (8 December 1542). Once more, a baby was to be crowned in Scotland. Next to her in hereditary succession stood a remote cousin, the head of the house of Hamilton, James Earl of Arran, the Châtelherault of after times. But his right depended on the validity of a divorce which some might call in question; and Matthew Stewart, Earl of Lennox, had pretensions. At the head of the Scottish clergy stood the able, though dissolute, Archbishop of St Andrews, Cardinal David Beton. For a moment it seemed as if a Reformed religion, or some northern version of Henricanism, was to have its chance. The nobles chose Arran for Regent; many of them envied the clergy; many were in Henry's pay. Arran for a while inclined towards England; he kept heretical chaplains; a parliament, in spite of clerical protest, declared that the Bible might be read in the vulgar tongue. Beton had been imprisoned; a charge of falsifying the late king's will had been brought against him. Henry's opportunity had come: the little Queen was to be wedded to Edward Tudor. But Henry was the worst of unionists. He bribed, but he also blustered, and let all men see that Scotland must be his by foul means if not by fair. A treaty was signed (1 July 1543); but within six months (11 December) it was repudiated by the Scots. Meanwhile the feeble Arran, under pressure of an interdict, had reconciled himself with Beton and had abjured his heresies. The old league with France was re-established. Henry then sent fleet and army. Edinburgh was burnt (May 1544). The Lowlands were ravaged with pitiless ferocity. The Scottish resistance was feeble. There were many traitors. The powerful Douglases played a double part. Lennox was for the English, and was rewarded with the hand of Henry's niece, Margaret Douglas. But Scotland could not be annexed, the precious child could not be captured, and Henry could not yet procure the murder of the Cardinal.

Patriotism and Catholicism were now all one. Not but that there were Protestants. One George Wishart, who had been in Switzerland and at Cambridge, was preaching the gospel, and some (but this is no better than a guess) would identify him with a Wishart who was plotting Beton's murder. He had powerful protectors, and among his disciples was a man of middle age, born in 1505, who as yet had done nothing memorable; he was priest, notary, private tutor; his name was John Knox. Wishart was arrested, tried and burnt for heresy (2 March 1546). Thereupon a band of assassins burst into the castle of St Andrews and slew Beton (29 May 1546). The leaders were well born men, Leslies, Kirkaldys, Melvilles. Their motives were various. Ancient feuds and hopes of English gold were mingled with hatred for a 'bloody butcher of the

saints of God'. They held the castle and the town. The ruffianly
and the godly flocked in. There was a strange mixture of debauchery
and gospel in the St Andrews of those days. John Knox appeared
there and was 'called' to preach to the congregation; reluctantly
(so he says) he accepted the call. The Regent had laid siege, but
had failed. At length came French ships with requisite artillery.
The besieged capitulated (July 1547); they were to be taken to
France and there liberated. John Knox was shipped off with the
rest, and was kept in the galleys for nineteen months, to meditate on
faith that justifies.

Meanwhile Henry of England had died (28 January 1547); but
the Protector Somerset was bent on marrying his boy king to the
girl queen. He had excellent projects in his head. He could speak
of a time when England and Scotland would be absorbed and
forgotten in Great Britain; but the French also were busy around
Mary Stewart. So he led an army northwards, and fought the
battle of Pinkie (10 September 1547). No more decisive defeat
could have been inflicted on the Scottish host and the Britannic
idea. Other events called Somerset home. The Scots could always
be crushed in the field, but Scotland could not be annexed. Then
came help from the good friend France, in the shape of French,
German, and Italian troops; the English employed Germans and
Spaniards. A parliament decided to accept a French proposal
(July 1548): the Queen of Scots should marry, not the English
king, but young Francis the Dauphin, and meantime should be
placed out of harm's way. She was shipped off at Dumbarton, and
landed in Brittany (13 August 1548) to pass a happy girlhood in
a lettered and luxurious court. The war was prosecuted with a
bloodthirst new in the savage annals of the borders; it was a war
fought by mercenary Almains. When peace was signed in 1550,
England had gained nothing, and upon the surface (though only
upon the surface) Scotland was as Catholic as ever it had been,
grateful to France, bitterly resentful against heretical England.

During the struggle Mary of Lorraine had borne herself bravely;
she appeared as the guiding spirit of a national resistance. She or
her advising kinsfolk were soon to make, though in less brutal sort,
the mistake that Henry VIII had made, and this time it was to
be irretrievable. During a visit to France (September 1550–
October 1551) she schemed with her brothers and the French king.
She was to take Arran's place as Regent; he had been compensated

with the duchy (no empty title) of Châtelherault, and his eldest
son (who now becomes the Arran of our story) was to command
the French King's Scots guard. The arrangement was not perfected
until 1554, for 'the second person in the kingdom' was loth to
relax his hold on a land of which he might soon be king; but the
French influence was strong, and he yielded. Mary of Lorraine
was no bad ruler for Scotland; but still the Scots could not help
seeing that she was ruling in the interest of a foreign power.
Moreover, there had been a change in the religious environment:
Mary Tudor had become Queen of England (6 July 1553). John
Knox, who after his sojourn in the French galleys had been one of
King Edward's select preachers and had narrowly escaped the
bishopric of Rochester, was fleeing to Geneva; and thence he went
to Frankfort, there to quarrel with his fellow exile Dr Cox over the
Book of Common Prayer. In Scotland Catholicism had been
closely allied with patriotism; but when England became Catholic,
Protestant preachers found refuge in Scotland. The King of France
was cherishing the intrigues of English heretics against the
Spanish queen; Mary of Lorraine was no fanatic, and her policy
was incompatible with stern repression. She was trying to make
Scotland more securely French; the task was delicate; and she
needed the support of nobles who had little love for the clergy.
A few high offices were given to Frenchmen; a few French soldiers
were kept in the fortresses; they were few, but enough to scatter
whole hosts of undrilled Scots. An attempt to impose a tax for
the support of troops was resisted, and the barons showed a strange
reluctance to fight the English. At length the time came for the
Queen's marriage (24 April 1558). The Scottish statesmen had
laboriously drawn a treaty which should guard the independence
of their realm and the rights of the house of Hamilton. This was
signed; but a few days earlier Mary Stewart had set her hand to
other documents which purported to convey Scotland for good
and all to the King of France. We may find excuses for the girl;
but, if treason can be committed by a sovereign, she was a traitor.
She had treated Scotland as a chattel. The act was secret, but the
Scots guessed much and were uneasy.

In the meantime Calvinism, for it was Calvinism now, was
spreading. After the quarrels at Frankfort, Knox had gone back
to Geneva and had sat at the master's feet. In 1555 he returned to
Scotland, no mere preacher, but an organiser also. He went

through the country, and 'Churches' of the new order sprang into being where he went. Powerful nobles began to listen, such as Lord Lorne, who was soon to be Earl of Argyll, and the Queen's bastard brother, the Lord James Stewart, who was to be Earl of Moray and regent. And politicians listened also, such as William Maitland, the young laird of Lethington. Knox was summoned before an ecclesiastical court (15 May 1556); but apparently at the last moment the hearts of the clergy failed them, and the prosecution was abandoned. It was evident that he had powerful supporters, especially the Earl of Glencairn. Moreover the natural leader of the clergy, John Hamilton, the Primate of Scotland, was a bastard brother of Châtelherault and, as a Hamilton, looked with suspicion on the French policy of Mary of Lorraine, so that the chiefs of church and state were not united. However, Knox had no mind for martyrdom; and so, after sending to the Regent an admonitory letter, which she cast aside with scornful words, he again departed for Geneva (July 1556). Then the bishops summoned him once more; but only his effigy could be burnt.

The preaching went on. In the last days of 1557 the first 'Covenant' was signed. 'The Congregation of Jesus Christ', of which Argyll, Glencairn, and other great men were members, stood out in undisguised hostility to that 'congregation of Satan' which styled itself the Catholic Church. They demanded that King Edward's Prayer Book (which was good enough for them if not for their absent inspirer) should be read in all the churches. The Regent was perplexed; the French marriage had not yet been secured; but she did not prevent the prelates from burning one Walter Milne, who was over eighty years of age (April 1558). He was the last of the Protestant martyrs; they had not been numerous, even when judged by the modest English standard; fanaticism was not among the many faults of the Scottish prelates; but for this reason his cruel death made the deeper mark. On St Giles' day (1 September) in 1558 that saint's statue was being carried through the town of Edinburgh, of which he was the patron. Under the eyes of the Regent the priests were rabbled and the idol was smashed in pieces. It was plain that the next year would be stormy; and at this crisis the face of England was once more changed.

A few weeks later Henry Percy, brother of the Earl of Northumberland, was talking with the Duke of Châtelherault. God, said the Englishman, has sent you a true and Christian religion. We are on the point of receiving the same boon. Why should you and we be enemies—we who are hardly out of our servitude to Spain; you who are being brought into servitude by France? The liberties of Scotland are in jeopardy, and the rights of the Hamiltons. Might we not unite in the maintenance of God's Word and national independence? This is the ideal which springs to light in the last months of 1558: deliverance from the toils of foreign potentates; amity between two sister nations; union in a pure religion. The duke himself was a waverer; his duchy lay in France; he is the Antoine de Bourbon of Scottish history; but his son the Earl of Arran had lately installed a Protestant preacher at Châtelherault and was in correspondence with Calvin. Percy reported this interview to an English lady who had once been offered to the duke as a bride for Arran and had just become Queen Elizabeth.

Mary, Queen of England and Spain, died on 17 November 1558. The young woman at Hatfield, who knew that her sister's days were numbered, had made the great choice. Ever since May it had been clear that she would soon be queen. The Catholics doubted and feared, but had no other candidate; King Philip was hopeful. So Elizabeth was prepared. William Cecil was to be her secretary, and England was to be Protestant. Her choice may surprise us. When a few months later she is told by the Bishop of Aquila that she has been imprudent, he seems for once to be telling the truth.

Had there been no religious dissension, her title to the throne would hardly have been contested among Englishmen. To say nothing of her father's will, she had an unrepealed statute in her favour. Divines and lawyers might indeed have found it difficult to maintain her legitimate birth. Parliament had lately declared that her father was lawfully married to Catharine of Aragon, and with this good Catholics would agree. But there was another scandal, of which good Protestants might take account. Elizabeth's godfather, the Henrician archbishop and Protestant martyr, had adjudged that Henry was never married to Anne Boleyn. His reasons died with him; but something bad, something nameless, might be guessed. It is sometimes said that Elizabeth's birth condemned her to be Protestant or bastard. But it would be truer to say that, had she cared much about legitimacy, she would have made her peace with Rome. Hints came to her thence, that the plenitude of power can set these little matters straight for the benefit of well disposed princes; and in papal eyes Cranmer's sentence would have been a prejudice in her favour. But pure legitimism, the legitimism of the divine entail, was yet in its infancy, and neither Protestant nor Catholic was bound to deny that a statute of the realm may set a bastard on the throne of William the Conqueror. For the people at large it would be enough that the Lady Elizabeth was the only living descendant of old King Henry, and that beyond her lay civil war. The thin stream of Tudor blood was running dry. Henry's will (but its validity might be questioned) had postponed the issue of his elder to that of his younger sister: in other words, the House of Scotland to the House of Suffolk. Mary Stewart was born in Scotland; she could not have inherited an acre of English land, and it was highly doubtful whether English law would give the crown to an alien who was the child of two aliens. Neither her grandmother's second marriage, namely that with Archibald Douglas (whence sprang Lady Lennox and her son Lord Darnley), nor the marriage of Mary Tudor with Charles Brandon (whence sprang Greys and Stanleys) was beyond reproach; few marriages were beyond reproach in those days of loose morals and conniving law. John Knox at Geneva had, to Calvin's regret, just blown a first blast of the trumpet against the monstrous regiment of women, and un- fortunately, though the tone was new, the tune was not. The Scottish gospeller could only repeat the biblical and other argu- ments that had been used a century ago by that Lancastrian sage, Chief Justice Fortescue. No woman had sat upon the English throne, save Mary, and she (it might be said) was a statutory queen. Many people thought that next in right to Elizabeth stood Henry Hastings, who was no Tudor but a Yorkist; and already in 1565 Philip of Spain was thinking of his own descent from Edward III. Thus Elizabeth's statutory title stood between England and wars of the roses which would also be wars of religion.

At this moment, however, she put a difference of creed between herself and the Dauphiness. It may be that in any case Henry II of France, who was in want of arguments for the retention of Calais, would have disputed Elizabeth's legitimacy; it was said that he had been prepared to dispute the legitimacy of her Catholic sister. But had Elizabeth been Catholic, the French and Scottish claim to her throne would have merely been an enemy's insult: an insult to England, a challenge to Spain. As it was, Henry might lay a strong case before the Pope and the Catholic world: Elizabeth was bastard and heretic to boot, and at this moment Paul IV was questioning Ferdinand's election to the Empire because some of his electors were Lutherans. That heretics are not to rule was no new principle; the Counts of Toulouse had felt its edge in the old Albigensian days.

After the fall of Calais in January (1558) England was panic-stricken. The French were coming; the Scots were coming; Danes and Hanseats were coming. German troops were being hastily hired to protect Northumberland. Philip's envoy, the Count of Feria, saw incompetence everywhere. The nobles held aloof, while some aged clergymen tried to conduct a war. He hardly dared to think what would happen if a few French ships touched the shore. Since then, there had been some improvement. No invader had landed, and Guise's capture of Thionville had been balanced by Egmont's victory at Gravelines. Shortly before Mary's death negotiations for a peace were begun at Cercamp; the outline of the scheme was a restoration of conquests. But Calais stopped the way. The French could not surrender that prize, and they were the more constant in their determination because the King of Spain would not much longer be King of England, and an isolated England would have no conquest to restore. When Elizabeth became queen, Calais was not yet lost; that was the worst of it. Both kings were weary of the war; behind both yawned gulfs of debt and heresy. But the ruler of the Netherlands was deeply concerned in the recovery of Calais—perhaps more materially, though less sentimentally, than were the English. Feria has reported the profound remark that when Calais was captured many Englishmen ceased to go to church. A Protestant Elizabeth might have to sign away the last memorial of old glories; and that would not fill the churches. Philip, it might be plain, would not suffer the French to invade England through Scotland; but the tie between Spain and an heretical England would be the coolest selfishness, the king's mind would be distracted between his faith and his policy, and if he were compelled to save England from the French, he certainly would not save England for the English.

True that for Protestant eyes there was light on the horizon. Anyone could see that there would be religious troubles in France and Scotland. Geneva was active, and Rome seemed to be doting.

That summer the psalms had gone up loudly from the Pré-aux-Clercs, and a Châtillon had been arrested. That autumn St Giles of Edinburgh had lain prostrate in the mud. Expectant heirs and royal cadets, Bourbons and Hamiltons, were wavering; Maximilian was listening to an enlightened pastor; France, Scotland, the Empire, might some day fall to evangelical lords. Good news came from Poland, Bohemia, and Hungary; it was even rumoured that the Pope would at last succeed in shaking Philip's faith. Still, the black fact of the moment was that Philip and Henry were making peace in order that they might crush their respective heretics. And England's military weakness was patent to all. Her soldiers and captains were disgracefully old-fashioned, and what gunpowder she had was imported from the Netherlands. 'To make a lewd comparison', said an Englishman, 'England is as a bone thrown between two dogs.' Was this bone to display an irritating activity of its own, merely because the two dogs seemed for the moment to be equal and opposite? To more than one mind came the same thought: 'They will make a Piedmont of England.'

Within the country the prospect was dubious. The people were discontented: defeat and shame, pestilence and famine had lately been their lot. A new experiment would be welcome; but it would miserably fail were it not speedily successful. No doubt, the fires in Smithfield had harmed the Catholic cause by confirming the faith and exasperating the passions of the Protestants. No doubt, the Spanish marriage was detested. But we may overestimate the dislike of persecution and the dislike of Spain. No considerable body of Englishmen would deny that obstinate heretics should be burnt. There was no need for Elizabeth to marry Philip or bring Spaniards into the land; but the Spanish alliance, the old Anglo-Burgundian alliance, was highly valued: it meant safety and trade and occasional victories over the hereditary foe. Moreover, the English Reformers were without a chief; beyond Elizabeth they had no pretender to the throne; they had no apostle, no prophet; they were scattered over Europe and had been quarrelling, Knoxians against Coxians, in their foreign abodes. Edward's reign had worn the gloss off the new theology. We may indeed be sure that, had Elizabeth adhered to the old faith, she must have quelled plots and rebellions or herself been quelled. We look at Scotland, France, and the Netherlands, and, it may be, infer that the storm would have overwhelmed her. Perhaps we forget how largely the tempests that we see elsewhere were due to the momentous choice that she made for England. It must probably be allowed that most of the young men of brains and energy who grew to manhood under Mary were lapsing from Catholicism, and that the educated women were falling faster and further. London too, Bonner's London, was Protestant, and London might be worth an abolished Mass. But when, after some years of fortunate and dexterous government, we see how strong is the old creed, how dangerous is Mary Stewart as its champion, we cannot feel sure that Elizabeth chose the path which was, or which seemed to be, the safest.

Of her own opinions she told strange tales. Puzzled by her shifty discourse, a Spanish envoy once suggested atheism. When a legal settlement had been made, it was her pleasure, and perhaps her duty, to explain that her religion was that of all sensible people. The difference between the various versions of Christianity 'n'estoit que bagatelle'. So she agreed with the pope, except about some details; she cherished the Augsburg confession, or something very like it; she was at one, or nearly at one, with the Huguenots. She may have promised her sister (but this is not proved) to make no change in religion; at any rate she had gone to mass without much ado. Nevertheless it is not unlikely that at the critical time her conduct was swayed rather by her religious beliefs or disbeliefs than by any close calculation of loss and gain. She had not her father's taste for theology; she was neither prig like her brother nor zealot like her sister; but she had been taught from the first to contemn the pope, and during Edward's reign she had been highly educated in the newest doctrines. John Hooper, the father of the Puritans, had admired her displays of argumentative divinity. More than one Catholic who spoke with her in later days was struck by her ignorance of Catholic verity. The Bishop of Aquila traced her phrases to 'the heretic Italian friars'. He seems to have been thinking of Vermigli and Ochino, and there may have been some little truth in his guess. Once she said that she liked Italian ways and manners better than any other, and sometimes seemed to herself half Italian. Her eyes filled with tears over Peter Martyr's congratulations. She had talked predestination with Fra Bernardino and had translated one of his sermons; the Puritans were persuaded that if she would listen to no one else, she would listen to him. All this might have meant little; but then she had suffered in the good cause. She had been bullied into going to mass; she had been imprisoned; she had nearly been excluded from the throne; some ardent Catholics had sought her life; and her suspected heresies had been at least a part of her offending. It would have been base to disappoint all those who had prayed for her and plotted for her, and pleasant it was when from many lands came letters which hailed her as the miraculously preserved champion of the truth. She had a text ready for the bearer of the good news: 'This is the Lord's doing and it is marvellous in our eyes.'

One point was clear. The Henrician Anglo-Catholicism was dead and buried. It died with Henry and was interred by Stephen Gardiner. In distant days its spirit might arise from the tomb; but not yet. The Count of Feria and Bishop Tunstall were at needless pains to explain to the young Queen that she was favouring 'Lutherans and Zwinglians', whom her father would have burnt. But in 1558 nothing was to be gained by mere schism. Her fellow sovereigns, more especially her brother-in-law, could have taught her that a prince might enjoy all the advantages of spotless orthodoxy and yet keep the pope at arm's length. Many Englishmen hated 'popery'; but by this time the core of the popery that they hated was no longer the papacy, but the idolatrous Mass. The choice lay between Catholicism with its pope and the creed for which Cranmer and Ridley died. It could scarcely be hoped that the bishops would yield an inch. Very shame, if no worthier motive, would keep them true to the newly restored supremacy of Rome. Happily for Elizabeth, they were few and feeble. Reginald Pole had hardly outlived Mary, and for one reason or another had made no haste in filling vacant sees; Feria thought that the 'accursed Cardinal' had French designs. And death had been and still was busy. Only sixteen instead of twenty-six bishops were entitled to attend the critical parliament, and only eleven with the Abbot of Westminster were present. Their constancy in the day of trial makes them respectable; but not one of them was a leader of men. The ablest of them had been Henry's ministers and therefore could be taunted as renegades.

A story which came from a good quarter[1] bade us see Elizabeth announcing to the Pope her accession to the throne, and not rejecting Catholicism until Paul IV declared that England was a papal fief and she a usurping bastard. Now, Caraffa was capable

[1] [See below, pp. 216–24.]

of any imprudence and just at this moment seemed bent on reviving the claims of medieval pontiffs, in order that he might drive a long-suffering Emperor into the arms of the Lutherans. But it is certain now that in the matter of courtesy Elizabeth, not Paul, was the offender. She ignored his existence. Edward Carne was living at Rome as Mary's ambassador. He received no letters of credence from the new Queen, and on 1 February 1559, she told him to come home as she had nothing for him to do. Meanwhile the French were thinking to obtain a bull against her; they hoped that at all events Paul would not allow her to marry her dead sister's husband. At Christmastide (1558), when she was making a scene in her chapel over the elevation of the host, the Pope was talking kindly of her to the French ambassador, would not promise to refuse a dispensation, but could not believe that another Englishwoman would want to marry a detestable Spaniard. A little later he knew more about her and detained Carne (a not unwilling prisoner) at Rome (27 March), not because she was base-born, but because she had revolted from the Holy See. He had just taken occasion to declare in a bull that princes guilty of heresy are deprived of all lawful power by the mere fact of their guilt (15 February). This edict, though it may have been mainly aimed at Ferdinand's three Protestant electors, was a salutary warning for Elizabeth and Anthony and Maximilian; but no names were named. Philip had influence enough to balk the French intrigue and protect his sister-in-law from a direct anathema. The Spaniard may in Paul's eyes have been somewhat worse than a heretic; but the quarrel with the other Habsburg, and then the sudden attack upon his own scandalous nephews, were enough to consume the few remaining days of the fierce old man. He has much to answer for; but it was no insult from him that made Elizabeth a Protestant.

No time was lost. Mary's death (17 November 1558) dissolved a parliament. Heath, Archbishop of York and Chancellor of the realm, dismissed it, and with loyal words proclaimed the new Queen. Within three weeks (5 December) writs went out for a new parliament. Elizabeth was going to exact conformity to a statutory religion. For the moment the statutory religion was the Roman Catholic, and she would have taken a false step if in the name of some higher law she had annulled or ignored the Marian statutes. At once she forbade innovations and thus disappointed the French who hoped for a turbulent revolution. A new and happy *et caetera* was introduced into the royal style[1] and seemed to hint, without naming, a Headship of the Church. Every change pointed one way. Some of the old Councillors were retained, but the new Councillors were Protestants. William Cecil, then aged thirty-eight, had been Somerset's and was to be Elizabeth's secretary. Like her he had gone to mass, but no Catholic doubted that he was a sad heretic. The Great Seal, resigned by Heath, was given to Nicholas Bacon. He and Cecil had married sisters who were godly ladies of the new sort. The imprisoned heretics were bailed, and the refugees flocked back from Frankfort, Zurich and Geneva. Hardly was Mary dead, before one bishop was arrested for an inopportune sermon (27 November). Another preached at her funeral (13 December) and praised her for rejecting that title which Elizabeth had not yet assumed; he too was put under restraint. Mary's chief mourner was not her sister, but, appropriately enough, the Lady Lennox who was to have supplanted Elizabeth. No bishop preached the funeral sermon for Charles V, and what good could be said of that Catholic Caesar was said by the Protestant Dr Bill (24 December). The new Queen was artist to the finger-tips. The English Bible was rapturously kissed; the Tower could not be re-entered without uplifted eyes and thankful words; her hand (it was a pretty hand) shrank, so folk said, from Bonner's lips. Christmas day was chosen for a more decisive scene. The bishop who was to say mass in her presence was told not to elevate the Host. He would not obey; so after the gospel out went Elizabeth; she could no longer witness that idolatry. Three weeks later (15 January) she was crowned while Calvin was dedicating to her his comments on Isaiah. What happened at the coronation is obscure. The bishops, it seems, swore fealty in the accustomed manner; the epistle and gospel were read in English; it is said that the celebrant was one of the Queen's chaplains and that he did not elevate the Host; it is said that she did not communicate; she was anointed by the Bishop of Carlisle, whose rank would not have entitled him to this office, had not others refused it. At length the day came for a parliament (25 January). A mass was said at Westminster early in the morning. At a later hour the Queen approached the Abbey with her choir singing in English. The last of the abbots came to meet her with monks and candles. 'Away with those torches' she

---

[1] [See below, pp. 211–16.]

exclaimed: 'we can see well enough!' And then Edward's tutor, Dr Cox, late of Frankfort, preached; and he preached, it is said, for an hour and a half, the peers all standing.

The negotiations between Spain, England and France had been brought to a pause by Mary's death, but were to be resumed after a brief interval, during which Elizabeth was to make up her mind. Some outwardly amicable letters passed between her and Henry II. She tried to play the part of the pure-bred Englishwoman, who should not suffer for the sins of the Spanish Mary. But the French were not to be coaxed out of Calais, and she knew that they were seeking a papal bull against her. It became plain that she must not detach herself from Spain and that, even with Philip's help, Calais could only be obtained after another war, for which England was shamefully unready. Then, in the middle of January, came through Feria the expected offer of Philip's hand. Elizabeth seemed to hesitate, had doubts about the pope's dispensing power and so forth; but in the end said that she did not mean to marry, and added that she was a heretic. Philip, it seems, was relieved by the refusal; he had laboriously explained to his ambassador that his proposal was a sacrifice laid upon the altar of the Catholic faith. He had hopes, which were encouraged in England, that one of his Austrian cousins, Ferdinand or Charles, would succeed where he had failed, secure England for orthodoxy, and protect the Netherlands from the ill example that an heretical England would set.

Meanwhile the great Treaty of Cateau-Cambrésis was in the making. Elizabeth tried to retain Philip's self-interested support; and she retained it. Without substantial aid from England, he would not fight for Calais; she would have to sign it away; but so earnest had he been in this matter that the French covenanted to restore the treasured town after eight years and further to pay half-a-million of crowns by way of penalty in case they broke their promise. No one supposed that they would keep it; still they had consented to make the retention of Calais a just cause for war, and Elizabeth could plausibly say that some remnants of honour had been saved. But the clouds collected once more. New differences broke out among the negotiators, who had half a world to regulate, and, before the intricate settlement could be completed, a marriage had been arranged between Philip and one of Henry's daughters. Elizabeth of France, not Elizabeth of England, was to be the bride. The conjunction was ominous for heretics.

From the first days of February to the first days of April the negotiations had been pending. Meanwhile in England little had been accomplished. It had become plain that the clergy in possession (but there was another and expectant clergy out of possession) would not yield. The Convocation of Canterbury met when parliament met, and the Lower House declared for tran-substantiation, the sacrifice of the Mass, and the Roman supremacy; also it idly protested that laymen were not to meddle with faith, worship, or discipline (17 February 1559). The bishops were staunch; the English Church by its constitutional organs refused to reform itself; the Reformation would be an unprecedented state-stroke. Probably the assembled Commons were willing to strike. The influence of the crown had been used on the Protestant side; but Cecil had hardly gathered the reins in his hand and the government's control over the electoral machinery must have been unusually weak. Our statistics are imperfect, but the number of knights and burgesses who, having served in 1558, were again returned in 1559 was not abnormally small, and with the House of 1558 Mary had been well content. Also we may see at Westminster not a few men who soon afterwards are 'hinderers of true religion' or at best only 'faint professors'; but probably the nation at large was not unwilling that Elizabeth should make her experiment. A few creations and restorations of peerages strengthened the Protestant element among the lords. The Earl of Bedford and Lord Clinton appeared as proxies for many absent peers, and, of all the lords, Bedford (Francis Russell) was the most decisively committed to radical reform. The Howards were for the Queen, their cousin; the young Duke of Norfolk, England's one duke, was at this time ardently Protestant, and in the next year was shocked at the sight of undestroyed altars.

Money was cheerfully voted. The Queen was asked to choose a husband, and professed her wish to die a maid. She may have meant what she said, but assuredly did not mean that it should be believed. A prudently phrased statute announced that she was 'lawfully descended and come of the blood royal'; another declared her capable of inheriting from her divorced and attainted mother; the painful past was veiled in general words. There was little difficulty about a resumption of those tenths and first-fruits which Mary had abandoned. Round the question of ecclesiastical supremacy the battle raged, and it raged for two months and more (9 February to 29 April).[1] Seemingly the Queen's ministers carried through the Lower House a bill which went the full Henrician length in its Caesaro-papalism and its severity. Upon pain of a traitor's death, everyone was to swear that Elizabeth was the Supreme Head of the Church of England. In the Upper House, to which the bill came on 27 February, the bishops had to oppose a measure which would leave the lives of all open Romanists at the mercy of the government. Few though they were, the dozen prelates could still do much in a House where there were rarely more than thirty temporal lords, and probably Cecil had asked for more than he wanted. On 18 March the project had taken a far milder form; forfeiture of office and benefice was to be the punishment of those who would not swear. Against this more lenient measure only two temporal lords protested; but a Catholic says that other 'good Christians' were feigning to be ill. The bill went back to the Commons; then back with amendments to the Lords, who read it thrice on the 22nd. Easter fell on the 26th, and it had been hoped that by that time parliament would have finished its work. Very little had been done; doctrine and worship had hardly been touched. Apparently an attempt to change the services of the Church had been made, had met with resistance, and had been abandoned.

Elizabeth was in advance of the law and beckoned the nation forward. During that Lent the Court sermon had been the only sermon, the preacher Scory or Sandys, Grindal or Cox. A papist's excited fancy saw a congregation of five thousand and heard extravagant blasphemy. On Easter day the Queen received the Communion in both kinds; the news ran over Europe; Antoine de Bourbon on the same day had done the like at Pau; Mary of Lorraine had marked that festival for the return of all Scots to the Catholic worship. The colloquy of Westminster follows. There was to be a trial by battle in the abbey between chosen champions of the two faiths. Its outcome might make us suspect that a trap was laid by the Protestants. But it is by no means certain that the challenge came from their side, and the Spanish ambassador took some credit for arranging the combat. The colloquy of Westminster stands midway between that of Worms (1557) and that of Poissy (1561). The Catholics were wont to get the better in these feats of arms, because, so soon as Christ's presence in the eucharist

[1] [See below, pp. 229–46.]

was mentioned, the Protestants fell a-fighting among themselves. Apparently on this occasion the rules of the debate were settled by Heath and Bacon. The Great Seal had passed from an amiable to an abler keeper. The men of the Old Learning were to defend the use of Latin in the services of the Church, to deny that a 'particular church' can change rites and ceremonies and to maintain the propitiatory sacrifice of the Mass. Their first two theses would bring them into conflict with national feeling; and at the third point they would be exposed to the united force of Lutherans and Helvetians, for the sacrifice, and not the presence, was to be debated. It was a less advantage for the Reformers that their adversaries were to speak first, for there was to be no extemporary argument but only a reading of written dissertations. In the choir of the abbey, before Council, Lords, Commons and multitude, the combatants took their places on Friday, 31 March. At once the Catholics began to except against the rules that they were required to observe. Dr Cole, however, maintained their first proposition and Dr Horne read the Protestant essay. The Reformers were well content with that day's work and the applause that followed. On Monday the second question was to be handled. Of what happened we have no impartial account; we do not know what had passed between Heath and Bacon, or whether the Catholic doctors were taken by surprise. Howbeit, they chose the worst course; they wrangled about procedure and refused to continue the debate. Apparently they were out of heart and leaderless. Two of the bishops were forthwith imprisoned by the Council for intemperate words, and thus the Catholic party in the House of Lords was seriously weakened at a critical moment. Moreover, the inference that men do not break off a debate with preliminary objections when they are confident of success in the main issue, though it is not always just, is always natural.

The next day parliament resumed its work. Meanwhile, Elizabeth had at length decided that she would not assume the Henrician title, though assuredly she had meant that it should be, as it had been, offered to her. Women should keep silence in the churches; so there was difficulty about a 'dumb head'. She had managed to get a little credit from Philip's envoy and a little from zealous Calvinists by saying that she would not be Head of the Church, and she could then tell appropriate persons that she scorned a style which the pope had polluted. So Cecil had to go to the Commons and explain that there must be a new bill and new oath. He met with some opposition, for there were who held that the Queen was Supreme Head *iure divino*. Ultimately a phrase was fashioned which declared that she was the only Supreme Governor of the realm as well in all spiritual or ecclesiastical things or causes as in temporal, and that no foreign prince or prelate had any ecclesiastical or spiritual authority within her dominions. However, among other statutes of Henry VIII, one was revived which proclaims that the King is Head of the Church, and that by the word of God all ecclesiastical jurisdiction flows from him. Catholics suspected that Elizabeth's husband would be head of the Church, if not head of his wife, and saw the old title concealed behind the new *et caetera*. Protestant lawyers said that she could take the title whenever she pleased. Sensible men saw that, having the substance, she could afford to waive the irritating name. On 14 April the bill was before the Lords. There were renewed debates and more changes; and the famous Act of Supremacy was not finally secured until the 29th.

In the last days of an unusually long session a bill for the Uniformity of Religion went rapidly through both Houses (18–28 April). The services prescribed in a certain Book of Common Prayer, and none other, were to be lawful. The embryonic history of this measure is obscure. An informal committee of Protestant divines seems to have been appointed by the Queen to prepare a book. It has been thought that as the basis of their labours they took the Second Book of Edward VI, but desired a further simplification of ceremonies. On the other hand, there are some signs that Cecil and the Queen thought that the Second Book, which had hardly been introduced before it was abrogated, had already gone far enough or too far in the abolition of accustomed rites. All this, however, is very uncertain. Our guess may be that, when men were weary of the prolonged debate over the Supremacy and its continuance was becoming a national danger (for violent speeches had been made), the Queen's advisers took the short course of proposing the Book of 1552 with very few changes. At such a moment relief might be found in what could be called a mere act of restoration, and the Edwardian Book, however unfamiliar, was already ennobled by the blood of martyrs. There are signs of haste, or of divided counsels, for the new Book when it came from the press differed in some little, but not trivial, matters from that which parliament had expressly sanctioned. The changes sanctioned by parliament were few. An offensive phrase about the Bishop of Rome's 'detestable enormities' was expunged, apparently by the House of Lords. An addition from older sources was made to the words that accompany the delivery of bread and wine to the communicant, whereby a charge of the purest Zwinglianism might be obviated. At the moment it was of importance to Elizabeth that she should assure the German princes that her religion was Augustan; for they feared, and not without cause, that it was Helvetian. A certain 'black rubric' which had never formed part of the statutory book fell away; it would have offended Lutherans; we have reason to believe that it had been inserted in order to meet the scruples of John Knox. Of what was done in the matter of ornaments by the statute, by the rubrics of the Book and by 'injunctions' that the Queen promptly issued, it would be impossible to speak fairly without a lengthy quotation of documents, the import of which became in the nineteenth century a theme of prolonged and inconclusive disputation. It must here suffice that there are few signs of any of the clergymen who accepted the Prayer Book either having worn or having desired to wear in the ordinary churches—there was at times a little more splendour in cathedrals—any ecclesiastical robe except the surplice. But, to return to Elizabeth's parliament, we have it on fairly good authority that nine temporal lords, including the treasurer (the Marquis of Winchester), and nine prelates (two bishops were in gaol) voted against the bill, and that it was only carried by three votes. Unfortunately at an exciting moment there is a gap, perhaps a significant gap, in the official record, and we cease to know what lords were present in the house. But about thirty temporal peers had lately been in attendance, and so we may infer that some of them were inclined neither to alter the religion of England nor yet to oppose the Queen. On 5 May, the bishops were fighting in vain for the renovated monasteries. On the 8th, parliament was dissolved.

At a moment of strain and peril a wonderfully durable settlement had been made. There is cause for thinking that the Queen's advisers had been compelled to abandon considerable parts of a lengthy programme; but the great lines had been drawn and were permanent. For this reason they can hardly be described in words that are both just and few; but perhaps we may make a summary of those points which were the most important to the men of 1559. A radical change in doctrine, worship and discipline has been made by Queen and parliament against the will of prelates and ecclesiastical councils. The legislative power of the convocations is once more subjected to royal control. The derivation of episcopal from royal jurisdiction has been once more asserted in the words of Henry VIII. Appeal from the courts of the Church lies to royal delegates who may be laymen. What might fairly be called a plenitude of ecclesiastical jurisdiction of the corrective sort can be, and at once is, committed to delegates who constitute what is soon known as the Court of High Commission and strongly resembles the consistory of a German Prince. Obstinate heresy is still a capital crime; but practically the bishops have little power of forcing heretics to stand a trial, and, unless parliament and convocation otherwise ordain, only the wilder sectaries will be in danger of burning. There is no 'liberty of cult'. The Prayer Book prescribes the only lawful form of common worship. The clergyman who adopts any other, even in a private chapel, commits a crime; so does he who procures this aberration from conformity. Everyone must go to church on Sunday and bide prayer and preaching or forfeit twelve pence to the use of the poor. Much also can be done to ensure conformity by excommunication which has imprisonment behind it. The papal authority is abolished. Clergy and office-holders can be required to swear that it is naught; if they refuse the oath, they lose office and benefice. If anyone advisedly maintains that authority, he forfeits his goods; on a third conviction he is a traitor. The service book is not such as will satisfy all ardent Reformers; but their foreign fathers in the faith think it not intolerable, and the glad news goes out that the Mass is abolished. The word 'Protestant', which is rapidly spreading from Germany, comes as a welcome name. In the view of an officially inspired apologist of the Elizabethan settlement, those who are not Papists are Protestants.

The requisite laws had been made, but whether they would take effect was very uncertain. The new oath was not tendered to the judges; and some of them were decided Romanists. Nor was the validity of the statutes unquestioned, for it was by no means so plain as it now is that an act against which the spiritual Lords have voted in a body may still be an act of the three Estates. Gradually in the summer and autumn the bishops were called upon to swear; they refused and were deprived. It is not certain that the one weak brother, Kitchin of Llandaff, actually swore the oath, though he promised to exact it from others. Futile hopes seem to have been entertained that Tunstall and Heath would at least take part in the consecration of their Protestant successors. Such successors were nominated by the Queen; but to make bishops of them was not easy. Apparently a government bill dealing with this matter had come to naught. Probably the Queen's advisers had intended to abolish the canonical election; they procured its abolition in Ireland on the ground that it was inconsistent with the royal supremacy; but for some cause or another the English parliament had restored that grotesque Henrician device, the compulsory election of a royal nominee. By a personal interview Elizabeth secured the conversion of the dean of the two metropolitan churches, that pliant old diplomat Nicholas Wotton. When sees and benefices were rapidly falling vacant, his adhesion was of great importance if all was to be done in an orderly way.

But given the election, there must still be confirmation and consecration; statute required it. The co-operation of four 'bishops' would be necessary if Matthew Parker was to sit where Reginald Pole had sat. Four men in episcopal orders might be found: for instance, William Barlow, of whose Protestant religion there could be no doubt, since Albert of Prussia had lately attested it; but these men would not be in possession of English sees. Moreover, it seems to have been doubted whether the Edwardian Ordinal had been revived as part of the Edwardian Prayer Book. Cecil was puzzled, but equal to the occasion. In a document redolent of the papal chancery Elizabeth 'supplied' all 'defects', and at length on 17 December, in the chapel at Lambeth, Parker was consecrated with Edwardian rites by Barlow, Scory, Coverdale and Hodgkin. The story of a simpler ceremony at the Nag's Head tavern was not concocted until long afterwards; it should have for pendants a Protestant fable which told of a dramatic scene between Elizabeth and the Catholic prelates, and an Anglican fable which strove to suggest that the Prayer Book was sanctioned by a synod of bishops and clergy.[1] A large number of deans and canons followed the example set by the bishops. Of their inferiors hardly more than two hundred, so it seems, were deprived for refusing the oath. The royal commissioners treated the hesitating priests with patient forbearance; and the meaning of the oath was minimised by an ably worded proclamation. We may conjecture

[1] [See below, pp. 247–58.]

that many of those who swore expected another turn of the always turning wheel. However, Elizabeth succeeded in finding creditable occupants for the vacant dignities; of Parker and some of his suffragans more than this might be said. The new service was introduced without exciting disturbances; the altars and roods were pulled down, tables were purchased, and a coat of whitewash veiled the pictured saints from view. Among the laity there was much despondent indifference. Within a dozen years there had been four great changes in worship, and no good had come of it all. For some time afterwards there are many country gentlemen whom the bishops describe as 'indifferent in religion'. Would the Queen's church secure them and their children? That question could not be answered by one who looked only at England. From the first, Elizabeth and Cecil, who were entering into their long partnership, had looked abroad.

The month of May 1559, which saw the ratification of the Treaty of Cateau-Cambrésis, is a grand month in the annals of the heresy which was to be destroyed. A hideous act of faith at Valladolid may show us that Catholicism is safe in Spain; but the English parliament ends its work, a French Reformed Church shapes itself in the synod of Paris, and Scotland bursts into flame. In 1558 we saw it glowing. Mary of Guise was temporising; she had not yet obtained the crown matrimonial for the Dauphin. In the winter parliament she had her way; the crown was to be (but never was) carried to her son-in-law. His father had just ceased his intrigues with English Protestants, and was making peace in order that he might be busy among the Protestants of France. The Regent of Scotland was given to understand that the time for tolerance was past. In March 1559, the Scottish prelates followed the example of their English brethren and uttered their *Non possumus*. They proposed to remedy many an indefensible abuse, but to new beliefs there could be no concession. The Queen-mother fixed Easter day for the return of all men to the Catholic worship. The order was disregarded. On 10 May the more notorious of the preachers were to answer at Stirling for their misdeeds. They collected at Perth, with Protestant lords around them. At this moment Elizabeth's best friend sprang into the arena. John Knox had been fuming at Dieppe. Elizabeth, enraged at his ill-timed 'blast', denied him a safe-conduct. François

Morel, too, the French Reformer, implored Calvin to keep this fire-brand out of England lest all should be spoilt. But if Knox chose to revisit his native land that was no affair of Elizabeth's, and he was predestinated to win for Calvinism the most durable of its triumphs. He landed in Scotland on 2 May and was at Perth by the 11th. Then there was a sermon; a stone was thrown; an image was broken, and the churches of St Johnston were wrecked. Before the end of the month there were two armed hosts in the field. There were more sermons, and where Knox preached the idols fell and monks and nuns were turned adrift. There were futile negotiations and disregarded truces. At the head of the belligerent Congregation rode Glencairn, Argyll, and Lord James. Châtel-herault was still with the Regent; and she had a small force of disciplined Frenchmen. At the end of July a temporary truce was made at Leith. The Congregation could bring a numerous host (of the medieval sort) into the field, but could not keep it there. However, as the power of the French soldiers was displayed, the revolutionary movement became more and more national. The strife, if it was between Catholic and Calvinist, was also a strife for the delivery of Scotland from a foreign army. None the less there was a revolt. Thenceforth, Calvinism often appears as a rebellious religion. This, however, is its first appearance in that character. Calvin had long been a power in the world of Reformed theology, and his death (1564) was not far distant; but in 1559 the Count of Feria was at pains to tell King Philip that 'this Calvin is a French-man and a great heretic' (19 March). Knox, when he preached 'the rascal multitude' into iconoclastic fury, was setting an example to *Gueux* and Huguenots. What would Elizabeth think of it?

Throughout the winter and spring Englishmen and Scots, who had been dragged into war by their foreign masters, had been meeting on the border and talking first of armistice and then of peace. Already in January Maitland of Lethington had a strong desire to speak with Sir William Cecil and since then had been twice in London. He was the Regent's Secretary, conforming in religion as Cecil had conformed; but it is likely that the core of such creed as he had was unionism. The news that came from Scotland in May can hardly have surprised the English Secretary. 'Some great consequences must needs follow': this was his quiet comment (26 May). Diplomatic relations with France had just been resumed. Nicholas Throckmorton, one of those able men who begin to collect around Elizabeth, had gone to reside there as her ambassador, had gone to 'practise' there and exacerbate the 'garboils' there. One of the first bits of news that he sends home is that Arran has been summoned to Court from Poitou, where he has been Calvinising, has disobeyed the summons and cannot be found (30 May). The Guises connect Arran's disappearance with Throckmorton's advent; and who shall say that they are wrong? In June Cecil heard from the border that the Scottish lords were devising how this young man could be brought home and married 'you know where'. 'You have a Queen', said a Scot to Throckmorton, 'and we our Prince the Earl of Arran, marriable both, and the chief upholders of God's religion.' Arran might soon be King of Scotland. The Dauphiness, who at the French Court was being called Queen of England, did not look as if she were long for this world: Throckmorton noted her swoons. Arran had escaped to Geneva. Early in July Elizabeth was busy, and so was Calvin, over the transmission of this invaluable youth to the quarter where he could best serve God and the English Queen. Petitions for aid had come from Scotland. Cecil foresaw what would happen: the Protestants were to be helped 'first with promises, next with money, and last with arms' (8 July). But to go beyond the first stage was hazardous. The late King of England was only a few miles off with his fleet and veteran troops; he was being married by proxy to a French Princess; he had thoughts of enticing Catharine Grey out of England, in order that he might have another candidate for the throne, if it were necessary to depose the disobedient Elizabeth. And could Elizabeth openly support these rebels? In the answer to that question lay the rare importance of Arran. The Scottish uproar must become a constitutional movement directed by a prince of the blood royal against a French attempt to deprive a nation of its independence. Cecil explained to Calvin that if true religion is to be supported it must first convert great noblemen (22 June).

Then the danger from France seemed to increase. There was a mischance at a tournament and Henry II was dead (10 July). The next news was that 'the House of Guise ruleth' (13 July). In truth, this was good news. Elizabeth's adversary was no longer a united France. The Lorrainers were not France; their enemies told them that they were not French. But the Duke and Cardinal were ruling France; they came to power as the uncles of the young

King's wife, and soon there might be a boy born who would be Valois-Tudor-Stewart-Guise. A Guise was ruling Scotland also, and the rebellion against her was hanging fire. So early in August Cecil's second stage was reached, and Ralph Sadler was carrying three thousand pounds to the border. He knew his Scotland; Henry VIII had sent him there on a fool's errand; there would be better management this time. In the same month Philip turned his back on the Netherlands, never to see them more. Thenceforth, he would be the secluded king of a distant country. Also, Paul IV died, and for four months the Roman Church had no supreme governor. The Supreme Governor of the English Church could breathe more freely. She kept her St Bartholomew (24 August). There was burning in Bartlemy Fair, burning in Smithfield—but only of wooden roods and Maries and Johns and such-like popish gear. 'It is done of purpose to confirm the Scottish revolt': such was a guess made at Brussels (2 September); and it may have been right, for there was little of the natural iconoclast in Elizabeth. A few days later (29 August) Arran was safely and secretly in her presence, and thence was smuggled into Scotland. Probably she took his measure; he was not quite sane, but would be useful. Soon afterwards Philip's ambassador knew that she was fomenting tumults in Scotland through 'a heretic preacher called Knox'. That was unkindly said, but not substantially untrue. Early in October 'the Congregation' began once more to take an armed shape. Châtelherault, that unstable 'second person', had been brought over by his impetuous son. The French troops in Scotland had been reinforced; the struggle was between Scot and Frenchman. So, to the horror of bishops-elect (whose consecration had not yet been managed), the table in Elizabeth's chapel began to look like an altar with cross and candles. 'She will not favour the Scots in their religion', said Gilles de Noailles the French ambassador. 'She is afraid', said the Cardinal of Lorraine. 'She is going to marry the Archduke Charles who is coming here in disguise', said many people. Surely she wished that just those comments should be made; and so Dr Cox, by this time elect of Ely, had to stomach cross and candles as best he might.

The host of the Congregation arrived at Edinburgh; a manifesto declared that the Regent was deposed (21 October). She and the French were fortifying Leith; the castle was held by the neutral Lord Erskine. But once more the extemporised army began to melt away. Treasure sent by Elizabeth was captured by a border ruffian, James Hepburn, Earl of Bothwell, who was to play a part in coming tragedies. The insurgents fled from Edinburgh (6 November). In negotiation with Cecil, Knox was showing the worldly wisdom that underlay his Hebraic frenzies; he knew the weak side of his fellow-countrymen; without more aid from England, the movement would fail. Knox, however, was not presentable at Court; Lethington was. The Regent's Secretary had left her and had carried to the opposite camp the statecraft that it sorely needed. He saw a bright prospect for his native land and took the road to London. Cecil's third stage was at hand. There were long debates in the English Council; there were 'Philipians' in it, and all that passed there was soon known at the French embassy. The Queen was irresolute; even Bacon was for delay; but, though some French ships had been wrecked, others were ready, and the danger to Scotland, and through Scotland to England, was very grave. At length Cecil and Lethington won their cause. An army under the Duke of Norfolk was to be raised and placed on the border. Large supplies of arms had been imported from the dominions of the Catholic king. Bargains for professed soldiers were struck with German princes. William Winter, Master of the Ordnance, was to take fourteen ships to the Forth. He might 'as of his own hand' pick a quarrel with the French; but there was to be no avowed war (16 December). On the morrow Dr Parker was consecrated. He had been properly shocked by Knox's doings. 'God keep us from such visitation as Knox hath attempted in Scotland: the people to be orderers of things!' (6 November). If in that autumn the people of Scotland had not ordered things in a summary way, Dr Parker's tenure of the archiepiscopate might have been precarious. A few days later and there was once more a pope (25 December): this time a sane pope, Pius IV, who would have to deplore the loss, not only of England, but of Scotland also. God of His mercy, said Lethington, had removed that difference of religion.

Once more the waves were kind to Elizabeth. They repulsed the Marquis of Elbeuf (René of Lorraine), and suffered Winter to pass. All the news that came from France was good. It told of unwillingness that national treasure should be spent in the cause of the Guises, of a dearth of recruits for Scotland, of heretics burnt and heretics rescued, of factions in religion fomented by the great.

Something was very wrong in France, for envoys came thence with soft words. 'Strike now', was Throckmorton's counsel; 'they only seek to gain time.' So a pact was signed at Berwick (27 February 1560) between Norfolk and the Scottish lords who acted on behalf of 'the second person of the realm of Scotland'. Elizabeth took Scotland, its liberties, its nobility, its expectant heir under her protection, and the French were to be expelled. On second thoughts nothing was published about 'the profession of Christ's true religion'. Every French envoy spoke softer than the last. Mary Stewart had assumed the arms of England because she was proud of being Elizabeth's cousin. The title of Queen of England was taken to annoy, not Elizabeth, but Mary Tudor. All this meant the Tumult of Amboise (14–20 March). Behind that strange essay in rebellion, behind la Renaudie, men have seen Condé, and behind Condé two dim figures, Jean Calvin and the English Queen. Calvin's acquittal seems deserved. The profession of Christ's true religion was not to be advanced by so ill laid a plot. But a very ill laid plot might cripple France at this critical moment, and, before we absolve Elizabeth, we wish to know why a certain Tremaine was sent to Brittany, where the plotters were gathering, and whether Chantonnay, Granvelle's brother, was right in saying that la Renaudie had been at the English court. Certain it is that Throckmorton had intrigued with Anthony of Navarre, with the Vidame of Chartres, with every enemy of the Guises; he was an apt pupil in the school that Renard and Noailles had founded in England. A little later (23 May) messages from Condé to the Queen were going round by Strassburg; and in June Tremaine brought from France a scheme which would put Breton or Norman towns into English hands: a scheme from which Cecil as yet recoiled as from 'a bottomless pit'.

Be all this as it may, the Tumult of Amboise fell pat into Cecil's scheme, and on 29 March Lord Grey crossed the border with English troops. The Scottish affair then takes this shape: A small but disciplined force of Frenchmen in the fortified town of Leith; the Regent in Edinburgh Castle, which is held by the neutral Erskine; English ships in the Forth; an English and Scottish army before Leith; very few Scots openly siding with the Queen-mother; the French seeking to gain time. We hasten to the end. An assault failed, but hunger was doing its work. The Regent died on 11 June; even stern Protestants have a good word for the gallant woman.

Cecil went into Scotland to negotiate with French plenipotentiaries. He wrung from them the Treaty of Edinburgh, which was signed on 6 July. The French troops were to quit Scotland. The French king and queen were never thereafter to use the arms and style of England. Compensation for the insult to her title was to be awarded to Elizabeth by arbitrators or the King of Spain. A pact concluded between Francis and Mary on the one hand and their Scottish subjects on the other was to be observed. That pact itself was humiliating. There was to be pardon for the insurgents; there were to be but six score French soldiers in the land; a Scottish Council was to be appointed: in a word, Scotland was to be for the Scots. But the lowest point was touched when the observance of this pact between sovereign and rebels was made a term in the treaty between England and France. Cecil and famine were inexorable. We had to sign, said the French commissioners, or four thousand brave men would have perished before our eyes and Scotland would have been utterly lost.

And so the French troops were deported from Scotland and the English army came home from a splendid exploit. The military display, it is true, had not been creditable; there had been disunion, if no worse, among the captains; there had been peculation, desertion, sheer cowardice. All the martial glory goes to the brave besieged. But for the first time an English army marched out of Scotland leaving gratitude behind. Perhaps the truest victory that England had won was won over herself. Not a word had been publicly said of that old suzerainty; no spoil had been taken, not a town detained. Knox included in his liturgy a prayer that there might nevermore be war between Scotland and England, and that prayer has been fulfilled. There have been wars between British factions, but never another truly national war between the two nations. Elizabeth in her first two years 'had done what none of her ancestors could do, for by the occasion of her religion she had obtained the amity of Scotland, and thus had God blemished the fame of the great men of the world through the doings of a weak woman': such was the judgment of a daughter of France and a mother in the Protestant Israel, of Renée, the venerable Duchess of Ferrara. Another observer, Hubert Languet, said that the English were so proud of the conversion of Scotland that they were recovering their old insolence and would be the very people to defy the imminent Council at Trent. The tone of Catholic correspondence changes: the Elizabeth who was merely rushing to her ruin will now set all Europe alight in her downward course. That young woman's conduct, when we now examine it, will not seem heroic. As was often to happen in coming years, she had been pursuing two policies at once, and she was ready to fall back upon an Austrian marriage if the Scottish revolt miscarried. But this was not what men saw at the time. What was seen was that she and Cecil had played and won a masterly game; and Englishmen must have felt that the change of religion coincided with a transfer of power from incapable to capable hands.

All this had been done, not only without Spanish help, but (so a patriot might say) in defiance of Spain. To discover Philip's intentions had been difficult, and in truth he had been of two minds. Elizabeth was setting the worst of examples. Say what she would, she was encouraging a Protestant revolt against a Catholic king. She was doing this in sight, and with the hardly concealed applause, of the Netherlanders; a friar who dared to preach against her at Antwerp went in fear of his life; whole families of Flemings were already taking refuge in England. Philip's new French wife was coming home to him; his mother-in-law, Catharine de' Medici, implored him to stop Elizabeth from 'playing the fool'. He had in some kind made himself responsible for the religious affairs of England, by assuring the Pope that all would yet be well. But the intense dread of France, the outcome of long wars, could not be eradicated, and was reasonable enough. He dared not let the French subdue Scotland and threaten England on both sides. Moreover he was for the moment miserably poor; Margaret of Parma, his regent in the Netherlands, had hardly a crown for current expenses, and the Estates would grant nothing. So in public he scolded and lectured Elizabeth, while in private he hinted that what she was doing should be done quickly. The French, too, though they asked his aid, hardly wished him to fulfil his promise of sending troops to Scotland. Then his navy was defeated by the opportune Turk (11 May); and the Spaniards suspected that the French, if guiltless of, were not displeased at the disaster.

This was not all. The Pope also had been humiliated. The conciliatory Pius IV had not long been on the throne before he sent to Elizabeth a courteous letter (5 May 1560). Vincent Parpaglia, the Abbot of San Solutore at Turin, once the secretary of Cardinal

Pole, was to carry it to her as Nuncio. She was to lend him her ear, and a strong hint was given to her that she could be legitimated. When she heard that the Nuncio was coming, she was perhaps a little frightened; the choice between recantation and the anathema seemed to lie before her; so she talked catholically with the Spanish ambassador. But Philip, when he heard the news, was seriously offended. He saw a French intrigue, and the diplomatic machinery of the Spanish monarchy was set in motion to procure the recall of the Nuncio. All manner of reasons could be given to the Pope to induce a cancellation of his rash act. Pius was convinced or overawed. Margaret of Parma stopped Parpaglia at Brussels. How to extricate the Pope from the adventure without loss of dignity was then the difficult question. Happily it could be said that Pole's secretary was personally distasteful to Philip, who had once imprisoned Parpaglia as a French spy. So at Brussels he enjoyed himself for some months, then announced to Elizabeth that after all he was not coming to her, and in the friendliest way sent her some Italian gossip (8 September). He said that he should go back by Germany, and, when he turned aside to France, Margaret of Parma knew what to think: namely, that there had been a French plot to precipitate a collision between Pius and Elizabeth. At the French Court the disappointed Nuncio 'made a very lewd discourse of the Queen, her religion and proceedings'. As to Elizabeth, she had answered this first papal approach by throwing the Catholic bishops into prison. And then, it is to be feared that she, or someone on her behalf, told how the Pope had offered to confirm her Book of Common Prayer, if only she would fall down and worship him.

In August 1560 a parliament met at Edinburgh, to do for Scotland what the English parliament had done in 1559. The pope's authority was rejected, and the Mass was abolished. Upon a third conviction the sayer or hearer of mass was to be put to death. A Confession of Faith had been rapidly compiled by Knox and his fellow preachers; it is said that Lethington toned down asperities. 'To see it pass in such sort as it did' surprised Elizabeth's envoy Randolph. The Scot was not yet a born theologian. Lethington hinted that further amendments could be made if Elizabeth desired them (13 September), and she made bold to tell the Lutheran princes that Scotland had received 'the same religion that is used in Almaine' (30 December). The Reforming preachers were few, but the few earnest Catholics were cowed. 'This people of a later calling', as an English preacher called the Scots, had not known the disappointment of a young Josiah's reign, and heard the word with gladness. There were wide differences, however, between the proceedings of the two parliaments. The English problem was comparatively simple. Long before 1559 the English Church had been relieved of superfluous riches; there was only a modest aftermath for the Elizabethan scythe. In Scotland the kirk-lands were broad, and were held by prelates or quasi-prelates who were turning Protestant or were closely related to Lords of the Congregation. Catholic or Calvinist, the possessor meant to keep a tight grip on the land. The bishops could be forbidden to say mass; some of them had no desire to be troubled with that or any other duty; but the decent Anglican process, which substitutes an Edmund Grindal for an Edmund Bonner, could not be imitated. The Scottish lords, had they wished it, could not have thrust an ecclesiastical supremacy upon their Catholic Queen; but to enrich the crown was not their mind. The new preachers naturally desired something like that proprietary continuity which had been preserved in England: the patrimony of the Church should sustain the new religion. They soon discovered that this was 'a devout imagination'. They had to construct an ecclesiastical polity on new lines, and they set to work upon a Book of Discipline. Elementary questions touching the relation between church and state were left open. Even the proceedings of the August parliament were of doubtful validity. Contrary to wont, a hundred or more of the 'minor barons' had formed a part of the assembly. Also, it was by no means clear that the compact signed by the French envoys authorised a parliament to assemble and do what it pleased in matters of religion.

An excuse had been given to the French for a refusal to ratify the treaty with England. That treaty confirmed a convention which the Scots were already breaking. Another part of the great project was not to be fulfilled. Elizabeth was not going to marry Arran, though the Estates of Scotland begged this of her and set a united kingdom of Great Britain and Ireland before her eyes. Perhaps it was well that Arran was crazy; otherwise there might have been a premature enterprise. A king of Scots who was husband of the English Queen would have been hateful in England; Scotland was not prepared for English methods of government; and

Elizabeth had troubles enough to face without barbaric blood feuds and a Book of Discipline. She had gained a great advantage. Sudden as had been the conversion of Scotland, it was permanent. Beneath all that was fortuitous and all that was despicable, there was a moral revolt. 'It is almost miraculous', wrote Randolph in the June of 1560, 'to see how the word of God takes place in Scotland. They are better willing to receive discipline than in any country I ever was in. Upon Sunday before noon and after there were at the sermons that confessed their offences and repented their lives before the congregation. Cecil and Dr Wotton were present....They think to see next Sunday Lady Stonehouse, by whom the Archbishop of St Andrews has had, without shame, five or six children, openly repent herself.' Elizabeth, the deliverer of Scotland, had built an external buttress for her English Church. If now and then Knox 'gave her cross and candles a wipe', he none the less prayed for her and everlasting friendship. They did not love each other; but she had saved his Scottish Reformation, and he had saved her Anglican Settlement.

Then, at the end of this full year, there was a sudden change in France. Francis II died (5 December 1560); Mary was a childless widow; the Guises were only the uncles of a dowager. A mere boy, Charles IX, was king; power had passed to his mother, Catharine de' Medici and the Bourbons. They had no interest in Mary's claim on England, and, to say the least, were not fanatical Catholics. After some hesitation Mary resolved to return to Scotland. She had hoped for the hand of Philip's son, Don Carlos; but her mother-in-law had foiled her. The kingdom that had been conveyed to the Valois was not to be transferred to the Habsburg, and a niece of the Guises was not to seat herself upon the throne of Spain. The Scottish nobles were not averse to Mary's return, as Elizabeth would not marry Arran, and there was no longer any fear that Scotland would be merged in France. Mary was profuse of kind words; she won Lord James to her side, and even Lethington was given to understand that he could make his peace. The treaty with England she would not confirm; she would wait until she could consult the Scottish Estates. Elizabeth regarded this as a dangerous insult. Her title to the crown had been challenged, and the challenge was not withdrawn. Mary's request for a safe-conduct through England was rejected. Orders were given for stopping the ship that bore her towards Scotland, but apparently were cancelled at the last minute. She landed at Leith on 19 August 1561. The long duel between the two queens began. The story of it must be told elsewhere; but here we may notice that for some years the affairs of Scotland were favourable to the Elizabethan religion. Mary issued a proclamation (25 August 1561) strikingly similar to that which came from Elizabeth on the first day of her reign. 'The state of religion' which Mary 'found publicly and universally standing at her home-coming was to be maintained until altered by her and the Estates of the realm.' But she and the Estates were not at one, and her religious position was that of a barely tolerated nonconformist. Lord James and Lethington were her chief advisers, and her first military adventure was a successful contest with turbulent but Catholic Gordons. Also it pleased her to hold out hopes that she might accept Elizabeth's religion, if her claim to be Elizabeth's heir presumptive were conceded. The ratification of the treaty she still refused, asserting (a late after-thought) that some words in it might deprive her of her right to succeed Elizabeth if Elizabeth left no issue. She desired to meet Elizabeth; Elizabeth desired to meet her; and the Scottish Catholics said that Mary would not return as 'a true Christian woman' from the projected interview. Her uncles were out of power. It was the time of the colloquy of Poissy (September 1561); it was rumoured that Theodore Beza was converting the Duke of Guise, who talked pleasantly with Throckmorton about the English law of in-heritance. The Cardinal of Lorraine publicly flirted with Lutheran-ism. Elizabeth learnt that her cross and candles marked her off from mere Calvinian Huguenots, though she kept in close touch with Condé and the Admiral. Moreover, the English Catholics were slow to look to Scotland for a deliverer; the alien's right to inherit was very dubious; they looked rather to young Darnley, who was born in England and by English law was an Englishman and the son of an English mother. So the Elizabethan religion had a fair chance of striking root before the General Council could do its work.

The invitation to the General Council came, and was flatly refused (5 May 1561). At this point we must turn for one moment to an obscure and romantic episode. From the first days of her reign the English Queen had shown marked favour to her master of the horse, Lord Robert Dudley—a young man, handsome and accom-plished, ambitious and unprincipled; the son of that Duke of Northumberland who set Jane Grey on the throne and died as a traitor. Dudley was a married man, but lived apart from his wife, Amy, the daughter of Sir John Robsart. Gossip said that he would kill her and marry the Queen. On 8 September 1560, when he was with the Queen at Windsor, his wife's corpse was found with broken neck at the foot of a staircase in Cumnor Hall.[1] Some people said at once that he had procured her death; and that story was soon being told in all the courts of Europe; but we have no proof that it was generally believed in England after a coroner's jury had given a verdict which, whatever may have been its terms, exculpated the husband. Dudley (the Leicester of after times) had throughout his life many bitter enemies; but none of them, so far as we know, ever mentioned any evidence of his guilt that a modern English judge would dream of leaving to a jury. We should see merely the unscrupulous character of the husband and the violent, opportune and not easily explicable death of the wife, were it not for a letter that the Spanish ambassador wrote to Margaret of Parma. That letter was not sent until its writer knew of Amy's death (which he mentioned in a postscript), but it professed to tell of what had passed between him, the Queen and Cecil at some earlier, but not precisely defined moment of time. It suggests (as we read it) that Elizabeth knew that Dudley was about to kill his wife. Cecil, it asserts, desired the ambassador to intervene and reduce his mistress to the path of virtue. Those who are inclined to place faith in this wonderful tale about a truly wonderful Cecil, will do well to remember that a postscript is sometimes composed before any part of the letter is written, and that Alvaro de la Quadra, Bishop of Aquila, was suspected by the acute Throckmorton of taking the pay of the Guises. At that moment the rulers of France were refusing ratification of the Edinburgh treaty, and were much concerned that Philip should withdraw his support from Elizabeth. The practical upshot of the letter is that Elizabeth has plunged into an abyss of infamy, will probably be deposed in favour of the Protestant Earl of Huntingdon (Henry Hastings), and will be imprisoned with her favourite. The sagacity of the man who wrote this can hardly be saved, except at the expense of his honesty. Howbeit, Elizabeth, whether she loved Dudley or no (and this will never be known) behaved as if she had thoughts of marrying him, and showed little regard for what was

[1] [For the latest light on this, see Ian Aird, 'The death of Amy Robsart', *E.H.R.*, January 1956.]

said of his crime. One reading of her character, and perhaps the best, makes her heartless and nearly sexless, but for that reason indecorously desirous of appearing to the world as both the subject and the object of amorous passions. Also she was being pestered to marry the Archduke Charles, who would not come to be looked at, or Arran, who had been looked at and rejected. Then (January 1561) there was an intrigue between the Bishop of Aquila and the suspected murderer. Philip was to favour the Queen's marriage with the self-made widower, and the parties to this unholy union were thenceforth to be good Catholics, or at any rate were to subject themselves and the realm to the authority of the General Council.

There was superabundant falsehood on all sides. Quadra, Dudley, Cecil and Elizabeth were all of them experts in mendacity, and the exact truth we are not likely to know when they tell the story. But the outcome of it all was that a papal Nuncio, the Abbot Martinengo, coming this time with Philip's full approval, arrived at Brussels with every reason to believe that Elizabeth would favourably listen to the invitation that he was bringing, and then, at the last moment, he learnt that he might not cross the Channel. There are signs that Cecil had difficulty in bringing about this result. Something stood in his way. He had to stimulate the English bishops into protest, and to discover a little popish plot (there was always one to be discovered) at the right moment. It is conceivable that Dudley and Quadra had for a while ensnared the Queen with hopes of a secure reign and an easy life. It is quite as likely that she was employing them as unconscious agents to keep the Catholics quiet, while important negotiations were pending in France and Germany. That she seriously thought of sending envoys to the Council is by no means improbable; and some stout Protestants held that this was the proper course. But while Quadra and Dudley were concocting their plot, she kept in close alliance with foreign Protestants. Arrangements for a reply to the Pope were discussed with the German Protestant princes at Naumburg (January 1561); and strenuous endeavours were made through the puritanic Earl of Bedford to dissuade the French from participation in the Tridentine assembly. The end of it was that the English refusal was especially emphatic, and given in such a manner as to be a rebuff not only to Rome but to Spain. An irritating reference to a recent precedent did not mend matters: King Philip and Queen Mary had repulsed a Nuncio. Another reason could be given. In Ireland the Elizabethan religion, which had been introduced there by act of parliament, was not making way. In August 1560, the Pope, who had already taken upon himself to dispose of two Irish bishoprics, sent to Ireland David Wolfe, a Jesuit priest, and conferred large powers upon him. He seems to have slipped over secretly from Brittany, where he had lain hid. Elizabeth could say, and probably with truth, that his proceedings were hostile to her right and title. As to a Council, of course she was all for a real and true, a 'free and general' Council; all Protestants were; but with the papistical affair at Trent she would have nothing to do. Pius had thought better of her; her lover's crypto-catholicism had been talked of in high places.

The papal legate at the French Court, the Cardinal of Ferrara, had some hope of succeeding where others had failed: 'not as Legate of Rome or the Cardinal of Ferrara, but as Hippolito d'Este', an Italian gentleman devoted to Her Grace's service. There were pleasant letters; cross and candles were commended; she was asked to retain them 'even as it were for the Cardinal of Ferrara's pleasure'; but hardly had the Council been reopened at Trent (18 January 1562) than Elizabeth was allying herself with the Huguenots and endeavouring to form a Protestant league in Germany. The dream of a France that would peacefully lapse from the Roman obedience was broken at Vassy (1 March 1562), and the First War of Religion began. In April Sechelles came to England as Condé's envoy and was accredited by Hotman to Cecil. The danger to England was explained by the Queen's Secretary: The crown of France would be in the hands of the Guisians; the King of Spain would help them; the Queen of Scots would marry Don Carlos, the Council would condemn the Protestants and give their dominions to a Catholic invader (20 July). On the other hand, Calais, Dieppe, or Havre, 'perhaps all three', might be Elizabeth's, so some thought; indeed 'all Picardy, Normandy, and Gascony might belong to England again'. The Queen had been thinking of such possibilities; already in June 1560, an offer of 'certain towns in Brittany and Normandy' had been made to her. She hesitated long, but yielded, and on 20 September 1562 concluded the Treaty of Hampton Court with the Prince of Condé. She was to help with money and men and hold Havre, Dieppe, and Rouen until Calais was restored. It was a questionable step; but Philip was interfering on the Catholic side, and Calais was covetable. Of course she was not at war with Charles IX; far from it; she was bent on delivering the poor lad and his mother from his rebellious subjects, who were also 'her inveterate enemies', the Guises. Of religion she said as little as possible; but the church of which she was the Supreme Governor affirmed in prayer that the Gallican Catholics were enemies of God's Eternal Word, and that the Calvinists were persecuted for the profession of God's Holy Name. The expedition to Havre failed disastrously. After the battle of Dreux (19 December 1562) and the edict of Amboise (19 March 1563), all parties in France united to expel the invader. The Earl of Warwick (Ambrose Dudley) and his plague-stricken army were compelled to evacuate Havre after a stubborn resistance (28 July), and the recovery of Calais was further off than ever. Elizabeth had played with the fire once too often. She never after this thought well of Huguenots; and friendship with the ruling powers of France became the central feature of her resolutely pacific policy. However, when at the beginning of 1563 she met her second parliament, and the Reformed Church of England held its first Council, all was going well. Since October an English army had once more been holding a French town; a foolhardy plot devised by some young nephews of Cardinal Pole had been opportunely discovered, and the French and Spanish ambassadors were supposed to have had a hand in it. Some notes of Cecil's suggest effective parliamentary rhetoric:

1559. The religion of Christ restored. Foreign authority rejected.... 1560. The French at the request of the Scots, partly by force, partly by agreement, sent back to France, and Scotland set free from the servitude of the pope. 1561. The debased copper and brass coinage replaced by gold and silver. England, formerly unarmed, supplied more abundantly than any other country with arms, munitions and artillery. 1562. The tottering Church of Christ in France succoured....

The Queen, it is true, was tormenting her faithful subjects by playing fast and loose with all her many wooers, and by disallowing all talk of what would happen at her death. It was a policy that few women could have maintained, but was sagacious and successful. It made men pray that her days might be long; for, when compared with her sister's, they were good days, and when they were over there would be civil war. We hear the preacher: 'How was this our realm then pestered with strangers, strange gods, strange languages, strange religion, strange coin! And now how peaceably rid of them all!' So there was no difficulty about a supply of money, and another turn might be given to the screw of conformity. Some new classes of persons, members of the House of Commons, lawyers, schoolmasters, were to take the oath of Supremacy; a first refusal was to bring imprisonment and forfeiture, a second death. The temporal lords procured their own exemption on the ground that the Queen was 'otherwise sufficiently assured' of their loyalty. That might be so, but she was also sufficiently assured of a majority in the Upper House, for there sat in it four-and-twenty spiritual Lords of her own nomination.

The Spanish ambassador reported (14 January 1563) that at the opening of this parliament, the preacher, Nowell, dean of St Paul's, urged the Queen 'to kill the caged wolves', thereby being meant the Marian bishops. Nowell's sermon is extant, and says too much about the duty of slaying the ungodly. Hitherto the Reformers, the men to whom Cranmer and Ridley were dear friends and honoured masters, had shown an admirable self-restraint. A few savage words had been said, but they had not all come from one side. Christopher Goodman desired that 'the bloody bishops' should be slain; but he had been kept out of England as a dangerous fanatic. Dr John Story, in open parliament, had gloried in his own cruelty, and had regretted that in Mary's day the axe had not been laid to the root of the tree. At a time when letters from the Netherlands, France or Spain were always telling of burnt Protestants, nobody was burnt in England and very few people lay in prison for conscience sake. The deprived bishops seem to have been left at large until Parpaglia's mission; then they were sent to gaol. Probably they could be lawfully imprisoned as contumacious excommunicates. Martinengo's advent induced Cecil to clap his hand on a few 'mass-mongers', and on some laymen who had held office under Mary. But in these years of horror it is a small matter if a score of Catholics are kept in that Tower where Elizabeth was lately confined; and her preachers had some right to speak of an unexampled clemency.

Rightly or wrongly, but very naturally, there was one man especially odious to the Protestants. When the statute of 1563 was passed, it was said among the Catholics that Bonner would soon be done to death, and the oath that he had already refused was tendered to him a second time by Horne, the occupant of the see of Winchester. The tender was only valid if Horne was 'Bishop of the diocese'. Bonner, who, it is said, had the aid of Plowden, the most famous pleader of the time, threatened to raise the fundamental question whether Horne and his fellows were lawful bishops. He was prepared to dispute the validity of the statutes of 1559: to dispute the validity of the quasi-papal power of 'supplying defects' which the Queen had assumed: to attack the very heart of the new order of things. Elizabeth, however, was not to be hurried into violence. The proceedings against him were stayed; her bishops were compelled to petition the parliament of 1566 for a declaration that they were lawful bishops; their prayer was not granted except with the proviso that none of their past acts touching life and property were to be thereby validated; and eleven out of some thirty-five temporal Lords were for leaving Dr Parker and his suffragans in their uncomfortably dubious position. Elizabeth allowed Lords and Commons to discuss and confirm her letters patent; she was allowing all to see that no Catholic who refrained from plots need fear anything worse than twelve-penny fines; but she had not yet been excommunicated and deposed.

A project for excommunication and deposition was sent to Trent from Louvain, where the Catholic exiles from England congregated. Like Knox and Goodman in Mary's reign, those who had fled from persecution were already setting themselves to exasperate the persecutor. The plan that found favour with them in 1563 involved the action of the Emperor's son, the Archduke Charles. He was to marry Mary Stewart (who, however, had set her heart on a grander match), and then he was to execute the papal ban. Englishmen, it was said, would never again accept as king the heir to the throne of Spain; but his Austrian kinsman would be an unexceptionable candidate or conqueror. The papal legates at Trent consulted the Emperor, who told his ambassadors that if the Council wished to make itself ridiculous, it had better depose Elizabeth; he and his would have nothing to do with this absurd and dangerous scheme (19 June). Soon afterwards he was allowing his son's marriage, not with the Catholic Mary, but with the heretical Elizabeth, to be once more discussed, and the negotiations for this union were being conducted by the eminently Lutheran Duke of Würtemberg, who apparently thought that pure religion would be the gainer if a Habsburg, Ferdinand's son and Maximilian's brother, became king of a Protestant England.

Philip too, though he had no wish to quarrel with his uncle, began seriously to think that, in the interest of the Catholic faith and the Catholic king, Mary Stewart was right in preferring the Spanish to the Austrian Charles; and at the same time he was being assured from Rome that it was respect for him which had prevented Pius from bringing Elizabeth's case before the assembled Fathers. She was protected from the anathema, which in 1563 might have been a serious matter, by conflicting policies of the worldliest sort. The only member of the English episcopate who was at Trent, the fugitive Marian Bishop of St Asaph, might do his worst; but the safe course for ecclesiastical power was to make a beginning with Jeanne d'Albret and wait to see whether any good would come of the sentence. Ferdinand, however, begged Elizabeth to take pity on the imprisoned prelates, and she quartered most of them upon their Protestant successors. The English Catholics learnt from the Pope, whom they consulted through the Spanish ambassadors at London and Rome, that they ought not to attend the English churches (October 1562).[1] As a matter of expediency this was a questionable decision. It is clear that the zealous Romanists over-estimated the number of those Englishmen whose preference for the old creed could be blown into flame. The State religion was beginning to capture the neutral nucleus of the nation, and the irreconcilable Catholics were compelled to appear as a Spanish party secretly corresponding with the Pope through Quadra and Vargas.

Simultaneously with the parliament a convocation of the province of Canterbury was held (12 January 1563), and its acts may be said to complete the great outlines of the Anglican settlement. A delicate task lay before the theologians: no other than that of producing a confession of faith. Happily in this case also a restoration was possible. In the last months of Edward's reign a set of forty-two Articles had been published; in the main they were the work of Cranmer. In 1563 Parker laid a revised version of them before the assembled clergy, and, when a few more changes had been made, they took durable shape and received the royal assent. A little more alteration at a later day made them the famous 'Thirty-nine Articles'. To all seeming the leaders of English theological thought were remarkably unanimous.

[1] [See below, pp. 224–6.]

A dangerous point had been passed. Just at the moment when the Roman Church was demonstrating on a grand scale its power of defining dogma, its adversaries were becoming always less hopeful of Protestant unanimity. In particular, as Elizabeth was often hearing from Germany, the dispute about the Lord's Supper was not to be composed, and a quarrel among divines was rapidly becoming a cause of quarrel among princes. Well intentioned attempts to construct elastic phrases had done more harm than good, and it was questionable whether the Religious Peace would comprehend the Calvinising Palsgrave. As causes of political union and discord, all other questions of theology were at this moment of comparatively small importance; the line which would divide the major part of the Protestant world into two camps, to be known as Lutheran and Calvinist, was being drawn by theories of the Holy Supper. It is usual and for the great purposes of history it is right to class the Knoxian Church of Scotland as Calvinian, though about Predestination its Confession of Faith is as reticent as are the English Articles. Had it been possible for the English Church to leave untouched the hotly controverted question, the Queen would have been best pleased. She knew that at Hamburg Westphal, a champion of militant Lutheranism, 'never ceased in open pulpit to rail upon England and spared not the chiefest magistrates'; it was he who had denounced the Marian exiles as 'the devil's martyrs'. Since the first moment of her reign Christopher of Würtemberg and Peter Paul Vergerio had been endeavouring to secure her for the Lutheran faith. Jewel, who was to be the Anglican apologist, heard with alarm of the advances made by the ex-Bishop of Capo d'Istria; and the godly Duke had been pained at learning that no less than twenty-seven of the Edwardian Articles swerved from the Augustan standard. Very lately he had urged the Queen to stand fast for a Real Presence. Now, Lutheranism was by this time politically respectable. When there was talk of a bull against Elizabeth, the Emperor asked how a distinction was to be made between her and the Lutheran princes, and could take for granted that no pope with his wits about him would fulminate a sentence against those pillars of the Empire, Augustus of Saxony and Joachim of Brandenburg. When a few years later (1570) a pope did depose Elizabeth, he was careful to accuse her of participation in 'the impious mysteries of Calvin', by which, no doubt, he meant the *Cène*. But though the

Augustan might be the safer creed, she would not wish to separate herself from the Huguenots or the Scots, and could have little hope of obtaining from her bishops a declaration that would satisfy the critical mind of the good Christopher. Concessions were made to him at points where little was at stake; words were taken from his own Würtemberg Confession. When the perilous spot was reached, the English divines framed an Article which, as long experience has shown, can be signed by men who hold different opinions; but a charge of deliberate ambiguity could not fairly be brought against the Anglican fathers. In the light of the then current controversy we may indeed see some desire to give no needless offence to Lutherans, and apparently the Queen suppressed until 1571 a phrase which would certainly have repelled them; but, even when this phrase was omitted, Beza would have approved the formula, and it would have given greater satisfaction at Geneva and Heidelberg than at Jena or Tübingen. A papistical controversialist tried to insert a wedge which would separate a Lutheran Parker from an Helvetic Grindal; but we find Parker hoping that Calvin, or, if not Calvin, then Vermigli will lead the Reformers at Poissy, and the only English bishop to whom Lutheran leanings can be safely attributed held aloof from his colleagues and was for a while excommunicate. It was left for Elizabeth herself to suggest by cross and candles that (as her German correspondents put it) she was living 'according to the divine light, that is, the Confession of Augsburg', while someone assured the Queen of Navarre that these obnoxious symbols had been removed from the royal chapel. As to 'the sacrifices of masses', there could be no doubt. The anathema of Trent was frankly encountered by 'blasphemous fable'. Elizabeth knew that her French ambassador remained ostentatiously seated when the host was elevated, for 'reverencing the sacrament was contrary to the usages established by law in England'.

Another rock was avoided. Ever since 1532 there had been in the air a project for an authoritative statement of English canon law. In Edward's day that project took the shape of a book (*Reformatio Legum Ecclesiasticarum*) of which Cranmer and Peter Martyr were the chief authors, but which had not received the king's sanction when death took him. During Elizabeth's first years we hear of it again; but nothing decisive was done. The draft code that has come down to us has every fault that it could have. In particular, its list of heresies is terribly severe, and apparently (but this has been doubted) the obstinate heretic is to go the way that Cranmer went: not only the Romanists but some at least of the Lutherans might have been relinquished to the secular arm. Howbeit, the scheme fell through. Under a statute of Henry VIII so much of the old canon law as was not contrariant nor repugnant to the word of God or to Acts of the English parliament was to be administered by the courts of the English Church. Practically this meant that the officials of the bishops had a fairly free hand in declaring law as they went along. They were civilians; the academic study of the canon law had been prohibited; they were not in the least likely to contest the right of the temporal legislature to regulate spiritual affairs. And the hands of the Queen's ecclesiastical commissioners were free indeed. Large as were the powers with which she could entrust them by virtue of the Act of Supremacy, she professedly gave them yet larger powers, for they might punish offenders by fine and imprisonment, and this the old courts of the church could not do. A constitutional question of the first magnitude was to arise at this point.[1] But during the early years of the reign the commissioners seem to be chiefly employed in depriving papists of their benefices, and this was lawful work.

But while there was an agreeable harmony in dogma and little controversy over polity, the quarrel about ceremonies had begun. In the Convocation of 1563, resolutions, which would have left the posture of the communicants to the discretion of the bishops and would have abolished the observance of saints' days, the sign of the cross in baptism and the use of organs, were rejected in the Lower House by the smallest of majorities. It was notorious that some of the bishops favoured only the simplest rites; five deans and a dozen archdeacons petitioned against the modest surplice. But for its Supreme Governor, the English Church would in all likelihood have carried its own purgation far beyond the degree that had been fixed by the secular legislature. To the Queen, however, it was of the first importance that there should be no more changes before the face of the Tridentine enemy, and also that her occasional professions of Augustan principles should have some visible support. The bishops, though at first with some reluctance, decided to enforce the existing law; and in course of time conservative sentiment began to collect around the rubrics

---

[1] [In 1610. See Coke, *Inst.* IV, c. 74.]

of the Prayer Book. However, there were some men who were not to be pacified. The 'Vestiarian controversy' broke out. Those who strove for a worship purified from all taint of popery (and who therefore were known as 'Puritans') 'scrupled' the cap and gown that were to be worn by the clergy in daily life, and 'scrupled' the surplice that was to be worn in church. Already in 1565 resistance and punishment had begun. At Oxford the Dean of Christ Church was deprived, and young gentlemen at Cambridge discarded the rags of the Roman Antichrist.

In the next year the London clergy were recalcitrant. The Spanish ambassador improved the occasion. In reply, Elizabeth told him that the disobedient ministers were 'not natives of the country, but Scotsmen, whom she had ordered to be punished'. Literal truth she was not telling, and yet there was truth of a sort in her words. From this time onwards, the historian of the English Church must be often thinking of Scotland, and the historian of the Scottish Church must keep England ever in view. Two kingdoms are drifting together, first towards a 'personal' and then towards a 'real' Union; but two churches are drifting apart into dissension and antagonism. The attractions and repulsions that are involved in this process fill a large page in the annals of Britain; they have become plain to all in the age of the Bishops' Wars and the Westminster Assembly; but they are visible much earlier. The attempt to Scoticise the English Church, which failed in 1660, and the attempt to Anglicise the Scottish Church, which failed in 1688, each of these had its century.

For a while there is uncertainty. At one moment Maitland is sure that the two kingdoms have one religion; at another (March 1563) he can tell the Bishop of Aquila that there are great differences; but undoubtedly in 1560 the prevailing belief was that the Protestants of England and Scotland were substantially at one; and, many as were to be the disputes between them, they remained substantially at one for the greatest of all purposes until there was no fear that either realm would revert to Rome. From the first the Reforming movement in the northern kingdom had been in many ways an English movement. Then in 1560 Reformation and national deliverance had been effected simultaneously by the aid of English gold and English arms. John Knox was a Scot of Scots, and none but a Scot could have done what he did; but, had he died in 1558 at the age of fifty-three, his name would have occurred rather in English than in Scottish books, and he might have disputed with Hooper the honour of being the progenitor of the English Puritans. The congregation at Geneva for which he compiled his Prayer Book was not Scottish but English. His Catholic adversaries in Scotland said that he could not write good Scots. Some of his principal lieutenants were Englishmen or closely connected with England. John Willock, while he was 'Superintendent' (Knoxian bishop) of Glasgow, was also parson of Loughborough. 'Mr Goodman of England' had professed divinity at Oxford, and after his career in Scotland was an English archdeacon, though a troublesome Puritan. John Craig had been tutor in an English family, and, instead of talking honest Scots, would 'knap suddrone'. But further, Knox had signed the English Articles of 1553, and is plausibly supposed to have modified their wording. A Catholic controversialist of Mary's day said that 'a runagate Scot' had procured that the adoration of Christ in the Sacrament should be put out of the English Prayer Book. To that book in 1559 Knox had strong objections; he detested ceremonies; the Coxian party at Frankfort had played him a sorry trick and he had just cause of resentment; but there was nothing doctrinally wrong with the Book. It was used in Scotland. In 1560 a Frenchman whom Randolph took to church in Glasgow, and who had previously been in Elizabeth's chapel, saw great differences, but heard few, for the prayers of the English Book were said. Not until some years later did 'the Book of Geneva' (Knox's liturgy) become the fixed standard of worship for the Scottish Church. The objection to all prescript prayers is of later date and some say that it passes from England into Scotland. This Genevan Use had been adopted by the chaplain of Elizabeth's forces at Havre, and, though he was bidden to discontinue it, he was forthwith appointed to the deanery of Durham. A Puritan movement in England there was likely to be in any case. The arguments of both parties were already prepared. The Leipzig *Interim*, the work of the Elector Maurice, had given rise to a similar quarrel among the Lutherans, between Flacians on the one side and Philipians on the other, over those rites and ornaments which were 'indifferent' in themselves, but had, as some thought, been soiled by superstition. The English exiles who returned from Zurich and Geneva would dislike cap, gown, and surplice; but their foreign mentors counselled submission; Bullinger was large-minded, and Calvin was politic. Scotland, however, was very near, and in Scotland this first phase of Puritanism was in its proper place. So long as Mary reigned there and plotted there, the Protestant was hardly an established religion; and, had Knox been the coolest of schemers, he would have endeavoured to emphasise every difference between the old worship and the new. It was not for him to make light of *adiaphora*; it was for him to keep Protestant ardour at fever heat. Maitland, who was a cool scheme, made apology to Cecil for Knox's vehemence: 'as things are fallen out, it will serve to good purpose'. And yet it is fairly certain that Knox dissuaded English Puritans from secession. In his eyes the Coxian Church of England might be an erring sister, but still was a twin sister, of the Knoxian Church of Scotland.

Elizabeth's resistance to the Puritan demands was politic. The more Protestant a man was, the more secure would be his loyalty if Rome were aggressive. It was for her to appeal to the 'neutral in religion' and those 'faint professors' of whom her bishops saw too many. It is not perhaps very likely that surplices and square caps won to her side many of those who cared much for the old creed. Not the simplest and most ignorant papist, says Whitgift to the Puritans, could mistake the Communion for the Mass: the Mass has been banished from England as from Scotland: we are full as well Reformed as are the Scots. But Elizabeth feared frequent changes, was glad to appear as a merely moderate Reformer, and meant to keep the clergy well in hand. Moreover, in Catholic circles her cross and candles produced a good impression. When she reproved Dean Nowell for inveighing against such things, this was soon known to Cardinal Borromeo, and he was not despondent (21 April 1565). Even her dislike for a married clergy, which seems to have been the outcome of an indiscriminating misogyny, was favourably noticed. It encouraged the hope that she might repent, and for some time Rome was unwilling to quench this plausibly smoking flax. But her part was difficult. The Puritans could complain that they were worse treated than Spanish, French and Dutch refugees, whose presence in England she liberally encouraged. Casiodoro de Reyna, Nicolas des Gallars, and Utenhove, though the Bishop of London was their legal 'superintendent', were allowed a liberty that was denied to Humphry and Sampson; there was one welcome for Mrs Matthew Parker and another for Madame la Cardinale.

The controversy of the sixties over rites and clothes led to the controversy of the seventies over polity, until at length Presbyterianism and Episcopalianism stood arrayed against each other. But the process was gradual. We must not think that Calvin had formulated a Presbyterian system, which could be imported ready-made from Geneva to Britain. In what is popularly called Presbyterianism there are various elements. One is the existence of certain presbyters or elders, who are not pastors or ministers of the Word, but who take a larger or smaller part in the government of the church. This element may properly be called Calvinian, though the idea of some such eldership had occurred to other Reformers. Speculations touching the earliest history of the Christian Church were combined with a desire to interest the laity in a rigorous ecclesiastical discipline. But Calvin worked with the materials that were ready to his hand and was far too wary to raise polity to the rank of dogma. The Genevan Church was essentially civic or municipal; its Consistory is very much like a committee of a town council. This could not be the model for a church of France or of Scotland, which would contain many particular congregations or churches. Granted that these particular churches will be governed by elders, very little has yet been decided: we may have the loosest federation of autonomous units, or the strictest subordination of the parts to some assembly which is or represents the whole. Slowly and empirically, the problem was solved with somewhat different results in France, Scotland, and the Low Countries. As we have said, the month which saw Knox land in Scotland saw a French Church taking shape in a national Synod that was being secretly held at Paris. Already Frenchmen are setting an example for constituent assemblies and written constitutions. Knox, who had been edifying the Church of Dieppe—that Dieppe which was soon to pass into Elizabeth's hands—stood in the full current of the French movement; but, like his teacher, he had no iron system to impose. Each particular congregation would have elders besides a pastor; there would be some general assembly of the whole church; but Knox was not an ecclesiastical jurist. The *First Book of Discipline* (1560) decides wonderfully little; even the structure of the General Assembly is nebulous; and, as a matter of fact, all righteous noblemen seem to be welcome therein. It gradually gives itself a constitution, and, while a similar process is at work in France, other jurisdictional and governmental organs are developed, until kirk-session, presbytery, synod and assembly form a concentric system of courts and councils of which Rome herself might be proud. But much of this belongs to a later time; in Scotland it is not Knoxian but Melvillian.

A mere demand for some ruling elders for the particular churches was not likely to excite enthusiasm or antagonism. England knew that plan. The curious church of foreign refugees, which was organised in the London of Edward VI's days under the presidency of John Laski, had elders. Cranmer took great interest in what he probably regarded as a fruitful experiment, and the Knoxian Church has some traits which, so good critics think, tell less of Geneva than of the Polish but cosmopolitan nobleman. Dr Horne, Elizabeth's Bishop of Winchester, had been the pastor of a Presbyterian flock of English refugees at Frankfort. With a portion of that flock he had quarrelled, not for being Presbyterian, but because the Presbyterianism of this precocious conventicle was already taking that acutely democratic and distinctly uncalvinian form, in which the elders are the annually elected officers of a congregation which keeps both minister and elders well under control. Among Englishmen a drift towards Congregationalism appears almost as soon as the ruling elder.

The enthusiasm and antagonism were awakened by a different cry: it was not a call for presbyters, but a call for 'parity', for an equality among all the ministers of God's Word, and consequently for an abolition of all 'prelacy'. As a battle cry this is hardly Calvinian; nor is it Knoxian; it is first audible at Cambridge. The premisses, it is true, lay ready to the hand of any one who chose to combine them. The major was that Protestant principle which refers us to the Primitive Church. The minor was a proposition familiar to the Middle Age: originally there was no difference between the *presbyter* and the *episcopus*. Every student of the canon law knew the doctrine that the prelacy of bishops is founded, not on divine command, but on a 'custom of the Church'. When the Puritan said that the episcopal jurisdiction was of popish origin, he agreed with Laynez and the pope; at least, as had been amply shown at Trent, the divine right of bishops was a matter over which Catholic doctors could quarrel bitterly. But the great Reformers had been chary of their words about ecclesiastical polity; there were many possibilities to be considered, and the decision would rest with princes or civic councils. The defenders of Anglican episcopacy occasionally told the Puritan that he was not a good Calvinist, and even Beza could hardly be brought by British pressure to a sufficiently dogmatic denunciation of prelacy. As to Knox, it is clear that, though he thought the English dioceses too large, he had no radical objection to such prelacy as existed in England. Moreover, the church that he organised in Scotland was prelatic, and there is but little proof that he regarded its prelatic constitution as a concession to merely temporary needs. The word 'bishop' was avoided (in Scotland there still were lawful bishops of another creed); but over the 'dioceses' stand 'superintendents' (the title comes from Germany), who, though strictly accountable to the General Assembly, are distinctly the rulers of the diocesan clergy. Between superintendent and minister there is no 'parity'; the one may command, the other must obey. The theory that valid orders can be conferred by none but a bishop, Knox would, no doubt, have denied; but some at all events of the contemporary English bishops would have joined him in the denial.

Apparently Thomas Cartwright, a young professor of divinity at Cambridge, spoke the word (1570) that had not yet been spoken in Scotland. Cambridge was seething with Puritanism; the bishops had been putting the vestiarian law in force; and the French Church had declared for parity. 'There ought to be an equality': presbyter and bishop were once all one. But if the demand for parity was first heard south of the Tweed, it was soon echoed back by Scotland; and thenceforth the English Puritan was often looking northward. In Scotland much had been left unsettled. From August 1561, to May 1568, Mary Stewart is there; Rizzio and Darnley, Bothwell and Moray, Lethington and Knox, are on the stage; and we hold our breath while the tragedy is played. We forget the background of unsolved questions and uncertain law. Is the one lawful religion the Catholic or the Protestant? Are there two established churches, or is one church established and another endowed? There is an *interim*: or rather, an armed truce. The Queen had not confirmed the statutes of 1560, though mass-mongers were occasionally imprisoned. Nothing decisive had been done in the matter of tithes and kirk-lands and advowsons. The Protestant ministers and superintendents were receiving small stipends which were charged upon the ecclesiastical revenues; but the bishops and abbots, some of whom were Protestant ministers, had not been ousted from their temporalities or their seats in parliament, and, as vacancies occurred, the bishoprics were conferred upon new occupants, some of whom were Catholics. The General Assembly might meet twice a year; but John Hamilton still went to parliament as a reverend father in God and primate of Scotland. If Mary had succeeded in re-establishing Catholicism, we should probably have said that it had never been disestablished. And when she had been deposed and a parliament held in her son's name had acknowledged the Knoxian Church to be 'the immaculate spouse of Christ', much was still unsettled. What was to be done with the bishoprics and abbacies and with the revenues and seats in parliament that were involved there-with? Grave questions of civil and ecclesiastical polity were open, and a large mass of wealth went a-begging or illustrated the beatitude of possession. Then in the seventies we on the one hand see an attempt to Anglicise the Church by giving it bishops, who will sit in parliament and be somewhat more prelatic than were Knox's superintendents, and on the other hand we hear a swelling cry for parity.

To many a Scot prelacy will always suggest another word of evil sound: to wit, Erastianism. The link is Anglican. The name of the professor of medicine at Heidelberg—it was Thomas Lüber, or in Greek Erastus—won a fame or infamy in Britain that has been denied to it elsewhere. And in some sort this is fair, for it was an English Puritan who called him into the field; and after his death his manuscript book was brought to England and there for the first time printed. His prince, the Elector Palatine Frederick III, was introducing into his dominions, in the place of the Lutheranism which had prevailed there, the theology that flowed from Zürich and Geneva; images were being destroyed and altars were giving place to tables. This, as Elizabeth knew when the Thirty-nine Articles lay before her, was a very serious change; it strained to breaking-point the professed unanimity of the Protestant princes. Theology, however, was one thing, church-polity another; and for all the Genevan rigours Frederick was not yet prepared. But to Heidelberg for a doctor's degree came an English Puritan, George Withers, and he stirred up strife there by urging the necessity of a discipline exercised by pastor and elders (June, 1568). Erastus answered him by declaring that excommunication has no warrant in the Word of God; and further that, when the prince is a Christian, there is no need for a corrective jurisdiction which is not that of the state, but that of the church. This sowed dissension between Zürich and Geneva: between Bullinger, the friend of the English bishops, and Beza, the oracle of the Puritans. Controversy in England began to nibble at the royal supremacy; and in Scotland the relation between the state (which until 1567 had a papistical head) and the Knoxian Church was of necessity highly indeterminate. Knox had written sentences which, in our rough British use of the term, were Erastian enough; and a great deal of history might have been changed, had he found in Scotland a pious princess, a Josiah or even a Deborah. As it fell out, the Scottish Church aspired to, and at times attained, a truly medieval independence. Andrew Melvill's strain of language has been compared with that of Gregory VII; so has Thomas Cartwright's; but the Scottish Church had an opportunity of resuming ancient claims which was denied to the English. In 1572 an oath was imposed in Scotland; the model was English; but important words were changed. The King of Scots is 'Supreme Governor of this realm as well in things temporal as in the conservation and purgation of religion'. The Queen of England is 'Supreme Governor of this realm as well in all spiritual or ecclesiastical things or causes as temporal'. The great continuity of ecclesiastical history is not wholly on one side of the border. The charge of popery was soon retorted against the Puritans by the Elizabethan divines and their Helvetian advisers: Your new presbyter in his lust for a usurped dominion is but too like old priest.

In controversy with the Puritans the Elizabethan religion gradually assumed an air of moderation which had hardly belonged to it from the first; it looked like a compromise between an old faith and a new. It is true that from the beginning of her reign Elizabeth distrusted Calvin; and when she swore that she never read his books she may have sworn the truth. That blast of the trumpet had repelled her. Not only had 'the regiment of women' been attacked, but Knox and Goodman had advocated a divine right of rebellion against idolatrous princes. Calvin might protest his innocence; but still this dangerous stuff came from his Geneva. Afterwards, however, he took an opportunity of being serviceable to the Queen in the matter of a book which spoke ill of her father and mother. Then a pretty message went to him and he was bidden to feel assured of her favour (18 September 1561). Moreover, in German history Elizabeth appears as espousing the cause of oppressed Calvinists against the oppressing Lutherans. Still as time went on, when the Huguenots, as she said, had broken faith with her about Havre and Calais, and the attack on 'her officers', the bishops, was being made in the name of the Genevan discipline, her dislike of Geneva, its works, and its ways, steadily grew. Though in the region of pure theology Calvin's influence increased apace in England and Scotland after his death, and Whitgift, the stern repressor of the Puritans, was a remorseless predestinarian, still the bishops saw, albeit with regret, that they had two frontiers to defend, and that they could not devote all their energy to the confutation of the Louvainists.

Then some severed, or half-severed, bonds were spliced. Parker was a lover of history, and it was pleasant to sit in the chair of Augustine, seeing to editions of Ælfric's Homilies and the Chronicles of Matthew Paris. But the work was slowly done, and foreigners took a good share in it. Hadrian Saravia, who defended English episcopacy against Beza, was a refugee, half Spaniard, half Fleming. Pierre Baron of Cambridge, who headed a movement against Calvin's doctrine of the divine decrees, was another Frenchman, another pupil of the law-school of Bourges. And it is to be remembered that at Elizabeth's accession the Genevan was not the only model for a radically Reformed Church. The fame of Zwingli's Zürich had hardly yet been eclipsed, and for many years the relation between the Anglican and Tigurine Churches was close and cordial. A better example of a purely spiritual power could hardly be found than the influence that was exercised in England by Zwingli's successor Henry Bullinger. Bishops and Puritans argue their causes before him as if he were the judge. So late as 1586 English clergymen are required to peruse his immortal *Decades*. There was some gratitude in the case. A silver cup with verses on it had spoken Elizabeth's thanks for the hospitality that he had shown to Englishmen. But that was not all; he sympathised with Elizabeth and her bishops and her Erastianism. He condemned 'the English fool' who broke the peace of the Palatinate by a demand for the Genevan discipline. When the cry was that the congregation should elect its minister, the Puritan could be told how in an admirably reformed republic Protestant pastors were still chosen by patrons who might be papists, even by a Bishop of Constance who might be the pope's own nephew and a Cardinal to boot, for a Christian magistracy would see that this patronage was not abused. And then when the bad day came and the Pope hurled his thunderbolt, it was to Bullinger that the English bishops looked for a learned defence of their Queen and their creed. Modestly, but willingly, he undertook the task: none the less willingly perhaps, because Pius V had seen fit to couple Elizabeth's name with Calvin's, and this was a controversialist's trick which Zürich could expose. Bullinger knew all the Puritan woes and did not like surplices; he knew and much disliked the 'semi-popery' of Lutheran Germany; but in his eyes the Church of England was no half-way house. As to Elizabeth, he saw her as no lukewarm friend of true religion, but as a virgin-queen beloved of God, whose wisdom and clemency, whose felicity and dexterity were a marvel and a model for all Christian Princes (12 March 1572).

The felicity and dexterity are not to be denied. The Elizabethan religion which satisfied Bullinger was satisfying many other people also; for (to say nothing of intrinsic merits or defects) it appeared as part and parcel of a general amelioration. It was allied with honest money, cheap and capable government, national independence, and a reviving national pride. The long Terror was overpast, at least for a while; the flow of noble blood was stayed; the axe rusted at the Tower. The long Elizabethan peace was beginning (1563), while France was ravaged by civil war, and while more than half the Scots looked to the English Queen as the defender of their faith. One Spaniard complains that these heretics have not their due share of troubles (November 1562); another, that they are waxing fat upon the spoil of the Indies (August 1565). The England into which Francis Bacon was born in 1561 and William Shakespeare in 1564 was already unlike the England that was ruled by the Queen of Spain.

NOTE

[The *Cambridge Modern History* repudiated footnotes, and Maitland's allusions offer many opportunities for research to the reader. It may be useful however to note here that the term 'Augustan' (pp. 176 ff.) means 'in accordance with the Confession of Augsburg'; that 'Flacians and Philipians' (p. 202) were the followers of Flaccus Illyricus and Philip Melanchthon respectively; that the 'thunderbolt' (above) was the Bull *Regnans in excelsis* of 1570 which excommunicated Elizabeth; that Bullinger's *Confutation of the Pope's Bull* was published in London in 1572; and that the two Spanish letters cited above are in the *Spanish Calendar*, pp. 269, 470.]

IX

ELIZABETHAN GLEANINGS

I. DEFENDER OF THE FAITH, AND SO FORTH[1]

For nearly 250 years the solemn style and title of the king or queen of this country ended with the words 'and so forth', or in Latin *et caetera*. On the first day of the nineteenth century a change was made. Queen Victoria's grandfather became king of a 'United Kingdom' of Great Britain and Ireland. He ceased to be king of France. He also ceased to be 'and so forth'.

Had this phrase always been meaningless? I venture to suggest that it had its origin in a happy thought, a stroke of genius.

If we look at the book to which we naturally turn when we would study the styles and titles of our English kings, if we look at Sir Thomas Hardy's Introduction to the Charter Rolls, we shall observe that the first sovereign who bears an 'etc.' is Queen Elizabeth. Now let us for a moment place ourselves in the first days of her reign. Shall we not be eager to know what this new queen will call herself, for will not her style be a presage of her policy? No doubt she is by the Grace of God of England, France, and Ireland Queen. No doubt she is Defender of the Faith, though we cannot be sure what faith she will defend. But is that all? Is she or is she not Supreme Head upon earth of the Church of England and Ireland?

The full difficulty of the question which this young lady had to face so soon as she was safely Queen may not be justly appreciated by our modern minds. We say, perhaps, that acts of parliament had bestowed a certain title, and had since been repealed by other acts of parliament. But to this bald statement we must make two additions. In the first place, one at least of the Henrician statutes had declared that the headship of the church was annexed to the kingship by a bond stronger and holier than any act of parliament: to wit, by the very word of God.[2] In the second place, one of the Marian statutes had rushed to the opposite limit. It had in effect declared that Henry's ecclesiastical supremacy had all along been

---

[1] [*E.H.R.* (January 1900): *Collected Papers*, vol. III, pp. 157–65.]
[2] Stat. 37 Hen. VIII, c. 17.

a nullity. It had indeed excused Queen Mary's temporary assumption of a title that was not rightfully hers, and documents in which the obnoxious phrase occurred were not for that reason to be invalid; but it applauded Mary for having seen the error of her ways, and having of her own motion rejected a title which no parliament could lawfully confer.[1]

It was a difficult problem. On both sides there were men with extreme opinions, who, however, agreed in holding that the solution of the question was not to be found in any earthly statute book. That question had been answered for good and all in one sense or the other by the *ius divinum*, by the word of God. We know that Elizabeth was urged to treat the Marian statutes as void or voidable, because passed by a parliament whose being was unlawful, since it was summoned by a queen who had unlawfully abdicated her God-given headship of the church.[2] This, if in our British and Calvinian way we make too free with the Greek version of Thomas Lüber's name, we may call the opinion of the immoderate Erastians: what God has joined together man attempts to put asunder 'under pain of nullity'. At the opposite pole stood a more composite body, for those who would talk of the vanity of all attempts to rob Christ's vicar of his vicariate were being reinforced by strange allies from Geneva, where Calvin had spoken ill of Henricianism. Then between these extremes there was room for many shades of doctrine, and in particular for that which would preach the omnicompetence of parliament.

Then a happy thought occurs. Let Her Highness etceterate herself. This will leave her hands free, and then afterwards she can explain the etceteration as occasion shall require. Suppose that sooner or later she must submit to the pope, she can still say that she has done no wrong. She can plead that, at least in some of his documents, King Philip, the Catholic King, etceterates himself. There are always, so it might be said, some odds and ends that might conveniently be packed up in 'and so forth'. What of the Channel Islands, for example? They are not parts of England, and they are hardly parts of France. Besides, even Paul IV would be insaner than we think him, if, when securing so grand a prize as England, he boggled over an 'etc.' And then, on the other hand, if Her Grace finds it advisable, as perhaps it will be, to declare that

[1] Stat. 1 & 2 P. et M. c. 8, secs. 42, 43.
[2] See the oration of John Hales in Fox, *Acts and Monuments*, ann. 1558.

the Marian statutes are null, she cannot be reproached with having been as bad as her sister, for we shall say that no reasonable man, considering all that has happened, can have doubted that the 'etc.' signified that portion of King Henry's title and King Edward's title which, for the sake of brevity, was not written in full. Lastly, suppose that the parliament which is now to be summoned is willing to go great lengths in an Erastian and Protestant direction, no harm will have been done. Indeed, hereafter the Queen's Highness in her exercise of her ecclesiastical supremacy may find it advisable to assert that this supremacy was in being before any parliament recognised its existence, and therefore is not to be controlled even by the estates of the realm. Therefore let her be 'Defender of the Faith, and so forth'. He who knows what faith is 'the' faith will be able to make a good guess touching the import of 'and so forth'.

And now it must be allowed that, though, so far as I am aware, Elizabeth is the first sovereign of this country who is solemnly etceterated, there may seem to be evidence to the contrary. It had been usual in certain classes of records to abbreviate the king's style. A king whose full style was Henry, by the Grace of God King of England, Lord of Ireland, Duke of Normandy and Aquitaine, and Count of Anjou, might well become upon a roll *H. d. g. Rex Angl. &c.* What I believe to be new in Elizabeth's reign is the addition of 'etc.' to an unabbreviated style.[1] When she has called herself Queen of England, France, and Ireland, and Defender of the Faith, she has given herself all the titles that were borne by her father and brother, save one only, and in the place of that one she puts 'etc.' The change is the more remarkable because of all people who have ever reigned in England her immediate predecessors had the best excuse for an etceteration. But no: whatever King Philip's Spanish chancery may have done, King Philip and Queen Mary are not etceterated in solemn English documents. The whole wearisome story must be told: Jerusalem must not be forgotten, nor Tyrol. Even the town-clerk at Cambridge, when he is writing out the borough accounts, will write of Flanders and Milan. Then comes Elizabeth with her conveniently short title, with no duchies, archduchies, and counties to be enumerated; and yet she must be 'etc.'

Now let us discover, if we can, the moment of time at which the

----

[1] [But see below, p. 216, *n.* 1.]

etceteration began. So to do is the more important because I am
not in a position to contend that this addition to the royal style is
to be found in every place in which, if my theory be true, it ought
to occur. In particular, any one who relied only on the officially
printed volumes of statutes might infer that the change took place
before the parliament of 1563, but after the parliament of 1559.
On the other hand, we may see the little syllable in a writ of
21 January 1559 which prorogued parliament from the 23rd to the
25th of that month. Occasionally a clerk will make a slip, an
omissive slip: especially by leaving unmodified an old formula
which he ought to modify. So let us look at the very first document
in which Queen Elizabeth announced her royal will and pleasure.
In Humfrey Dyson's collection at the British Museum lies the
proclamation, 'imprynted at London by Richard Jugge', which
tells us how it hath pleased Almighty God to call to his mercy out
of this mortal life, to our great grief, 'our deerest suster of noble
memory', and how the kingdoms of England, France, and Ireland,
'with all maner titles and rights thereunto in any wise apper-
teyning', have come to Us, 'Elizabeth, by the grace of God Queene
of Englande Fraunce and Ireland defendour of the fayth. etc.'[1]

A little later Mary's body was borne to the grave, and there was
heraldic display, of which an apparently official account is extant.[2]
Heralds are bound to be careful of titles. The late queen had a
lengthy title, but it must be recited at full length. Then, when the
dirge has been chanted and the crowd is questioning whether many
more dirges will be chanted in England, comes the demand for
a loyal shout for a new queen, whose title is brief, but who is
something that her sister was not: for she is 'etc.'

Then we know that parliament had hardly assembled (25
January) before the Commons appointed (30 January) a committee
to consider the validity of the summons which had called them
together, and of the writs by virtue whereof some of Mary's last
parliaments were holden. The committee reported (3 February)
that the omission of the words *Supremum Caput* was no cause of
nullity. I should suppose that Elizabeth's ministers had by this

[1] Brit. Mus., Grenville 6463. I refer to this precious volume because, as
I understand, what is there to be seen is one of the very papers that came
from Jugge's office.

[2] *State Papers, Domestic*, vol. I, no. 32 (MS.); see *Foreign Calendar* for
1559–60, p. cxxviii.

time decided—and surely it was a wise decision—that whatever ecclesiastical changes were to be made should be made in a straight-forward manner by repeal, and should not be attempted by means of a theory which Roman Catholics and Calvinists would accuse of blasphemy and the plain man would charge with chicane. It may be, therefore, that they never had to rely on their 'etc.'; but some of us would gladly have been present at the deliberations of that committee.

Some years later certain English members of the Roman Church were consulting some high authority—not the Pope himself, but some high authority—touching the course of conduct that they ought to pursue towards a queen whom Pius V had denounced as excommunicate and deposed. Their questions and the answers that were given thereto were published by Dr Creighton in this *Review*.[1] These scrupulous persons desire to know whether Elizabeth may be called Queen of England, and, if so, whether the 'etc.' may be added. Question and answer run as follows:

Cum Elizabetha in forma titulorum adiungat in fine 'et caetera', quo intelligitur esse ecclesiae supremum caput, quoniam eo excepto omnes alii tituli expresse nominantur, an catholici hoc intelligentes possunt salva fidei professione etiam illam particulam 'et caetera' adiungere?

Licet haeretici per illam vocem 'et caetera' intelligant caput ecclesiae Anglicanae, non coguntur tamen catholici ita eam intelligere: ea enim vox indifferens est ad alia multa: immo vox est quae ut plurimum apponi solet in titulis aliorum regum.

If, then, we see significance in this 'etc.', we are only seeing what was seen by some at least of Elizabeth's subjects, and the brain to which *illa particula* occurred seems to deserve credit for its ingenuity. Catholic and Calvinist can say that this is a *vox indifferens* common in regal styles. On the other hand, the champions of a divinely instituted caesaro-papalism will observe that all Elizabeth's possible titles, except one, have been expressly named.

For all this we might fear that we were making much ado about nothing, and discovering deep policy in some clerk's flourish, were it not for a piece of evidence that remains to be mentioned. At the Record Office is preserved a paper on which Cecil has scribbled memoranda.[2] It is ascribed to 18 November 1558, the second day of Elizabeth's reign. Apparently the Secretary is taking his mis-tress's pleasure about a great variety of matters, and, as he does

---

[1] *E.H.R.* (1892), p. 81.   [2] *State Papers, Domestic* (1892), no. 3.

so, he jots down notes which will aid his memory. Ambassadors must be sent to foreign princes; a new great seal must be engraved; a preacher must be selected to fill the pulpit at Paul's Cross next Sunday. Then, among these notes—which should be photographed, for no print could represent them—we find the following:

A commission to make out wryttes for y^e parlement touchyng &c. in y^e style of wryttes.

This seems to me proof positive that 'etc. in the style of writs' was the outcome, not of chance but of deliberation that took place at the first moment of the reign in the highest of high quarters.

So we might expand the symbol thus:

Etc. = and (if future events shall so decide, but not further or otherwise) of the Church of England and also of Ireland upon earth the Supreme Head.[1]

II. QUEEN ELIZABETH AND PAUL IV[2]

A well-known story about Elizabeth and Paul IV was told by Sarpi,[3] endorsed by Pallavicino,[4] and believed by Ranke.[5] Lingard,[6] after accepting, saw cause to reject it, and his example has been very generally followed by English historians, though often they manifest their disbelief rather by silence than by contradiction. Still the tale is not quite dead, and I do not know that the evidence which disproves it has ever been fully stated, albeit that evidence lies in obvious places. It is concerned with an important matter—namely, the immediate causes of those ecclesiastical changes which were heralded by the death of Mary Tudor.

It runs thus in Sarpi's history. Elizabeth began her reign with hesitation. She was hurried into decisive measures by the insensate arrogance of the Pope. Sir Edward Carne was residing at Rome as Mary's ambassador. The new Queen sent him letters of credence, and bade him announce to the Pope her accession to the throne. Thereupon Paul broke into reproach and menace. She was a

---

[1] [Mary had employed the same 'etc.' until 26 March 1554, when her triumph over Wyatt enabled her to defy the legal scruples of her clergy and dispense with her supremacy over the Church. A. F. Pollard, *Political History of England, 1547–1603* (1910), p. 192.]

[2] [*E.H.R.* (April 1900): *Collected Papers*, vol. III, pp. 165–77.]

[3] *Hist. Conc. Trid.* ed. 1620, p. 333; transl. Le Courayer, vol. II, p. 53.

[4] *Vera Conc. Trid. Hist.* vol. II, p. 532.

[5] *Englische Geschichte*, vol. I, p. 301. [Transl. Boase (1875), vol. I, pp. 229–30.]

[6] *Hist. Engl.* ed. 1823, vol. V, p. 146; ed. 1854, vol. VI, p. 3.

bastard, England was a papal fief, and her assumption of the crown was insolent usurpation. Nevertheless, if she would submit herself to his discretion, he would do in her favour all that was compatible with the dignity of the holy see. Many people, says Sarpi, thought that this rude reception of Elizabeth's advances was due not only to Paul's imperious temper, but also to the solicitations of the French, who were concerned to prevent a marriage between the Queen of England and the King of Spain. Then, having suffered this rebuff, Elizabeth decided to have no more to do with Rome, and allowed the English Protestants to have their way.

Pallavicino accepted Sarpi's facts, but defended the Pope's conduct. Rude Paul might have been, and tactless; but Elizabeth was a hypocrite, and substantially the Pope was in the right. Lingard at one time apologetically told his readers that 'it was the misfortune of Paul, who had passed his eightieth year, that he adopted opinions with the credulity and maintained them with the pertinacity of old age'. Afterwards the Catholic doctor found reason to withdraw his well-turned sentence.

Now this was a lifelike story. Had it not been likelife, Sarpi would not have told, Pallavicino would not have endorsed, Ranke would not have believed it. There was a real danger that Pope Paul would do just what he is said to have done. This danger was evident to Feria in England. A week after Elizabeth's accession he wrote thus to his master, King Philip:

I am very much afraid that if the Queen do not send her obedience to the Pope, or delay doing so, or if he should take it into his head to recall matters concerning the divorce of King Henry, there may be a defect in the Queen's title, which, more than anything else, will upset the present state of affairs in this country.[1]

Paul was imprudent enough for anything. Even if Elizabeth did all that a Catholic sovereign should do, it was quite possible that the hot-headed old man would fling her bastardy in her face, and declare that England was a fief moving from St Peter. At the moment he was asserting that, without his sanction, Charles V's abdication of the empire was a nullity, and he was doing all that mortal pope could do to drive the patient Ferdinand into Lutheranism.

[1] *Spanish Cal.* 1558–67, p. 6; Kervyn de Lettenhove, *Relations Politiques*, vol. I, p. 309.

Perhaps it was just this that prevented some such explosion as that which Sarpi has recorded. Paul had one great quarrel on his hands, and even he—for he was human—could hardly afford another. As a matter of fact, during the months that will concern us he was showing some desire to stand well with the Spanish while he denounced the Austrian Habsburg, and a declaration in favour of Mary Stuart's claim to the English crown would have been very much like a declaration of war against Philip. Little good had come to Pope Paul of his alliance with France; and the ascendancy of his nephew Carlo Caraffa, whom we shall see as the French advocate, was almost at an end.

Be all this as it may, Sarpi's story cannot be true.

Let us remember that Elizabeth became queen on 17 November 1558. Now it is apparent in notes written by Cecil during the first hours of the new reign that no sooner was Mary dead than he was thinking of the embassies that must be sent to foreign potentates. Not only was the pope included in his list, but, having mentioned the emperor before the pope, the exact minister was at pains to correct his mistake and to give the accustomed precedence to the Holy Father.[1] These notes may have been written before Cecil had met his young mistress. Then it is apparent from other notes that this project was abandoned or suspended.[2] Envoys were to go to Ferdinand and Philip and some other friendly powers; but seemingly there was to be no mission to Rome.

To the first weeks of the new reign we must attribute the remarkable paper of advice tendered by Richard Goodrich.[3] Some part of the counsel that he gave was rejected. It was extremely cautious counsel. He did not believe that the parliament which was being summoned could be induced to abolish the papal and restore the royal supremacy over the church. What the estates of the realm actually did a few months afterwards was, in his eyes, something too good to be expected. This estimate of affairs, made by an able man who lived in their midst, should be weighed by those, if such there be, who think that Elizabeth's revolt from Rome was an inevitable concession to an irresistible demand. But

[1] *Domestic*, vol. i, no. 2 (MS.).

[2] Nothing of the pope in the paper ascribed to 18 November: *Domestic*, vol. i, no. 3 (MS.).

[3] *Domestic*, vol. i, no. 68 (MS.). Froude made good use of this discourse, but has not referred to the portion that will concern us.

one part of Goodrich's advice seems to have been taken, that, namely, which is given in the following words:

I would also...have letters sent to the agent there [i.e. at Rome] to continue his residence, and to advertise as occasion shall be given without desire of any audience, and, if he should be sent for, that he should signify that he understood from hence that there was a great embassy either despatched or ready to be despatched for the affairs, whose despatch I would should be published with the persons' names, and yet treated so as it should pass for the most part of next summer, and in the meantime to have good consultation what is to be done at home, and do it, and thereafter send.

The plan is that Carne is to have no new letters of credence, but is to remain at Rome as an 'intelligencer', and, if pressed by inquiries, is to say that a grand embassy is coming. The mission of that embassy can be delayed until the parliament is over, and meanwhile Elizabeth can make her own arrangements untroubled by an embarrassing correspondence with His Holiness.

The rest of the story can be told by notes of letters and events.

1 December 1558. A letter is sent to Carne at Rome, telling him that, 'as he was theretofore placed there as a public person by reason of his ambassade', he is not to act as solicitor in a certain matrimonial suit that is depending before the curia.[1]

17 or 18 December. Carne has just heard of Elizabeth's accession, and writes to congratulate her.[2]

20 December. Probably a letter is sent to Carne in the sense advised by Goodrich—namely, to the effect that, if asked about this matter, he may say that a grand embassy is being prepared. The contents of this letter, which does not seem to be forthcoming, we learn in a manner that will be explained hereafter.[3]

25 December. Carne to Elizabeth. He sends some Italian news, and also informs her that the Pope intends to depose the three Lutheran electors and give their dominions to Catholic princes.[4]

25 December. Elizabeth refuses to witness the elevation of the host, and thus chooses a great festival of the church for an act which must, at this moment, be regarded as a display of unequivocal Protestantism.

25 December. The Bishop of Angoulême to the King of France. With great difficulty the bishop has obtained an audience of the

---

[1] *Foreign*, 1558–9, no. 56.   [2] *Foreign*, 1558–9, nos. 123, 162.
[3] See below under 16 February.   [4] *Foreign*, 1558–9, no. 123.

Pope. Paul cannot believe that Elizabeth will wish to marry Philip, but will not promise to refuse a dispensation.[1] It seems quite clear from this interesting letter that Paul had not pronounced, and was not prepared to pronounce, against Elizabeth's title to the throne. The French ambassador did not, according to his own account, say a word about bastardy or about the hereditary right of the dauphiness. He contented himself with the endeavour to prevent a marriage between Elizabeth and her brother-in-law, and even in this modest enterprise was not very successful, for the Pope would make no definite promise. Also it seems clear that at this moment Paul did not suspect—and indeed he had little reason for suspecting—that the English queen was joining the number of the schismatical and heretical princes. He talked kindly of her, and could not believe that she was foolish enough to marry a Spaniard.

31 December. Carne to Elizabeth. A mutilated letter which was thus summarised in England:

Sir Edward Carne (ambassador resident at Rome from Queen Mary, and after by a letter from her majesty continued) writeth unto her that the ambassador of France laboureth the Pope to declare the Queen illegitimate. Cardinal Caraffa is their instrument. The French likewise labour to withdraw the King of Spain, if they can, from affecting the Queen of England.[2]

31 December. Carne to Cecil. He offers his services to the Queen, though he would like to be recalled. He desires to know the Queen's pleasure, as his old commission has expired. [He has not as yet received the letter of 20 December.[3]]

25 January 1559. The English parliament meets, and by this time it is abundantly plain in England that the Queen means to abolish the papal supremacy. Any further dissimulation at Rome would be useless.

1 February. Resolution of the Queen's council. A letter is to be sent to Carne telling him that he is to come home, as there is no cause why he should remain at Rome.[4] On 4 February the letter is sent.[5]

15 February. Bull 'Cum ex Apostolatus', declaring that heretical princes are deposed by the mere fact of heresy.[6]

---

[1] Ribier, *Mémoires*, vol. ii, p. 776.   [2] *Foreign*, 1558–9, nos. 160, 161.
[3] *Ibid.* no. 162.   [4] *Ibid.* no. 299.   [5] *Ibid.* no. 474.
[6] *Magnum Bullarium* (Luxemb. 1727), vol. i, p. 846.

16 February. Carne to the Queen. He had written on the 11th. The French here can obtain nothing from the Pope against her; 'he [Paul] has such respect to herself and her realm that he will attempt nothing against either unless occasion be given therehence [i.e. from England].' The Pope means to send a Nuncio, but waits until an ambassador shall come from Elizabeth.[1]

An abstract of the last-mentioned letter runs thus: 'A Nuncio intended for England, but stayeth until the Queen first sendeth to the Pope, according to the message he [Carne] had delivered by the Queen's directions by her letters of 20 December.'[2] It is thus that we learn of the letter of 20 December and of the attempt to keep the Pope quiet by talk of a coming embassy.

10 March. Carne receives the letter of 4 February which recalls him. He then tries to obtain from the Pope licence to leave Rome, giving various excuses—for example, that he wants to see his wife and children and will soon return. He learns, however, from Cardinal Trani that Paul knows of the recall.

21 March. Trani tells Carne that the Pope is 'sore moved' and will not hear of Carne's departure.

27 March. Trani tells Carne that the Pope forbids his departure, since Elizabeth and her realm have revolted from obedience to the Roman see.

1 April. Carne to Elizabeth. He tells of his detention. From this letter are derived the facts stated in our last three paragraphs. That Carne reports them accurately must not be assumed.[3]

3 April. Carne to Elizabeth. Again he tells how he is detained and is compelled by the Pope to take charge of the English hospital at Rome. 'He perceives the French have obtained somewhat of their purpose the month before, but in what particular he cannot learn.'[4]

24 April. Philip to Feria. As Elizabeth has refused the title of 'supreme head' when it was offered to her, there may still be some hope. Seeing this, and seeing how damaging it would be if the Pope were to declare her a bastard, which he might decide to do, 'since I am not to marry her', I have endeavoured to stay his hand by assuring him that there are hopes of her amendment.[5]

30 May. Throckmorton to Cecil. He has heard from the Venetian

---

[1] *Foreign*, 1558–9, no. 331. [2] *Ibid.* no. 333.
[3] *Foreign*, no. 474. [4] *Ibid.* no. 492.
[5] *Spanish Cal.* 1558–67, p. 60; Kervyn de Lettenhove, *Relations Politiques*, vol. I, p. 508.

ambassador at the court of France that Carne was a willing prisoner at Rome, and thankfully accepted the charge of the hospital.[1]

Now from all this it seems plain enough that Sarpi's story is radically untrue, and Pallavicino's defence unnecessary. Whether Paul ever made any attack against Elizabeth on the score of her base birth is very doubtful. That he never made any public and solemn attack against her on that score, or even on the score of heresy and schism, is fairly certain: many would have preserved copies of a bull that denounced her, whether as heretic or as usurper. But at least it should be indubitable that she was not driven into Protestantism by his insults. Apparently he did and said nothing against her until he learnt that she was withdrawing her minister from his court, and that her talk of sending an embassy had been deceitful.

Whether she was one of the people who were in his mind when the bull that is dated on 15 February was being prepared would be a delicate question. Primarily he was thinking of the three Protestant electors who had dared to take part in the choice of an emperor. In the background may have stood Maximilian, who was leaning towards Luther, and Anthony, who was leaning towards Calvin. We should suppose that by the middle of February Paul had heard of a scene enacted in a royal chapel on Christmas Day by a young actress, who planned her scenes with admirable art. Still even at the date of the bull Carne was saying that the Pope was Elizabeth's friend, and to find a reason why the ambassador should lie about this matter would not be easy. Not until later would the Pope have serious cause to doubt the truth of Philip's repeated assurances that all would go well in England, and already the miserable man had on his hands his own scandalous nephews, besides a wrongfully elected emperor. But even if it were in some sort true that 'Cum ex Apostolatus' was aimed at Elizabeth as well as some other people, still no names were named in it, and if, according to canonical reckoning, her reign ends in the spring of 1559, that is not because King John held England of Pope Innocent, nor because King Henry and Queen Anne were adulterers, but because Elizabeth, as she had frankly admitted, was a heretic: *porque era erege*.[2] Sometimes truth speaks through truthless lips.

[1] *Foreign*, 1558–9, no. 789.
[2] *Spanish Cal.* 1558–67, p. 37; Kervyn de Lettenhove, *Relations Politiques*, vol. I, p. 475.

When did Elizabeth's reign end? I do not know. English historians, so far as I have observed, say nothing of Paul's bull, and I gather from the *Bullarium* that it may not have been 'published' in the technical sense of that term.[1] At a later date the English Catholics were told that the question whether an heretical prince was *privatus lata sententia* or merely *privandus sententia ferenda* was a somewhat doubtful question, and therefore it was somewhat doubtful whether Elizabeth was queen until Pius V denounced her. According to a 'probable opinion' his denunciation merely declared to the world an effect which her heresies had produced without the aid of any sentence; but the contrary was said to be 'the commoner opinion'.[2] Be that as it may (and with such subtleties we had better not meddle), we have little reason for accusing Paul IV of striking Elizabeth before, or even after, he was stricken.

Who started the story that Sarpi told? There were times when Elizabeth explained to the right people—to Spanish ambassadors and the like—that in the early days of her reign she had been forced to seem less Catholic, more Protestant, than really she was. Whatever else she may have been, she was a great storyteller, and I am not sure that this lifelike legend of a reasonable young woman and an impracticable old pope would have been unworthy of her genius.

By way of appendix to a paper which perhaps has repeated too much that is generally known, I will add an account of Elizabeth's Christmas escapade which is lying among the 'Roman Transcripts' at the Record Office. At this moment I am not able to describe the source whence this extract was taken, but apparently we learn that the news of Elizabeth's unfinished mass and of her almost contemporary edict touching epistle and gospel soon reached Rome. As we should expect, the story was improved by transmission; but to me it seems that very fairly might the as yet uncrowned queen be charged at Rome with having openly declared herself a heretic (or in the Italian of the time a Lutheran) if, rather than witness the elevation of the host, she ostentatiously quitted her chapel.[3]

---

[1] It was confirmed in 1566 by a bull of Pius V—*Inter multiplices* (*Bullarium*, vol. II, p. 214; Hinschius, *Kirchenrecht*, vol. v, p. 682).

[2] *E.H.R.* (1892), p. 87 (answer to Question 14).

[3] The evidence is good. See Feria's letter, *Spanish Cal.* 1558–67, p. 17; Kervyn de Lettenhove, *Relations Politiques*, vol. I, p. 365; Il Schifanoya's letter, *Venetian*, 1558–80, p. 2; Letter of Sir W. Fitzwilliam, Ellis, *Orig. Letters*, 2nd ser. vol. II, p. 262; extracts printed in Bridgett and Knox, *Queen Elizabeth and the Catholic Hierarchy*, p. 65.

Corsini 38 *F* 6. *Diario Pontificum.* 1327–1561

1559

La Regina d'Inghilterra finalmente di questo mese (Gennaro) si dichiara Luterana, e fece un decreto che non se douesse predicar altro che l'Evangelio e l'Epistola di San Paolo, et essendo alla messa non uolse stare a ueder consecrare, anzi uolse impedire il uescouo che non consecrasse, e permise a ciascuno di uiuere a suo modo sin tanto che ella dichiaraua per decreto il [*sic*] Parlamento che si hauesse da uiuere nella uera e pura fede, qual intendeua, secondo che dicono i Luterani.

Il Re Filippo fece intendere alla detta regina, che poi ch'ella non uoleua uiuere catolicamente, ch'egli le protestaua, che non uoleua hauerla piu per confederata, ne tener conto delle cose di quel regno d'Inghilterra.

7 *Marzo*

Le cose della religione in Inghilterra andauano di male in peggio, et haueuano fatti Inquisition contra Papistam [*sic*] che cosi si chiamauano questi heretici.

III. PIUS IV AND THE ENGLISH CHURCH SERVICE[1]

It has long been known that Pope Pius IV did something in the way of prohibiting those Englishmen who were likely to attend to papal commands from participating in the worship of the English Church. I am not aware, however, that the document in which he spoke his mind has been printed, though a copy of it is lying very close to our hands among the transcripts which Froude brought from Simancas.[2] My attention was drawn to this copy by a short note contained in Major Hume's *Calendar of Spanish Papers*, who apparently thought that its subject matter was of too little interest to deserve any but the briefest notice. Yet I think that the following 'Case and Opinion' are none too well known even among professed students of ecclesiastical history.[3]

On 7 August 1562, Alvaro de Quadra, the Spanish ambassador in England, wrote to Francesco de Vargas, the Spanish ambassador at Rome, to the following effect:

The enclosed paper has been given to me on behalf of the catholics of this realm. They desired that it should be sent to Trent, but I think

---

[1] [*E.H.R.*, July 1900: *Collected Papers*, vol. III, pp. 177–80.]

[2] B.M. Add. MS. 26056, pp. 182, 185.

[3] *Spanish Calendar*, 1558–67, p. 258. 'Sends an address from the English catholics asking for an authoritative decision as to the legality of their attending the reformed services. Sets forth the arguments in favour of their being allowed to do so.'

that you had better lay it before His Holiness, for he is more perfectly informed about the circumstances of the case than those at Trent are likely to be. The case is novel and unusual; it is very different from an ordinary case of communicating with excommunicates. The question *Si est metus aut coactio?* cannot be seriously raised; the coercion is absolute, for capital punishment is imposed on every one who will not live as a heretic. Also in this instance we have only to do with presence at what are called 'common prayers', and these contain no impiety or false doctrine, for they consist of Scripture and prayers taken from the catholic church, though what concerns the merits and intercession of saints has been omitted. Moreover we have not to deal with the communion, which is celebrated only at Easter and other great festivals. The question is solely as to presence at these 'common prayers'.

The writer adds that he has been chary of giving advice to those who have consulted him, since he wished neither to condemn the feeble nor to damp the ardour of the strong. As I understand him, he doubts whether any general rule will adequately meet all possible cases.[1]

The question that was submitted to the Pope and the answer that he gave to it—the answer seems to have been dated on 2 October—run in the following words:

Casus est:
Quidam principatus lege et statutis prohibuit sub poena capitali ne aliquis sit catholicus, sed omnes vitam hereticam agant, et intersint psalmis eorum more lingua vulgari decantandis, et lectionibus ex Bibliis lingua item populari depromptis, nec non concionibus quae ad eorum dogmata aprobanda apud populum frequentius habentur, commemorantur et fiant.
Quaestio:
An subditi fideles et catholici sine periculo damnationis aeternae animae suae supradictis interesse possint.
Ad casum respondemus quod neque vitam catholicam relinquere, nec hereticam ducere, neque eorum psalmis, lectionibus et concionibus interesse licet: cum in casu proposito non esset cum hereticis comunicare et cum eis participare sed vitam et errores illorum protestari, cum non velint aliam ob causam interesse nisi ut tanquam heretici reputati poenas catholicis impositas effugiant; et scriptum est Obedire oportet Deo dicenti Qui me erubuerit et meos sermones,[2] quanquam hominibus vitam et ritus Deo et ecclesiae contrarios precipientibus, et eo magis cum nobiles et magnates non sine pusillorum scandalo supradictis interesse possint.

[1] This covering letter is in Spanish. The 'Case and Opinion' are, I think, in Froude's own handwriting. I will give them as they stand; some small emendations will occur to the reader.

[2] Here, I suppose, an *etc.* should mark the end of an unfinished text.

It seems pretty clear that those who 'settled this case for opinion' desired an answer very different from that which they received. We can hardly acquit them of grossly exaggerating their woes. To listen to them one would think that non-attendance at church was a capital crime, instead of being cause for a twelve-penny fine. Quadra is guilty of a similar misrepresentation when he says *siendo prohibido aqui por ley el ser catolico y puestas penas capitales a quien no viviere como herege*, unless indeed every one is living as a heretic if he refrains from actively proclaiming the papal supremacy. At any rate we must allow that the very utmost that could be done to induce a soft answer was done by those who thus brought capital punishment into contact with absence from church. Moreover they do not ask for any counsel of perfection. All that they want to know is whether church-going is deadly sin. And, again, Quadra makes it quite plain that there is no talk of any participation in the Lord's Supper—the devilish supper, as even moderate English Catholics could call it[1]—and in favour of 'the common prayers' he seems to say all that could fairly be said by a prelate who was in communion with Rome. But no, Pius, the conciliatory Pius, will have none of it. If the choice lies between church and gallows the gallows must be chosen.

IV. THOMAS SACKVILLE'S MESSAGE FROM ROME[2]

Pius IV, though he had serious thoughts of denouncing Elizabeth as an excommunicate heretic and deposed queen, made at least four attempts to secure her conversion. A good deal is generally known about the mission of Vincent Parpaglia in 1560 and the mission of Martinengo in 1561. Something also is easily discoverable about the efforts made by the cardinal of Ferrara in 1562, and they were sanctioned by Pius, though by this time he was no longer hopeful.[3] Then we may learn a little of an episode in which Thomas Sackville was the principal actor. He is the Thomas Sackville who wrote poetry that is admired, and became Lord Buckhurst and Earl of Dorset.

In the winter of 1563–4 he was in Rome and was arrested as a spy; but he was soon liberated, and held converse with some

---

[1] See *E.H.R.* (1892), p. 85.

[2] [*E.H.R.* (October 1900): *Collected Papers*, vol. III, pp. 180–5.]

[3] Among the Roman transcripts are two letters of 3 January and 15 March 1562 about this negotiation.

illustrious people. In January Cecil was anxious about his fate; Cecil's Italian 'intelligencers' were to find out what had happened. Then from a letter written in February we may gather that Cecil did not know whether Sackville had or had not a commission from the queen.[1] Then in November Guzman de Silva, the Spanish ambassador in England, had something to tell King Philip about Sackville's proceedings. The Pope, so the Spaniard said, had conversed with Sackville, and had assured him that if what was preventing Elizabeth from making dutiful submission was the fear that she would be deposed as illegitimate, or the fear that she would not be allowed to marry whom she pleased, she might set her mind at rest. The ambassador added that Sackville, having journeyed from Rome to Flanders, thence wrote to the Queen, who wrote in reply without the knowledge of Cecil or Cecil's friends. Despite this secrecy Silva did not believe that Elizabeth was in earnest. He suspected, and so may we, that she was endeavouring to keep the Catholics quiet by the semblance of a confidential correspondence with His Holiness.[2]

Among the Roman transcripts at the Record Office are two which bear upon this story. The first is a curious document signed by Goldwell, Bishop of St Asaph, and others of the English refugees at Rome. It is dated on 19 January 1564 at the English hospital. In effect it is a certificate of respectability given by these refugees in Sackville's favour. Richard Sackville is the Queen's cousin, one of her councillors, and a very wealthy man. Thomas is his son and heir apparent. Moreover Thomas is a man of good behaviour and of such pleasant discourse that many of the nobles take great delight in his conversation.[3]

Then there is a paper dated at Rome on 3 May 1564. At its end the writer calls himself 'Vincentius Parpaglia Abbas S. Solutoris Turini'. It sets forth what Thomas Sackville may report to Elizabeth as having been heard by him from the mouth of Pius IV on two different occasions when the Pope gave him audience. In the final and attestatory clause Parpaglia states that he was present at these interviews as well as at others which Sackville had with Cardinals Boromeo and Morone. To be brief, Sackville may say that the Pope expressed surprise at Elizabeth's refusal to admit

---

[1] *Foreign Calendar*, 1564–5, nos. 109, 113, 159.

[2] *Spanish Calendar*, p. 390.

[3] This document is printed in Brady, *Episcopal Succession*, vol. I, p. 87.

into England the Nuncios (first Parpaglia and then Martinengo) who had been sent to her. Pius, however, had been given to understand that two causes had weighed with Elizabeth—first the divorce of her parents, and secondly the alienation of church property.

Ad quae sua Sanctitas hunc in modum responsum dedit: se non velle ullo modo tantam rationem et curam rerum temporalium et humanarum haberi ut animarum salus impediatur: atque ideo si quando serenissima regina ad unionem ecclesiae et obedientiam huius sanctae sedis reverti voluerit, sua Sanctitas pollicetur se paterno affectu et quanto amore desiderari possit eam recepturam; et illis difficultatibus quas supradixi[1] ea remedia adhibituram quae reginae maiestas, parlamentum generale et totius regni consensus indicaverit ad coronam stabiliendam et pacem atque quietem totius populi confirmandam esse aptissima, et in omni re quod iustum piumque iudicabitur confirmaturam.

Sackville was to beg Elizabeth to be merciful to the bishops and other Catholics in her realm, and was to add that if she publicly or privately sent an envoy to Rome he would be honourably treated, and an endeavour would be made to satisfy all pious and honest demands that he might make.

It would hardly, I think, be too much to say that Elizabeth was once more told that if she would enter the Catholic fold she might be as legitimate as the Pope could make her, and that there would be no trouble about the spoils of the monasteries. On the other hand, no hint is given of any approval of her prayer book or any compromise in matters of faith or worship.

What seems to be an allusion to this episode occurs in the semi-official answer to Nicholas Sanders which was published in 1573, and is ascribed to the pen of Bartholomew Clerk. Seven years ago, he says, it happened that a noble Englishman was at the court of Rome and had converse with Pius IV. The Pope professed his inability to understand how a wise and literate queen could fall away from the faith. He suspected, so he said, that Elizabeth's defection was due to the holy see's condemnation of her mother's marriage, and added that were that so he was prepared to reverse the sentence if his primacy were recognised. Then Clerk, having told this tale, exclaims to Sanders, 'If you doubt me there are extant among us the articles written by the hand of the abbot of S. Salute, and there are extant the letters of Cardinal Morone, in

---

[1] Parpaglia is speaking.

which he strenuously exhorts the nobleman in question earnestly to solicit our Queen in this matter.'[1]

It has been suggested that Clerk's nobleman was the Earl of Arundel. It has been suggested also that the boast about the existence of articles in Parpaglia's handwriting was untrue.[2] There can now—so I submit—be little doubt that Sackville was the man whom Clerk had in mind, and the document that has been described above looks as if it were the articles to which Sanders was rhetorically referred.[3]

Parpaglia's signature enables us to identify the abbey of which he was the titular head. Too long he has figured as abbot of San Saluto, San Salute, San Salvatore, Saint Sauveur, St Saviour's, and so forth. Really the abbey was that of SS. Solutore, Avventore ed Ottavio de Sangano at Turin; it seems to have been suppressed in 1536, and in 1570 its revenues were given to the Jesuits.[4]

V. SUPREMACY AND UNIFORMITY[5]

It may seem rash to suppose that about those two famous statutes of the first year of Elizabeth anything remains to be said. They have been approached by innumerable writers from almost every conceivable point. Still I am not sure that 'diplomatic' has yet said its say about them, or, to use a less lofty and therefore a more becoming phrase, I am not sure that any one has had the curiosity to examine those acts in the hope of learning something from the external aspect of the parchment and the work that has been done thereon by pens and knives. But, whatever else an act of parliament may be, it is a piece of parchment. It is preserved in the palace at Westminster. It can be inspected by the public. It may tell tales, and such tales as an official editor of the statutes of the realm is not authorised to repeat. Having seen enough to persuade me that in this manner a few grains of information might be gleaned, I asked my friend Mr H. C. Barker to make a careful

---

[1] *Fidelis Servi Subdito Infideli Responsio*, Lond., Jo. Daye, 1573, sig. k, II.

[2] Estcourt, *Question of Anglican Orders*, pp. 361, 366.

[3] In 1573 nine, rather than seven, years would have elapsed since the Sackville episode.

[4] Döllinger, *Beiträge zur Geschichte der sechs letzten Jahrhunderte*, vol. II, p. 238.

[5] [*E.H.R.* (July 1903): *Collected Papers*, vol. III, pp. 185–209. For another interpretation of the evidence here set forth see J. E. Neale, 'The Elizabethan Acts of Supremacy and Uniformity', *E.H.R.* (July 1950).]

inspection of the acts in question, with an eye to all marks of erasure, cancellation, and interlineation. The results of his labours may, so I think, be of some interest to others besides myself. But before I state them two or three prefatory words should be said.

A bill, as we all know, had to pass through both houses of parliament. Before the first house (that is, the house in which it originated) had done with it, it was engrossed. From that time forward there was a piece of parchment which was the bill. If then we find that the text which was written on that piece of parchment shows signs of erasure, cancellation, and interlineation, we are entitled as a general rule to the inference that amendments were made either in the second house or else at a late stage in the transit of the measure through the first house.[1] In a given case this inference may be wrong. It may happen that the engrossing clerk, while he is at his work, makes a mistake and then corrects it with knife and pen. The two acts of which we are speaking show a considerable number of instances in which two or three letters of a word seem to be written over an erasure, while the rest of the word stands on parchment that to all appearance has not felt the knife. We have, therefore, to exercise a little common sense in endeavouring to distinguish between corrected slips of the pen and amendments made in parliament after the text has been engrossed.[2] For example, if we see that on many occasions the phrase 'the last day of this session of parliament' is so written that the first part of it stands over an erasure and the second part of it is interlined, we shall hardly talk of clerical error, but we shall infer that an amendment was moved and carried. In the following remarks no notice will be taken of what clearly seem to be slips of the pen and the correction of such slips. For instance, we will not record that in the word 'metropolitan' two or three of the middle letters seem to stand upon an erasure. All that may be significant we will mention.

What lies before me as I write is a copy of Dr Prothero's *Statutes and Constitutional Documents*, annotated by Mr Barker. As that book is deservedly in common use and very handy, I will refer to its pages and lines, but will in every instance give words enough

---

[1] Smith, *Commonwealth*, [ed. L. Alston (1906), p. 57]. A bill may be committed and amended before it is engrossed, 'yea, and some time after'.

[2] Such amendments were said to be 'made at the table'. I take it that the actual erasing and so forth was done in the view of the assembled members.

to enable a reader to find in any other collection of statutes the passage which is the subject of remark.[1] Dr Prothero spells words in modern fashion, and in this we will follow him. Words that are written over an erasure will be printed in italics. Words that are interlined will be printed within square brackets. An erasure over which nothing has been written will be indicated by three asterisks. As to the length of such an erasure, a word will be said in a foot-note. The number of words in a line of the manuscript is a varying number; but when it is said that a line is erased this will mean that some twenty words have disappeared. It will be understood that when we speak of erasure we speak of the work done by a knife. If words are struck through by a pen, we shall say that they are, not erased, but cancelled.[2]

1. *The Act of Supremacy* (*1 Eliz. c. 1*)

The roll consists of three skins, fastened end to end, and affixed to the last are four small 'schedules' or 'followers'. These are fastened to the left-hand side of the roll by a narrow strip of parchment. The words which express the royal assent are easily legible. The top right-hand corner of the roll is soiled and creased, and this makes the direction for delivery to the second house difficult to read. A crease has run along the line of words which express the assent of the second house and has defaced the inscription. Perhaps, were there any lack of other evidence, we could just discern that in this instance the second house was the House of Lords. We should also see that the bill went to the second house with two provisos annexed and received that house's assent with four provisos annexed.

We may now proceed to the work of annotation.

Sec. I (Prothero, p. 2, ll. 24–5): 'may from *the last day* [of this session of parliament] by authority...' Of this and similar indications of a change affecting the commencement of the act we shall speak below.

Sec. II (p. 3, ll. 1–5): 'and one other act ***[3] made in the twenty-fifth [year of the said late king, concerning restraint of payment of annates

---

[1] [The references given by Maitland can be readily traced in Tanner's *Tudor Constitutional Documents*.]

[2] It will be remembered that on the roll the sections are not numbered and that the numeration is not authoritative; also that the text in the official edition was taken, not from the original act, but from the clean transcript enrolled in the chancery.

[3] An erasure of the length of three or four letters.

and firstfruits of archbishoprics and bishoprics to the see of Rome and one other act in the said twenty-fifth] year....' This may be the correction of a clerk's blunder occasioned by the recurrence of 'twenty-fifth year'; or the draftsman may have forgotten that there were two acts about annates which required mention.

Sec. II (p. 3, ll. 23–4): 'all times *after the last day of this* [session of parliament] shall be revived....'

Sec. IV (p. 4, ll. 14–20): 'all other laws and statutes and the branches and clauses of any act or statute repealed and made void by the said act of repeal made in the time of the said late King Philip and Queen Mary ***[1] and *not* in this present act especially mentioned and revived, shall stand, remain, and be repealed and void in such like manner and form as they were before the making of this act....' Here we find an extensive alteration made at an important point; but we can hardly guess the cause. This section prevents the revival of certain Henrician statutes by the repeal of Mary's repealing act. The erased words may have been of the exceptive sort, and may have been struck out by the conservatives in the House of Lords. To speculate about this matter would, however, be dangerous.

Sec. V (p. 4, ll. 25–8): 'an act against such persons as shall unreverendly speak against the sacrament of the body and blood of Christ, commonly ***[2] called the sacrament of the altar, and for receiving thereof *under* both kinds....' It seems possible that there was some hesitation between 'under' and 'in'. In the body of the Edwardian act that was being revived we see 'under both kinds', while the title of that act on the chancery roll has 'in both kinds'.[3]

Sec. V (p. 4, ll. 30–1): 'from *the last day* [of this session of parliament] be revived, and from *th*enceforth....'

Sec. VI (p. 5, ll. 8–9): 'from the *last day of this* [session of parliament] deemed....'

Sec. VII (p. 5, ll. 18–19): 'any time *after the last day* [of this session of parliament] use....'

Sec. VII (p. 5, ll. 23–4): 'but fro*m th*enceforth the same shall....'

Sec. IX (p. 7, ll. 9–10): 'as well in all spiritual [or ecclesiastical] things or causes as temporal....' This occurs in the oath of supremacy. If the interpolated words are an amendment we have at first sight some little difficulty in imagining the motives of those who desired it; but perhaps they thought that 'or ecclesiastical' would so explain 'spiritual' that any claim to jurisdiction *in foro conscientiae* would be excluded.

Sec. X (p. 7, l. 24): 'archbishop, bishop, or other ecclesiastical *officer* or minister.' Possibly 'officer' took the place of 'person'.[4]

Sec. XI (p. 8, ll. 24–6): 'shall presently be judged disabled in the law to receive, take, or have *the same* promotion spiritual or ecclesiastical, *the same* ***[5] temporal office, ministry, or service....' An amendment

---

[1] An erasure of just two lines, equal to the space between 'all' and 'Mary'.

[2] An erasure of one or two letters.

[3] *Statutes of the Realm*, vol. IV, pp. 1–3.   [4] See §IX.

[5] An erasure of the length of 'the same'.

narrowing the scope of a disabling clause seems a possible cause of these alterations.

Sec. XIII (p. 9, ll. 22–3): 'the said refusal, *and shall and may use and exercise the said office in such manner and form.*[1] . . .'

Sec. XIV (p. 9, l. 27): 'and for *the more* [sure] observation of this act. . . .'

Sec. XIV (p. 10, l. 3): 'of your highness, or ***[2] shall advisedly. . . .'

Sec. XIV (p. 10, ll. 30–1): 'or do the said offences or any of them [in manner and form aforesaid] and be thereof duly convicted. . . .'

Sec. XIV (p. 11, ll. 1–2): 'or any of them [in manner and form aforesaid] and be thereof duly convicted. . . .' This and the last amendment seem to come from those who would have the definitions of the offences strictly construed.

Sec. XV. In this section the phrase 'one half-year next' occurs twice. On the second, but not on the first, occurrence, the 'half' is interlined. The context seems to show that this is only the correction of a blunder.

Sec. XV. At the end of this section occur seven lines of writing that are cancelled by a pen. Of them we shall speak below.

Sec. XVIII (p. 12, ll. 5–6): 'for any offence that is *revived* [or made premunire or] treason by this act. . . .'

Sec. XVIII. At the end of this section occur six and a half lines of writing which are cancelled by a pen. Of them we shall speak below.

Here the roll ends. We pass to the schedules.

The first schedule is marked with a direction for delivery to the Lords. It therefore originates in the Commons. It contains the proviso which is printed as section XIX. It is a curious proviso, coming apparently from the Reforming side, to the effect that nothing done by this present parliament shall hereafter be judged heresy or schism. Not a very useful proviso, one would think, if ever the conservative party returned to power.

The second schedule contains three provisos which are printed as sections XX, XXI, XXII. These originated in the House of Lords, for on the schedule stand the order for delivery to the Commons, and a note that the Commons have assented.

Sec. XX. This section says that the persons, whom for the sake of brevity we may call the high commissioners, 'shall not in any wise have authority or power to order, determine, or adjudge any matter or cause to be heresy, but only such as heretofore have been determined, ordered, or adjudged to be heresy [by the authority of the canonical Scriptures or by the first four general councils or any of them, or by any other general council wherein the same was declared heresy by the express and plain words of the said canonical Scriptures],[3] or such as hereafter

---

[1] The parchment seems to have been scraped, but it is not clear that any writing was erased.

[2] An erasure of fourteen to sixteen letters.

[3] Interlined in very small letters.

shall be ordered, judged, or determined to be heresy by the high court of parliament of this realm with the assent of the clergy in their convocation; anything in this act contained to the contrary notwithstanding'.

The two portions of this section seem to proceed from different parties, and, whether we have here a clause added by the Lords and amended by the Commons, or a clause proposed in the Upper House (perhaps by the committees) and altered in that House, we have reason to infer the occurrence of an interesting episode. It strikes the conservatives in the Upper House that, unless something be said to the contrary, these royal commissioners may soon be adjudging heretical many of the old beliefs—for example, a belief in transubstantiation. So a limit must be set, and it takes a very conservative form: only what has been adjudged heresy in the past is to be adjudged heresy in the future, unless convocation, which has lately shown its conservatism, consents to a change. But this adoption of the old standard, though only in a one-sided fashion, would hardly suit the reforming party. A clause is inserted which expresses a certain theory about ecclesiastical history, and even if we cannot call that theory definitely Protestant it is opposed to traditional teaching. It draws a line among the general councils of the church. The result makes for toleration. To put the matter briefly and roughly, none of the old beliefs, nor any of those new beliefs that are held by decent people, are to be heretical; but we may think it lucky for the Reformers that this section was not administered by the conservatives, for have not councils which called themselves general seen a good deal that Protestants cannot see 'in the express and plain words of the said canonical Scriptures?' At any rate, however, we have warrant for saying that the Lords materially modified the bill in a conservative and also a tolerant sense.

Sec. xxi. This proviso is substituted for a clause which stood at the end of section xv and which has been cancelled. They both aim at the requirement of two witnesses if any one is to be convicted for an offence against the act, but the cancelled words were singularly clumsy. The House of Lords seems to have desired to make perfectly clear a rule favourable to accused conservatives.

Sec. xxii. This proviso is substituted for a clause which stood at the end of section xviii. In this instance it may be well to print the text in such wise that the action of the lords in protecting the accused may be plainly seen.

Original version	*Amended version*
Provided always and be it enacted by the authority aforesaid that if any person or persons shall hereafter happen to give any relief, aid, or comfort, or in any wise to[1] be aiding, helping, or comforting[2] the person or persons of any that	[1] *Omit* to. [2] *Insert* to.

Original version	Amended version
shall hereafter [3]offend[3] in any matter or case of premunire[4] revived or made by this act [5]not knowing of such offence to be committed or done by the same person or persons at the time of such relief, aid, or comfort, that every such relief, aid, or comfort shall not in any wise be judged or taken to be any offence,[5] any thing in this act[6] to the contrary notwithstanding.	[3-3] *Substitute* happen to be any offender. [4] *Insert* or treason. [5-5] *Substitute* that then such relief, aid, or comfort given shall not be judged or taken to be any offence, unless there be two sufficient witnesses at the least that can and will openly testify and declare that the person or persons that so gave such relief, aid, or comfort had notice and knowledge of such offence committed and done by the said offender at the time of such relief, aid, or comfort so to him given or ministered. [6] *Insert* contained or any other matter or cause.

Sec. XXIII. This curious section touching the pending cause of Richard Chetwood, Esq., stands on the third schedule. It evidently proceeds from the Commons. A direction for delivery to the Lords and a notice of the Lords' assent are endorsed upon it.

Sec. XXIV is on the fourth schedule, and this also represents the work of the Lower House. It is concerned with the case of Robert Harecourt.

It will be noticed that in section I, which repeals an act of Philip and Mary, and in section II, which revives certain acts of Henry VIII, and in section V, which revives an act of Edward VI, and in section VI, which repeals an act of Philip and Mary, and in section VII, which declares that no foreign prince, etc., shall exercise jurisdiction, etc., the phrase 'the last day of this session of parliament' has been substituted for some other and much shorter phrase. Apparently that phrase was 'henceforth' or something equivalent thereto. In section V and again in section VII we may see a 'henceforth' changed into 'thenceforth'. Also in section III, which revives certain earlier acts, the word 'henceforth' still stands: the revival is to take place immediately. Perhaps we may ascribe to mere carelessness the fact that the change made in sections I, II, V, VI, and VII was not made in section III. The cause of the alteration we may probably find in the rule that 'all acts of parliament relate to the first day of parliament, if it be not otherwise provided by the act'.[1] It may occur to us that a certain

---

[1] Coke, *Fourth Institute*, p. 25.

retrospectivity had been desired by those who drew the bill. But I do not think that such a wish can be laid to their charge. When the bill was first engrossed it already contained section XVII, which explicitly says that the act is not to extend to any offence against any of the revived acts if that offence is committed 'before the end of thirty days next after the end of the session of the present parliament'. Moreover section XIV, which creates the offence of advisedly maintaining the authority of a foreign prelate, was careful to allow a similar immunity until 'after the end of thirty days next after the determination of this session of this present parliament'. I think therefore that we may fairly absolve the framers of the measure of any intent to punish men for doing what was no offence at the time when it was done. The change, however, that was made in five sections may in the eyes of the conservatives have been worth making. Awkward consequences might flow from retrospective revivals and repeals, even though those consequences did not extend to the infliction of punishment on men who had broken no existing law.

At this point I may be allowed to say that I am by no means so willing as some commentators are to apply to the historical interpretation of an act of 1559 the well-known rule about the 'relation' of statutes to the first day of the session. We know that rule well, because it stands in the Fourth Institute; but in 1559 Edward Coke was yet a little boy. I have never minutely explored the history of the rule, but I fancy that at the beginning of Elizabeth's reign the amount of written authority at its back consisted of a single dictum of a certain clerk of parliament which is found in the Year Book of 1455.[1] From the nature of the case it was a rule that could only come into play on extremely rare occasions, and I much doubt whether we ought to construct lofty edifices on the assumption that this canon of interpretation was generally known to laymen or even to lawyers before it found a place in the works of our great dogmatist. And so (to revert to our starting-point) the substitution of a reference to the end of the session for some such word as 'henceforth' may be regarded rather as the removal of an ambiguity than as anything of greater significance.

[1] Y.B. 33 Hen. VI, f. 17 (Pasch. pl. 8). The rule, however, passed into Broke's *Abridgement*, 'Exposicion de certein parolx', pl. 33. Broke died in 1558; the *Abridgement* was published in 1568. In the medieval period the Statute Roll shows no date except that of the first day of the parliament, so interpreters would hardly have any choice [see C. R. Cheney, *Handbook of Dates* (1945), p. 71.]

We may now consider how the information that we have obtained by the contemplation of this parchment accords with what we may learn from other sources.

Apparently the long session of 1559 saw three attempts to deal with the question of ecclesiastical supremacy. Bill no. 1 was introduced into the Lower House, read a first time on 9 February, read a second time on the 13th, debated on the 14th, committed on the 15th, and then to all appearance withdrawn or abandoned. Bill no. 2[1] was read a first time on the 21st, read a second time and ordered to be engrossed on the 22nd, read a third time on the 25th, with two provisos relating respectively to Richard Chetwood and Robert Harecourt. It was sent up to the Lords on the 27th, read a first time on the 28th, and read a second time (after a fortnight's interval) on 13 March, and then committed to the Duke of Norfolk, the Bishops of Exeter and Carlisle, and Lords Winchester, Westmoreland, Shrewsbury, Rutland, Sussex, Pembroke, Montagu, Clinton, Morley, Rich, Willoughby, and North. It was read a third time, with certain provisos added by the Lords and sundry other amendments on 18 March. On that day it was carried to the Commons, who read it (or the new matter in it) a first time on the 20th, a second time on the 21st, and a third time on the 22nd. Then it, with a new proviso annexed by the Commons, was read thrice in the Upper House on the 22nd. To that bill the royal assent was not given. The Easter recess and the Colloquy of Westminster here intervene.

Bill no. 3 was read a first time in the Commons on 10 April. It was read a second time and ordered to be engrossed on the 12th, and it was read a third time on the 13th. Therefore I take it that the now existing engrossment was made between the session of the 12th and the session of the 13th. Then it was delivered to the Lords on the 14th, and a note upon it tells that two schedules went with it. These will be the third and fourth concerning Chetwood and Harecourt, and they are represented in modern editions by sections XXIII, XXIV.[2] The bill was read a first time in the Lords on the 15th.[3] On the 17th it was read a second time and committed to the Bishops of Ely and Carlisle, the Duke of Norfolk, Lords

---

[1] Expressly marked as *nova* in the *Commons' Journal*.

[2] We have seen that similar or perhaps the very same schedules were annexed to Bill no. 2.

[3] The existing journal records no sitting between the 13th and the 17th.

Arundel, Shrewsbury, Worcester, Rutland, Sussex, Bedford, Montagu, Clinton, Howard of Effingham, Rich, Hastings, and St. John. On the 25th[1] a proviso to be annexed to the bill was read thrice and ordered to be engrossed. This I take to be the second schedule, containing sections XX, XXI, XXII. Then the bill was read a third time and returned to the Commons on the 26th. On the 27th it was returned with a new proviso to the Lords, who seem to have read that proviso thrice on the 29th. This proviso I take to be the first schedule, or in other words section XIX.

On the whole, then, as fairly certain conclusions, we may hold (1) that the Commons send up a measure consisting of sections I—XVIII, XXII, and XXIV; (2) that the Lords add section XX (restriction of the scope of heresy), section XXI (requirement of two witnesses), and section XXII (aiding and comforting offenders), and at the same time cancel certain parts of sections XV and XVIII, which the new clauses have made unnecessary; and (3) that the Commons at the last moment add section XIX, declaring that no act in this present parliament shall be adjudged to be 'any error, heresy, schism, or schismatical opinion'.

Other inferences must be much less certain. In particular we cannot tell how those interesting words about the first four councils forced their way into a section which as originally drawn seems to have been meant merely to protect the adherents of the old learning. Unfortunately erasure was permitted where we would rather have seen cancellation. However, in a given context a free use of the knife may not be insignificant.

Without making this paper too long I may be suffered to refer to the interesting question why that supremacy bill—'No. 2', as I call it—which had with great difficulty been forced through all its stages before Easter, was abandoned, so that a new bill had to be introduced. It seems to me that Froude, having access to Feria's letters, really solved a problem which had perplexed his predecessors; but, having a soul above parliamentary detail, he hardly made his solution sufficiently plain. There can, I think, be little doubt that Bill no. 2 declared that Elizabeth was Supreme Head of the Church of England, though perhaps in its ultimate form, when the Lords had amended it, she was given an embarrassing option of saying whether she was Supreme Head or not.

---

[1] Here we become dependent on Dewes and the material that he had before him.

And further there can, I think, be little doubt that at the last moment, and when the bill, having passed both houses, was no longer amendable, she decided (or for the first time published her decision) that she would not assume the irritating title.

Thus we obtain an explanation of a speech delivered by Archbishop Heath which, as many observers have seen, was a foolish, irrelevant speech if the bill that he was opposing did not profess to bestow or to acknowledge a supreme headship.[1] Then we have Feria's despatches. On 19 March[2] he relates how he has recently (since the 6th) had an interview with Sir Thomas Parry, who came, with Elizabeth's knowledge, to speak with him in private, and at the outset gave a promise that she would not take the title 'head of the church'. The ambassador further says that since then Elizabeth had by her own mouth made him the same promise. On the 15th, so Feria adds, 'these heretics' had moderated their original proposal and were providing that the Queen might take the title if she pleased. (On the 13th, we may observe, the bill was before the Lords and had been sent to a committee on which conservatives and waverers were well represented.) Then on the 24th[3] Feria tells how he had by letter begged Elizabeth not to confirm what parliament had been doing until she had seen him after the Easter recess. He then states that Elizabeth sent for him, that he saw her at nine o'clock in the morning of the 24th (Good Friday), that she had resolved to go to parliament that day at one o'clock after dinner for the purpose of giving her assent to what had been done, but that she had postponed her going until Monday, 3 April, and that the heretics were downcast. On 11 April[4] Feria takes credit to himself for this change in the Queen's intentions: on Good Friday she was resolved to confirm

---

[1] Dixon, *History of the Church of England*, vol. v, p. 67, note: 'A great part of Heath's speech is fired against "supreme head", but "supreme head" was not in the bill. Hence nearly half of Heath's speech was thrown away.' If Canon Dixon had attended to Froude he would not have said so confidently that 'supreme head' was not in the bill. Dr Gee (*The Elizabethan Prayer Book*, p. 100) has come to another conclusion. Froude's only mistake, so it seems to me, is that he speaks as if after Easter 'a variation of phrase was all that was necessary', and as if the bill was at once 'conclusively passed'. Really a new bill was necessary, was opposed in the House of Lords, amended and re-amended, before it became law.

[2] Kervyn de Lettenhove, *Relations Politiques*, vol. i, p. 475.

[3] *Ibid.* p. 481.

[4] *Ibid.* p. 493.

what parliament had done, but almost miraculously the blow had been averted. He proceeds to say that the Queen has declared in parliament (this might be by a minister) that she does not wish to be called head of the church, also that on the 10th (the day on which Bill no. 3 makes its first appearance in the journals) Cecil went to the Lower House and explained that, though the Queen was grateful for the offered title, she, out of humility, would not assume it, but desired that some other form of words concerning supremacy or primacy might be devised. Thereupon, so the Spaniard asserts, Cecil was told that what he was doing was contrary to the word of God, and that honourable members were surprised at his coming every day to the house with some new scheme. Then on the 15th Feria can inform his master that *cabeza* is changed into *gobernadora*.

This tale seems consistent with itself and with what we read in the journals of the two houses. Moreover it seems to let in light upon a very puzzling episode. Bill no. 2 passed its last stage on 22 March (Wednesday in Holy Week), and, if it ever became law, it would revive the Edwardian act touching the reception of the communion in both kinds. Now by a proclamation dated the 22nd[1] the Queen says that in 'the present last session' of parliament she, with the assent of Lords and Commons, 'made' a statute reviving this act of her brother's reign, which statute, however, cannot be printed and published abroad in time for the Easter festival, being of great length; and that therefore the Queen, by the advice of sundry of her nobility and Commons 'lately' assembled in parliament, declares to all her subjects that the Edwardian act is revived and in force. With some confidence we may infer that the man who drafted this proclamation believed that before it was issued the supremacy bill would have received the royal assent, and seemingly he also believed that parliament would have been dissolved or prorogued; and then Feria explains to us that almost by a miracle the Queen determined at the very last moment to withhold her approbation.[2]

[1] Gee, *Elizabethan Prayer Book*, p. 255. [Steele, *Tudor and Stuart Proclamations*, vol. i, p. 53.]

[2] Since the above sentences were in type I have seen the article in the *Dublin Review* (January 1903) in which Father J. H. Pollen has forestalled what I had to say of Bill no. 2 and the proclamation of 22 March. It was with great pleasure that I read what he had written. I thought of suppressing this part of my note, but will leave it standing, as he and I have approached

And then Elizabeth reaped her reward. She rarely acted without consideration; and by 'consideration' we mean what the lawyers mean. On 24 April Philip tells Feria that, as she has refused the supreme headship when it was offered to her, he has told the Pope that there are hopes of her amendment and has endeavoured to prevent the issue of any decree concerning her bastardy.[1] What King Philip and the Count of Feria were too orthodox and too haughty to know was that the amendment in Elizabeth's conduct, which they ascribed to the fear of Spain and of Rome, was ascribed by despicable heretics to the persuasive words of the godly Mr Lever. She was an economical woman and thought one stone enough for two birds.[2]

But Romanists and Calvinists were not the only people to be considered. What of the Caesaro-papalists: of the people who were for holding that the Marian statutes were void, because Mary had abandoned her divine office:[3] the people who talked about the word of God when Cecil came after Easter and explained that there must be a new bill? Perhaps these men saw in the new bill something that was sufficiently satisfactory. At any rate we ought to

the matter from different points. His surmise that the proclamation, of which we have an apparently unique copy, may never have been issued seems by no means improbable. He also remarks that Supremacy Bill no. 2 seems to have contained clauses concerning public worship, so that had the royal assent been given to it no Act of Uniformity would have been necessary and parliament might have been dissolved before Easter. When Mr Alfred Harrison was courteously showing to me the original of the Lords' Journal, he pointed out to me that already the clerk who wrote it had been confused by the plurality of Supremacy Bills. At the end of the session there is a list of the acts that have been passed. The twenty-fourth item in it is 'An Act for restoring the Supremacy of the Imperial Crown of this Realm and repealing divers Acts of Parliament made to the contrary'. The thirty-second item is (or was, for it has been cancelled) 'An Act restoring to the Crown the ancient Jurisdiction over the State Ecclesiastical and Spiritual and abolishing all Foreign Power repugnant to the same'. Then one of these two items having to be cancelled, the clerk struck his pen through the wrong one—namely, that which accurately gives the title of our Act of Uniformity. In the printed journal (vol. I, p. 579) the cancelled passage is simply omitted. Editors should know that cancelled passages sometimes tell interesting tales.

[1] Kervyn de Lettenhove, *Relations Politiques*, vol. I, p. 508.

[2] Sandys to Parker, 30 April 1559, Parker's *Correspondence*, p. 66: 'The bill of supreme government, of both the temporality and clergy, passeth with a proviso that nothing shall be judged heresy which is not condemned by the canonical Scriptures and four general councils. Mr Lever wisely put such a scruple in the queen's head that she would not take the title of supreme head.' Sandys would hardly be telling Parker this at the end of April if all along it had been clear that Elizabeth was only to be supreme governor.

[3] See *E.H.R.* vol. xv, pp. 121–3.

notice a fact too little noticed in recent books, namely, that Elizabeth's parliament certainly did not make it clear that the King of England is not supreme head of the Church of England. It expressly revived what must have seemed both to Catholics and Calvinists, if they looked into the matter, the most offensive of all King Henry's statutes, that concerning the doctors of the civil law (37 Hen. VIII, c. 17). That act states that Henry's 'most royal Majesty is and hath always been, by the word of God, supreme head in earth of the Church of England, and hath full power and authority to correct, punish, and repress all manner of heresies . . . and to exercise all other manner of jurisdiction commonly called Ecclesiastical jurisdiction'. It also states that his Majesty 'is the only and undoubted supreme head of the Church of England, and also of Ireland, to whom by Holy Scripture all authority and power is wholly given to hear and determine all manner of causes ecclesiastical'. These words were revived in 1559, and, as I understand, remained on our statute book until 1863, when they were repealed by one of the Statute Law Revision Acts, which said, however, that the repeal was not to affect 'any principle or rule of law'.[1] This declaration, which we well might call the *Unam sanctam* of the royal supremacy, since it bases that supremacy upon the very word of God, was statute law in the reign of Elizabeth, and, unless repealed by implication, was statute law in the reign of Victoria. But we must return to our parchments.

2. *The Act of Uniformity* (*1 Eliz. c. 2*)

The roll, which consists of two skins without any schedules, shows an order for delivery to the Lords, the assent of the Lords, and the assent of the Queen.

Sec. I (p. 14, l. 9): 'the feast of *the Nativity* [of St John Baptist] next coming. . . .'

Sec. I (p. 14, ll. 13–14): 'the said feast of *the Nativity* [of St John Baptist] in full force. . . .' This at first sight would seem to point to a change in, and probably to a postponement of, the date fixed for the commencement of the act. But 'the feast of the Nativity of St John Baptist' occurs twice in section II, twice in section III, once in section IV, and twice in section VII, and in none of these instances are there signs of interpolation. It does not seem likely that the different sections were to take effect at different times. The alteration in the text of the first

---

[1] Stat. 26–7 Vict. c. 125.

two sections may be traceable to some general change of dates which was made in the bill while it was in the Lower House, and to a change that was insufficiently obvious on the paper document that lay before the engrossing clerk.

Sec. II (p. 14, ll. 28–32): 'with one alteration or addition of certain lessons to be used on every Sunday in the year [and the form of the litany altered and corrected,] and two sentences only added in the delivery of the sacrament to the communicants, and none other or otherwise....' This is an interesting interpolation. It looks like a Lords' amendment. We may well imagine that there were some temporal peers who, though willing to vote for the Prayer Book as a whole, yet scrupled to use hard words of the bishop of Rome. However, there seems to be a little evidence that the offensive phrase had already disappeared out of 'the Letanye used in the Quenes Maiesties Chappel, according to the tenor of the Proclamation'.[1] Also those who are versed *in re diplomatica* will notice the recurrent 'and' as a possible source of mischief. On the other side we may note that if there is not a change of hand there certainly seems to be a change of ink.

Sec. II (p. 14, ll. 33–4): 'and that if any manner of *parson*, vicar or other whatsoever....'

Sec. II (p. 15, ll. 2–10): 'or shall wilfully or obstinately (standing in the same) use ***[2] any other rite, ceremony, order, form or manner of celebrating of the Lord's Supper openly or privily, or Matins, Evensong, administration of the sacraments, or other open prayers *than is mentioned and set forth in the said book* ([3]*open prayer in and throughout this act is meant that prayer which is for other* [to come unto or hear] either in common churches or private chapels or oratories, commonly called the service of the church), or shall preach, declare....' Here the change is extensive, but possibly represents what we should call a draftsman's amendment. Even as it is we find an 'interpretation clause' let into the middle of the enactment, and perhaps the original text was yet clumsier.

Sec. II (p. 15, ll. 27–30): 'it shall be lawful to all patrons or donors of all and singular the same spiritual promotions *or of any of them to present or collate to the same as though the persons so offending were dead*; and that if....'

Sec. II (p. 15, ll. 33–5): 'the person so offending and convicted the third time [shall be deprived *ipso facto* of all his spiritual promotions, and also] shall suffer imprisonment during his life....' The repetition of 'shall' may have caused a careless omission. If this be not so a penalty is increased. It is not, perhaps, uncharitable to suppose that some wavering noblemen may have been reconciled to the bill by thoughts of patronage. Nothing, it will be remembered, is being said that will deprive of his rights a patron who adheres to the old creed. That is a remarkable feature in the settlement; there is no test for patrons.

---

[1] Clay, *Liturgies set forth in the Reign of Queen Elizabeth* (Parker Soc.), pp. x–xii, 12. [2] Erasure of three letters.

[3] Dr Prothero, for the convenience of modern readers, inserts '[by]'.

Sec. XIII (p. 20, ll. 12–15): 'such ornaments of the church and of the ministers thereof shall be retained and be in use as was[1] in this[2] church of England....' Unless some one thought fit deliberately to substitute 'as was' for the 'as were' which we nowadays expect, we seem to have here only the correction of some slip of the pen. In the many commentaries that have been written on this famous clause has it ever been noticed that the term 'the metropolitan of this realm' is very curious? There never was any such person. If Archbishop Heath had been a kindly critic of the bill he would not have protested against a phrase which in the eyes of the uninstructed might seem to give an undue pre-eminence to Canterbury. In the face of this trace of hasty draftsmanship we can hardly make the common assumption that the words 'by the authority of parliament in the second year of the reign of King Edward VI' must have had some one precise meaning for all the then members of parliament. Few indeed are the critics of documents who have made allowance enough for mere carelessness and forgetfulness.

If there is anything significant in the somewhat unusual form of the enacting clause in this act—'be it enacted by the Queen's Highness with the assent of the Lords and Commons in this present parliament'—we can say with some certainty that this form had been chosen before the bill had left the House of Commons, for the parchment shows no alteration at this point. It is possible that the bishops' dissent was discounted by the framers of the original bill; but it is not impossible that the omission of 'spiritual and temporal' was an accident.[3] The Act of Supremacy has the usual words, and on the face of that act 'the lords spiritual and temporal' are party to the abolition of the papal jurisdiction and the repeal of the Marian statutes. Also the general heading of the chancery roll for the session proclaims the assent *omnium dominorum tam spiritualium quam temporalium* to, among other acts, this Act of Uniformity.[4]

What we see upon the parchment agrees with what we read elsewhere. The bill was introduced in the Lower House, had its three readings on 18, 19, and 20 April, and when read the second time was ordered to be engrossed. It was brought in before the Lords on the 25th, and had its three readings on the 26th, 27th, and 28th. Apparently it was not again sent to the Commons; but from this fact we are not, I believe, entitled to infer that the Lords

---

[1] The writing just fills the erasure.
[2] So the act. The official edition gives 'the'.
[3] See Pike, *Const. Hist. of the House of Lords*, p. viii.
[4] *Statutes of the Realm*, vol. IV, p. 9.

made no amendments. The theory of the time seems to have required a return of the bill to the first house if the second house amended it in such a way that it would do more than the first house originally intended, but no return was necessary if the amendment made by the second house was of such a kind that it reduced the amount of work that the bill would do—for example, if the second house struck out one of a series of clauses which aimed at the creation of new offences. This is a matter about which further information is desirable. Some day we ought to have of these and some others of our acts of parliament a 'diplomatic' edition such as Frenchmen or Germans would have made long ago.

It is well known that the *Journal of the House of Lords* becomes suddenly silent at the most exciting moment of this momentous session. It leaps from Saturday, 22 April, to Monday, 1 May: in other words, it leaps over the days on which the Supremacy Bill (no. 3) and the Uniformity Bill were receiving the assent of the House of Lords. Is this due to accident or is it due to fraud? This question springs to our lips, for we have every reason to believe that the journal ought to have recorded the fact that not one lord spiritual voted for these bills and that every prelate who was present voted against them. This fact might indeed be notorious; but notoriety is not evidence, and in the then state of constitutional doctrine the Queen's ministers may have wished to deprive their adversaries of the means of 'averring by matter of record' that the first Estate of the realm was no party to the religious settlement. With some slight hope that the hand-writing might be more eloquent than print I obtained permission to see the original journal. It made no disclosure. In the first place, the work is so neat and regular that it looks, not like a journal kept day by day, but like a fair text made at the end of the session from notes that had been taken as the session pro-ceeded. In the second place, the practice was to devote one page —or rather one side of a page—to every day, whether there was much or little to record. The session of Saturday, 22 April, is described on the back of a page and ends with an adjournment to the next Tuesday; the session of Monday, 1 May, is described on the front of the next page. Even if the book were unbound it would, I fear, reveal no more; for, as we apparently have to deal with a clean text made at the end of the session, any inference that we might be disposed to draw from the distribution of quires and sheets would be highly precarious, and 'This may or may not have been an accident' would have to be our last word. There is, I may add, another omission which has not attracted so much attention. There is no record of the House having sat on 14 and 15 April. That it did sit on these days we know. The third Supremacy Bill was brought to it on the 14th, and read a first time on the 15th. Whether or not this increases the probability that the more serious omission was the result of mere carelessness is not very plain. We are dealing with a problem in which one of the quantities—the coefficient of negligence, we might call it—is very much unknown.

X

CANON MacCOLL'S NEW CONVOCATION[1]

With 'the crisis in the Church' and 'the Lambeth decision' this paper will have nothing to do. In the one I take no interest; the other I have not read. But I have been constrained of late to make some acquaintance with the first years of Elizabeth's reign, and whatever is written about that time by Mr Malcolm MacColl seems to me a serious matter; at all events, when it consists of the suggestion of hitherto unknown or disregarded facts. Mr MacColl has the public ear, and what he says, even by way of hypothesis, will soon be believed by the many, and will pass into the manuals. Therefore, I will venture to make public an appeal to him for the reconsideration of a doctrine that he has promulgated,[2] touching the events of the year 1559, and more particularly touching a newly discovered convocation of the clergy.

He will agree with me that the Roman Church has not permanently profited by the consecration that was perpetrated at the sign of the Nag's Head. He will agree with me that the Anglican Church will not permanently profit by a convocation that is holden at the sign of the Cock and Bull. He will agree with me that the year 1559 is so fruitful of documents of all sorts and kinds, that it is scarcely a time at which guess-work should assemble bishops and clergy in synods, of which no direct evidence has descended to us. We think of Parker's collections and Cecil's memoranda, of the Zürich letters, of Feria, Quadra, and Noailles, of the Roman attacks and Anglican apologies. We think how easy it would be to prove, for example, that in 1559 a colloquy between champions of two creeds took place in Westminster Abbey during the Easter recess of parliament. We think of these things, and we say that at such a time important events are hardly to be multiplied except at the call of contemporary testimony. Let us leave room for the stroke of genius. Every now and again some master of the

[1] [*Fortnightly Review*, December 1899: *Collected Papers*, vol. III, pp. 119–36.]
[2] *Fortnightly Review*, October 1899.

historic art may be able to demonstrate that a parliament or a synod must have been assembled, although he can show us no text that describes its doings, or none that is not too late, anonymous and of unknown origin. Such exploits are for those who by years of toil have taught themselves to fly. Most of us have to walk on foot.

Now Sir William Harcourt, so I understand, said that 'the Crown and Parliament enacted the Prayer Book in the teeth of the bishops and clergy'. I am not concerned to defend the phrase, and it is not that which I should have chosen; but if we are speaking of what happened in the first year of Elizabeth's reign, then we must either admit that Sir William's saying does not fly very wide of the mark, or else we must produce some facts that have been neglected. We supposed that no bishop voted in favour of the Act of Uniformity. We supposed that every bishop who was present in the House of Lords voted against it. We supposed that the lower house of Convocation, at least in the southern province, uttered its mind in articles which breathe out Roman Catholicism of an uncompromising and militant sort. This being so, we had perhaps no warrant for talking of the clergy's teeth, but we seemed to have ample warrant for denying that the changes in worship that were effected in 1559 were authorised by any constitutional organ of the English Church. So far as I am aware, those historians and controversialists whose names Mr MacColl would more especially revere have been content to leave the matter thus, and to say (as well they might) that the Church accepted or received a book that it did not enact or propound.

In passing, let us notice Mr MacColl's treatment of the old evidence, for I must confess that I do not like it:

Of the twenty-six sees then existing, ten were vacant through death, leaving sixteen bishops as peers of Parliament. Nine of those voted against the third reading of the Act of Uniformity. One was absent through illness, and seven for no assignable reason. The Bill was thus opposed by just one more than a third of the whole bench.[1]

Now the Canon's memory seems to me as faulty as the equation $9 + 1 + 7 = 16$. One bishop, he says, was absent through illness, and seven for no assignable reason. Is not imprisonment an assignable reason? Winchester and Lincoln were in gaol because of the part they played in the Colloquy with the Protestants. St Asaph

[1] *Fortnightly Review*, October 1899, p. 646.

had received no writ, and had mildly complained that he ought to have been summoned. There is good authority for saying that the bill was carried by a majority of three.[1] So if Goldwell had been summoned, and White and Watson had been liberated, the bill might have been lost, and, for anything that I know to the contrary, Mr MacColl and I might be believing in transubstantiation at this day. Then Peterborough had given a proxy to York, London, and Lichfield; Durham to York; Bath to York, London, and Exeter; St David's to York, London, and Peterborough. If these proxies were used, assuredly they were used on the Conservative side. Indeed the solidarity of the English episcopate at this critical moment seems to me as wonderful as it is honourable. That is not the point. What is to the point is, that Mr MacColl's statement of the case can only be saved from a charge of unscrupulous partisanship by a confession that highly important facts were forgotten.

Then I see an argument that bewilders me. Some of the Marian bishops were, we are told, intruders:

> Now the first step which Elizabeth took in ecclesiastical legislation was to repeal the repealing Acts of Mary, thus reviving the state of things which existed when Mary came to the throne. The effect of this astute policy was to disqualify the Marian bishops to vote either in Parliament or Convocation, and they were thus disqualified when the Act of Uniformity came before them, and had, in fact, subjected themselves to heavy penalties by voting at all....More than half were disqualified by canonical and statutory law....[And so] their votes [against that Act] were—quite legally and canonically—regarded as null and void.

The author of these sentences must forgive a pedagogue for saying that, had they been written in the hurry of an examination, they would have been regarded as signs of ingenuity—but of indolence also. Coming, as I hope they come, from a comfortable study, I can only wonder at them. As to the disqualification of Marian 'intruders', I will say nothing now, though Mr MacColl calls Erastianism what I should have called the highest of high Catholicism. But to his argument, the short answer is, that Elizabeth did not 'repeal the repealing Acts of Mary' until after the Act of Uniformity had passed the House of Lords. That House had not done with the Act of Supremacy when it finished its work on the Act of Uniformity. The two bills received the royal assent on the

---

[1] 10 May 1559: Feria to Philip: Kervyn de Lettenhove, *Relations Politiques*, vol. I, p. 519.

same day. But further, the Act of Supremacy expressly said that the Marian Acts were to be repealed 'from the last day of this session of parliament', thus carefully excluding the doctrine of retrospective operation. Furthermore, there was a creditable clause declaring that no one was to suffer under the revived statutes of Henry and Edward for anything done before the end of thirty days next after the end of the session. Why, even the Court of Rome was given sixty days wherein to dispose of some pending appeals! That marvellous clause I have long regarded as the most splendid instance of our English reverence for possession. It is colossal.

Where then is the astuteness? Well, perhaps there was astuteness; but it was that of the statesman, not that of the pettifogger. There were hot-headed Protestants advising Elizabeth to act much as Mr MacColl thinks that she acted, and to ignore the changes made in Mary's day. Wisely she at once called a parliament. Wisely she sent writs to the Marian bishops. Wisely she treated the Roman Catholic religion as a religion by law established. Wisely (to mention the small but crowning instance), she allowed Richard Chetwood and Ann his wife to pursue their appeal to the Bishop of Rome. Wisely she cast her burden on parliament; and she had her reward. I do not mean that there was no astuteness of a lower kind. Bishop Goldwell, it might be said, deserved no writ, as he was in a state of transition between St Asaph and Oxford. Two more voters and two orators were excluded when Watson and White luckily misconducted themselves, and were laid by the heels. But of any attempt to treat as nullities the votes given by the Marian intruders, there is no sign whatever.

Yes, says Mr MacColl, there is; and now, having shown us his surety of foot, he prepares us for his flight through the void. In letters patent, dated in 1560, Elizabeth spoke of the Act of Uniformity as one of the statutes that were passed in her first year 'by the consent of the three estates of our realm'. Therefore, it is urged, the votes of the Marians must have been ignored, and we must look about us for some other clergymen who will serve as warrantors for the queen's words about the three estates.

Will the Canon suffer me to strengthen his argument, or does he dread the gifts of the infidels? The Act of Supremacy begins with a prayer to the queen that she will suppress the 'foreign usurped power', deliver the nation from 'bondage', and repeal the Marian statutes. Who, let us ask, put up this prayer? We shall here find no brief talk of 'three estates', but a far more explicit statement; for the petitioners are 'the Lords Spiritual and Temporal, and the Commons in this your present parliament assembled'. But this is not all. Canon MacColl can easily find a highly official statement made in the year 1559, to the effect that the two famous and thirty-eight other Acts were passed with the assent of all (yes, all) the Lords Spiritual and Temporal.[1] Clearly, therefore, not only were the votes of the Marian bishops and the papistical noblemen ignored, but at least two other spiritual lords (shall we say Barlow and Scory?) must have been present in parliament.

Or else (for there is an alternative) it was already law that two estates of the realm vote as one House, and that the will of the majority of that House is the will of all the Lords Spiritual and Temporal in parliament assembled. Since then many and many an Act bears on its face the consent of the Lords Spiritual, and yet no bishop voted for it. Are not their votes and defaults registered in a Black Book kept by the Radicals? But, says Mr MacColl, 'the spiritual peers constitute the first of the three estates of the Realm, and whatever lawyers may think now, it is unquestionable that, in the time of Elizabeth and previously, an Act of Parliament would have been considered of doubtful authority, if not altogether invalid, [if it were] passed in a parliament where the spiritual state was ignored'.[2] To this let us answer, first, that the bishops are not 'ignored' whenever a bill is carried against their votes; secondly, that the judges of Henry VIII's day, holding (rightly or wrongly) that the bishops derived their seats in parliament from their baronies, declared that a parliament would be a good parliament though no bishops had been summoned to it;[3] and, thirdly, that Sir Thomas Smith and Sir Edward Coke knew something about the English law of Elizabeth's day, and clearly teach us that 'the Upper House' gives or withholds its assent as one and only one of the three legislating units: to wit, King, Lords, and Commons. Coke treasured, as precedents, two statutes of Richard II's reign. The two archbishops, for the whole clergy of their provinces, made their solemn protestations in open parliament, that they in no wise meant or would assent to any statute or law in restraint of the Pope's authority; 'and yet', says Coke, 'both bills passed by the King,

[1] Heading of the Acts of 1559.   [2] *Reformation Settlement*, p. 349.
[3] Keilwey's *Reports*, 184 b.

Lords, and Commons'. 'Whatever lawyers may think now', that is what my Lord Coke thought.[1]

I am always unwilling to read lectures on Elizabethan law to Sir Edward Coke, but still he wrote after the great precedent of 1559 had settled the question for ever; and just at this point I am inclined to make a concession to Canon MacColl. In 1559 our rule, that the bishops may all be in the minority and the Act never the worse, was certainly in the making, but I doubt it was already past discussion. The Spanish ambassador, on 18 June, says that 'the doctors' (he means the lawyers) are doubting whether the bishops can be deprived, since the Act of Supremacy was passed in contradiction to the whole ecclesiastical estate.[2] He adds that the oath has not been tendered to the judges; and, I fear, that some of those judges (Browne and Rastell) were little better than papists. It is generally known, and Mr Pike has noted,[3] that, just at the critical time, a mysterious silence falls upon the official journal of the House of Lords. I do not wish to be uncharitable to Cecil and Bacon, but cannot help remarking that had Bonner, or any of his fellows, wished to give proof that the Act of Supremacy was carried against the voices of the bishops, there would have been no official document ready to hand. And Bonner, with the expert Plowden to guide him, did wish to prove that the Act was invalid. Mr MacColl speaks as though no contradiction was offered to Elizabeth's statement about the consent of the three estates. Bonner flatly contradicted it. When indicted, he threatened to argue before a jury that the Act of Supremacy had never received the assent of the Lords Spiritual and Temporal, and of the Commons.[4] He was never put upon his trial, but was left untried in gaol. I have seen the original record on the rolls of the Queen's Bench. Now, I do not say, and do not think, that he had a good case, and he would have had the utmost difficulty in giving a legally acceptable proof of the dissent of the bishops. My humble guess would be that an impartial court (had impartiality been possible) would have decided in favour of our modern doctrine of two estates in one House; and the most that we can say against those who spoke of the Acts of Uniformity and Supremacy as

[1] *Second Institute*, p. 587.
[2] Kervyn de Lettenhove, *Relations Politiques*, vol. I, p. 540.
[3] In the important Preface to his *Constitutional History of the House of Lords*.
[4] Strype, *Annals*, vol. I, pt. 2, p. 4.

bearing the consent of the Lords Spiritual is, that they gave expression to a constitutional theory which might possibly have been overruled in a court manned by zealous Catholics. Therefore, on this occasion, I do not hear Elizabeth telling a lie. At the very worst, she begs a question—a question that must be begged, if her Anglican settlement is to be maintained.

Mr MacColl, noticing the official statement about the three estates, and not noticing the official statements about the Lords Spiritual in parliament assembled, proceeds to say that 'something evidently took place which has escaped the scrutiny of our historians', and he then argues that this something was a second Convocation. But where, we must ask, did he learn that the clergy in Convocation is one of the three estates of the realm? Where did he learn that every Act to which those three estates have assented was laid before a Convocation? Where, above all, did he learn that the assent of Convocation is the assent of the Lords Spiritual in parliament assembled? Not by a Convocation, real or fictitious, can Elizabeth's accuracy be saved, if it needs saving. Not by a Convocation, real or fictitious, can we dispel the doubts reported by Bishop Quadra. And, by the way, I should like to ask some Spanish scholar whether Sir William Harcourt's 'in the teeth of the bishops and clergy' is a very bad translation of this Catholic prelate's 'en contradicion de todo el estado eclesiastico'.

Having persuaded himself that 'something evidently took place which has escaped the scrutiny of our historians', Mr MacColl finds the requisite something in a document 'discovered' by Mr Wayland Joyce in the State Paper Office,[1] and of that document he prints a portion. I will print the whole. It so happens that when I first saw it at the Record Office I did not know that any part of it had been published, nor had I read Mr MacColl's book or article. For a moment I enjoyed the little thrill that comes to us when we fancy that we have unearthed a treasure, and then I said 'Rubbish!' and turned the page. Was I wrong?

The document begins thus:

Ther returned into England upon Queene Maryes death that had bin bishops in K. Ed. 6 tyme.

1. Coverdale.	3. Chenye.
2. Scorge.	4. Barlowe.

---

[1] Joyce, *The Civil Power in its Relations to the Church* (1869), pp. 135-7.

Ther remained Bishops for sometyme that were Bishops in Queen Maryes tyme.

1. Oglethope B. of Carleile who crowned Q. Eliz.
2. Kichin B. of Landafe.

Ther were Bishops in the Parlament holden primo Eliz. and in the Convocation holden at the same tyme.

Edmonde B. of London.	Ralph B. of Covent. and Lichfeilde.
John B. of Wintone.	Thomas B. of Lincolne.
Richard B. of Wigorne.	James B. of Exon.

The above is not printed by Mr MacColl. Straightway upon this there follows what he does print.

The booke of Common prayer, published primo Eliz., was first resolved upon and established in the Church in the tyme of K. Ed. 6. It was re-examined with some small alterations by the Convocation consistynge of the said [*sic*][1] Bishops and the rest of the Clergy in primo Eliz., which beinge done by the Convocation and Published under the great seal of Englande, ther was an acte of parlament for the same booke which is ordinarily printed in the begininge of the booke; not that a booke was ever subiected to the censure of the parlament, but being aggreed upon and published as afforesaid, a law was made by the parlament for the inflictinge of penalty upon all such as should refuse to use and observe the same; further autority then to [*sic*] is not in the parlament, neyther hath bin in former tymes yealded to the parlament in thinges of that nature but the judgment and determination thereof hath ever bin in the Church, thereto autorised by the kinge, which is that which is yealded to H. 8 in the statute of 25 his raygne.

What shall we say of this stuff? Canon MacColl, knowing only the latter half of it, set himself to guess that a second and un-papistical Convocation was summoned to sanction the Prayer Book, the Marian bishops having effaced themselves by opposition. Canon MacColl laboured under the misfortune of knowing something about the votes that these Marians gave in parliament, and something about a Convocation that upheld the power of the Pope. The writer of our document was not so well informed. Indeed, his mention of 'Chenye' (to choose but one blunder) shows that he was recklessly ignorant. Now we must take his story or we must leave it; we cannot pick and choose just what will suit our opinions or our party. His Convocation of the year 1559 is held when parliament is held. In it sit Bonner, White, Pate, Bayne, Watson, and Turberville; and this is the Convocation that

---

[1] Mr Joyce and Mr MacColl give *same* not *said*.

approves the Prayer Book. Whether good Father Coverdale was sitting cheek by jowl with bloody Bonner; whether the Reverend Mr Barlow, who, as late as 1 March, was out in Germany with Melanchthon, hurried home in time to meet those Holy Confessors White and Watson ere they went to the Tower; whether Cheyney was made bishop for this occasion only; whether Thirlby was still in the Netherlands; all this is not so plain as it might be, and the history of the northern Province is wrapped in its accustomed darkness. But one thing seems perfectly clear, namely, that this writer knows nothing of two Convocations, the earlier of which was all for papal supremacy, while the later enacted the Prayer Book. In his eyes, the Convocation which gives us the Prayer Book is no such select body of divines as that which Mr MacColl has conjured up for us—an assembly which, to my mind, looks little better than a Protestant caucus—but the genuine Convocation of the southern Province, in which, for want of an archbishop, Edmund Barker presides.

Is what stands before us a lie? Its audacity seems to crave a more merciful verdict, and I do not know that its writer intended it for publication. One (and probably the later) of the two copies that exist was said by an endorser to be in the handwriting of Sir Thomas Wilson, who was Keeper of the State Papers under James I.[1] From its presence among the State Papers no inference can be drawn; odds and ends of many sorts and kinds are there. Before we acquit its composer of fraud, we have to remember, first, that the tale of the Nag's Head was silly and impudent, and yet generally believed by Roman Catholics. Secondly, that Anglicans, who were twitted about their 'parliamentary' church by Romanists, and who resented the Puritanic interference of the House of Commons, were under a temptation to disseminate some such story as this; and thirdly, that the risk of immediate detection was not very serious, since few documents were in print. However, as at present advised, I incline to a lenient judgment. Perhaps we may see an idle romance that was meant for the fire. Perhaps an attempt to write history *a priori*, and an attempt that did not satisfy its maker. Perhaps an inchoate lie that never got beyond

[1] Public Record Office, *State Pap. Eliz. Dom.* vol. VII, nos. 46 and 47. The spelling of 47, which is attributed to Wilson, is nearer to modern usage than is that of 46. Canon MacColl talks of Sir Thomas Weston; but, though the name is ill-written, there can be no doubt that Wilson is meant.

a first draft. These are only guesses; but, in all seriousness, I venture to counsel Canon MacColl and other honest controversialists to beware of this paper.

The argument from smoke to fire is a favourite with some minds, and, needless to say, it is sometimes legitimate; but the Roman Catholic champions of the present day have good cause to regret that their predecessors would only surrender bit by bit the story of the Nag's Head, instead of branding it as a good round lie. Even so, Anglicans will run a needless danger if they argue that the paper at the Record Office, though not exactly truthful, must enshrine some core of truth. After all—or perhaps before all—men do endeavour to write history out of their own heads. Here, for example, is Mr MacColl sending into a world in which Jesuits and Erastians live an argument which supposes that the Marian bishops sat and voted in the House of Lords after the Marian Acts had been repealed. We do not say that 'there must be some truth' in this. We say that the Canon's arm-chair was comfortable, and that the statute book and the journals of parliament stood just beyond his reach. And if we know ourselves we do not scream at him; so to do would be both unkind and imprudent. We are sinners, all of us. The guess-working spirit is so willing; the verifying flesh is often weary.

It will hardly have escaped the scrutiny of Mr MacColl that the 'something' that 'escaped the scrutiny of our historians' seems also to have escaped the memory of those who must once have known all about it, and were deeply concerned to tell what they knew. Canon MacColl and Sir William Harcourt, modern though they may be, fill the place of controversialists who long ago went to their rest. Profoundly convinced though I am of Sir William's ability and eminence, I am not sure that he is a more formidable foe than was Dr Nicholas Sanders, especially now that a crisis in the Church is far more likely to end in smoke ('good, strong, thick, stupefying incense smoke') than in the thrust of a dagger aimed at our Queen. Now Sanders' bitter pen touched the point that we have been examining. By three votes, he said, and three only, you subverted the faith of your forefathers, and the bishops, to a man, were against you. He could not be left unanswered. Inspired by Parker and Cecil, Bartholomew Clerke took the field. He wrote, what seems to me, an effective pamphlet; but Sanders' facts were not to be denied. As to the victory by three votes, Clerke says (and with some truth) that immediately after the end of Mary's reign this was a marvellously creditable result. As to the bishops (he adds), well, perhaps they did not resist to a man,[1] but they were a seditious and abusive, yet timid crew, and their retreat from the Westminster Colloquy made them contemptible. Now this will not seem to divine or lawyer a very appropriate reply. It was, however, the best that Parker and Cecil could contrive. Why was not Canon MacColl there to crush the malignant papist by proof that the votes of the Marian bishops were 'legally and canonically' null, and, by proof, that the spiritual estate of England was its own reformer? But poor Clerke lived too soon. The benighted man thought that the two parties to the Westminster Colloquy were rightly called 'Papists' and 'Protestants'; and we have changed all that. He lived before the Oxford movement. Indeed, he lived—but let us forget it—when a Cambridge movement was in full flood.

The name of one bishop, and one only, has Canon MacColl risked, as that of a possible occupant of a chair in his astutely selected (I had almost said 'jerrymandered') Convocation. It is the name of Tunstall. The writer of the paper that lies in Chancery Lane did not risk this name, probably because he knew that a bishop of Durham would not be at home in a synod of the southern Province; and were I in Mr MacColl's place I would not bring Tunstall away from his statesmanly employment on the Scottish border until after the Act of Uniformity is secured. Nor would I make myself a sponsor for his adhesion to the Elizabethan form of religion. Henricianism he might have accepted. But we have it from one who was on the spot that, after the session was over, the moribund old man journeyed to London in order to persuade the Queen to abandon the heresies that had been adopted, and to pay respect to her father's will, even if she could not accept the Church in its entirety. And laughter, we are told, was his reward.[2] Now Scory we may hand over to Canon MacColl. Barlow he may have, and Coverdale, if he can bring the one from Russia, the other from Geneva, in time for a meeting, the date of which is not yet

---

[1] *Fidelis Servi Responsio*, ed. 1573, sig. L. iiii: 'Resistebant itaque fortasse (ut ais) omnes ad unum episcopi.'

[2] Kervyn de Lettenhove, *Relations Politiques*, vol. I, p. 595: Quadra to Philip: 13 August 1559. When this letter is read with Tunstall's, his position seems clear: but 'they laughed at him'.

fixed. *Tres faciunt collegium.* Straining a point, we might admit a suffragan, or even Bale. Whether an Upper House of Convocation that is thus concocted would supply the Prayer Book with any valuable amount of synodical authority, is a question that I gladly leave to Mr MacColl. Perhaps a wholly new light might fall on 'the ornaments rubric' if we could be quite sure that it came from the pen of Miles Coverdale.

As a subsidiary argument, the Canon has argued that it is not like Elizabeth to ignore the clergy and to allow laymen to settle ecclesiastical affairs. I am not prepared to discuss this matter at any length, but still may suggest that he and others should distinguish between the Queen who has obtained her Act of Uniformity and the young woman who could hardly induce a bishop to anoint her. To me it seems that the Elizabeth of those first few months was wholly unable to dictate to the Lords and the beneficed clergy, and was bidding high for the support of the Protestants. This is the Elizabeth who made Europe ring by leaving her chapel on Christmas day rather than witness the elevation of the host. When the legal settlement had been made, and the Protestants were satisfied, then came the time for an appeal to the moderate, neutral, wavering nucleus of the nation, for hints of crypto-Catholicism, and even for flirtations with the unmarrying bishop of Rome. As to the Prayer Book and the Act of Uniformity, if Canon MacColl will look at the latter—I mean no page in a printed volume, but a sheet of parchment lying at Westminster—he will, so I think, see reason to suspect that the House of Lords amended the bill and, in effect, erased from the litany that rude prayer for deliverance from the detestable enormities of the pope. Be that as it may, I would respectfully submit to him that evolving history from half a document when you know that the whole is close at hand, and that you and others have a right to see it, is to expose yourself, your cause, your party, to needless jeopardy. The party to which Canon MacColl belongs has been learned.

XI

ROUND'S 'COMMUNE OF LONDON'[1]

The short title of Mr Round's new book raised hopes that the full title[2] dashed. In the compass of three hundred and twenty pages thirteen 'other studies' accompany two admirable papers on the history of London, and we receive a prefatory letter from Sir Walter Besant into the bargain. Such a letter would have been needless, and indeed misplaced, if Mr Round had written that book on medieval London which he is well qualified to write. Speaking in a daily newspaper about Mr Round's exploits, Sir Walter has lately said that 'since the work of research is so slow and laborious. . .it is impossible to be both historian and antiquary'. We doubt the justice of the severe judgment which the learned novelist has thus published to the City and the world, but must confess that it derives a certain plausibility from Mr Round's habit of clothing the results of his inquiries in short papers. Then those who sit in the seats of the scornful—Mr Harrison, for example, and Mr Lang —bewail the decadence of noble history and the prevalence of petty-minded antiquarianism. On the other hand, some who would fain be on Mr Round's side when he goes up against these unbelievers as a champion of the Great Unedited suffer qualms and bad moments. Sir Walter Besant's impossibility may seem to them null. But then there is Renan's impossibility: 'On ne peut être à la fois bon controversiste et bon historien.'

Let us first perform the unpleasant part of our task. Once more Mr Round gives his readers too much controversy and too little history. Their interest in the twelfth century is always being distracted by the castigation of some unfortunate being who lived in the nineteenth. In an essay on 'The Conquest of Ireland' Mr Round collects forcible phrases descriptive of the manners and customs of the natives. The kings go 'battle-axing' around; Ireland is 'a shaking sod between them' or 'a vast human shambles'; a king 'relieved his feelings by gnawing off the nose of his butchered foe'. Sympathy with these proceedings Mr Round disclaims; but

[1] [*The Athenaeum*, 21 October 1899.]
[2] [*The Commune of London and other studies.*]

too many of his papers look as if the pleasure of 'battle-axing' had got the better of him. Of two cases we are debarred from speaking by consideration for a suffering public. It must suffice, therefore, that on many pages Mr Oman and Mr Hall are trounced and battle-axed. Now be it granted that the exposure of error is necessary work, and let it be supposed that Mr Oman and Mr Hall have erred; still Renan's *bon historien* will execute justice in an appendix as noiselessly and painlessly as may be. But it cannot be said that Mr Round has always done this. To give one example: he has obtained our ear for an interesting episode in the history of London. He tells his readers that Henry II was offered *quingentas marcas*, and then adds, 'Miss Norgate says "five thousand"; but one must not be severe on a lady's Latin.' That takes their thoughts from King Henry and sets them waiting for the moment when this ungracious remark will come home to roost. If Mr Round or his printer misspells the name of Scheffer-Boichorst, we do not say that his acquaintance with the German tongue is but gentlemanly. Miss Norgate, however, must be dragged in and battle-axed; she took part in the modern battle of Hastings. Also the reader is informed that 'a little *clique* of Oxford historians, mortified at my crushing *exposé* of Mr Freeman's vaunted accuracy, have endeavoured, without scruple, and with almost unconcealed anger, to silence me at any cost'. They must be simple folk down there at Oxford if they think that Mr Round will ever be silent about his own 'crushing' rightness and the crushed wrongness of Freeman and his followers. That is the pity of it. And so, after all these fierce joys, the book ends in a minor key. Its last melancholy words tell the reader that 'in England, at the present time, there is neither inducement nor reward' for original research. We are unfeignedly sorry that Mr Round should feel discouraged. But if he be not content with the unstinted praise bestowed upon his books by reviewers, then he must make a reasonable concession to the large public. It is not averse to original research, but it wants continuous history. Froude perused vast quantities of manuscript materials, and yet died an admired author and a Regius Professor. George Norton's book about London had behind it hard work among unprinted records, and, though it was more learned than lively, attained the honour of a third edition. But we know of no country in the world where there is any pressing demand for short studies of disconnected themes, and we know of one country which (if a pedantic phrase be allowed) prefers an objective to a subjective style of historiography.

Mr Round's topics are miscellaneous—'Place-Names in Sussex and Essex', 'Anglo-Norman Warfare', 'The Origin of the Exchequer', 'The Inquest of Sheriffs (1170)', 'The Conquest of Ireland', 'The Struggle of John and Longchamp', 'Castleward and Cornage', 'Bannockburn', 'The Marshalship of England', and some others. In almost every case he says what was well worth saying, and says it lucidly. We see the acute ingenuity and the diligent prosecution of trails which by this time we expect, and we are generally inclined to agree with his inferences. Opinions will vary; howbeit, for our part, we think him at his best when he is dealing with financial affairs, but the essay on the marshalship must also be highly placed, and he has an unrivalled power of making historical material out of corrected pedigrees.

Occasionally he is rather puzzling. Thus, speaking of the *ing* which terminates some English place-names, he says, or appears to say, that 'in its French form *igny* this suffix seems as distinctive of the "Saxon" settlement about Bayeux as it is absent in that which is found in the Boulogne district'. We are forced to ask whether this sentence is truly printed, or whether Mr Round has really discovered that the *-igny* common throughout large tracts of France is not a 'French form' of the Latin *-iniacus*. In the latter case the new light should be set upon a candlestick for the sake of those learned Frenchmen who are quite sure that the Aubigny of Calvados and some seventeen other Aubignys are safe in the Romance fold, and beyond the reach of the greediest Germanism. Can it be that Mr Round was jesting at Kemble's expense, and has not seriously said that Macedon is the Greek form of Monmouth? And, again, we are puzzled when told that the writer formerly described as Benedictus Abbas is 'now virtually known to have been Richard Fitz Nigel'—puzzled, for we cannot remember that Mr Round or any one else has met the argument which convinced Dr Stubbs that his 'chance hypothesis' was not worth defence. Mr Round's memory, however, may be better than our own, and stumbling-blocks such as those that we have noted are rare. Of a tendency to believe the worst of his fellow-countrymen he cannot be acquitted. Is the grant of Dowgate to the men of Rouen 'a fact unknown to English historians'? Some of them, even if they never look beyond books published in darkest Oxford, may have read of this grant, may even have seen Dowgate behind a printed Dunegate, and yet have said nothing about it.

'The Pope and the Conquest of Ireland' is an attractive title, and we were eager to see how Mr Round would deal with one of the most intricate of the minor problems of medieval history. 'Meritoriously and suggestively rather than conclusively' will, so we should guess, be the verdict of the few adepts. 'Wishful to approach the subject from an independent standpoint, I have not,' says Mr Round, 'studied the German papers dealing with the subject.' We share—and perhaps Mr Round shares—Freeman's dislike for 'the last German book', and our author's desire for independence is praiseworthy. Still in this instance he had to explore a many-faced story or set of stories, and we doubt whether he was wise in publishing his judgment until he had heard every version of the case. He rejects *Laudabiliter* and the confirmation thereof, but accepts the three letters of Alexander III which are in the *Black Book*, and about the impetration of which he gives some valuable tidings. Thus far we are disposed to agree with him. Then, however, there is a sixth text, the well-known passage in the *Metalogicus*, touching which he pronounces no definite opinion. Now 'one thing at a time' is a good rule, but until we have decided whether or no John of Salisbury wrote what has been ascribed to him we shall hardly put the other pieces of the tale into their proper places. Mr Round thinks that Giraldus concocted *Laudabiliter* and the confirming bull. That seems possible, though some difficulty lies before an attribution of both documents to one hand, and Scheffer-Boichorst's conjecture that they were once neither better nor worse than school exercises deserves a hearing in the United Kingdom. But when Mr Round suggests that Gerald joined in a conspiracy with some official English historians, then doubts begin to flow in flood.[1] *Laudabiliter* is papistical: perhaps too papistical to be papal: certainly too papistical to be royal. It looks like an attempt to base Henry's dominion over Ireland, and over England also, upon a certain rock, whereon Pope Adrian and his erudite English friend, but not King Henry II, may have wished to edify two insular and pence-paying realms. There remains the possibility that in the royal treasury at Winchester lay a document, at the contents whereof *Laudabiliter* makes a guess—a

---

[1] [For all this, see A. L. Poole, *Domesday Book to Magna Carta* (1951), p. 300, n. 1.]

document which was not what Henry wanted and which he never used, since it said too much of St Peter, his rights, his islands, and his pence. Had not Mr Round passed that self-denying ordinance, he would have had the pleasure of telling English readers that the *Metalogicus* deposits the ring with which Henry was to have been invested, not 'in curiali archivo publico', but 'in cimiliarchio publico', and perhaps of remarking that very few Englishmen besides John of Salisbury were learned enough to put it there. However, the essay perceptibly loosens some strings in the knot, and should advance the day when all will see that no race, church, or party among us can make useful capital out of any moderately probable version of the story of *Laudabiliter*.

We have reserved for high praise the two papers on London. To say that they satisfy us would not be true. They are too good to be satisfactory; but they have dispelled some of the darkness which wrapped the history of our chief city. All have heard of the commune of 1191, and some have guessed, as with Giry's books before them they could hardly help guessing, that French ideas were at work among the citizens when they extorted a commune from Longchamp and John of Mortain. But hitherto these London communards have been dim figures; we knew little of what they wanted and less of what they won. They become plainer by some shades in Mr Round's pages. His sagacity has discovered in a manuscript which lies at the Museum 'the Oath of the Commune in the time of Richard I', and then from John's reign an almost equally important 'Oath of the Twenty-four'. Upon the disinterment of these oaths and of a few other relevant documents Mr Round is heartily to be congratulated, and he makes a profitable investment of his treasure. It becomes, he urges, highly probable that Mayor and Common Council and freeman's oath are the permanent outcome of the stormy movement of 1191. It becomes, he urges, highly probable that the commune of Rouen was the model of the conjurators. It is a happy coincidence that Rouen's influence upon London should be thus asserted by Mr Round just at a time when Miss Bateson has shown that it was the laws, not of Bristol, but of Breteuil, to which some of our western boroughs aspired. Assuredly we must keep our eyes on France, and Mr Round has used his eyes well in the capital town of Normandy. Once he goes so far as to speak of a foreign organisation 'transplanted bodily' into London. This recalls Norton's catastrophic doctrine that the existence of London 'as one body politic' derives from this Act of 1191. We will not quarrel with Mr Round's trenchant phrase; but it is of spiritual rather than bodily transplantation that we have to think, and the Englishman who is tempted 'to belong to other nations' generally contents himself with the imitation of superficial traits. Mr Round, who 'remains an Englishman', although (or perhaps because) he writes '*exposé*' and means 'exposure', would, we take it, admit that the differences between London with its folk-moot and Rouen with its hundred peers were deep-set and vital. That the Mayor of London comes to us with and not before the commune will be disputed by few who know the evidence or have been taught by Dr Stubbs. We have learnt from Dr Gross that the Knights' Gild was not the governing body of the town. But the recovered oath is of no little importance. In vain we ask at present how long Londoners were suffered to swear it. Lord Kitchener, as Mr Round remarks, vowed to obey the Mayor and 'to keep the City harmless'; but he did not bind himself 'to hold the commune'. Did even Richard I allow those words to be said? We have our doubts. He granted to the men of London but a niggardly charter, and within five years after the concession of the commune his justiciar's hand was heavy upon aggrieved plebeians in the City. On the other side, to expel the 'commune' from Glanvill's text would be a hardy feat, and Mr Round might have done more for us at this awkward point than refer us to Dr Gross's cautious remarks. Be all this as it may, the oath is important. If in the evolution of medieval communities towards corporateness one moment must be fixed at which the new quality is attained, there is certainly something to be said for choosing the time when the freemen begin to swear troth to their town.

Then, as to the ruling organs of the City, the latent curiosity of Londoners will be stimulated by the new evidence. In the Twenty-four of John's reign Mr Round inclines to see 'the germ of the Common Council', and not, as some others have seen, the nascent Court of Aldermen. The negative half of this doctrine seems to be more probable than the positive. It is amply clear that later on in the thirteenth century the Mayor and Aldermen, acting collegiately, were the governing body of London. If there then was any other conciliar organ of the City, it has marvellously contrived to conceal its activity. We do not understand Mr Round to assert that the Twenty-four of John's reign are the Common Council of

Edward III's day in an early stage of an unbroken existence, and about 'germs' it were difficult to dispute. Some germs are sterilised by an unkind environment; others, which look noxious, are called microbes, and are extirpated by prudent man. One of Mr Round's most precious discoveries is that the communards of 1191 swore to obey the Mayor and 'skevins'. London, however, was destined to be ruled not by a council of mayor and skevins, but by a council of mayor and ward-aldermen. Our interest in these excellent essays will not be diminished if we suspect that the Londoners' attempt to live up to the foreign ideal of a 'sworn commune' was not permanently successful.

Financial relief they seem to have obtained at or about this time. Mr Round was not likely to ignore this side of the matter. Already he had done good service by illustrating the long contest between a city which wished to pay but £300 a year for its 'farm' and a king who exacted somewhat more than £500. He now informs us that when the 'commune' was granted, in October 1191, the farm was 'simultaneously' and 'suddenly' reduced from more than £500 to £300. That he has added no strict proof of this assertion must be due to some mischance. He presumably speaks of the Pipe Rolls of 1189 and 1191; but we look in vain for information about the intermediate roll. Thereon, as Mr Turner has lately remarked, three men, 'as wardens', account for a little less than £300. Now Mr Round would probably say, and with truth, that these three men were in strictness no 'farmers', though as a matter of fact the roll speaks of the *firma* of London and Middlesex. Still we must regret that he left his readers unguided at this critical spot, without even referring them to Mr Turner's researches. The intervention of a year in which there was no farming between the years of the high farm and those of the low is a matter which an historian of the commune must have explored, and ought to explain. But Mr Round has taught his readers so much that they should not be ungrateful.

Much more might be said in commendation of these essays, for there is good and novel matter in them concerning the civic justiciars, whom Mr Round discovered, and the civic families and the English Knights' Gild. But we may hope to have made it clear that his book must be studied by those who would know the London of the twelfth century. If the hitherto invertebrate history of the greatest of all cities ever develops a constitutional backbone, Mr Round's work will be thankfully remembered.

XII

WILLIAM STUBBS, BISHOP
OF OXFORD[1]

No readers of the *English Historical Review*, no English students
of history, no students of English history can have heard with
indifference the news that Dr Stubbs was dead. A bright star had
fallen from their sky. This is not an attempt to speak on behalf of
those who had been his close friends, or even of those who, without
being his close friends, yet knew him well. Evidently there is
much to be told which only they are privileged to tell of a man
who was good as well as great, of a kindly and generous, large-
minded, warm-hearted man. Then there is the bishop to be
remembered, and the professor, the colleague in the university,
and the counsellor of other historians, whose ready help is acknowledged in many prefaces. Evidently also there is something to be
added of good talk, shrewd sayings, and a pleasant wit. Of all this
some record has been borne elsewhere, and fuller record should be
borne hereafter. But to this journal rather than to any other there
seems to fall the office of endeavouring to speak the grief of a large
but unprivileged class—namely, of those to whom Dr Stubbs was
merely the author of certain books, but who none the less cordially
admired his work and who feel that within our English realm of
historical study there has been a demise of the crown, or rather
that they have had a king and now are kingless.

Representatives of this unprivileged multitude would, I take it,
be hard to find among Oxford men unless they were too young to
remember the days when the great books were coming from the
press. It is with many misgivings that I shall endeavour to say
a little part of what should be said. But when I was asked to do
so, some battered and backless volumes told me of happy hours
and heavy debts. Also I was not sorry that an opportunity for
some expression of gratitude to the historian of the English
constitution should be given to one whose lot is that of teaching
English law.

[1] [*E.H.R.* (July 1901): *Collected Papers*, vol. III, pp. 495–511.]

The bishops of London and Oxford have but just left us, and our thoughts may naturally go back to the year 1859, when Hallam's death was followed by Macaulay's. It is to be remembered, however, that some years have already fled since Stubbs and Creighton retired from the active service of history. Already we may think of them as belonging to a past and a remarkable time. Was there ever, we might ask, any other time when an educated, but not studious Englishman, if asked by a foreigner to name the principal English historians, would have been so ready with five or six, or even more names? Freeman and Froude, Stubbs, Creighton, Green, and Seeley he would have rapidly named, and hardly would have stopped there, for some who yet live among us had already won their spurs. It is fair to say that the English historian who wishes to have numerous readers in his own country had better give to that country a large share of his attention. I fancy that Creighton gained the public ear somewhat slowly, and that the well-known Seeley was not the Seeley who wrote of Stein. Still it was a remarkable time, prolific of work that not only was good but was generally praised. Also we may notice the close connection that existed between these masters of history and the English universities, but more especially the university of Oxford. The time when the active labourers had been Grote and Carlyle, Buckle and Palgrave, men in whom neither Oxford nor Cambridge could claim anything, and Edinburgh could not claim much, had been followed by a time when Oxford had become a centre of light whence historians proceeded and whither they returned. History seemed to be in the ascendant, and an Historical Review was needed. Now it might be too much to say that if a laurel crown had been at the disposal of the public that reads history this prize would certainly have fallen to Dr Stubbs, but there can, I think, be little doubt about its destination if the only awarders had been the generally recognised historians and votes for self (which in some cases may properly be given) had been excluded. Of some weighty voices we can be very sure, for they have spoken in prefaces and dedications.

At least there should, so it seems to me, be no doubt about the award that should be made in this journal. The greatness of historians can be measured along many different standards, and far be it from any one to speak slightingly of the man who, without adding to what was known by the learned, has charmed and delighted and instructed large masses of men. His place may be high, and even the highest, provided that he be honest and reasonably industrious in the search for truth. But such a man will find his reward in many places. Here we have to think first of the augmentation of knowledge—the direct augmentation which takes place when the historian discovers and publishes what has not been known, and the indirect augmentation which takes place when his doings and his method have become a model and an example for other scholars. And here Dr Stubbs surely stood supreme.

No other Englishman has so completely displayed to the world the whole business of the historian from the winning of the raw material to the narrating and generalising. We are taken behind the scenes and shown the ropes and pulleys; we are taken into the laboratory and shown the unanalysed stuff, the retorts and test tubes; or rather we are allowed to see the organic growth of history in a historian's mind and are encouraged to use the microscope. This 'practical demonstration', if we may so call it, of the historian's art and science from the preliminary hunt for manuscripts, through the work of collation and filiation and minute criticism, onward to the perfected tale, the eloquence and the reflections, has been of incalculable benefit to the cause of history in England and far more effective than any abstract discourse on methodology could be. In this respect we must look to the very greatest among the Germans to find the peers of Dr Stubbs, and we must remember that a Mommsen's productive days are not cut short by a bishopric. The matter that lay in the hands of our demonstrator was, it is true, medieval, and the method was suited to the matter, but in those famous introductions are lessons of patient industry, accurate statement, and acute but wary reasoning which can be applied to all times and to every kind of evidence. The very mingling of small questions with questions that are very large is impressive. The great currents in human affairs, and even 'the moral government of the universe', were never far from the editor's mind when he was determining the relation between two manuscripts or noting a change of hand, and then if he turned for a while to tell big history it was with a mind that still was filled to the full with tested facts and sifted evidence.

In 1857 a project in which the honour of England was deeply concerned took shape: the Rolls Series was planned. Looking back now we may see that a considerable risk was run. A supply of competent editors was wanted, and the number of men who had already proved their fitness for the task was by no means large. We may fairly congratulate ourselves over the total result, though some indifferent and some bad work saw the light. In such matters Englishmen are individualists and libertarians. The picture of an editor defending his proof sheets sentence by sentence before an official board of critics is not to our liking. We must take the ill along with the unquestionable good that comes of our free manners. It would be in the highest degree unjust were we in the present case so to distribute light and shade that one bright figure should stand out against a gloomy background. There were accomplished men and expert and industrious men among the editors. There was the deputy keeper himself, and Dr Stubbs, who measured his words of praise, called Sir Thomas Hardy illustrious. Luard there was, and Madden and Brewer; but we have no wish to make what might look like a class list. However, it must be past all question that Dr Stubbs raised the whole series by many degrees in the estimation of those who are entitled to judge its merits. Not a few of his fellow editors would gladly have admitted that they learned their business from him, and that they were honoured when their books were placed on one shelf with his. We cannot say that without him there would have been failure, but the good work would have had some difficulty in floating the bad. His output was rapid, and yet there was no sign of haste. In the course of twenty-five years seventeen volumes were published, besides such a trifle as the *Constitutional History*; and every one of those volumes might fearlessly be put into the hands of learned foreigners as an example—a carefully chosen example, it is true—of English workmanship. Praise was not grudged by learned foreigners. When extracts from the English chronicles were being published in the *Monumenta Germaniae*, men who well knew good from bad work, and the best work from the second best, carefully examined what Dr Stubbs had done, and pronounced it perfect. His knowledge of the manuscript contents of English libraries, episcopal registries, muniment rooms, and similar places must have been unrivalled, and he seemed to have at his fingers' ends all the information that had been collected by the Hearnes and Bales and Tanners. But also from the first he was distinguished by the sureness with which he trod on foreign ground, and though no Englishman will blame him for devoting his best powers to English history we may often wish that he had interpreted medieval Germany, or even modern Germany, to Englishmen. Though very English he was never insular.

Meanwhile it was becoming evident that under the pretext of introducing chroniclers Dr Stubbs was writing excellent history on a large scale. Whether in an adequately governed country he would have been allowed to do this we need not inquire. A 'brief account of the life and times of the author' was permitted by official instructions, and 'any remarks necessary to explain the chronology' might be added. These elastic terms were liberally construed. Sir Thomas Hardy must have seen that he had found the right man, and the vicar of Navestock proceeded to explain chronology in his own manner and to the delight of many readers. To begin with, he explained the chronology of the crusades so freshly and so vigorously that after many years we turn back with joy to his explanation. There is room for differences of opinion touching the relative merit of the various introductions: each of us may choose his favourite. The Hoveden was the first that I read, and, perhaps because it is an old friend, there is none that I like better. Into these earliest introductions Dr Stubbs poured the contents of a mind that was brimming over not merely with facts but with thoughts. What, we may ask, could be better conceived or better executed than the sketch of Henry II's foreign policy and its consequences? Where but in the 'Walter of Coventry' shall we look for the quarrel between John and Innocent? Whither do we go for the age of Dunstan or for the age of Edward II? Then there is the gallery of portraits in which the statesmen and the prelates and the men of letters of the twelfth century stand before us real, solid, and living. We feel that every scrap of available knowledge about them and their families and their surroundings has been fused and utilised by a constructive and sympathetic mind which has found details and has given us men—'erring and straying men'. Dr Stubbs's men err and stray in a most life-like manner.

The worst of this plan of writing history in the guise of introductions was that Dr Stubbs never received at the hands of the large public just that palm which the large public was competent to bestow. He was, so it seems to me, a narrator of first-rate power: a man who could tell stories, and who did tell many stories, in sober, dignified, and unadorned but stirring and eloquent words. If an anthology were to be made of tales well told by historians, and the principle of selection paid no heed to the truthfulness of the passages, but weighed only their verisimilitude and what may be called their aesthetic or artistic merits, Dr Stubbs would have a strong right, and hardly any among the great historians of his day would have a stronger, to be well represented. But the large public knows or guesses that constitutional history is arid; the little book on the early Plantagenets is highly compressed; some of the seventeen lectures are—as many lectures may properly be —a little too garrulous to be good reading; and the well-told stories and the life-like portraits are where the large public will not look to find them.

It is not a little surprising that a man who could paint men so well, and so well tell stories, a man (we may add) who loved a pedigree and was fond of tracing the hereditary transmission of landed estates and psychical traits, should have decided to make the great effort of his life in the history of institutions. That he had a strong taste for law—and the history of institutions is the history of public law—cannot be denied. It has often seemed to me that if he had changed his profession he might have been a very great judge. But if there was taste there was also—this often appears—a strong conviction that constitutional history is the absolutely necessary background for all other history, and that until this has been arranged little else can be profitably done. I do not suppose that the great task was irksome, but still it was a task to which duty called.

What are we to say of the *Constitutional History*? Perhaps I have just one advantage over most of its readers. I did not read it because I was set to read it, or because I was to be examined in it, or because I had to teach history or law. I found it in a London club, and read it because it was interesting. On the other hand it was so interesting, and I was so little prepared to criticise or discriminate, that perhaps I fell more completely under its domination than those who have passed through schools of history are likely to fall. Still, making an effort towards objectivity, must we not admire in the first instance the immense scope of the book—a history of institutions which begins with the Germans of Caesar and Tacitus and does not end until a Tudor is on the throne? Then the enormous mass of material that is being used, and the ease with which this immense weight is moved and controlled. Then the risks that are run, especially in the earlier chapters. This last is a point that may not be quite obvious to all; but is it not true that the historian runs greater and more numerous dangers if he tells of the growth and decay of institutions than if he writes a straightforward narrative of events? Would Gibbon's editor find so few mistakes to rectify if Gibbon had seriously tried to make his readers live for a while under the laws of Franks and Lombards? Then, again, we recall the excellent and (to the best of my belief) highly original plan which by alternating 'analytical' and 'annalistic' chapters weaves a web so stout that it would do credit to the roaring loom of time. While the institutions grow and decay under our eyes we are never allowed to forget that this process of evolution and dissolution consists of the acts of human beings, and that acts done by nameable men, by kings and statesmen and reformers, memorable acts done at assignable points in time and space, are the concrete forms in which the invisible forces and tendencies are displayed. When compared with other books bearing a like title Stubbs's *Constitutional History* is marvellously concrete.

It is possible that by trying to blend or interlace two styles of history Dr Stubbs sometimes repelled two classes of readers. The man who wants events and actions, characters and motives, may find more than he likes of institutional development and even of technical law, while there may be too many facts and details, names and dates and moral judgments for those who desire a natural history of the body politic and its organs. But to both these classes of students it may be suggested that in the present state of our knowledge concerning men and their environment both methods must be used, and that our highest praise should be reserved for one who can use them concurrently. Also Dr Stubbs's book is extremely 'well documented', as the French say, and those who have had occasion to criticise any part of it would willingly confess that its footnotes were the starting-points of their own investigations. A word too should surely be said of the art—unconscious art, perhaps, but still art—whereby our interest is maintained not only throughout the long crescendo but also throughout the long diminuendo. Dr Stubbs saw English history and taught others to see it in a manner which, if I am not mistaken, was somewhat new. Somewhere about the year 1307 the strain of the triumphal march must be abandoned; we pass in those well-known words 'from the age of heroism to the age of chivalry, from a century ennobled by devotion and self-sacrifice to one in which the gloss of superficial refinement fails to hide the reality of heart-less selfishness and moral degradation'. It was no small feat for an historian who held this opinion to keep us reading while the decades went from bad to worse, reading of 'dynastic faction, bloody conquest, grievous misgovernance, local tyrannies, plagues and famines unhelped and unaverted, hollowness of pomp, disease and dissolution'. And yet he kept us reading, and even those whose unfortunate experience compels them to think of the book chiefly as one whence pupils must be taught can, if they get a spare hour, still read and still admire. It is so solid and so real, so sober and so wise; but also it is carefully and effectively contrived.

As regards permanence, probably we ought to distinguish. It is difficult to believe that the account of the twelfth and three next following centuries will become antiquated until many a long day has gone by, though mistakes will be found and additions will be made. On the other hand it would be foolish to say that Dr Stubbs knew the earlier centuries as he knew the twelfth. That is impossible; the evidence is too small in quantity and too poor in quality. Many an investigator will leave his bones to bleach in that desert before it is accurately mapped. It may be doubted whether Dr Stubbs himself was fully aware of the treachery of the ground that he traversed. He had studied the evidence for himself with his usual thoroughness. Nevertheless he was under the guidance of German explorers. This an Englishman who means to do good work in those ages is likely to be. The Germans have some advantages over us. For one thing, legal education has been good in Germany, and consequently the German historian, be he lawyer or no, can use a much more accurate set of terms and concepts than such as are at our disposal. This may lead him to make about old times theories that are too sharp to be true, but he sees possibilities that are concealed from us in our fluffier language, and the sharp one-sided theory will at least state the problem that is to be solved.

Dr Stubbs chose his guides well. In particular any one who is praising his first chapters should turn aside for a moment to do reverence to the great Konrad Maurer. It is pleasant to think that Dr Liebermann has been able to dedicate his edition of the Anglo-Saxon laws to this veteran scholar—*dem Altmeister der germanischen Rechtsgeschichte*. When Dr Stubbs published his book those first chapters well represented the best learning of the time; but *die germanische Rechtsgeschichte* did not stop in 1873, and Dr Stubbs stopped there or thereabouts. No doubt the author of a work which is obviously becoming classical has a difficult question before him when new editions are demanded. How much to alter in order that the book may keep abreast of advancing knowledge? How much to leave unaltered in order that the book may still be itself? Dr Stubbs made some changes, but not many that were of importance. It is allowable to regret that he made so many and yet so few. He sometimes leaves us doubting whether he is deliberately maintaining in the nineties a position that he held in the seventies. It is apparent that he was slow to change opinions when he had once formed them; but we do not always know precisely how much he is reaffirming and how much he is simply leaving alone. To have altered the footnotes would have been laborious, for the books, especially the German books, to which students were rightly sent in 1873 can hardly have been the first to which the bishop would have wished to send them in 1897. Conservatism, however, is the note of the methodological preface prefixed to the last edition of the *Select Charters*, which one of its readers must confess that he does not altogether understand. Some one is being reprimanded. But who? Fustel de Coulanges? We can only guess. A laudable desire to avoid controversy, coupled with a desire to warn the young against seductive guides, seems to have made the bishop's words for once obscure, and this at an interesting moment, for he was publishing what might be called his last will and testament. But whether those early chapters are destined to wear ill or to wear well, they represented an almost immeasurably great advance beyond anything that had previously been written in England; nor can we say that, as a general picture of the first age of English history, they are likely to be superseded in the near future. This being so, the conservatism that their writer displayed was, to say the least, pardonable. He wished to hold fast that which had been good.

Conservative Dr Stubbs was in another sense, but it may be a testimony to his fairness and to his rigorous and praiseworthy exclusion of modern politics from the middle ages if I say that it was possible to know the *Constitutional History* fairly well and yet not know how its author would vote at a parliamentary election; my own guess would have been wrong. It even seems possible that at some time hence those who, ignoring the contents of English ballot-boxes, assign to historiographers their respective places in the thought of the nineteenth century, will reckon Dr Stubbs's version of English history among the progressive rather than among the conservative forces. If the study of history had in some sort made him 'sad', he was hopeful; and he was hopeful at a time when great changes were following each other in swift succession. Was there ever so profound a medievalist who was so glad when he had done with the middle ages? 'The charm', he said, 'which the relics of medieval art have woven round the later middle ages must be resolutely, ruthlessly broken.' Even his high-churchmanship, if it is more apparent than anything that could accurately be called political conservatism, is by no means prominent in the *Constitutional History*. A large collection might be made of passages in which archbishops, bishops, monks, and clergy are castigated in terms which a layman would have scrupled to use. I open the second volume by chance at a page where the clergy of the fourteenth century 'are neither intelligent enough to guide education nor strong enough to repress heresy'; the best prelates are apparently being blamed for being 'conservative rather than progressive in their religious policy', while the lower type represented by Arundel is charged with 'religious intolerance'. Certainly Stubbs was just, and to read his great book is a training in justice.

To those for whom he was no more than a writer of books the seventeen lectures revealed him in some new lights. We will pass by the pleasant chat and the too frequent groans over statutory lectures. The attempt to formulate 'the characteristic differences between medieval and modern history' might, so I venture to think, be taken as an instance of the sort of work which Dr Stubbs could not do very well. He loved the concrete, and was not happy among abstractions of a high order, such as a contrast between 'rights, forces, and ideas'. We think how Seeley's agile mind would have played round, and perhaps played with, such a theme. On many pages, however, Dr Stubbs indicated the shape that some comparatively modern history would take if he wrote it. For example, a dislike for the puritans, or at any rate for the puritan cause, came out strongly. These indications were new to some of us who stood outside. That his history was not carried beyond 1485 is deeply to be regretted. The two admirable lectures on Henry VIII are tantalising, though worthy of the man who drew Henry II. We see that he sees the great problem, and a solution is suggested; but we are left to doubt whether an unwillingness to admit that many people wanted Henry to do what he did in ecclesiastical affairs is not compelling the historian to imagine not only a king who is almost super-human in his self-will, but also a clergy and a nation which are sub-human in their self-abasement. Still, though he seems inclined to steer a course that looks difficult, Dr Stubbs was so wise and equitable and sympathetic that it is possible, and more than possible, that he would have kept his head where many heads have been lost, and would have done good justice both to papist and to puritan. Certain it is that those statesmen and churchmen whose cause he thought the good cause would at times have felt the weight of his chastening hand. He never spared a friend who erred and strayed.

Nothing has yet been said of the *Councils and Ecclesiastical Documents*. What is published is enough to make us wish that Dr Stubbs had given one of many lives to the Anglo-Saxon charters. Other lives should have been devoted to the constitutional history of Scotland and France and Germany; yet another to a history of medieval scholarship. Nothing, again, has been said of the *Select Charters*—that fertile book, which is becoming the mother of a large family in England and elsewhere. Few books have done more to make a school than that book has done, and the school at Oxford may well be proud of it. Nothing, again, has been said of the laborious and lucid historical appendix which redeems the report of certain commissioners from the limbo to which such things tend. It may be doubted whether history can be written upon commission, for the historical inference, when it is set to do practical work, is apt to degenerate into the legal dogma. Still, even when it was produced under unfavourable conditions, Dr Stubbs's work could never fail to be good.

But I must end. The last words of the great history are familiar, so familiar that I will not repeat them. Few historians have a right to speak in that solemn strain about the attainable maximum of truth and the highest justice that is found in the deepest sympathy with erring and straying men. Few indeed have had a better right to speak in that strain than had Dr William Stubbs. His place among historians we do not attempt to determine. Assuredly it will be high. I fancy that those who fix it high among the highest will be those who by their own labours have best earned the right to judge.

XIII

MARY BATESON[1]

To many residents at Cambridge it still seems hardly credible that Miss Mary Bateson is no longer at work among them. We thought it so certain that twenty years hence her generous enthusiasm for learning, her dogged tenacity of purpose, her cool and sober common sense, would still be serving mankind, that we might well be dazed by the disaster that has befallen us. Yet some things are clear. If we have to think of promise, we can also think with some comfort of performance. For much more we confidently hoped; but we have much that cannot be taken away. I shall not endeavour to tell the whole tale, but will speak only of the last book. The admirably edited *Records of the Borough of Leicester* and the brilliant papers on the 'Laws of Breteuil' had shown that Miss Bateson's knowledge of the history of our medieval towns was almost, if not quite, unrivalled. Thereupon she was asked to undertake for the Selden Society a sort of digest of the borough custumals, published and unpublished. The first volume appeared in 1904; the second and last appeared this summer, with a long and learned introduction, which is in truth a full and elaborate commentary. When the first volume only had been issued, the Lord Chief Justice told the Selden Society that Miss Bateson knew more about English legal history than nine lawyers out of ten. After seeing the second volume, his lordship may doubt whether his words were quite strong enough. Such a book cannot make its mark in a couple of months, nor yet in a couple of years. It cannot attract 'the general reader'; it can be only a book for a few students of history. Moreover, Miss Bateson, a true daughter of Cambridge, felt such scorn for what she would call 'gas' that it was difficult to persuade her that a few sentences thrown in for the benefit of the uninitiated are not to be condemned by the severest taste. Of such a work I should not like to speak confidently at short notice. But it was my good fortune to see this book in every stage of its growth: in manuscript, in slip, and in page. Good fortune it was. The hunger and thirst for knowledge, the keen delight in the

[1] [*The Athenaeum*, 8 Dec. 1906: *Collected Papers*, vol. III, pp. 540–3.]

chase, the good-humoured willingness to admit that the scent was false, the eager desire to get on with the work, the cheerful resolution to go back and begin again, the broad good sense, the unaffected modesty, the imperturbable temper, the gratitude for any little help that was given—all these will remain in my memory, though I cannot paint them for others. As to the book —friendship apart—I do think it good. Given the limits of space and time, which were somewhat narrow, I do not see how it could have been much better. Given those limits, the name of the Englishman who both could and would have done the work does not occur to me. Unless I am much mistaken, that book will 'sup late', but in very good company. I see it many years hence on the same shelf with the *History of the Exchequer* and the *History of Tithes*. Neither Thomas Madox nor yet John Selden will resent the presence of Mary Bateson.